A Dialectical Pedagogy of Revolt

Studies in Critical Social Sciences Book Series

Haymarket Books is proud to be working with Brill Academic Publishers (www.brill.nl) to republish the *Studies in Critical Social Sciences* book series in paperback editions. This peer-reviewed book series offers insights into our current reality by exploring the content and consequences of power relationships under capitalism, and by considering the spaces of opposition and resistance to these changes that have been defining our new age. Our full catalog of *SCSS* volumes can be viewed at www.haymarketbooks.org/category/scss-series.

Series Editor
David Fasenfest, Wayne State University

Editorial Board
Chris Chase-Dunn, University of California–Riverside
G. William Domhoff, University of California–Santa Cruz
Colette Fagan, Manchester University
Martha Gimenez, University of Colorado, Boulder
Heidi Gottfried, Wayne State University
Karin Gottschall, University of Bremen
Bob Jessop, Lancaster University
Rhonda Levine, Colgate University
Jacqueline O'Reilly, University of Brighton
Mary Romero, Arizona State University
Chizuko Ueno, University of Tokyo

A Dialectical Pedagogy of Revolt

Gramsci, Vygotsky, and the Egyptian Revolution

Brecht De Smet

Haymarket Books
Chicago, IL

First published in 2014 by Brill Academic Publishers, The Netherlands.
© 2014 Koninklijke Brill NV, Leiden, The Netherlands

Published in paperback in 2015 by
Haymarket Books
P.O. Box 180165
Chicago, IL 60618
773-583-7884
www.haymarketbooks.org

ISBN: 978-1-60846-560-6

Trade distribution:
In the U.S. through Consortium Book Sales, www.cbsd.com
In the UK, Turnaround Publisher Services, www.turnaround-uk.com
In all other countries by Publishers Group Worldwide, www.pgw.com

Cover design by Ragina Johnson.

This book was published with the generous support of Lannan Foundation and the Wallace Action Fund.

Printed in Canada by union labor.

10 9 8 7 6 5 4 3 2 1

Library of Congress Cataloging-in-Publication Data is available.

Contents

Foreword IX
Preface XIII
Acknowledgments XV
Abbreviations XVI

Introduction 1

PART 1
Subject and Activity

1 In Want of the People 21

2 Individual and Collective 28

3 Concept of the Subject 37

4 Cultural–Historical Activity Theory 48

PART 2
Subject and Struggle

5 Class as Subject 63

6 The Modern Prince 75

7 A Pedagogy of Revolt 89

8 Revolution 102

9 Pathologies 110

PART 3
Historical Lineages

10 Roots of the 25 January Uprising 123

11	Colonial Subjects	135
12	Colonial Crisis	145
13	Nasserism	158

PART 4
Neoliberal Capitalism

14	Sadat's *Infitah*	175
15	Mubarak's Détente	193
16	Neoliberal War of Movement	206
17	The Civildemocratic Project	214

PART 5
The Workers' Movement

18	The Mahalla Strikes	233
19	Development of the Strike	240
20	The Strike's Intellectuals	255
21	Pedagogies of Revolt	272
22	Adequate Assistance	288

PART 6
Tahrir

| 23 | Story of an Uprising (I) | 301 |
| 24 | Story of an Uprising (II) | 314 |

25	The Activity of Tahrir	327
26	The Organization of Tahrir	335
27	The Mass Strike	345
28	Revolutionary Pathologies	352
29	Revolution Beyond Tahrir	362
	Conclusions	376
	References	391
	Index	414

Foreword

Andy Blunden

What could be a more exhilarating and engrossing reading than a blow-by-blow account of a revolution, and one as recent and significant as the Egyptian Revolution of 2011? But De Smet's account is far from being a simple chronology. De Smet has synthesized a unique and original conceptual framework which has allowed him to make an understandable plot from this immensely complex story.

The first third of the book is devoted to introducing the reader to the array of concepts to be deployed, for it is important to understand just how De Smet renders the revolutionary process intelligible. For all those who have an interest in social change these are practical questions: revolutions do not just happen, they are made.

The main threads of theory which De Smet has woven together are Gramsci's social and political theory and Vygotsky's Cultural Psychology and Activity Theory as I have reconstructed it by mediating Vygotsky and Hegel with each other. There is no doubt that the marriage of my work with that of Gramsci is extraordinarily appropriate, but I came to an appreciation of Gramsci only late in life and De Smet has carried through a synthesis which I now happily accept as a fait accompli.

The body of theory which I have developed was always intended for use in the class struggle, to which all my adult life had been devoted, but in the course of overcoming the gulf which had opened up between social theory and psychology, I plumbed such a degree of generality that it was left to Brecht De Smet to seek out the specific insights which could bring the concepts to bear on the historical and political problems of the workers' movement. No amount of philosophy of science can substitute for that insight which is required to open up for analysis such a complex process of development.

Nowadays, it is quite common for writers and researchers to emphasize the importance of grasping things 'as a whole' and seeing the world as 'processes rather than things'. But this is easier said than done. In "Capital," Marx left us the paradigm for such a 'dialectical' science, although the key ideas can be traced back through Hegel and Goethe to Herder's attempt at a philosophy of history. Vygotsky took Capital as his model, and a few remarks about "Capital" will serve to prepare the reader for De Smet's work which is to follow.

In the first preface to "Capital," Marx (1867) explains that "in bourgeois society, the commodity-form of the product of labor – or value-form of the commodity – is the economic cell-form." Marx elaborates his analysis of bourgeois society, i.e., capitalism, by unfolding the inherent and necessary tendencies within the simple relation of an exchange of products. He is able to do this because he sees bourgeois society as essentially a market place, that is, just thousands and thousands of commodity exchanges. "Essentially," because exchange of commodities is in reality something which, as such, very rarely happens in modern capitalist society; it would seem more precise to say that everything is bought and sold, for money. This conception, that capitalism is all about money, is exactly how not to elucidate the nature of bourgeois society, however, because money acquires its nature only thanks to bourgeois society. In Section 3 of Chapter 1 of "Capital," Marx gives us a schematic history of the development of exchange as an incidental practice in ancient society up to the formation of money, and shows how both money and wage labor are forms of commodity. That is, the commodity relation is both a 'unit of analysis' in the sense that "everything is a commodity" and a "germ cell" in that the commodity relation develops from its own logic into money, and finally accumulations of capital – a new molar unit of value.

Vygotsky used this concept of 'unit of analysis' or 'germ-cell' to solve a number of longstanding problems in psychology, and De Smet has adopted the approach to understand the development of the working class and its interconnection with a developing national popular consciousness.

The point of determining a "germ cell" or "unit of analysis" as the starting point for analysis is to find that simplest possible relation or action which can be grasped and understood practically, sensuously, almost viscerally, and so provides a firm basis for tracing the process which unfolds itself from that simple relation. The germ cell must be a real, singular, sensuously perceivable event or action, not some force or 'law of history' or principle – some abstraction like 'class forces' or 'mode of production', which acts on the subject matter from behind the scenes, so to speak. It is the unit or cell which gives to the whole process its intrinsic unity, allowing those phenomena which genuinely belong to the process at issue to be distinguished from what is accidental or extraneous.

It was by using this method that De Smet had solved the problem which had eluded me – the leap from trade union consciousness and solidarity to national political consciousness and the formation of a hegemony in relation to other subaltern groups. De Smet's solution to this problem in the context of the outbreak of an insurrection in the largest and most industrialized country in the Arab world is exceptionally important. Significantly, it is not just a descriptive account, but a *practical* account which shows us the successive predicaments in which social actors find themselves, making transparent the dynamics of development which arise from such predicaments. It is this practical character of his analysis which is made possible by the "germ cell" approach.

By mediating Vygotsky and Hegel with each other, I have been able to utilize the universal scope of Hegel's "Logic" to transform Vygotsky's psychology into a general theory of subjectivity. A general theory does not absolve the theorist from the obligation for concrete investigation of whatever kind of subject-formation is problematized, but the scope of Hegel's "Logic" is testament to the viability of such a theory. However, Vygotsky's psychology is an experimental and empirical science, not a speculative philosophy; it arose out of a critique of existing psychological theory, just as Marx's "Capital" arose out of a critique of British political economy.

It should be noted, too, that Vygotsky's psychology is not some relic of the past, but is continued by a substantial community of researchers and teachers across the globe, which enriches and develops Vygotsky's legacy across a range of disciplines. Because many of the concepts have their origins in psychology, they have retained their psychological names, but this is no metaphor or analogy, like the way critical theorists have used Freud or Piaget in the past. Vygotsky reconstructed his concept of the psyche exclusively on the basis of the observation of behavior. Further, he concluded that "[...] every higher mental function was formerly a unique form of psychological cooperation, and only later was converted into an individual method of behavior, transferring into the psychological systems of the child the structure that, even in the transfer, retains all the basic traits of symbolic structure" (1934b, 41). Furthermore, at the heart of his analysis of the intellect was the use of artifacts (products of the wider culture) mediating every action. Thus, in a very profound way, the wider culture penetrates and constitutes the very substance of an individual's thinking. But while Vygotsky observed that a "concept arises and is formed in a complex operation that is directed toward the resolution of some task…tasks that are posed for the maturing adolescent by the social environment – tasks that are associated with his entry into the cultural, professional, and social life of the adult world" (1934a, 124, 132), he never investigated the processes of formation of the social environment itself. This was a task taken up by Activity Theory, and which I have continued, and which De Smet has brought to bear on the Egyptian Revolution.

To do this, De Smet has chosen units of analysis, or germ cells, whose inner contradictions and dynamics will be well-known to readers. In the process of immersing himself in the events in Egypt (over and above the use of Gramsci, Lukács, Trotsky, Marx, Lenin et al.), De Smet made the important breakthroughs mentioned above, and has also been able to further develop a number of aspects of my work which have either remained implicit in the reading of Hegel, or have occupied no more than a footnote in my own writing.

I should mention the nesting of projects; a relation which is quite inescapable but to which I have hitherto paid no attention, focusing instead on external relations between projects which were sufficient to outlines the principal characteristics.

De Smet has also appropriated Vygotsky's thesis that instruction *leads* development, rather than following along behind development as was proposed by Piaget. De Smet shows that projects develop not spontaneously, simply according to a logic implicit in the predicaments in which the actors find themselves, but are *made* according to a process which can be conceived of as a dialectic of learning and instruction.

Finally, De Smet develops the idea of prolepsis in terms of projection – how a movement projects an image of its future self as a guide for its activity – showing that this projection appears to others as an *imaginary*, inviting or interpellating them according to its conceptions. De Smet thereby introduces the concepts of autoprolepsis and heteroprolepsis – concepts vital to understanding the formation of hegemony.

These ideas fit well with the Gramscian philosophy of praxis, and his ideas about organic intellectuals and the struggle for hegemony, and De Smet deserves great credit for the conceptual synthesis he has accomplished. But the writing of this book was no bookish exercise: it involved an extended immersion in Egyptian politics and social life which long predated the stunning events of January and February 2011. This new and original constellation of concepts has been put to good use in bringing to us an exhaustive account of the Egyptian Revolution.

References

Marx, Karl. 1867. "Preface to the First German Edition of 'Capital'." In: *MECW* Volume 35, 7–11, Lawrence & Wishart.

Vygotsky, Lev S. 1934a. "Thinking and Speech." In *LSVCW* Volume 1, 39–285, M.E. Sharpe.

——. 1934b. "Tool and Sign in the Development of the Child." In: *LSVCW* Volume 6, 3–68, M.E. Sharpe

Preface

This book is an elaboration of a doctoral dissertation I wrote in 2012 on the relation between political activists and the workers' movement in Egypt in the face of the 25 January uprising. It builds on previous publications such as "Egyptian Workers and 'Their' Intellectuals: The Pedagogy of the Mahalla Strike Movement" (2012) and "Tahrir: A Project(ion) of Revolutionary Change" (2014). Although this project is primarily based on field work and literature research accomplished between 2008 and 2012 it fits within the intellectual framework of a longer personal engagement with questions of self-emancipation, subject constitution, and the role of 'external' actors in assisting such developments. It is also part of a wider collaboration of activists and scholars who are trying to make sense of emancipatory struggles in order to enhance their outcomes. As such this project does not claim any political neutrality, but it explicitly places itself on the standpoint of the oppressed and dominated subaltern groups within contemporary, global capitalism, and wishes to be judged on its scientific merits accordingly.

This study brings together different disciplinary approaches, engages in philosophical contemplation, historical investigation, and political analysis, and deploys fieldwork sources as well as a wide-range of literature. It is a work of synthesis and construction rather than one of analysis and deconstruction. In order to understand complex phenomena it is a scientific duty to weave together different threads and to actively construct instead of merely unravel the logic behind the tapestry of social reality. Such an endeavor is not an exercise in reductionism or simplification. On the contrary, it aims to bring out the rich concreteness of emancipatory activity.

However, a synthetic study is too often neglected, sometimes out of fear to step outside one's scholarly comfort zone and sometimes because the task simply appears as too daunting and ambitious. And perhaps it is. The transdisciplinary character of my investigation leaves it wide open for criticism of specialists from each discrete domain. Bringing together an analysis of Hegel's concepts, of the Egyptian political economy, of Vygotsky's cultural psychology, of the dynamic of Tahrir, and so on, within a single work necessarily means that those subjects cannot be elaborated as exhaustively as their separate discussion in multiple volumes might. Moreover, the divided nature of the social sciences and my own limited education as a historian, orientalist, and political scientist in the light of the vast and diverse production of scientific knowledge renders any personal attempt at a transdisciplinary synthesis incomplete and imperfect.

However, I prefer to see this deficiency as an opportunity to complement and improve the argument I present in this book in collaboration with experts from different domains. This critical feedback is what drives the social sciences as a cooperative project.

Acknowledgments

I would like to thank David Fasenfest for giving me the opportunity to publish this book in such an innovative series as Studies in Critical Social Sciences. I also wish to express my appreciation for my colleagues at the Department of Conflict and Development Studies at Ghent University, especially Koenraad Bogaert and Sami Zemni for our past collaborations and discussions. I also appreciate the critical comments of Maha Abdelrahman and Gilbert Achcar on the original dissertation. Special thanks go out to Jelle Versieren for our enduring effort to make sense of Egypt's political economy and transition to capitalism.

Andy Blunden and Colin Barker, I am most grateful for your continued support for and confidence in my attempts to connect Vygotsky to a Marxist theory of social movements. Andy, your lucid 'practical-critical' appropriation of Hegel has rendered dialectical logic comprehensible and operational for a new generation of Marxists, social movement activists, and critical scholars.

I also thank Estelle Cooch for proofreading and copy-editing the text, and sharing her insightful remarks with me. Needless to say, I take full responsibility of any lingering methodological, factual, grammatical, and spelling errors in the text.

Finally, a warm thanks to my friends and comrades in Egypt without whom this work would not have been possible and who are still struggling today to build a genuine project of political and human emancipation. You deserve our lasting respect and solidarity.

Abbreviations

AAPSO	African-Asian Peoples' Solidarity Organization
ADNP	Arab Democratic Nasserist Party
ASU	Arab Socialist Union
CETU	Congress of Egyptian Trade Unions
CHAT	Cultural-Historical Activity Theory
CPE	Communist Party of Egypt
CSF	Central Security Forces
CSS	Center for Socialist Studies
CTWS	Center for Trade Union and Workers Services
CYR	Coalition of the Youth of the Revolution
DMNL	Democratic Movement for National Liberation
EASP	Egyptian Arab Socialist Party
ECP	Egyptian Communist Party
ECESR	Egyptian Center for Economic and Social Rights
EDLC	Egyptian Democratic Labor Congress
EFITU	Egyptian Federation of Independent Trade Unions
EMNL	Egyptian Movement for National Liberation
EPCSPI	Egyptian Popular Committee in Solidarity with the Palestinian Intifada
ESDP	Egyptian Social Democratic Party
ESP	Egypt Socialist Party
GFETU	General Federation of Egyptian Trade Unions
GFLU	General Federation of Labor Unions
GFLUKE	General Federation of Labor Unions in the Kingdom of Egypt
HMLC	Hisham Mubarak Law Center
IAEA	International Atomic Energy Agency
ILO	International Labor Organization
MTWU	Metro and Tram Workers Union
NAC	National Association for Change
NCWS	National Committee for Workers and Students
NDF	National Democratic Front
NDP	National Democratic Party
NFTUE	National Federation of Trade Unions in Egypt
NSF	National Salvation Front
RETAU	Real Estate Tax Authority Union
RS	Revolutionary Socialists (Tendency)
SCAF	Supreme Council of armed forces
SLCHR	Sons of Land Center for Human Rights

ABBREVIATIONS

SMT	Social Movement Theory
SPAP	Socialist Popular Alliance Party
SRC	Socialist Renewal Current
SWP	Socialist Workers Party
UESY	Union for Egyptian Socialist Youth
UPY	Union of Progressive Youth
WCNL	Workers' Committee for National Liberation
WNDP	Workers National Democratic Party
ZPD	Zone of Proximal Development

Introduction

On 25 January 2011 a diverse group of Egyptian social media activists, leftists, youth organizations, political opposition forces, human rights proponents, Islamists, and hardcore football supporters – the so-called Ultras – had called for a demonstration in *Midan Tahrir* – Liberation Square. The demands of the organizers were relatively modest: "[…] the sacking of the country's interior minister, the cancelling of Egypt's perpetual emergency law, which suspends basic civil liberties, and a new term limit on the presidency that would bring to an end the 30-year rule of president Hosni Mubarak" (Shenker 2011a).

No one expected the protests to attract tens of thousands of ordinary Egyptians, let alone be the harbinger of revolution (Sowers 2012, 4). "Before the revolution it was a success to have 100 people demonstrating in the street. So we were laughing: tomorrow we will have a revolution,"[1] leftist journalist Haisam Hassan recalled. "We wanted to challenge the cops by protesting that day. A lot of people were surprised to see that we had more than 25,000 people at Tahrir that day and things escalated from there,"[2] shrugged youth activist Ahmed al-Gourd. Political cartoonist Salah Abd al-Azim had originally planned his wedding on 22 January. When he heard of the protest organized on the 25th, he decided to postpone his marriage to the 26th, so he could participate in the demonstration:

> I imagined it would only be one day of protests as usual. So I delayed my wedding to 26 January. So on 25 January we went to the protests. No one of my guests could make it to my wedding on the 26th, because half of them were protesting and the other half were escaping the police![3]

The security apparatus was surprised by the massive turnout and followed the events relatively passively, at first. In the afternoon Central Security Forces (CSF) tried to break up the protests with water cannons, sound bombs, batons, rubber bullets, and tear gas, and the peaceful demonstrations turned violent as protesters retaliated with rocks and bricks. Central Cairo became a war zone with continuous street battles between police forces and tens of thousands of demonstrators. The protests in Cairo sparked off massive demonstrations in

---

1 Interview with Haisam Hassan, Cairo, 7 March 2011.
2 Interview with Ahmed al-Gourd, Cairo, 24 March 2011.
3 Interview with Salah Abd al-Azim, Cairo, 22 March 2011.

Alexandria and in cities in the Delta, the Canal Zone, and Upper Egypt. The next 18 days saw an ebb and flow of mass protests and violent countermeasures, throughout which the original tame demands were transformed into the revolutionary slogans of "the people want the fall of the régime," and "bread, freedom, and social justice." Tahrir Square in Cairo was occupied, and across the whole country police stations and the party offices of the ruling National Democratic Party (NDP) were burned down. Suddenly people began to realize they were making a revolution and that there was no way back. Their mass uprising eventually pressured Hosni Mubarak, who had been Egypt's president since 1981, to step down.

Return of Mass Politics

The revolutionary events, first in Tunisia and then in regional heavyweight Egypt, reinvigorated practices of mass politics throughout the Middle East and the world at large. Protest movements such as the *Indignados* and Occupy Wall Street were directly inspired by the apparent success of the Tahrir occupation. The so-called Arab Spring[4] also stimulated an intellectual, ideological, and academic debate on the contemporary character of mass agency and the methodology of societal transformation. Within the domain of Middle Eastern Studies, it reinforced the position of scholars who had opposed the dominant research paradigm that framed the region's populations as passive objects of religion, tradition, and authoritarianism (Beinin and Vairel 2011, 1).[5] The Iraqi poet and novelist Sinan Antoon mused that in the eyes of the world the Middle East had become: "[…] a place where the burden of the past weighed so heavily and the cultural DNA somehow preconditioned those who carried it to feel more at home with tyrants and terror" (Antoon 2012, 7).

The roots of this defeatist discourse stretched back to the era of Western colonialism, which presented the Arab masses as uneducated, backward and thus incapable of self-emancipation. At the end of the nineteenth century Lord Cromer[6] emphatically ruled out the possibility of self-determination of the Egyptian people:

---

4 A problematic term with orientalist overtones, suggesting a previous era of 'winter' where nothing really happened and a cyclical nature to protests.
5 For an example of a *mea culpa* of such scholars: Tarek Masoud (2011) and Jeremy Kinsman (2011).
6 As consul-general, Evelyn Baring (1841–1917), First Earl of Cromer, was Britain's chief colonial administrator of Egypt from 1883 to 1907.

> Can any sane man believe that a country which has for centuries past been exposed to the worst forms of misgovernment at the hands of its rulers, from Pharaohs to Pashas, and in which, but ten years ago, only 9.5 percent of the men and 0.3 percent of the women could read and write, is capable of suddenly springing into a position which will enable it to exercise full rights of autonomy with advantage to itself and to others interested in its welfare? The idea is absurd.
> SEIKALY AND GHAZALEH, 2011

More than a century later, on the first day of the 25 January Revolution, an article appeared on the BBC website, observing that "Egypt has many of the same social and political problems that brought about the unrest in Tunisia – rising food prices, high unemployment and anger at official corruption" (Egypt Protests 2011). Yet, it immediately downplayed the possibility of a revolutionary Tunisian scenario in Egypt by echoing Cromer: "However, the population of Egypt has a much lower level of education than Tunisia. Illiteracy is high and internet penetration is low" (Egypt Protests 2011). The colonial premise of Lord Cromer that despotism and a lack of formal education constituted absolute obstacles to the self-determination of a people was still shared by political commentators and scholars of the region today. Moreover, the Arab Spring came as a shock, not only for Western 'colonial' observers, but also for Arab activists and intellectuals, as Seikaly and Ghazaleh pointed out:

> It is not simply colonial overlords, authoritarian régimes, and Western arms dealers that attempt to produce the Arab people as children to be herded. Arab elitist discourse has played one of the most crucial and sustaining roles in producing the people as passive, easily manipulated children. Arab intellectuals reproduce a pervasive and ongoing divide between the 'educated' and the 'uneducated' [...] Elites are reproducing the very infantilization of the people that has buttressed colonial, authoritarian, and neo-colonial domination.
> SEIKALY AND GHAZALEH, 2011

A majority of Arab intellectuals were not able to imagine the 'people' – *al-sha'b* as a self-determining agent. Although most of them acknowledged 'the masses' as a formidable social force, they saw them as a power that could be mobilized by a third party instead of a self-conscious collective actor in their own right. In the end, al-sha'b was just a category from which 'Savior-Rulers'[7] such as

---

7 Cf. Draper 1971. The concept of the 'Savior-Ruler' is explained in chapter nine "Pathologies."

Gamal Abd al-Nasser drew their legitimacy. However, the paternalist pedagogy of many Arab intellectuals did not reflect a regional history without mass movements. Eliott Colla reminded us that:

> [...] making revolution is not something new for Egyptians – having had no less than three "official" revolutions in the modern era: the 1881 Urabi Revolution which overthrew a corrupt and comprador royalty; the 1919 Revolution, which nearly brought down British military rule; and the 1952 Revolution which inaugurated 60 years of military dictatorships under Nasser, Sadat and Mubarak… In other words, despite what commentators might say, modern Egyptians have never passively accepted the failed colonial or postcolonial states that fate has dealt them.
> COLLA, 2012, 47–48

Indeed, the contemporary Arab revolts did not wake the region from an eternal slumber of Oriental despotism. Nevertheless, the salient display of mass agency *did* encourage and reinforce a conception of the popular masses as a collective agent. People were not only conscious agents; they became conscious of their agency as a people. The salient victories and failures of the Egyptian 25 January uprising and other contemporary mass movements emphasize the need for an understanding of the mechanics behind their formation, mobilization, organization, development, transformation and, often, collapse.

Social Movements and Capitalism

The intellectual development of the academic study of social movements is strongly entwined with the history of the capitalist system contested by these movements. Interest within Western academia for popular protests largely grew out of fear of the threat that socialist and fascist street mobilizations posed to bourgeois democracy in the 1920s and 1930s. Social movements were negatively perceived as forms of non-institutionalized, irrational, and spontaneous collective behavior, in which agency was largely absent (Eyerman and Jamison 1991, 10–11). The emergence of 'new social movements' in the late 1960s necessitated novel perspectives on the formative causes and developmental dynamics of collective action. In the 1970s, authors such as Charles Tilly and Sidney Tarrow investigated social movements through a critical and productive engagement with Marxist theories of struggle and contestation, discussing the relation between everyday life and 'repertoires of contention', and between societal transformation and immediate forms of resistance (cf. Barker et al. 2013). Since the 1980s, social movement theory (SMT) scholars tried to incorporate the role of the 'cultural', the 'ideological', and the 'pedagogical' by borrowing concepts from symbolic interactionism and frame theory (Johnston 2009, 3).

However, frame theory has been criticized for being an apolitical, fragmentary, and superficial conception of how thoughts and artifacts mediate collective agency. It is a "marketing approach to movement mobilization" that "[...] arises precisely when marketing processes have come to dominate social movements [...]" (Oliver and Johnston 2000, 47). In their seminal work "Social Movements: A Cognitive Approach" (1991) Ron Eyerman and Andrew Jamison observed that: "There is something fundamental missing from the sociology of social movements, something that falls between the categories of the various schools and is left out of their various conceptualizations" (Eyerman and Jamison 1991, 45). SMT lacked a conceptualization of movements as "processes in formation" and "forms of activity" with a "cognitive praxis" (Eyerman and Jamison 1991, 2–3).

The criticism of Eyerman and Jamison addressed a cultural-historical[8] gap in the study of social movements. Firstly, as 'movements', they not only imply a quantitative 'crossing of distance' or 'being in motion', but also an internal *development* from a certain phase, level, or state towards another one: "[...] existing forms of activity and organization (and of passivity and disorganization) need to be understood as transitory, inwardly contradictory and open to large- or small-scale transformation" (Barker et al. 2013, 15). Through a struggle to change the status quo, social movements (and their participants) are themselves transformed. Secondly, they are specific forms of human *activity*, of people 'coming together' and collaborating around shared goals. Thirdly, social movements are sites of *learning*, of the production of practices, knowledge, and self-consciousness. In other words, the study of social movements should not only focus on how preexisting actors, reacting to emerging political opportunities, collectively mobilize resources; it should also investigate how such a collaboration actively produces new forms of agency and subjectivity.

Nevertheless, the development of self-conscious, cohesive, and coherent[9] practices of collective activity – i.e., the subjective component of social movements – remained largely a black box for SMT scholars. The emergence of social movement studies in the 1970s and 1980s coincided with a growing aversion

---

8 "The recognition that culture plays a central role in generating and sustaining movements was slow to develop and remains the model's least developed concept" (Morris 2000, 446).

9 Cohesion is unity at the level of organization or structure, coherence is unity at the level of thought. Note that unity does not mean identity. On the contrary, for two phenomena to become united, their difference is presupposed.

toward conceptions of the (mass) subject, the theorization of which had been tainted with the 'modernist' legacy of authoritarianism, eschatologism, determinism, and/or monologism.[10]

Taken as a broad paradigmatic historical movement, (post)structuralist philosophy and postmodern thought conceptually emancipated the subaltern[11] from his or her intellectual subsumption under 'homogeneous subjects' and 'motors of history', and emphasized the heterogeneity, multi-vocalism, and non-linearity of identity or discourse formation (cf. Mouffe 1993). The influential structuralist Louis Althusser claimed that "[…] Marxist philosophy must break with the idealist category of the 'Subject' […]" (Althusser 1976, 94) In works such as "For Marx" (1969) and "Reading Capital" (1970), he embarked on an intellectual project that aimed to purge Marxist thought from both its Hegelian subjectivist-humanist and Kautskyan objectivist-economist legacies. The subject's agency was replaced by the interpellative force of ideology. Michel Foucault, for his part, criticized the modernist metaphysics and replaced its central notion of the (individual, Kantian) subject with a productive concept of power: "The individual is not a pre-given entity which is seized on by the exercise of power. The individual, with his identity and characteristics, is the product of a relation of power exercised over bodies, multiplicities, movements, desires, forces" (Foucault 1980, 73–74).

The poststructuralist paradigm stimulated scholars from the social and political sciences and humanities to unearth the *petite histoire* of subaltern actors that had been buried under the grand narratives and subjects of liberalism, nationalism, fascism, and communism. Attention was diverted from the traditional institutions and sites of contestation and struggle, as power itself was rediscovered as a dispersed, capillary, everyday, and decentralized force, which opened up entirely new fields of research of the 'microphysics' of oppression and domination. Functioning as critique, poststructuralist and postmodern thought "[…] raised important questions about how large collectivities constitute themselves around certain descriptive categories and claim them as their own" (Barker et al. 2013, 26). Many critical thinkers influenced by poststructuralism sought ways to combine their critique of modernity with a practical theory of emancipation. Judith Butler, for example, appropriated and

---

10 'Monologism' allows only one 'voice' to speak, thus generating homogeneity and claims for an 'ultimate truth'. Conversely, 'dialogism' offers a platform to many 'voices', thereby inspiring difference, variation, and a relative conception of truth (Cf. Bakhtin 1985).

11 Gramsci's term to denote groups that are subordinated to the power and hegemony of ruling groups.

developed ideas of Althusser and Foucault in order to criticize the particularism of feminist identity politics (cf. Butler 1993).

However, as a general intellectual trend, poststructuralism and postmodernism represented a paradigmatic *shift within* rather than an *expansion of* the study of contemporary relations of power and resistance. The modernist celebration of sameness and the universal was exchanged for an overemphasis on difference and the particular (cf. Fraser 2013). The novel philosophical interpretations of agency, subjectivity, and power implied crucial changes for emancipatory politics. If the nature of power was essentially decentralized, diffuse, and pluralist, it could only be resisted in a local and capillary form; otherwise a new apparatus of domination with its own universalist claims would be established, as presumably happened, for example, in the Soviet Union.[12] This means that there are no 'primary' struggles to be waged, no 'essential' sites of power that have to be conquered, controlled, or defeated by emancipatory movements.[13]

When faced with the reality of mass demonstrations, general strikes, and revolutionary uprisings, the poststructuralist turn begs the question of how the theoretical elision of the mass subject and an emphasis on the decentralized and dispersed character of capillary power and everyday forms of resistance constitute a political strategy to transform society (cf. Moore 2011, 8). As Barker et al. concluded: "One result [...] has been a narrowing of the understanding of movements and their place in large-scale processes of social change" (Barker et al. 2013, 5) Instead of an emancipatory breakthrough, the embrace of localized and everyday micro-strategies of resistance by activists and engaged social scientists alike appears as a practical and theoretical retreat from mass politics. Especially postmodernist thought, built upon poststructuralist philosophical premises (cf. Callinicos 1989), presented itself as the final negation of the grand 'modernist' narratives, be they liberal or Marxist – but did not the new paradigm itself represent a metadiscourse of defeat in the face of a triumphant neoliberal capitalism? The comment of the Soviet philosopher Evald Ilyenkov (1924–1979) on the entanglement of the development of a science and its object springs to mind:

> Here the history of science itself serves as a kind of mirror for the history of the object. Changes in the science reflect major historical changes in the structure of the object itself. The object develops fast enough, and the

---

12 For a critique: Callinicos 2001.
13 For a critique: Barker et al. 2013.

historical periods in its development coincide with those of the development of the science and its categories.

ILYENKOV, 2008B, P. 205

In "The Condition of Postmodernity" (1990), a play on Jean-François Lyotard's "The Postmodern Condition" (1984), David Harvey argued that the rise of the postmodern paradigm is tightly connected to the restructuring of capitalism in the 1970s. With regard to the rise of 'identity politics' that replaced struggles for material redistribution, Nancy Fraser observed that: "The shift from redistribution to recognition has occurred just as an aggressively globalizing US-led capitalism is exacerbating economic inequality" (Fraser 2013, 160). Furthermore, the poststructuralist and postmodern turns coincided with a general decline of trade unionism and the Left in the same period (cf. Barker et al. 2013, 25–26).

Before the 1970s, the rise of national liberation movements and the crisis of 'actually existing socialism', both in its Stalinist and social-democratic appearances, encouraged intellectuals such as Jean-Paul Sartre (1905–1980)[14] and Frantz Fanon (1925–1961)[15] to reconstruct existing theories of praxis as tools for emancipation. The failure of newly established postcolonial régimes, new social movements, and New Left tendencies such as Maoism, Italian workerism, autonomism, and so on, to offer a credible, organic, and stable alternative in a crisis-ridden, post-war capitalism signaled a real decline of mass agency and subjectivity. Throughout the 1970s and 1980s the emerging neoliberal narrative partly absorbed, appropriated, and pacified the anti-authoritarian, anti-hierarchical, and anti-bureaucratic agency that the 1960s movements represented.[16]

Becoming the dominant intellectual paradigm in the 1980s and 1990s, poststructuralist and postmodernist thought thus appear as the critical expression of a newly emerging shape of capitalist modernity and of the defeat or pacification of traditional and new social movements. Just as the political practices of Stalinism and social democracy constituted inadequate negations of capitalism, poststructuralist and postmodernist thought represented an incomplete, distorted, and halted negation of the ontology of modernity. Vast problems for

---

14 Cf. "Critique of Dialectical Reason" (2004).
15 Cf. "Wretched of the Earth" (1963).
16 "Neo-liberalism with its proclamation of the end of conformism and its attack on the 'nanny state' can in this context be understood as a policy designed to absorb the agility of the emerging subject for the new potential of a more flexible mode of production, while at the same time keeping this new subject from gaining the necessary experience to challenge the old positions of individual profits and leadership" (Barfuss 2008, 846).

human emancipation, such as enduring poverty, inequality, uneven development, state violence and oppression, could not be solved through micropolitics and dispersed instances of resistance, but required formidable solutions, in the shape of material revolutions and intellectual 'grand' theories.

The emergence of the alterglobalization and antiwar movement, resurgent trade union militancy, the Arab uprisings, and other local and global forms of mass struggle, forcefully express the necessity for a negation of the contemporary order. But this negation cannot be simply a sublation of poststructuralist thought and politics as it still has to fulfill the original task of the complete negation of capitalist modernity. While the current incarnation of capitalism differs in important ways from its postwar, interwar, and nineteenth century predecessors, it remains a social formation dominated by generalized commodity production, the accumulation of capital, and the proletarianization of the labor force. The unresolved problems of previous capitalist forms are continuously dragged into freshly reconfigured world orders. This prolonged *duration*[17] of the capitalist mode of production is veiled by a seemingly accelerating 'velocity of history' (Schlesinger 1999), which constantly presses critical thinkers to reinvent the wheel in order to keep up with 'change'. In other words, the actuality of capitalism encompasses a burden of the past as well as of the present.

Toward a Pedagogy of Revolt

Contemporary social movements encounter the burden of the past or the 'non-contemporaneity of the present' (cf. Thomas 2009, 282) in the concrete shape of both 'old' and 'new' political problems of organization, mobilization, institutionalization, leadership, and internal democracy. The central theme of the work at hand is the enduring contradiction between the ethico-political principle of emancipation and the historical legacy of the division of labor.

Alan Johnson defined emancipation as: "[...] a political process in which the oppressed author their own liberation though popular struggles which are educational, producing a cognitive liberation, and instrumental, enabling the defeat of their oppressors" (Johnson 2001, 98). The idea that the only real form of emancipation is self-emancipation goes back to Marx's adage in his critique

---

17   "[...] duration is the modality of the development of an inert time [...] when an historical form persists, reproducing itself consistently in the force of the equilibrium between its own capacity of innovation and the progressive development of its own powers of 'viscosity' [...] duration is the 'normal phase' of life of individual social formations: the formal time of annals, an empty time" (Alberto Burgio in Thomas 2009, 152).

of the Gotha Program: "The emancipation of the working class must be the act of the workers themselves" (Marx 2008, 28). At the time, this slogan constituted a revolutionary principle that rejected previous paternalist traditions whereby an enlightened elite, Blanquist vanguard, or 'Savior-Ruler' acted as the emancipator of a subaltern group, substituting their own power for the agency of those that desired liberation (cf. Levant 2012). Real emancipation entails the development of the capacity of a group to emancipate itself.

Yet, in "The German Ideology" (1976), Marx and Engels also drew attention to a fundamental predicament of human emancipation: the historical separation between theory and practice,[18] mental and material labor: i.e., the social division of labor constitutive of class society:

> From this moment onwards consciousness can really flatter itself that it is something other than consciousness of existing practice, that it really represents something without representing something real; from now on consciousness is in a position to emancipate itself from the world and to proceed to the formation of 'pure' theory, theology, philosophy, ethics, etc.....
> MARX AND ENGELS, 1976, 45

The growing social division of labor created a distinction between practice and thought by separating a category of professional 'ideologists' from the rest of society. This social separation between theory and practice, further deepened by the development of modern education and science in capitalist modernity, brought Karl Kautsky (1854–1938), the leading theoretician of the Second International, to the conclusion that the idea of socialism had to be brought to the workers from without.[19] Even though other Marxists, such as Vladimir Lenin (1870–1924)[20] and Rosa Luxemburg (1871–1919), rejected Kautsky's paternalist view of workers as the passive receivers of 'theory' from bourgeois intellectuals, they did not develop a coherent theory of their own role as non-proletarian[21]

---

18 Obviously there is no 'pure' historical dichotomization between theory and practice. Gramsci remarked that "[...] in any physical work, even the most degraded and mechanical, there exists a minimum of technical qualification, that is, a minimum of creative intellectual activity [...]" (Gramsci 1971, 8). Marx rather drew attention to the emergence of 'pure' theory as opposed to theory that is continuously encapsulated by everyday practice.
19 Cf. Chapter 6 "The Modern Prince" and Chapter 7 "A Pedagogy of Revolt."
20 For a discussion of Lenin's presumed elitism or substitutionism: Au 2007, Draper 1990, and Levant 2012.
21 Throughout the text, I use 'proletarians' and 'proletariat' in its broadest sense of modern wage laborers who, as a population, are the product of the historical process of

actors within the development of the workers' movement. As some of the great 'thinkers' and 'leaders' of the socialist movement emerged from the ranks of the (petty) bourgeoisie, how could and should they assist the development of the workers' movement without appropriating it for their own benefit? From the perspective of the self-emancipation of the working class, what forms of 'external' instruction and assistance were necessary, possible, and ethical?

Yet the question of leadership, theory, and authority did not only flow from a *social* division of labor, separating worker activists from petty bourgeois leaders; within the workers' movement itself there were forms of both a spontaneous and institutionalized *technical* division of labor between organizers and organized, leaders and led. As Johnson suggests, the existence of leadership in emancipatory movements expresses a general obstacle in the process of subject formation, as well as a situational, strategic necessity:

> The idea of self-emancipation, in liberating people from the need for liberators, can seem to deny the need for leaders at all. It certainly denies the necessity for a Power From Above to deliver liberation to the poor benighted subjects below. Yet there are two reasons why we can't get rid of leadership so easily: unevenness in the consciousness of the emancipatory subject, and the organised opposition of the adversary.
> JOHNSON, 2001, 113

Thus the question of leadership is entwined with, on the one hand, the problem of power, and, on the other, processes of education, learning, and instruction. Within every emancipatory movement there is an implicit theoretical and practical pedagogy of revolt at work, which governs relations of assistance, learning, and power between internal and external forces. Political pedagogies play a fundamental part in the formation and development of the self-consciousness, activity, theory, organization, and leadership of an emancipatory subject. The work at hand constructs an outline of a *general* pedagogy of revolt and confronts it with the *particular* politicized forms of learning and assistance within the Egyptian 25 January Revolution. As such, it aims to be a modest intellectual contribution to the reconstruction of (a theory of) the emancipatory subject.

In order to establish the basic premises of a political pedagogy, I draw on concepts developed within the tradition of cultural-historical activity theory (CHAT),

---

proletarianization: i.e., the separation of producers from their means of production. Naturally this does not mean that 'the proletariat' is a homogeneous force with a single consciousness, as I elaborate further in the text.

a term coined by Michael Cole and Yrjö Engeström in the 1990s to represent the emergence of an interdisciplinary school of thought that combined insights from Lev Vygotsky's cultural psychology and Alexei N. Leontyev's Activity Theory (Blunden 2010, 3). Despite its interdisciplinary ambitions and potential applicability to the study of social movements, CHAT's historical roots in the domains of cultural psychology, pedagogy, communication studies, and anthropology have prevented the paradigm from being used extensively in studies of mass protest and revolution.[22] Hence I appropriate concepts and insights from CHAT and Vygotsky in particular and reintegrate them in a *politicized* cultural-historical framework. I use the Italian Marxist Antonio Gramsci as the main[23] political 'translator' of Vygotsky's pedagogy, by connecting cultural-psychological

---

[22] Notable exceptions are Deborah Kilgore's "Understanding learning in social movements: a theory of collective learning," Wayne Au's "Vygotsky and Lenin on Learning: The Parallel Structures of Individual and Social Development" (2007), and Mastaneh Shah-Shuja's "Zones of Proletarian Development" (2008). Kilgore's article opened up the debate around a Vygotskian approach toward collective learning processes. However, by basing herself on Melucci she framed Vygotsky's dialectics within the SMT paradigm, which is less useful for my project.

Au's groundbreaking piece investigated the possibility to 'translate' Vygotsky's notion of ontogenetic learning and instruction into the domain of sociogenetic development, using Lenin as a middleman. However, Gramsci is probably an even better sociogenetic 'translator' of Vygotsky than Lenin because of his more profound elaboration of the distinction between 'common sense' and 'philosophy'; 'organic' and 'traditional' intellectuals; and 'proletarian' and 'national-popular' dimensions of emancipation (cf. Levant 2012).

Shah-Shuja, for her part, takes credit for her innovative applying of elements of Vygotsky's cultural psychology and Activity Theory in an analysis of protest movements. She articulates them within an Autonomist-like theoretical framework that fundamentally differs from my ('subject-constructivist', Hegelian-Marxist'?) approach. For example, she melds Vygotsky's notion of 'zone of proximal development' with the libertarian communist or anarchist idea of 'temporary autonomous zones', which becomes a 'zone of proletarian development': a social learning space liberated from state and capital. However, there is no real definition of what 'the proletariat' is (Davis 2010), let alone how it develops as a subject. Furthermore, despite its creativity, "Zones of Proletarian Development" suffers from a lack of conceptual coherence and from an ultraleftist 'all or nothing' attitude toward imperfect forms of organizational mediation (Cox 2010). Our opposing philosophical premises and methods render a constructive dialogue between our approaches difficult, if not impossible.

[23] Supported by a cast of other Marxist and critical authors, such as Marx, Lenin, Luxemburg, Lukács, Trotsky, Sartre, Ilyenkov, and so on. The relevance of a reinvigorated Marxist approach towards the study of contemporary social movements has been argued convincingly by Barker et al. in "Marxism and Social Movements" (2013).

concepts such as social situation of development, interiorization, prolepsis, central neoformations, and zone of proximal development (ZPD) to key Gramscian notions such intellectuals, hegemony, and (philosophy of) praxis. As such this work is *synthetic* rather than *analytic* in its approach. It does not offer detailed philological or hermeneutic readings of Vygotsky and Gramsci, assessing their ideas in order to arrive at the most correct interpretation. Instead it appropriates, reconstructs, and mobilizes their concepts for an interpretation of the emancipatory struggle that is relevant today.

Vygotsky and CHAT

Lev Semyonovich Vygotsky (1896–1934) was born in a banker's family and raised in the Belarusian city of Gomel. Despite his Jewish origins, he was admitted to study law in Moscow in 1913. Vygotsky graduated in 1917 from university and also took a course in psychology and philosophy, which would determine his further career. Returning to Gomel he taught literature and psychology at the local high school. There Vygotsky also engaged with the education of impaired children, which encouraged him to construct a general theory of human development that could direct a pedagogical practice of overcoming 'defects' in child development (Yasnitsky 2012, 113). The Russian Revolution and the ensuing foreign military interventions and civil war turned both the theory and practice of education upside down. After a lecture given in 1924 at the Second All-Russian Congress of Psychoneurology, Vygotsky was invited to take up a position at the Moscow Institute of Pyschology. His own theory took form as an immanent critique of the dominant behaviorist paradigm developed by Vladimir Bekhterev (1857–1927) and Ivan Pavlov (1849–1936), and was motivated by their vulgar materialist liquidation of consciousness as a valid concept of psychology. In 1925 he completed his doctoral thesis, "The Psychology of Art," which engaged with the ideological-aesthetic struggle between the schools of Constructivism, Formalism, Futurism and Symbolism.

In the Moscow Institute, together with two young assistants, Alexander R. Luria (1902–77) and Alexei N. Leontyev (1903–79), he laid the foundations of a Marxist cultural psychology that overcame the limitations of the dominant objectivist-materialist approach to the human mind. This cultural psychology was the result of a group effort, an enduring collaboration between Vygotsky, Luria, Leontyev and a few graduate students, whose work was the outcome of a continuous interaction between a theoretical critique of key psychological thinkers – Freud, Piaget, Pavlov, and so on – and the practical feedback of psychological and pedagogical experiments. The primary research topics of the group were issues of ontogenesis (child development), defectology (psychological disablement), learning processes, and methodology (Blunden 2010, 13–17). The ambitious goal was to construct a unified and comprehensive theory and methodology of psychological development. The concept of cultural mediation, in the form of signs and material tools, was crucial to their approach (Yasnitsky 2012, 116–117).

The rapid rise of Marxist cultural psychology in the second half of the 1920s was brought to a standstill by a general deterioration of the intellectual climate in the Soviet Union. In 1931 the Soviet state restored the prerevolutionary curriculum in schools. More than ever Pavlov's behaviorism was raised to the status of theoretical dogma and cultural psychology was denounced and its prominent figures harassed. Vygotsky never lived to see his ideas fully suppressed, however, as in 1934 he died of tuberculosis, a disease which he had struggled with throughout his whole life. Luria, for his part, left the dangerous field of psychology and fully embraced the 'safe' study of medicine (Blunden 2010, 17–18).

After the death of Stalin in 1953, the intellectual climate in the Soviet Union relaxed somewhat. Leontyev (1978) took Vygotsky's ideas in a new direction with Activity Theory, which investigated the concepts of activity, action, and operation and the role of motivation in human activity. Through Scandinavian scholars, and in particular Yrjö Engeström's work "Learning by Expanding" (1987), Activity Theory was introduced in Western Europe in the 1980s. Meanwhile other Soviet scholars were rediscovering Vygotsky. Luria's student Alexander Meshcheryakov (1923–74) redeployed the insights of cultural psychology in the field of the defectology of deaf-blind children. The philosopher Evald Ilyenkov (1924–79) developed the connection between the concepts of activity and the 'ideal'. This generation began to criticize Leontyev's Activity Theory from the perspective of the rediscovered work of Vygotsky himself. However, even in the Soviet Union of the 1960s and 1970s there were clear *political* limits to the development of a Marxist cultural psychology (Blunden 2010, 19).

In the next decades, cultural psychology was largely developed outside the Soviet Union through the translations of Vygotsky's work by Michael Cole, an American graduate student who studied in 1962 for one year in Moscow under supervision of Luria. This connection in fact re-established a previous dialogue between American progressive educational theory and Vygotsky's cultural psychology, when John Dewey had visited Moscow in 1928 (Blunden 2010, 20). Finally, in his work "An Interdisciplinary Theory of Activity" (2010), Andy Blunden (1945-) reassembled the different strands of CHAT and highlighted the methodological connection with predecessors such as Goethe, Hegel, and Marx.

Gramsci

Antonio Gramsci (1891–1937) was born in a middle-class family in Ales, Sardinia, an island off the west coast of Italy. As a boy he suffered from social hardships, due to his father's imprisonment, and health problems, which left him hunchbacked and with a weak physique for the rest of his life. In 1911 the young Gramsci won a scholarship to the University of Turin. Two years later he joined the Italian Socialist Party, becoming an editor and journalist. His political views were influenced by socialist and Sardinian nationalist circles and by the salient industrialization of Turin, which attracted proletarianized farmers from the Italian South. Building on thinkers such as Antonio Labriola (1843–1904) and Benedetto Croce (1866–1952), Gramsci complemented the 'vulgar' Marxism that circulated in the party with a more sophisticated Hegelian outlook.

During the First World War Gramsci was active in the organization and education of Turin workers and he became one of the leading socialist leaders. After the war, he set up the revolutionary socialist weekly *L'Ordine Nuovo* (The New Order) which became the voice of Bolshevik politics in Italy. In 1920, the group around *L'Ordine Nuovo* played a crucial role in assisting the workers' councils that emerged spontaneously[24] during the general strike and factory occupations in Turin in 1919 and 1920. The compromise negotiated between moderate trade union leaders, the Socialist Party, and the state representing the interests of land and factory owners not only stabilized the capitalist system for a brief period, but it also blocked the self-emancipatory movement of the Italian working class (Le Blanc 1996, 281). Disillusioned with the reformist policies of the Socialist Party, Gramsci and many other Italian socialists founded the Italian Communist Party in 1921.

Until 1924, the leadership of the party was in hands of Amadeo Bordiga (1889–1970), who was criticized by Lenin in his "Left-Wing Communism: an Infantile Disorder" (1964a) for his ultra-left politics. Whereas Gramsci advocated a united front against the rise of Fascism, Bordiga insisted on shielding the party from 'bourgeois' influences such as the Socialist Party. In 1924 he was elected into parliament. In the same year Bordiga was arrested and Gramsci took over the leadership of the Italian Communist Party until he was himself confined in 1926, despite his parliamentary immunity. He remained in prison

---

24   Spontaneous does not mean unorganized, because any economic or political action requires a minimum of organization. It means organization 'from below', as a direct reaction against circumstances, instead of called for by a trade union or party organ (cf. Levant 2012).

until 1937, when he died due to a deterioration of his already weak health condition. While imprisoned, he wrote thirty-four notebooks, which dealt with diverse topics, ranging from political theory, over philosophy, to Italian history.

Only after the Second World War did Gramsci's ideas begin to circulate through the publishing by the Italian Communist Party of select sections of his "Prison Notebooks." Gramsci's thought was appropriated by the Italian 'Eurocommunist' movement, which sought to anchor its reformist politics in the works of the respected Marxist. In "The Antinomies of Antonio Gramsci" Perry Anderson famously criticized this reformist instrumentalization of Gramsci's ideas. In defending a revolutionary project, Anderson rejected the coherence of Gramsci's thought, which, due to Fascist censorship, the use of obscure terminology, and its fragmented form, appeared contradictory and multi-interpretable. Recent scholarship, however, has affirmed the internal consistency of Gramsci's concepts (cf. Thomas 2009).

Outline

"Part 1 Subject and Activity" aims to sketch a general theory of the subject. First it engages with the problematic notion of 'the people' as a collective actor (Chapter 1). Subsequently, it criticizes philosophical conceptions of the subject as the individual person (Chapter 2). Then a conception of the collective subject is offered, following Goethe, Hegel, and Marx (Chapter 3). This perspective is enriched with concepts from cultural-historical activity theory, such as social situation of development, interiorization, neoformation, prolepsis, zone of proximal development, activity-system, and collaborative project (Chapter 4). Finally I present my own reflections on and additions to Blunden's concept of project collaboration.

Having constructed an outline of a general theory of the collective subject, "Part 2 Subject and Struggle" turns to the emancipatory subject and the particular activity of revolt. The formation of proletarian and national-popular subjects through the cell-forms of, respectively, 'strike' and 'demonstration' are discussed from a logical and conceptual point of view (Chapter 5). Working class neoformations are understood in Gramscian terms: as trade unionism, political parties, and the Modern Prince (Chapter 6). Next, the motor of sociogenetic development is interpreted as a process of collective learning and instruction, in which 'organic' and 'traditional' intellectuals play a crucial role (Chapter 7). This analysis is followed by a differentiation of modes of struggle into 'war of position' and 'war of movement', emphasizing that in revolutionary times, the development of strikes and demonstrations happens with leaps and bounds (Chapter 8). Finally, a few pathologies of development are discussed: bureaucratism, passive revolution, inadequate instruction, and substitutionism (Chapter 9).

"Part 3 Historical Lineages" deals with the long-term historical process of 'original accumulation' of the 25 January Revolution. It starts with a few methodological remarks on fusing logical development with historical process, explaining the concepts of uneven and combined development, historical bloc, and (deflected) permanent revolution (Chapter 10). Then follows a brief historical excursus of the making of the Egyptian working class and the first nationalist revolution in 1919 (Chapter 11). Subsequently, the problems of partial political and economic independence are discussed, as well as the gradual emergence of trade unionism after the First World War (Chapter 12). Lastly, the Nasserist intervention is interpreted as a developmental pathology from the perspective of proletarian and national-popular sociogenesis (Chapter 13).

"Part 4 Neoliberal Capitalism" reveals the short-term 'original accumulation' of the 25 January Revolution. It starts with Sadat's 'Open Door Policy', which was a first attempt to implement neoliberal reform and which reignited the development of strikes and demonstrations in the 1970s (Chapter 14). In the 1980s this development was cut short by the contingent rise of a rentier economy and Mubarak's successful 'transformist' policies (Chapter 15). However, financial problems necessitated a reconfiguration of the historical bloc in the 1990s, which led to an intensification and acceleration of neoliberal reform, backed up by increasing politics of violence and exclusion (Chapter 16). Political and social violence and exclusion encouraged the rise of 'economic' and 'political' protest movements. The formation of a new left in the 1990s and the resurgence of street politics in the 2000s constituted a civildemocratic project, which was one of the pillars of the 25 January uprising (Chapter 17).

"Part 5 The Workers' Movement" offers a detailed analysis of proletarian subject formation in the years preceding 25 January 2011 through processes of collective learning and instruction. The primary case study is the Mahalla strike movement (Chapter 18). Through this specific case the general development of the strike into trade unionism is investigated (Chapter 19). The role of different organic and especially traditional intellectuals in building the strike project is disclosed (Chapter 20). Subsequently the various forms and modes of instructive assistance are discussed (Chapter 21). Lastly, the internal debates on the adequacy and limits of the offered instruction is represented from a 'zone of proximal development'-perspective (Chapter 21).

"Part 6 Tahrir" deals with the 'extended reproduction' of the 25 January Revolution: the uprising and its aftermath. The first two chapters give a detailed description of the 18 Days (Chapters 23 and 24). The next two chapters analyze the activity and self-organization of the 'Republic of Tahrir' (Chapters 25 and 26). Subsequently, the role of strikes in the wider revolutionary project is investigated (Chapter 27). Attention is paid to the limits and deformations of the uprising (Chapter 28). Finally, a brief overview of developments after the insurrection is presented, alongside a discussion of problems and possibilities of subject formation.

The last part, "Conclusions," is divided in two sections. "Permanent Deflections of Revolution" summarizes the historical trajectory of the proletarian and national-popular subjects through the lens of collective processes of learning and instructive assistance. "A Pedagogy of Revolt" recapitulates the theoretical synthesis of Vygotsky and Gramsci.

PART 1
Subject and Activity

∴

CHAPTER 1

In Want of the People

In this introductory chapter I explore the tension between the organically emerging, but abstract concept of 'the people' in the 25 January Revolution and its real composition, i.e., as 'population'. It distinguishes between 'the people' as a descriptive category and as a political construction, which paves the way for the subsequent chapters on subject formation.

People and Population

When the Egyptian demonstrations on 25 January 2011, planned by small groups of political, human rights, and social media activists, turned into mass protests, the dominant slogan became *al-sha'b yurid isqat al-nizam* (the people want the fall of the régime), which was "a direct import from Tunisia" (Khalil 2012, 144). During the Tunisian uprising, this demand was loudly chanted at the Avenue Habib Bourguiba until president Ben Ali stepped down. The phrase "the people want" referred to a popular poem of the Tunisian poet Abu al-Qasim al-Shabbi (1909–34), of which the final two lines had been incorporated in the national anthem: "If the people want life someday, fate will surely grant their wish. Their shackles will surely be shattered and their night surely vanish" (Achcar 2013, 13). With regard to the medium of the message, Eliott Colla observed that the chant's rhythm "[...] is a familiar part of the soundtrack of Arabic-language activist public culture. While [...] this particular couplet is not rhymed, it can be sung and shouted by thousands of people in a unified, clear, and preordained cadence – and that seems to be a key factor in why it has worked so well" (Colla 2012, 50).

Both in Tunisia and Egypt, protesters presented themselves as 'the people' wanting the fall of 'the régime'. The powerful slogan implied the existence of a collective, national-popular political actor who expressed a universal and sovereign will. Moreover, it pushed those social elements belonging to 'the régime' outside of popular legitimacy. Either you were with al-sha'b, or against it. Casting the 25 January uprising in Lenin's appraisal of the Paris Commune of 1871 and the Russian Revolution of 1905:

> [...] it was undoubtedly a 'real people's' revolution, since the mass of the people, their majority, the very lowest social groups, crushed by oppression and

exploitation, rose independently and stamped on the entire course of the revolution the imprint of their own demands, their attempt to build in their own way a new society in place of the old society that was being destroyed.
LENIN 1964B, 416

Nevertheless, critical scholars were quick to dismiss the binary between 'people versus dictatorship', which, along other oppositions such as 'seculars versus Islamists' and 'old guard versus frustrated youth', was picked up by the media and appropriated to frame the revolutionary process in simplistic categories (Amar 2012). As a political and sociological analysis of the main protagonists and antagonists of the protest movement, these three binaries mutually excluded one another. With regard to the opposition between 'youth' and 'old guard', even though young men and women initiated and spearheaded the protests (al-Bendary 2011), their important role did not *define* the process. This frame narrowed the scope of the revolution and undermined the legitimacy of the protests as a broad, popular movement, as Jessica Winegar warned at the time:

> [...] transitional government figures have started referring to the uprising as a 'youth' uprising and the demands of the people as demands of the 'youth' in a familiar paternalistic way that diminishes not only the importance of what has happened, but also the demands that the vast majority of Egyptians, no matter their age, have of the post-Mubarak government
> WINEGAR 2011

Furthermore, it was unclear which actors were actually meant by 'the youth', as Rabab al-Mahdi pointed out:

> In this construct, the media and academic analysts lump together the contradictory and often conflictual interests of 'yuppies' (young, urban, professionals of the aforementioned connections and backgrounds) with those of the unemployed, who live under the poverty line in rural areas and slum-areas. Under this banner of 'youth' the 'yuppies' and upper middle-class young people are portrayed as the quintessential representative of this uprising.
> AL-MAHDI 2011A

The archetype of the Egyptian revolutionary became a particular youth, such as the Google employee Wael Ghoneim, who, perhaps, reflected more the predominant social composition of the international media than that of the revolutionary actors (Salvatore 2013, 223–224).

The second frame of 'secularists versus Islamists' had no roots whatsoever in the process of 25 January uprising, but only came to the surface during the referendum on the constitutional amendments on 19 March 2011. Subsequent elections and referenda reinforced this opposition. During the '18 Days' of insurrection the prevalent discourse, saliently expressed in slogans, graffiti, and cartoons, was one of popular union and against religious sectarianism. The symbol of the Crescent and Cross was omnipresent, representing unity between believers.[1] Whereas religious activity played a small role in the mobilization of the masses – for example via the mass gatherings after midday Friday prayers or the rallying calls by some preachers – the protesters did not put forward any religious demand.

From a sociological perspective, the 25 January protests were joined by young and old people, men and women, rich and poor, Christians and Muslims. Blogger and activist Hossam al-Hamalawy observed that:

> All social classes in Egypt participated in the uprising from the first stages. Hosni Mubarak's régime succeeded in creating a state of alienation between it and all the social classes, with no exceptions. Even among the Egyptian elite except for those businessmen who surrounded HM [=Hosni Mubarak], were relieved when he resigned.
>
> HADDAD 2011B

The sociologist Muhammad Bamyeh stressed the diverse social composition of the revolutionaries:

> While the youth were the driving force in the earlier days, the revolution quickly became national in every sense; over the days I saw an increasing demographic mix in demonstrations, where people from all age groups, social classes, men and women, Muslims and Christians, urban people and peasants – virtually all sectors of society, acting in large numbers and with a determination rarely seen before.
>
> BAMYEH 2011

The claim that the protest movement represented 'all sectors of society' reinforced its legitimacy in the face of state repression. However, it also revealed the sociological diversity represented by the universalist signifier of 'the people' – a

---

1 Farida Makar explained that the history of the symbol dates back to the 1919 revolution, and that it had re-emerged in the month before the 25 January Revolution after a church bombing in Alexandria (Makar 2011, 309).

heterogeneous gathering of individuals from different social, political, economic, and cultural backgrounds and from distinct age, sex, and belief groups.

The People and the Régime

'The revolutionary people' was far from being a stable category during the development of the revolution: its numbers increased and decreased with the ebb and flow of the mobilizations; and the allegiance of individuals and groups shifted sometimes from participating in the protests to supporting Mubarak and vice versa. While there was a mass contestation of the régime, the population was not consistently and continuously united against the dictator. Apart from those supporters of the president who remained passively at home, the state was able to mobilize substantial social reserves, especially NDP members, semi-criminal elements, and plainclothes police. On Monday 31 January the first pro-Mubarak demonstration was staged outside the ministry of information, rallying some 300 demonstrators. State television focused on these first signs of 'division' among the popular masses. Tuesday 1 February saw an increasing number of pro-Mubarak protests. The military for its part, continued to avoid a direct confrontation with the protesters, but closed off roads and train services to sabotage the mobilization of the masses. This episode served to discredit the claim of the protesters that they represented 'the people' against 'the régime', implying that the demonstrators only defended particularist demands and not the general interest. The president could then present himself as the arbiter of the conflict between different factions within al-sha'b, agreeing with some but not all demands of the protesters in order to further the 'common good' of the nation. This tactic had a big impact on the less politicized layers of the movement, as anthropologist Samuli Schielke observed:

> The Pro-Mubarak demonstration was clearly organised by the government, with trucks with loudspeakers and pictures of Mubarak riding through the streets and distributing photocopied paper sheets in handwriting saying "Yes to Mubarak, no to destruction." But it gained genuine popular support and there were really a lot of people spontaneously joining the march for Mubarak.
> SCHIELKE 2011

Political scientist Sabry Zaky explained that, if Mubarak had proceeded in this mock-conciliatory fashion he probably would have been able to separate the political vanguard from the popular masses and diffuse the movement.[2] Schielke concluded that:

> One camp firmly supports the president, be it out of personal interest, out of belief in strong leaders, or out of fear of chaos. Another camp is critical of the president and the system but optimistic and ready to accept the concessions the government offered. Which way this camp turns in the next days and weeks will be decisive. And one camp, the revolutionary camp, either supports the demonstrators on Tahrir Square, or is standing there right now.
> SCHIELKE 2011

At the very least the president would have won precious time to reorganize the counterrevolutionary forces and reinforce his own position within the régime. However, the increasing clashes between pro-Mubarak supporters and revolutionary protesters, culminating in the infamous 'Battle of the Camel' on Wednesday 2 February, destroyed any wishful thinking about Mubarak's sincerity: "[...] the short pro-Mubarak euphoria had again given way to a more critical albeit by no means unified mood" (Schielke 2011). In contradistinction to the relatively small 'hard core' of thousands of protesters whose revolutionary activity was incessant and relentless, the real mass base of hundreds of thousands of demonstrators was constantly in flux. Furthermore, after the fall of Mubarak, the people as a unified category appeared to collapse almost as fast as the régime embodied by the figure of the president. Political and labor activist Saud Omar complained that: "The revolution was a group work. But now everyone is talking about the revolution as if he owns it."[3]

After the 18 Days a process of differentiation and crystallization of revolutionary opposition forces disintegrated the unity of the people. Activist Gihan Shabeen of the Socialist Revolutionary Current (SRC) explained that: "There are those people who want to demobilize the people and there are those who want the mobilization to continue and to let the people feel that there is a change in their life."[4]

Similar to al-sha'b, *al-nizam*, the 'régime', was a heterogeneous and dynamic category. Even though the 25 January protesters demanded the straightforward overthrow of the unequivocal evil that Mubarak's reign represented, they faced

---

2   Interview with Sabry Zaky, Cairo, 10 March 2011.
3   Interview with Saud Omar, Suez, 18 March 2011.
4   Interview with Gihan Shabeen, Cairo, 16 March 2011.

a multi-tentacled monster. The Egyptian nizam was vertically and horizontally layered; not only did it consist of different and often opposing elite factions (cf. Kandil 2012), but it also incorporated the various scales of surplus extraction and state power, ranging from the lowly bureaucrat to the regional governor; from the ordinary policeman in the street to the officer in the ministry of interior; from the corrupt public sector manager to the international investor; and from Cairo to Washington. Is a soldier who fraternizes with the protesters or a member of Mubarak's National Democratic Party who participates in a strike during the revolution, part of al-sha'b or al-nizam? From an objectivist sociological perspective, such a question seems impossible to answer.

And so, in the face of hundreds of thousands of protesters chanting 'the people want the fall of the régime', one may arrive at a surreal ontological suspicion: do 'the people' as a collective actor even exist? The empirical facts of the January 25 movement – its diversity and fluidity – show that there was no protagonist simply waiting behind the curtains of history only to make his scripted appearance at the scene of revolution. 'The people' do not coincide with 'the population', which merely represents the passive collection of individuals in a given society. The slogan of 'the people want' indicates a transformation of a passive 'population' into an active 'people', of objective existence into subjective self-consciousness. Thus the politico-philosophical question whether 'the people' *exists*, shifts from an epistemological perspective – is 'the people' a true or false representation of the agent at Tahrir Square – to an ontological one: how do 'people' *become* 'the people'. In order to understand the mass agency of an emancipatory movement, it is necessary to understand how it is *constructed* as an actor. Salwa Ismail posited that:

> The revolutions in Egypt and Tunisia invite us to consider the question of the relationship between subjectivities, on one hand, and political agency and collective action, on the other. In both revolutions the people formed as a collective agent asserting a collective will and putting forward demands for radical transformation. The people, as a collective actor, engaged in sustained protests, formulated unified demands, and developed a shared discourse that affirmed the will to bring about specific changes.
> ISMAIL 2011, 990

Ismail correctly focused on the question of the *formation* of collective agency. Especially the study of revolutionary societal change and transformation requires a concept of *which* entity 'does' things and *how* it is able to act. Revolution, then, is not only the product of the activity of certain actors, it is a productive process in its own right, in which new political subjects emerge, or existing actors are transformed in fundamental ways. An investigation into the emergence of a revolutionary subject during the 18 Days requires an understanding of subject formation *in general*, which I elaborate in this part of the work; the development of a *particularly* emancipatory agency in the context of capitalist society, which I discuss in the second part; and the *individual* case of the Egyptian revolution, of which the investigation makes up the remainder of the book.

CHAPTER 2

Individual and Collective

In the previous chapter I highlighted the agency of 'the people' as a political construction. In order to understand the formation of such a subject, this chapter briefly discusses the tension between individual and collective forms of subjectivity through an exploration of the philosophical roots of the modern concept of the subject.

Mind and Body

In modern society the dominant conception of the subject is *the individual person*. Ideologically this concept is expressed by laws and rights that constitute an individual human being as an actor in the civil and political sphere and by the prevailing paradigm of methodological individualism in the social sciences, especially economics and psychology. From a legal perspective, in most countries, being part of the human species is not a sufficient condition to qualify for *subjectness* – by which I mean the capacity to act as a subject. Whereas human subjectness has to manifest itself in an individual body, the body itself is not a subject. Age and mental health are additional parameters that distinguish those members of society who are *responsible* for their own acts from those that are not. In order to be responsible, the individual has to act as a *rational* and *self-conscious* being. The individual subject has to be a *knowing* actor who *reflects* on his or her own nature as a subject and who *directs* its actions according to this cognitive process.

The English word 'subject' had emerged in the fourteenth century in political and philosophical circles and was directly derived from the Latin *subjectum*, which, in turn, was a translation of Aristotle's concept of *hypokeimenon* – meaning ontological substance (Blunden 2005/6). It was used to designate individuals that were *subjected* to the power of a sovereign, such as a monarch. Subjects formed the passive substance of a king's active power. In the seventeenth century, the French rationalist philosopher René Descartes (1596–1650) coined the term subject as the *individual* cognizing actor, consolidating the humanist conception developed during the Renaissance of the individual philosopher, scientist, and thinker as the active and creative constructor of knowledge. For Descartes, the undeniable fact of his own, personal consciousness was the premise of his philosophy. The French philosopher could doubt the input of his senses, but not the fact that he doubted – i.e., the consciousness of doubting. Descartes also pointed out that the movement of his consciousness was not of his own volition, that it reacted against and upon stimuli from 'outside'. His rational approach established his individual consciousness and the world outside consciousness as *facts*.

Inscribing himself within premodern dualist philosophical traditions, Descartes conceived of thought and the material world as radically different and even opposite substances. As part of the material world, the body was but the mechanical vehicle of the individual knowing subject. This line of thought, however, posed the problem of the *relation* between the mind and the body. How could the subject ever act if the thought-forms of her mind and the movements of her body could not correspond in any rational way, for they belonged to two opposite planes of existence? In principle, there could be no correspondence between thinking and acting, but in practice individuals continuously acted according to thoughts.

The Dutch philosopher Baruch Spinoza (1632–77) solved the Cartesian problem in a manner "[...] brilliant in its simplicity for our day as well as his: the problem is insoluble only because it has been wrongly posed" (Ilyenkov 2008a, 31). Descartes's initial premise, a consciousness separate from its body, was incorrect: "There are not two different and originally contrary objects of investigation – body and thought – but only one single object, which is the thinking body of living, real man [...]" (Ilyenkov 2008a, 31). The mind thinks not *for* the body, operating it like a machine; it is the body *itself* that thinks. Conversely, thinking is not the causal product of a mechanical action, but a property of the action itself. At this point the problematic shifted from the relation between thinking and being *within* the individual human to the relation *between* the mind-body and the things external to it: "[...] why and how the thinking body feels and perceives the effect caused by an external body within itself *as an external body*, as its, and not as its own shape, configuration, and position in space" (Ilyenkov 2008a, 38–39).

Thus the philosophical problem of the interaction between mind and body was sublated by the question of the relation between *subject* – i.e., the agent of cognition – and *object* – i.e., the external world of things.

Transcendental Subject

The German philosopher Immanuel Kant (1724–1804) granted the subject its full modern content of unity between individual morality, cognition, and self-consciousness. Kant engaged with the barren debate between skepticists, who claimed that the only true source of knowledge was the individual sensory apparatus, and dogmatists, who built their philosophical systems on ontological premises that were not verifiable by experience. To Kant it seemed logically impossible to create a unified philosophical system that comprised both schools, therefore he aimed to develop a general 'legislation' of reason, delimiting the rational boundaries wherein a civilized dialogue between the two trends of thought could take place.

Kant recognized that all knowledge was derived from experience, but that experience itself was only possible through the existence of *transcendental* categories that preceded experience, e.g. quality and quantity, identity and difference, time and space. This form of *a priori* transcendental cognition belonged to the *transcendental subject*, which was a purely *abstract* and *universal* subject – i.e., that which remained of the individual cognizing actor after its consciousness had been purged of cultural-historical categories. Cartesian dualism was reproduced in Kant's system through his conception of the individual, knowing subject, which was the unity of a *phenomenal* and *noumenal* (or transcendental) subject, respectively operating in the realm of sensual understanding and of transcendental reason. Outside the realm of human knowledge there existed the world of things *an sich*, 'in themselves', which escape our experience. Such things may or may not exist, but we can neither deny nor assert their existence.

Apart from a *rational observer*, the individual human subject was by definition a *moral actor*, a person who carried responsibility for her own acts. For Kant, this morality was not a cultural-historical construct, but it belonged to the domain of the transcendental subject: "[...] conscience is not a thing to be acquired, and it is not a duty to acquire it; but every man, as a moral being, has it originally within him" (Kant 2008, 105). Similar to cognition, morality was a human universal that preceded the particular teachings of any secular or religious tradition. That which was *right in general* could not be deduced empirically, but had to be derived logically, free from contingent factors or cultural-historical preferences. This basic logical axiom or categorical imperative was the principle of universalizibility: "Act according to a maxim which can be adopted at the same time as a universal law" (Kant 2008, 78). In other words, if an act can be universalized without it leading to logical contradictions, it is a moral act. The fact that human beings are naturally endowed with, on the one hand, a transcended morality, and, on the other, a (conditional) free will, means that obeying the categorical imperative is a matter of ethical duty. Kant's modern conception of moral agency refers to duty not as an external bond between the individual and a higher power, but as a relation *internal* to the subject: between its free will and the universal categorical imperative. Interior, individual self-discipline instead of exterior, social force emerged as the instrumentality of moral duty.

From an emancipatory perspective Kant's claims about the transcendental universality of human cognition and morality stressed the fundamental equality of individuals *as* human beings. However, in order to arrive at this universality, the human subject was stripped from its rich cultural-historical determinations and reduced to a mere logical apparatus. Moreover, the universality of Kant's cognizing and ethical subject was derived from a particular Western trajectory. In order to establish his 'general legislation of reason', Kant had purged the accumulated history of Western thought of its disagreements and dissimilarities, thus disclosing *empirically* the handful of ideas about reason that were shared by all Western thinkers. The German philosopher then uncritically elevated this historical-empirical generalization to the status of universal truth about the formal rules of thought (Ilyenkov 2008a, 80–81). The 'transcendental' subject that survived the logical purification process was not universal human reason, but a far-reaching abstraction of Western philosophical thought. Representing the musings of a small circle of Western philosophers as the meta-historical and meta-cultural universality of human thought constituted an intellectual colonization of subaltern groups, both inside and outside Western societies.

Activity

Instead of resolving the intellectual conflict between skeptic and dogmatist schools of thought, Kant proposed peaceful coexistence, compromise, and respect within the scientific community. However, as the age of revolutions drew nearer, his radicalized successors became less satisfied with this philosophical gentleman's agreement. Inspired by the revolutionary tide in France (1789–93), the German philosopher Johann Gottlieb Fichte (1762–1814) disagreed with Kant's philosophical armistice and argued for a singular theory of thought that could unite the opposing categories and paradigms. Kant's claim that there were two different worlds of thought, governed by respectively experimental understanding and logical reason, suggested a schizophrenic cognizing subject, whose transcendental categories were completely disconnected from contemplation of the conceivable world of objects. Fichte criticized Kant's concept of the thing *an sich*. He did not question the existence of a world of unknowable things-in-themselves, but the logical consistency of its Kantian concept:

> […] *in the concept* 'of a thing as it exists before and outside any possible experience' there was included a bit of nonsense not noted by Kant: to say that the Ego was *conscious* of a thing *outside consciousness* was the same as to say that there was money in one's pocket outside one's pocket.
> ILYENKOV 2008A, 117

In order to solve the contradiction in Kantian thought, Fichte took human activity as the substance of his philosophy. He rejected Descartes's *cogito ergo sum* as a viable premise for an ontology, for that cohesive being which is the Self, the Ego or the I, is itself a product of our own activity. The individual human being continuously discovers the world through its free and creative activity. For Fichte: "Practical activity was the 'third' thing on which all mutually contradictory systems came together as on common soil" (Ilyenkov 2008a, 137). Through activity the separate worlds of the thinking subject and the contemplated object could encounter one another and form relations of correspondence:

> If philosophy begins with a fact, then it places itself in the midst of a world of being and finitude, and it will be difficult indeed for it to discover any path leading from this world to an infinite and supersensible one. If, however, philosophy begins with an Act, then it finds itself as the precise point where these two worlds are connected with each other and from which they can both be surveyed in a single glance.
> FICHTE 1994, 51

Self-consciousness is nothing else than human activity reflected back on itself. There is no abstract transcendental subject that forms the universal, rational kernel of every 'real' individual human being. The thinking subject and the object of thought are not a priori categories, but they *emerge* from the primordial substance of activity.

Fichte also rejected the other dualisms of the Kantian system, such as the opposition between natural necessity and human freedom, and between practical (ethics) and theoretical philosophy. In his time of revolution, he posited that the development of a philosophical position was not only a rational, but also an ethical act. Notwithstanding the peculiarities and problems of Fichte's system, the radical thinker played a crucial role in the development of a philosophy of the subject by positing that the subject is something that is constructed from human activity. Consequently, the study of the subject becomes an investigation of activities and how these practices bring forth forms of agency, cognition, and morality.

Collective Subjectivity

Fichte still took for granted that the subject was first and foremost an individual human being, and that 'society' or 'culture' somehow could be derived from this singular unit of life. Since the rise of modernity, however, the concept of the subject as an individual person exists side by side with other notions of human agency. In common discourse broad categories such as class, race, and gender, and institutions such as the family, school, company, state, and market are endowed with the power to act and to form opinions. Most legal systems recognize institutional agents by differentiating between *natural* and *juridical* persons. Whereas natural persons are individual human beings, juridical persons are entities that are treated as persons before the law. This practice reveals that a subject can be something else than a singular human being, and, in fact, that its prevalence often necessitates an explicit recognition by law. Conversely, it discloses that the conception of the subject as an individual human being has become so self-evident that in order to be recognized as a subject and to be able to function in society, a non-individual agent has to be subsumed under the category of 'person'.

The philosophical issue at hand – with obvious political and ethical consequences – is the character of the non-individual actor and its relation to individual persons. Together with the mind/body and subject/object dichotomies, the opposition between the 'individual' and the 'collective' has been one of the determinants of modern thought. Arguably, there is little to gain in explanatory power by simply reducing one pole of the opposition to the other. The movement, rationality, and morality of a macroeconomic system cannot be extrapolated from the economic behavior of a single person. Conversely, the complex behavior and personality of a singular human being cannot be deduced from her participation in a single activity, group or institution.

The formative process of subjects, both individual and collective, reveals that they constitute one another. Taking the individual mind-body as a starting point, it is clear that non-individual entities require the existence of separate and distinct individual human beings. A circle of friends, a demonstration, or a business are created at a certain point in time by individuals who come together. Such a group can become a subject, or remain a loose collection of persons. The effect of their collaboration is either a merely quantitative aggregation of individual capacities and predispositions, or it entails a qualitative expansion of agency, cognition, and consciousness – an outcome that is bigger than the simple sum of its individual parts. In the latter case, the logic and dynamic of collaboration cannot be straightforwardly derived from the behavior of a single participant, but only investigated as a *system*. For example, in her investigation of the formation of the 25 January 2011 movement, Salwa Ismail posited that: "[…] we need to consider the individual selves that formed the collective […] a process through which intersubjective understandings of individual experiences become constitutive of a social imaginary and translate into shared sentiments and agreed ideas and aspirations" (*Ismail 2011, 990*).

However, taking the individual mind-body as a premise is problematic, as the modern person is as much the *effect* as the *cause* of collective subjects. For example, the Marxist philosopher of language Valentin Voloshinov (1895–1936) distinguished between a singular human being and his or her 'individuality':

> To avoid misunderstandings, a rigorous distinction must always be made between the concept of the individual as natural specimen without reference to the social world [...] and the concept of individuality which has the status of an ideological-semiotic superstructure over the natural individual and which, therefore, is a social concept.
> VOLOSHINOV 1973, 34

Likewise, Gramsci claimed that:

> [...] one must conceive of man as a series of active relationships (a process) in which individuality, though perhaps the most important, is not, however, the only element to be taken into account. [...] The individual does not enter into relations with other men by juxtaposition, but organically, in as much, that is, as he belongs to organic entities which range from the simplest to the most complex.
> GRAMSCI 1971, 352

Obviously, a human being is not born as a fully-formed person, but is the product of his participation in diverse 'organic entities' such as family, school, friends, workplace, and the communities in which he matures. It is impossible to think of ourselves as a person isolated from these units of social life that have produced our 'individuality' and through which we continue to reproduce ourselves as a person. Individual and collective subjects presuppose one another logically and historically.

However, even though an investigation of the 'individual' and the 'collective' discloses potential *modes* of the subject, it does not reveal its *substance*. What is a subject made of? How do collective subjects constitute a person? How does a person 'come together' with others to constitute a group? How do persons and non-individual entities act, know, and reflect? Individual and collective bodies do not move through an empty social space, but they swim through a thick cultural-historical fluid. A *subjectivity* – by which I mean the *specific content* of any subject – consists of various practices, semiotic systems, and material artifacts – i.e., forms of human activity. By its past and present collaborations with other humans and by its appropriation and use of socially produced signs and tools the individual mind-body cannot escape being a social creature. Each of its 'personal' actions, be it a thought, an utterance, or a movement immediately presupposes a preexisting cultural framework. Its unique 'individuality' is the refraction, combination, and semi-stable crystallization of different subjectivities – i.e., the nature of the particular activities in which the person has taken part. Ilyenkov pondered that:

> The separate individual is only human in the exact and strict sense of the word, insofar as he actualizes – and just by his individuality – some ensemble or other of historically developed faculties (specifically human forms of life activity), some fragment or other of a culture formed before and independently of him, and mastered by him during upbringing (the moulding of the person). From that angle the human personality can rightly be considered as an individual embodiment of culture, i.e. of the universal in man.
> ILYENKOV 2008A, 359

Instead of a horizontal, quantitative axis, ranging from the singular to the plural, the relation between individual and collective subject appears as a vertical, qualitative movement of the folding and unfolding of subjectivities in increasingly complex units. In a manner of speaking, the 'highest' level of the subject, human society-culture-history, i.e., the totality of subjectivities, is folded (incompletely) into the individual person, who becomes a *microcosm* of the world, as Vygotsky commented:

> When our Marxists explain the Hegelian principle in Marxist methodology they rightly claim that each thing can be examined as a microcosm, as a universal measure in which the whole big world is reflected. On this basis they say that to study one single thing, one subject, one phenomenon *until the end*, exhaustively, means to know the world in all its connections. In this sense it can be said that each person is to some degree a measure of the society, or rather class, to which he belongs, for the whole totality of relationships is reflected in him.
> VYGOTSKY 2004, 316

In methodological terms the singular person is a source of knowledge; an index of society in general and the specific collective subjects in which she participates (or has participated). However, the subject matter of her individual life trajectory should not be confused with the subjectivities of the organic entities to which she belongs (or has belonged). The individual and the collective are different modes of existence of the same substance: human activity, in the sense of both "[…] the freely conscious creativity of the subject and the whole vast sphere of the 'dead', congealed, fossilized creative activity, the world of objects" (Ilyenkov 2008a, 154). The collective subject has a life process in its own right, a development as a distinct whole, which cannot be reduced to the path of a singular participant or represented as the simple aggregate of the discrete life stories of all partakers. Moreover, from the standpoint of human agency and emancipation, the subjectness that emerges from the collaboration of individual human beings as a collective subject, is not a mere addition of distinct wills, but a cultural and historical force. An understanding of human subjectness cannot be derived from an abstract scheme of 'transcendental' logic, but requires a cultural-historical conception of activity.

CHAPTER 3

Concept of the Subject

In the previous chapter, the dichotomy between the individual and the collective has been revealed as an opposition between modes of subjectness, which share the same substance: human activity, both in its direct, living and indirect, 'dead' (cultural-historical) forms. Before engaging with CHAT proper, I engage with its philosophical roots which, as Blunden (2010, 2012a, 2014) showed, can be traced back to Goethe, Hegel, and Marx.

Gestalt, Bildung, Urphänomen

Blunden saw in the rise of 'Romantic Science' of the late eighteenth and nineteenth centuries a precursor to current cultural-historical activity theory. Romantic Science was not a complete, explicitly formulated theoretical system, but a loose body of ideas that reacted against the abstraction of human nature posited by the Enlightenment philosophers: "The human being was simultaneously flattened out into a uniform type and broken up, analysed into so many separate faculties and isolated from the world" (Blunden 2012a, 96).

The two key thinkers of this movement were the Germans Johann Gottfried Herder (1744–1803) and Johann Wolfgang von Goethe (1749–1832). Contrary to Kant, who posited reason as a universal human faculty, independent from temporal and spatial circumstances, Herder emphasized the historical and cultural particularity of thought. The consciousness of an individual was an expression of the general consciousness of his time (*Zeitgeist*) and of the consciousness of a people with a specific history, culture, and language (*Volksgeist*). Although his concept of *Volksgeist* could be appropriated for a conservative nationalist political project, the Romantic philosopher himself rejected racial nationalist theories by affirming that there was but one human species and he explicitly supported the French Revolution and democratic politics. Influenced by Spinoza, Herder conceived of Nature as an active force and humanity as an integral part of this dynamic, organic whole (Blunden 2012a, 96–97).

The outline of such an organic natural philosophy was developed by Goethe, whose ideas directly inspired Marx, Vygotsky, and Luria (Blunden 2012a, 96). Three concepts are at the core of Goethe's Romantic Science: *Gestalt*, *Bildung*, and *Urphänomen*. Understanding a phenomenon consisted of a *structural* and a *genetic* movement of thought. With regard to the structural movement,

Goethe claimed that: "In an organic being, first the form as a whole strikes us, then its parts and their shape and combination" (Blunden 2010, 27). Scientific understanding should neither take as its object the organism as an undifferentiated whole, nor should it mechanically reduce the whole to its constituent elements. Instead, the organic being should be approached as a *Gestalt*, an organic unity of the whole and its elements: "[…] the whole was present in every part, and every part was connected to the whole. The whole must therefore be perceptible in every part" (Blunden 2010, 27). Unlike the abstractions of positivist science, concrete knowledge was realized by a movement of thought from the whole to its parts and then back again to the whole. In the domain of biology, for example, the function of a kidney could not be deduced from its constituent parts, but by its relations with other organs and the organism as a whole.

However, a phenomenon could not be understood simply by taking a snapshot of its current organic structure or *Gestalt*. To Goethe, Nature was not a static entity, but an ever-changing organism. Organisms were not just things, but processes: things-in-development. As an author, Goethe invented the *Bildungsroman*, which emphasized the inner development and education of the central character. The story of Nature and its organisms was a *Bildungsroman* in its own right. Central to an understanding of an organic being was an insight into its growth and development, i.e., its *Bildung*. Thought had to grasp the organic being not only as a structural-organic *Gestalt*, but it had to position its momentary state within a temporal-genetic sequence of *Gestalten*, its *Bildung*.

To understand an organic being as a structural *Gestalt* and a process of *Bildung*, the Romantic scientist had to avoid a reduction and abstraction of its complexity and offer an explanation instead of a mere description of its nature. The solution was to find the *Urphänomen* of the object: "[…] the most easily understood, simplest, or archetypical form of the thing, a form which allowed the nature of the whole phenomenon to be understood" (Blunden 2010, 28). The *Urphänomen* is a representation of a complex phenomenon by a more primitive or embryonic form, in which the many determinations of the object are folded. Here 'primitive' means the logically most simple form of the object, not its historical origin. Moreover, the movement of abstraction necessary to discern the *Urphänomen* is not a reduction of the phenomenon to a general principle, a definition, or a set of attributes, but its conceptualization as another 'real' object that incorporates the essential characteristics of the phenomenon under investigation. Discovering the folded form of the phenomenon is the first, analytic, movement of scientific investigation. For Goethe, this was not the result of a rigorous application of scientific laws, but of a largely intuitive and contemplative process of 'being with' the object of study, which reveals, often with a leap of insight, an inroad to the problem. Such an *Aha-Erlebnis* or eureka moment is followed by a second, synthetic, movement, which, takes on the shape of an unfolding of the various facets of the phenomenon, rendering explicit what remains implicit in the *Urphänomen*. Goethe speculated about the existence of the biological cell as the *Urphänomen* of all organic life, which carried in itself the *Gestalt* of the developed being in an embryonic form – an intuition that was later vindicated by the actual discovery of the cell through microscopic research.

Although Goethe's rough concepts of *Gestalt*, *Bildung*, and *Urphänomen* remained unsystemized and were developed in the framework of a natural philosophy, they do offer a perspective on the subject that escapes the classical Kantian dichotomies. Firstly, a subject is not an undifferentiated thing, but an ensemble of different parts that function as a whole. 'The people', as a revolutionary actor, consists of various elements that claim to be one and the same. Even though together the parts form the whole, their own function, position, meaning, or role is *constituted* by the whole – which means that they cannot be understood individually without grasping their relation to the whole. Conversely, the *Gestalt* cannot be understood by an analysis of single part. Throughout the 25 January uprising the activities of men, women, Muslims, Copts, the youth, workers, shopkeepers, and so on, were determined and rendered meaningful not by their own, particular position, but by their continuous reference to the whole, i.e., the people. Reducing the revolution to a youth or Facebook revolt ignores its many facets.

Secondly, a subject is something that emerges, grows, develops, and dies. A subject lives its own *Bildungsroman*, moving through different phases and taking on new forms. The *Gestalt* of the people at one point differs from its form at another moment, even though its signifier remains the same. From a Romantic, emancipatory perspective, one could argue that revolution is the *Bildungsroman* of the people, the story of how the people as an actor emerges, develops, and, sometimes, falls apart, and perishes.

Thirdly, due to its character as a complex ensemble of different forces, an understanding of the formation and development of a subject such as the people requires a degree of abstraction that should not lapse into simplistic reductions or empty generalizations. A statistical analysis of which individuals and groups participated in the occupation of Tahrir Square may be an interesting tool of scientific investigation, but it does not enhance our concept of what the people *is* and how these disparate elements function together as a whole. The notion of *Urphänomen* offers a different perspective: through an unfolding of the most primitive, archetypical form of the subject, its complexity and multi-determinateness can be peeled off, layer by layer.

Formation of Consciousness, Concept

Goethe's unsystemized notions of *Gestalt*, *Bildung*, and *Urphänomen* were appropriated by the German philosopher Georg W.F. Hegel (1770–1831) and transposed from the field of natural science to the domain of human consciousness in its broadest sense (Blunden 2012a, 102–105). Hegel rejected the traditional presumption that thought presented itself to its observer only in the form of language. Language was a form of mediation of thought, the means by which thought became conscious of itself as thought, but it was far from the only form. Hegel posited that thought was objectified, not only in words and signs, but in all human actions, events, and material artifacts:

> Practice, the process of activity on sense objects that altered things in accordance with a concept, in accordance with plans matured in the womb of subjective thought, began to be considered here as just as important a level in the development of thought and understanding, as the subjective-mental act of reasoning (according to the rules) expressed in speech.
> ILYENKOV 2008A, 209

In other words, thought was expressed in the whole development of human history and culture. Hegel's early writings such as the 1802–3 draft "System of Ethical Life" still conceived of *Geist* (mind, spirit, or thought) as the expression of everyday, quite material, practices. Three years later, he had reversed this approach, thinking of real human activities as the objectifications of thought. This evolution marked Hegel's turn to philosophical idealism (Blunden 2010, 37).

Nevertheless the significance of this philosophical innovation could hardly be underestimated, as Ilyenkov stressed: "It was on that basis that Hegel also acquired the right to consider in logic the objective determinations of things outside consciousness, *outside the psyche of the human individual*, in all their independence, moreover, from that psyche" (Ilyenkov 2008a, 176). Hegel did not deduce the character of society from the individual, but took the existence of society *before* individual consciousness as a premise of his philosophy. In Hegel's philosophy Goethe's *Gestalt* became a *formation of consciousness*: a "[…] dissonant unity of a *way of thought*, a *way of life* and a certain *constellation of material culture*" (Blunden 2010, 47). Prefiguring modern anthropological notions, Hegel's formation of consciousness is nothing else than *culture*: an ensemble of ideas and mindsets, practices and activities, material and semiotic artifacts. Culture – the whole system of raising children, creating and using tools and signs – *mediates* between individual human beings and Nature.

Whereas history reveals the actual, accidental, and specific development of thought-forms, logic reveals its general and necessary forms. The *Bildung* of a formation of consciousness, the development of a culture, has both a historical and logical path. The historical process presents itself in actuality, but the discovery of the logic of development is a conceptual challenge. In his "Science of Logic" (1969), Hegel appropriated the thought-form of thinking – in its ideal and material aspects – as the subject matter of a critical investigation. In order to understand the complexity of thought, Hegel had to begin his investigation from its simplest, archetypical form. *Begriff* (Concept, Notion), not as a sign or representation, but as "the gist of the matter" (Ilyenkov 2008a, 9), fulfilled the same function as Goethe's *Urphänomen*. The Concept was not established by a process of abstraction, which eradicated the rich particularities of the object in order to arrive at its general, aggregated, or abstract universal properties. On the contrary, the Concept had to reveal its object in all its concreteness, or the totality of its determinations (Ilyenkov 2008a, 187). The dialectical process of unraveling the determinations of a thought-form generated logical contradictions. These contradictions were not the consequence of a logical deficiency or error, but represented a real phase in the development of the thought-form that had to be overcome or negated. Hence, the traditional logical categories should not be taken for granted, but studied critically through their historical development in correspondence with their contemporary cultural objectifications.

The first two books of the "Logic" – *Being* and *Essence* – contain the logical determination of the Concept. As a starting point, *Being* represents the prehistory and precondition of thought. *Essence* unravels thinking by an analytic movement of contradictory categories that supersede one another until its simplest determination emerges: the abstract concept. In the third book, the *Concept*, this unit of thought becomes more and more concrete as it unfolds itself in various directions.

Hegel argued that the (subjective) Concept was constituted by a mediated unity between that which is *Allgemein* (general, universal), *Besonder* (specific, particular), and *Einzeln* (singular, individual). The German philosopher stressed that: "For the sake both of cognition and of our practical conduct, it is of the utmost importance that the real universal should not be confused with what is merely held in common" (Hegel 2001, 124). *Das Allgemeine* was not a shared attribute or common property of a number of *individuals*, but a principle or idea that directly expressed the *whole*. Hegel illustrated this notion with Rousseau's distinction between the *volonté générale* (general will) and the *volonté de tous* (the will of all). Returning to the case of the 25 January Revolution, 'the people' invoked in the slogan 'the people want the fall of the régime' expressed a whole, i.e., the population as an active political force, and not a common attribute of otherwise atomized citizens.

When stripped from its obscure terminology and filled with the substance of the social world, Hegel's *Begriff* becomes a conceptual representation of the collective subject, as Blunden argued: "[The subject] entails an all-sided relation between the consciousness of finite, mortal *individuals*, the *particular* forms of on-going activity and relations entailed in the relevant social practice, and the *universal* products through which the subject is represented (Blunden 2010, 63). This can be considered a *general definition* or *abstract concept* of the collective subject.

Note that the full conception of the *subject* already comprises its *object*. Hegel sublated the Cartesian dualism between being and thinking, and the Kantian dichotomy between things-as-they-appear and things-in-themselves by stressing the interpenetration of subject(ivity) and object(ivity). In Hegel's system, the relation between subject and object is not a relation between humanity and Nature, or between the ideal and the material, but of humanity to itself. Firstly, an object is understood as that which is 'external' from the perspective of a particular subject. From the viewpoint of one subject, another subject is an object: subjects are continuously objectified by other subjects. Secondly, a subject can only exist as a subject by objectifying itself 'into' the world. Thought is objectified into speech, sorrow into tears, protests into committees, and these objectifications are in turn appropriated by the subject. In the human world, an object is always an object *for* a subject, and a subject always exists through its objectifications:

> [...] Hegel, in his logic, quite exactly expressed, in scholastically disguised form, the fundamental features of human life activity: man's faculty (as a thinking creature) to look at himself 'from outside' as it were; or in other words to transform *the schemas of his own activity into its own object*.
> ILYENKOV 2008A, 232

In other words, a subject's agency and existence in the world is constantly mediated by the ideal/material artifacts that it produces or appropriates.

Hegel criticized Kant's transcendental subject, arguing that logical categories were not inherent in each individual consciousness, but that they matured as the product of a collective activity within the developing totality of human culture. Individuals appropriated these thought-forms uncritically as ready-made schemes, fetishizing them as transhistorical categories of true knowledge. There was no correspondence between individual consciousness and objective consciousness materialized in human culture and especially in science and philosophy as the highest developed forms of thought. The individual consciousness was *alienated* from its own human thought, objectified in their history and culture. For Hegel, the solution was to bring individual consciousness back in accordance with objective consciousness. Thought *an sich*, in itself, had to become thought *für sich*, for itself, which meant thinking that would be fully conscious of itself as thought. Logic was the process in which thought became both object (as a thing reflected upon by thinking) and subject (thought actively thinking). Logic, however, was not constituted by merely presenting an overview of historical thought-forms, but by the active and critical rethinking of these thought-forms. Such was the momentous task of the science of logic and its agent: the individual philosopher.

Blunden draws our attention to the fact that "[...] Hegel saw the revolutionary impact of capitalism, both the enlightenment and the misery it brought with it, but never saw a movement of the oppressed, a modern social movement" (Blunden 2010, 33). Hegel recognized the *alienation* of humanity, but to him this process did not take place in the sensuous world by inhuman practices such as exploitation and domination, but was due to the fact that humanity "[...] *objectifies* itself in *distinction* from and in *opposition* to abstract thought" (Marx 1992, 384). Alienation in the social world was only an appearance of the estrangement of man from pure thought. Hegel reduced the substance of humanity to thought and turned human sensuousness, labor, and artifacts into attributes of the abstract mind and self-consciousness. While the German philosopher had witnessed the events of the French Revolution in his youth, it was the process of restoration and the 'revolutionary' role played by Napoleon Bonaparte in transforming ancien régime structures 'from above' that defined his thought. Hegel could not fathom emancipation of the oppressed as a process of *self*-emancipation and conceived of the formation of the modern state as the primary tool of liberation.

Practical-Critical Activity

As one of the radical 'Young Hegelians', Ludwig Feuerbach (1804–72) criticized Hegel for 'solving' the contradiction between subject and object merely in the realm of thought, i.e., by positing an idealist monism. Hegel grasped the world of things as objective thought-forms and the task of a philosophy of identity (logic) as the bringing into correspondence of objective and subjective thought. Hegel's philosophical premise was not *sensuous* being, but being as a *thought-form*. His investigation of human thought, abstracted from its material character, turned into an elaboration of an immaterial, supernatural subject – a new theology.

Feuerbach advanced that philosophy should take real being, including "[…] not only stones, trees, and stars, but also the thinking body of man […]" (Ilyenkov 2008a, 215), as its starting point. The traditional distinction between thought and being, subject and object, had taken for granted the existence of thought as a category separated from being, whereas being already entailed thinking (and vice versa) in the form of the mind-body:

> If we had brain matter in mind, then it was quite ridiculous in general to ask how thought was 'linked' with it, how the one was connected with the other and 'mediated' it, because there simply was no 'one' and 'the other' here, but only one and the same thing; *the real being of the living brain was also thought, and real thought was the being of the living brain.*
> ILYENKOV 2008A, 216

In Feuerbach's materialist monism there was no domain of thinking separated from the domain of being. Hence the philosophical question of the correspondence and mediation between thinking and being became superfluous: if thinking was a purely material process taking place in the individual brain, its thought products would *directly* correspond to material objects.

The chief problems of Feuerbach's philosophy and "[…] of all hitherto-existing materialism […]" were summed up by Karl Marx (1818–1883) in his "Theses on Feuerbach" (1976a, 6–9).[1] While Feuerbach successfully criticized the idealist content of Hegel's philosophy, he failed to develop the important dialectical insights of his erstwhile teacher from a materialist perspective. The philosophical advances he made in drawing attention to the sensuous and corporeal character of subjectivity, were negated by his neglect of Hegel's cultural-historical concept of the subject and his premise of *contemplation* instead of *activity*.

First, Marx reproached Feuerbach for returning to a Kantian view of the subject as an isolated individual actor in which a transhistorical essentialist 'human nature' is crystallized: "The essence therefore can by him only be regarded as 'species', as an inner 'dumb' generality which unites many individuals only in a natural way." Outside the individual thinking brain there was not only nature proper, but also a humanized nature, historically appropriated by labor and integrated in society: "Feuerbach consequently does not see that […] the abstract individual that he analyses belongs in reality to a particular social form." Marx emphasized that: "[…] the essence of man is no abstraction inherent in each single individual. In reality, it is the ensemble of the social relations."

---

[1] For a similar discussion of the Theses: Blunden 2012a, 189–193.

Second, because of Feuerbach's disregard for the all-encompassing reality of *humanized* nature and society, he only understood the world of things *objectively*, i.e., from the standpoint of the object, or from the perspective of an individual subject that passively perceived the object and was determined by it. What vulgar or 'contemplative' materialism lacked was a conception of the object from the perspective of the subject: "[...] as human sensuous activity, practice [Praxis]"; and, conversely, the subject from the standpoint of the object: "[...] human activity itself as objective activity [...]."

Third, if the substance of human existence was neither contemplated being nor active thought, but 'practical-critical activity' then the traditional philosophical problem of correspondence between the world of thoughts and the world of things – the question of objective truth – could not be solved only theoretically, but practically:

> Man must prove the truth, i.e., the reality and power, the this-sidedness of his thinking, in practice. The dispute over the reality or non-reality of thinking which is isolated from practice is a purely scholastic question. [...] All social life is essentially practical. All mysteries which lead theory to mysticism find their rational solution in human practice and in the comprehension of this practice.

Fourth, if humankind must prove the truth in practice, then a rational critique of political and religious thought-forms was a necessary but insufficient activity, as it left the real, worldly contradictions intact. Marx's eleventh thesis that "Philosophers have hitherto only interpreted the world in various ways; the point is to change it" was not only directed against Hegel's idealist concept of the task of the philosopher, but also against the materialists. Contemplative materialism postulated that humans "[...] are products of circumstances and upbringing, and [...] therefore, changed men are products of changed circumstances and changed upbringing [...]" but in doing so it "[...] forgets that it is men who change circumstances and that the educator must himself be educated." Emancipation, as "revolutionary practice" required both a "changing of circumstances" and "self-change."

Social Formation, Cell-Form

For Hegel, objectification was always alienation as it separated humanity from pure thought. Marx distinguished between *objectification*, which was part of the 'neutral' process of subject formation, and *alienation*, which was an inhuman form of objectification. The radical thinker inverted Hegel's understanding of alienation, and claimed that alienation in thought was but the appearance of estrangement in the social world. Idealist reductionism had mystified and concealed the potential for an emancipatory criticism of Hegel's philosophy. Whereas thought appropriates its object logically or conceptually, the object itself is produced historically, i.e., as the product of human activity. The movement of the world is not a derivative of the development of thought, springing from the head of the philosopher as the goddess Athena, and neither is the real, historical production of the subject matter mechanistically and directly 'reflected' in the thought process. Rather, the apprehension of a phenomenon in thought is always conceptually mediated. Marx then concluded that there were two forms of dialectical logic, a mystified and a rational one (Marx 1990, 103): "Hegel's dialectic is the basic form of all dialectics, but only after being stripped of its mystical form, and it is precisely this which distinguishes my method" (Marx 1982, 544).

Marx appropriated Hegel's dialectic logic of thought-forms as the conceptual form of human activity (cf. Ilyenkov 2008a, 8). Instead of thought, the substance of his 'materialist dialectics' was: "[…] the real individuals, their activity and the material conditions under which they live, both those which they find already existing and those produced by their activity" (Marx and Engels 1976, 31). Hegel's 'formation of consciousness' is re-conceptualized in materialist terms as a 'social formation'.

Both Goethe and Hegel had struggled with the process of understanding a totality without reducing the whole to one of its elements, and eventually they had solved the methodological issue by approaching a phenomenon through a simple archetype: the *Urphänomen* and Concept, respectively. Their conceptual movement consisted of two moments: an analytical one, which determined an appropriate archetype of the object; and a synthetic one, which developed the many determinations of the subject matter. In the "Grundrisse," Marx discussed the same method with regard to the notion of 'population'. When dealing with the phenomenon of 'population', one inevitably starts from "[…] a chaotic conception of the whole […]" (Marx 1986, 37) – i.e., the direct appearance of the subject matter, which is already concrete in social reality but still abstract in thought: "In thinking, it therefore appears as a process of summing-up, as a result, not as the starting point, although it is the real starting point, and thus also the starting point of perception and conception" (Marx 1986, 38).

Subsequently, the object should be studied in detail: "[…] through closer definition one would arrive analytically at increasingly simple concepts; from the imagined concrete, one would move to more and more tenuous abstractions until one arrived at the simplest determinations." (Marx 1986, 37). The phase of investigation entails the process of gathering empirical data and of abstraction (generalization). The end point of the 'descending movement' of abstraction was the *cell-form* of a phenomenon. Likewise, in his "Critique of Hegel's Philosophy of Right," the young Marx deployed 'private property' as the cell-form of the bourgeois state (Blunden 2010, 66, 108–112); and in "Capital," the mature thinker posited the simple commodity form as the archetype of the complex capital form: "The wealth of societies in which the capitalist mode of production prevails appears as an 'immense collection of commodities'; the individual commodity appears as its elementary form. Our investigation therefore begins with the analysis of the commodity" (Marx 1990, 125).[2]

Once the cell-form had been established, the ascending movement began, in which the subject matter was conceptually reconstructed. In the "Grundrisse," Marx emphasized the structural aspect of the movement from the abstract to the concrete: the conceptual representation of a phenomenon as a coherent *Gestalt*: "From there it would be necessary to make a return journey until one finally arrived once more at population, which this time would be not a chaotic conception of a whole, but a rich totality of many determinations and relations." (Marx 1986, 37). In "Capital" Marx highlighted the genetic or developmental operation, the process of *Bildung*: "We perceive straight away the insufficiency of the simple form of value: it is an embryonic form which must undergo a series of metamorphoses before it can ripen into the price-form" (Marx 1990, 154).

Unlike Hegel, Marx never elaborated his methodology in a systematic way. Moreover, after criticizing Hegel from a 'practical-critical' philosophical perspective, he did not develop his implicit *general* theory of human activity, but principally engaged with a rigorous critique of bourgeois political economy and a more fragmented discussion of the *particular* activity of class struggle in the capitalist formation. The central collective subject of this activity is the proletariat. Before dealing with class subjectivity, the outline of a general theory of activity and the subject that is emerging from my narrative has to be completed in a few more broad strokes in the next chapter.

---

2 Cf. "Marx first analyses the simplest, most ordinary and fundamental, most common and everyday *relation* of bourgeois (commodity) society [...]. In this very simple phenomenon (in this 'cell' of bourgeois society) analysis reveals *all* the contradictions (or the germs of *all* contradictions) of modern society" (Lenin in Ilyenkov 2008a, 318).

CHAPTER 4

Cultural–Historical Activity Theory

In the preceding chapter, the philosophical lineages of contemporary cultural-historical activity theory have been laid bare. Goethe's Romantic Science, Hegel's idealist dialectic, and Marx's practical-critical appropriation thereof, revealed the contours of a general theory of the subject, understood in constructivist and cultural-historical terms. In the following chapter three intertwined threads of thought – Vygotsky's cultural psychology, Activity Theory, and Blunden's 'collaborative project'-approach – are shown to offer a clear framework of analysis to investigate human activity.

Unit of Analysis

The Russian Revolution of 1917 created a fertile climate for innovative and creative artistic, philosophical, and scientific production. Although Pavlov's reflexology became the dominant trend in Soviet psychology – because of its 'materialist' rejection of the 'idealist' notion of consciousness – in the decade following the 1917 there was still room for heterodox ideas, even within the academic institutions of the young state. Soviet Cultural Psychology grew out of Lev Vygotsky's immanent critique of Pavlovian behaviorism and reflexology. The consolidation and concentration of state power in the hands of Stalin who preferred the mechanical theories of Pavlov to Vygotsky's dialectical approach, blocked the further development of a Marxist cultural psychology in the 1930s.

Even though evidence that Vygotsky was directly influenced by Hegel is, at best, tenuous, his methodology was formed through a profound engagement with Marx's 'early' writings, "Capital," Engels's popularizations, and Lenin's "Philosophical Notebooks," which, for their part, presented a materialist critique of Hegelianism (Blunden 2010, 122–126). As a psychologist, Vygotsky's object of study was the behavior and consciousness of the *individual* subject, which he approached as a whole of interconnected parts – i.e., as a *Gestalt*. Human speech, memory, perception, and so on, do not develop independently from each other: their formation is intertwined. Their individual function can only be understood through their reciprocal relation and to the connection of each part to the whole. Moreover, the *structure* of the individual subject could only be comprehended as a moment within a process of *development*: "[…] the basic task of research obviously becomes a reconstruction of each stage in the development of the process: the process must be turned back to its initial stages" (Vygotsky 1978, 62).

Clearly, Vygotsky's methodology was strongly influenced by the structural-genetic approach that was rooted in Goethe's *Gestalt* and *Urphänomen*, Hegel's formation of consciousness and Concept, and Marx's social formation and cell-form. Unlike the *Gestalt* psychologists, whose starting point of psychological investigation was the whole mind, Vygotsky realized that the complex behavior and consciousness of the individual subject could not be grasped directly as a totality – the unfolding of its understanding had to be mediated by an archetype:

> In our view, an entirely different form of analysis is fundamental to further development of theories of thinking and speech. This form of analysis relies on the partitioning of the complex whole into *units*. In contrast to the term 'element', the term 'unit' designates a product of analysis that possesses *all the basic characteristics of the whole*. The unit is a vital and irreducible part of the whole. The key to the explanation of the characteristics of water lies not in the investigation of its chemical formula but in the investigation of its molecular movements. In precisely the same sense, the living cell is the real unit of biological analysis because it preserves the basic characteristics of life that are inherent in the living organism.[1]
>
> VYGOTSKY 1987A, 46

According to Blunden, Vygotsky deployed 'joint artifact-mediated action' as his unit of analysis of individual consciousness (Blunden 2010, 191).[2] Vygotsky criticized the methodology of the subjective psychologists, as thought cannot be investigated directly by introspection – observation of one's own consciousness remains a form of consciousness – it has to be studied objectively through behavior, i.e., activity. The basic unit of conscious activity is an *action* – an idea developed later on by Leontyev. However, Vygotsky also criticized the paradigm of the objective psychologists – the behaviorists and reflexologists – for it is equally impossible to investigate an action as a conscious, i.e., subjective action, from a purely objective standpoint. This criticism

---

[1] Also: Vygotsky 2012, 4–5, 11, 224.
[2] For the more advanced unity between thinking and speaking he deployed "word meaning" as a unit of analysis (Yasnitsky 2012, 127).

echoed Marx's rejection of Feuerbach's 'contemplative' materialism. Outside the laboratory, individual human consciousness was constructed through social interaction with others, mediated by cultural-historically developed material tools and ideal signs. In order to treat consciousness as both an objective and subjective phenomenon, this 'real' process had to be reproduced in the laboratory. Instead of minimizing the subjectivity of the researcher and reducing her role to that of passive observer, the Russian psychologist took the interaction between observer and observed as his methodological point of departure.

To study the formation of concepts among children, Vygotsky deployed the 'method of double stimulation': "Two sets of stimuli are presented to the subject, one set as objects of his activity, the other as signs that can serve to organize that activity" (Vygotsky 2012, 110–111). Through the gradual introduction of the means of solution the whole process of concept formation could be investigated step by step.

Learning and Development

Similar to non-Marxist psychologists such as Piaget, Vygotsky argued that the formation of the child's mind moves through a number of stages and takes place in relation to a particular social context. Vygotsky's novel approach was, firstly, to interpret the open-ended concept of 'context' or 'situation' as those specific external circumstances and relations that were relevant to the development of the child. Secondly, he understood the relation between the child and his social situation as a *predicament* from which the child has to emancipate itself. The child can only liberate himself from the restraints of its social situation by making a *development*: "[…] by a qualitative transformation of their own psychological structure and the structure of their relationship with those who are providing for their needs […]" (Blunden 2010, 154). The social environment does not offer new psychological structures on a plate; on the contrary, the child has to create those mental functions – *neoformations* in Vygotsky's jargon – which allow him to make a qualitative development that overcomes his condition.

The child's 'social situation of development' is not an absolute category, but a cultural-historical product: the whole field of expectations that parents and society at large develop vis-à-vis a child of a certain biological age. Through these expectations a child perceives the limits of its actual developmental phase. The conflict between, on the one hand, the child's desire and will to overcome his current social situation of development, and, on the other, the constraints of his condition, is the 'motor' behind the creation of new psychological functions and mental development as a whole: "If the milieu presents no such tasks to the adolescent, makes no new demands on him, and does not stimulate his intellect by providing a sequence of new goals, his thinking fails to reach the highest stages, or reaches them with great delay" (Vygotsky 2012, 115). Vygotsky conceptualized this contradiction as a situation of *crisis*, induced by the need for a certain neoformation while this function has not yet been developed. Major transition points are defined in terms of a revolution in the forms of mediation of the child, which enable new modes of interaction between the child and its social environment (cf. Wertsch 1985, 19).

Vygotsky observed that for each stage of development, one neoformation and one 'line of development' play a central part in developing the entire mental structure. Central or leading neoformations and lines of development of a previous phase continue to exist in the current stage, but lose their decisive role in the maturation of the whole (Vygotsky 2012, 114–116). For example, the development of memory as a psychological function pushes forward the maturation of the whole mental structure, opening up a new social situation of development for the child. In early school years the child 'thinks' by remembering. When this line of development has run its course, another neoformation takes over this leading role, and, continuing the example, the child remembers by thinking (Vygotsky 1987d, 309). This also means that 'learning' is different from 'development'. Learning to ride a bike at a certain age may push forward the whole motoric development of the infant, whereas mastering the same activity at a later age in adolescence merely adds a new competence to the repertoire.

Conceiving of development as a predicament for the child leads to the question of how the child develops the means to overcome its condition. When considering the activity of learning it seems logical to put competence before performance. For how can one perform a task before knowing how to do it? Vygotsky rejected the nativist argument that *a priori* structures allowed the child to learn and perform certain tasks: it were not already existing capacities that enabled performance, but the activity of performance itself that constructed capacities (Ratner 1991, 182–183; Wertsch 2007, 188). Simply put, a child develops speech by trying to speak. A neoformation matures as the result of overcoming the current social situation of development.

But how do 'external' performances create 'internal' competences? Vygotsky observed that: "An operation that initially represents an external activity is reconstructed and begins to occur internally" '(Vygotsky 1978, 56). The notion of *interiorization* or 'ingrowth' is key to Vygotsky's 'general genetic law of cultural development', which claims that every neoformation appears twice: first 'inter-mentally', then 'intra-mentally' (cf. Bakhurst 2007, 53–54; Daniels 2007, 309; Meshcheryakov 2007, 162). The Russian psychologist noticed that: "[…] learning awakens a variety of internal developmental processes that are able to operate only when the child is interacting with people in his environment and in cooperation with his peers. Once these processes are internalized, they become part of the child's independent developmental achievement" (Vygotsky in Del Rio and Alvarez 2007, 279). The activity or performance is not simply 'copied' into an existing plane of consciousness as a competence, but the inward transference of neoformations is the process that develops such a mental plane. The practice is transformed during its interiorization, becoming similar yet different to its original objectification (Bakhurst 2007, 54).[3]

Vygotsky emphasized the importance of *instruction* as a motor of ontogenesis. Whereas Piaget argued that instruction should closely *follow* the independent and 'natural' path of ontogenesis, Vygotsky argued that instruction had to *lead* development. There is a difference between the degree to which a child can solve a problem on its own, and its capacity to accomplish a task in collaboration with others (Vygotsky 2012, 198). Vygotsky described this tension as the *zone of proximal development* (ZPD): "[…] the distance between the actual developmental level as determined by independent problem solving and the level of potential development as determined through problem solving under adult guidance, or in collaboration with more capable peers" (Vygotsky 1978, 86).

The role of instruction in the learning process is to motivate development, i.e., to assist the individual subject in creating those neoformations that allow it to overcome its social situation of development. Vygotsky emphasized that instruction is only effective when it is 'proleptic'; when it anticipates or imagines competence through the representation of a future act or development as already existing: "[…] the only good kind of instruction is that which marches ahead of development and leads it; it must be aimed not so much at the ripe as at the ripening functions. […] instruction must be oriented toward the future, not the past" (Vygotsky 2012, 200).

Meshcheryakov (2007) distinguished between two forms of proleptic instruction: *autoprolepsis* and *heterolepsis*. Autoprolepsis is a form of self-instruction, whereby a child casts itself in the role of a future, more developed self. A classic example from ontogenesis is that of a child playing adult roles, projecting itself

---

3   The concept of interiorization appears as a cultural-psychological appropriation of the philosophical understanding that "The so-called inner world (and all processes connected with it) arises as a result of the outer activity of a subject mediated by intersubjective relations. In order to create or to change 'inner' or subjective phenomena, it is necessary to create some objective thing" (Lektorsky 1999, 67).

in a more advanced stage of its own trajectory. *Heterolepsis*, on the other hand, is the interpellation of a potential capacity of a child by another agent. For example: a parent speaking to her young child as if it were a more mature conversation partner, even though it has not yet (fully) developed the capacity to engage in such a dialogue. The potential development of the child is called into being by the proleptic instruction of the parent.

Activity as Collaboration

Aleksei N. Leontyev, a student of Vygotsky's and the founder of Activity Theory, criticized the unit of analysis of his mentor, arguing that 'joint artifact-mediated action' lacked the crucial element of *motivation*. Leontyev (1978) posited that, historically, human beings engaged in activities to satisfy a certain need. The development of complex activities entailed the disarticulation of activities (e.g. 'hunting') into a chain of discrete actions of which the direct goal differed from the motivation of the activity as a whole. The routine execution of some actions internalized these as subliminal operations. Thus Leontyev differentiated between activities, actions, and operations. Activities are a societally produced series of individual, conscious, object-oriented, and artifact-mediated actions, which, in turn, consist of unconscious, 'incorporated' routine operations.

Engeström (1987, 1990) expanded Leontyev's theory with the notion of 'system of activity'. An activity-system is not only an activity involving humans and their object-oriented actions, mediated by material tools and conceptual signs; it is also a cohesive and coherent but often contradictory system comprising rules, relations, and divisions of labor, which organize the subject's actions and relations towards (1) its object; (2) co-participants in the activity; and (3) other agents who are engaged in separate and distinct activities that are oriented towards the same object.

Blunden (2010, 2014) disagreed with Leontyev and Engeström with regard to the concept of the cell-form of human activity, contending that they confused the *substance* (Leontyev) or a *model* (Engeström) of activity with *its unit of analysis*. Reiterating Vygotsky's concept of a unit of analysis in the tradition of Goethe, Hegel, and Marx, Blunden listed three requirements. Firstly, "It is the conception of a singular, indivisible thing" (Blunden 2010, 190). A unit of analysis is not a group of objects or a combination of different objects. Leontyev's notion of activity was, by his own definition, a whole unit of actions. An action itself could not be a unit of analysis because it missed the 'final motivation' that was an essential characteristic of the activity as a whole. Secondly, "It exhibits the essential properties of a class of more developed phenomena"

(Blunden 2010, 190). A unit of analysis is an archetype, the most primitive form, the simplest determination that can be developed into a mature and concrete form of thought and practice. While obviously useful for the analysis of certain advanced forms of activity, Engeström's 'system of activity' was already a *developed* form. Thirdly, "It is itself an existent phenomenon (not a principle or axiom or hypothetical force or such like non-observable)" (Blunden 2010, 190). A unit of analysis is not a property or attribute of an object, it is an object in its own right. This last requirement connects the unfolding of a phenomenon in thought, its conceptual *Bildung*, to its development in reality. A unit of analysis should be "[...] both a concept and an existent reality [...]" *that* "[...] must be conceived and chosen so as to provide the building block for conception as well as actuality" (Blunden 2010, 191). Even though the movement of a phenomenon in thought does not necessarily [4] replicate its real, historical trajectory, its unit of analysis is the starting point of both its actual and comprehended development.

In the spirit of Romantic Science, Blunden stressed that the discovery of a unit of analysis that is appropriate for a certain subject matter is not a question of the rigorous application of scientific rules and categories, but required "[...] a transition from reflection and being-with the object, until a certain aperçu makes possible the leap to an abstract representation of the complex whole in the form of an archetype" (Blunden 2012a, 100). Rather than a process of deduction or induction, the unit of analysis emerges from the activity of the researcher in her field, when her intuitions about the object of research mature into scientific concepts. Many social scientists engaged in field work recognize such a moment of *aperçu* or *Aha-Erlebnis*, when they find a road into the complex problematic they are investigating.

Blunden himself proposed 'collaborative project' as a unit of analysis of human activity. A collaborative project is a system of human actions and mediating

---

4 Marx remarked in the "Grundrisse" that it was *possible* for the conceptual and historical movements to operate in parallel: "[...] the simple categories express relations in which the less developed concrete may have realised itself without as yet having posited the more complex connection or relation which is conceptually expressed in the more concrete category; whereas the more developed concrete retains the same category as a subordinate relation. Money can exist and has existed in history before capital, banks, wage labour, etc., came into being. In this respect it can be said, therefore, that the simpler category can express relations predominating in a less developed whole or subordinate relations in a more developed whole, relations which already existed historically before the whole had developed the aspect expressed in a more concrete category. *To that extent, the course of abstract thinking which advances from the elementary to the combined corresponds to the actual historical process.* (Marx 1986, 39. Emphasis added.).

artifacts (material tools and ideal signs), which projects itself forward to a certain goal or ideal. This can be a social form as humble as a knitting group or as grand as a nation state. Essentially project collaboration is the archetype or cell-form of the collective subject, because it is the smallest unit of activity that generates subjectness. I will use collaborative project and collective subject as synonyms throughout the text, keeping in mind, however, that all projects are subjects, but most subjects are *developed* projects, i.e., matured systems of activity.

Blunden emphasized that the object or goal of a system of activity is not only an 'external' aim to which the collective subject directs itself; but that it is immanently projected from the 'internal' activity of its participants. This is a critique of Leontyev's teleological and functionalist view, which conceived of activity as an object-oriented process of gratification.[5] In traditional Soviet Activity Theory the object overdetermines the subject's activity, which stands in clear opposition to the ethics of an emancipatory science where agency and immanence are at the core of the project. Activities are not passively constituted by motivations, they themselves give rise to new aims and principles. The object of an activity-system emerges from the process of collaboration of its participants and entails both cooperation and conflict.

Drawing on Hegel's 'theory of recognition', Blunden distinguished between three archetypical relations *between* subjects: colonization, commodification, and solidarity (cf. Blunden 2004a, 2004b). A relation between projects cannot be understood as anything but a budding collaboration itself, because something has to be *shared* by the subjects: "If there is no international law, no shared ethos, no language or *anything* mediating the interaction, then how is any relationship possible?" (Blunden 2007). A real encounter between projects presupposes that they do something together; that they participate in a shared activity, that they become a joint project themselves. If unmediated, neither subject recognizes the other as a subject: inevitably the result of such an unmediated interaction is war and destruction of the other (in a physical and/or cultural sense), or withdrawal from the interaction, whereupon both projects continue their separate ways.

Mediated contact between two projects creates specific forms of collaboration. Domination, enslavement, or *colonization* describes an asymmetrical relation between a dominant and submissive subject, wherein the objectifications of the servant-subject (language, customs, practices, cultural artifacts,

---

5 Compare with Vygotsky's critique of psychologists that: "[...] took a wrong turn with their purely teleological interpretation, which amounts to asserting that the goal itself creates the appropriate activity via the determining tendency – i.e., that the problem carries its own solution" (Vygotsky 2012, 110).

and property rights) are destroyed and replaced by those of the master-subject. The subjectivity that develops from the interaction between master and servant is polarized by the division between theory and practice. The servant can only recognize himself as a subject through the subjectness of the master. The colonizer directs and determines the objectifications of the servant, enforcing his own self-consciousness on the other. However, the master can only achieve his subjectness in a roundabout way: through the controlled activity and objectifications of his servant. While the servant is subjectively dependent on the master, the colonizer is objectively dependent on the activity of the colonized for his existence as a subject. Both subjects find the means of mediation in each other, and are able to recognize themselves as subjects, but in a distorted way. The classical Hegelian 'master-servant dialectic' is not only appropriate for the grand archetypical examples of historical slavery or colonization, but can also be found in more trivial and benign encounters between subjects, such as patron-client relations and charity – as I explain below.

Commodification, exchange, or trade, happens when two subjects meet on relatively equal terms and both of them have something that the other subject needs or desires. Gratification is realized through exchange and this interaction creates its own types of collaboration. Trade acts as a form of mediation through which both subjects recognize each other and themselves as subjects. The relation between two exchanging subjects is relatively symmetrical, based on mutual respect for the other; they recognize each other as a subject and this recognition is expressed as 'rights'. Through their trade the two projects constitute a new form of collaboration, while, at the same time, remaining separate subjects. However, the other is but a means to an end, and its worth is only calculated according to its capacity to satisfy the needs of the own project. For example, in the capitalist economy only the circulation of commodities is of interest to its participating subjects, not the life activities and humanity of the other. The other is treated as a means to the end of the self, instead of an end-in-itself; the other is objectified and commodified. The dominance of the commodity relation has a tendency to 'reify' all human relations (cf. Lukács 2000).

The third mode of interaction between two projects is *solidarity*. Blunden defines solidarity as a collaboration between different subjects that strengthens the subjectness of the shared project and of each participant. Solidarity is offering assistance in the development of another project "[…] by voluntarily lending one's own labor to the support of the other's project according to their direction" (Blunden 2010, 284). Solidarity entails the freely chosen submission of the provider of assistance to the beneficiary, in order to increase the agency of the other. Solidarity stands in sharp contrast to charity, which is a 'benign' form of colonization. Whereas charity may alleviate the direct suffering or plight of the other, it increases at the same time the dependency of the recipient and only strengthens the agency and autonomy of the donor. Conversely, solidarity is oriented towards the self-emancipation of the other, as the benefactor assists in developing the means within the other to emancipate itself: "Solidarity is the opposite of philanthropic colonization, because in assisting someone, the other remains the owner of the project and is thereby assisted in achieving self-determination" (Blunden 2010, 284).

Conclusions

Blunden's conception of collaborative project as a unit of analysis of human activity is of paramount importance for the renewal of a theory of the emancipatory subject. In contrast to the Kantian ahistorical individual actor or mystical conceptions of a homogeneous actor as the predestined 'motors' of history, the subject appears here as a historically developing, self-conscious, cultural-historical unit of human life and activity. Furthermore, unlike determinist conceptions of class, nation, or race, collective agency is presented as the practical and historical outcome of conscious human collaboration, instead of its philosophical *a priori*. In order to understand the process of subject formation, and emancipatory struggle in particular, it is necessary to investigate how people come together around a shared objective; how they deploy, appropriate, and produce signs, tools, and practices during their collaboration; and how these objectifications in turn transform their original activity and goals, for better or for worse. In other words, human subjects are nothing more than collaborative projects engaged in a developmental process, and emancipatory movements are but the politicized form of this ontology.

My deployment of the concept of project in the study of the Egyptian 25 January Revolution, has fine-tuned some of its aspects (cf. De Smet 2014b). A first thought concerns the relation between 'teleology' and 'immanence'. Blunden criticized Leontyev for his functionalist and teleological understanding of the relation between motivations and activities. His critique opens up a much more dynamic perspective of how activities *generate* goals. I suggest, however, that the notion of project collaboration encompasses both movements, i.e., *teleologically* from goal to activity, and *immanently* from activity to goal. A goal is the ideal form of the outcome of an activity, i.e., its projection, and the outcome is the material form of the goal. Marx observed that:

> [...] what distinguishes the worst architect from the best of bees is that the architect builds the cell in his mind before he constructs it in wax. At

the end of every labor process, a result emerges which had already been conceived by the worker at the beginning, hence already existed ideally.
MARX 1990, 284

The first rallies on 25 January 2011 clearly illustrated this notion, as the activity of demonstrating was directly constituted by the call to protest of the organizing activists. The idea of the protests already existed before the materialization of the demonstrations. However, from 25 January onward, the goals of the developing collaboration seemed to lag behind its actual activities. Even though some activists had hoped that 25 January would initiate a revolutionary uprising,[6] the organizers only demanded the implementation of basic democratic reforms, rather than the dismissal of Mubarak, let alone a revolutionary change of the relations of power.[7]

However, the sheer numbers of protesters in the streets swiftly transformed the goals of the demonstrations 'from below'. Already at noon it was clear to some participants that the massive protests could be "an opportunity to bring down the Mubarak régime" (Guardian News Blog 25/1, 2011) and the slogan of "the people want the fall of the régime" was heard among some of the demonstrators.[8] As the actions of the protesters became more radical, their aims followed suit. No one who came to the protests of 25 January would have dared to dream that in the following days they would torch NDP and state security offices throughout the whole country, and by strength of numbers defeat the dreaded Central Security Forces (CSF) in the streets. In successive waves, elements of the state apparatus were disorganized and defeated by the masses; with each victory the call for a 'régime change' became louder. The goal that was rendered explicit was not an external object that constituted the activity, but, on the contrary, it was a reflection in consciousness of the real collaborative process that was unfolding. People became conscious of what they were already doing in practice: creating a revolutionary project. This illustrates how the imagination of a project sometimes lags behind its actual collaboration and tries to catch up theoretically with its own radical practice, or sometimes moves ahead of it, pulling the activity toward it, as it were.

A second contemplation about the concept of project concerns its relationality toward other projects. Blunden discusses modes of recognition that are largely 'horizontal' – although 'colonization' and 'solidarity' entail relations of

---

6 Interview with Khaled al-Balshy, Cairo, 14 March 2011.
7 Interview with Sabry Zaky, Cairo, 10 March 2011.
8 Interview with Haisam Hassan, Cairo, 7 March 2011.

'vertical' integration as well. Their primary relation is that of two intersecting circles with an overlapping part that represents the shared forms of mediation. This picture is complicated by the fact that projects are also 'vertically' related with one another: they are 'nested', as some circles completely envelop others. There is a vertical line of relations, going from the individual subject, over the activity-systems of groups and institutions, to the whole social formation. A project is positioned within a matrix of horizontal and vertical relations with other forms of collaboration. This reveals a need to theorize thoroughly the concept of *space* and *scale* in the study of projects, which is beyond the scope of this work. However, I implicitly address the verticality of projects when I discuss the formation of the worker subject and revolution in the next chapters.

A third remark deals with the relation between Vygotsky's cultural psychology and the development of projects. In "For Ethical Politics" Blunden (2003) investigated the development of collective emancipatory subjects from a Hegelian perspective. Here, the developmental dynamic of the different phases of the subject remained largely conceptual. Today, Blunden would probably emphasize real processes of learning and instruction as the *actual* drive behind development, which is exactly what I try to elaborate in this work. Projects go through a developmental process, in which specific activities and organizational structures take up a leading role, pushing the development of the total project forward, while other forms sink into the background. Vygotsky's insights in the field of ontogenesis offer a key to an understanding of sociogenesis as a process of collective learning and instruction.

A fourth comment draws on Ilyenkov, who, discussing Hegel's study of the Concept, observed, in the language of Marx's "Capital":

> The Hegelian logic described the system of the objective forms of thought within the limits of which revolved the process of *extended reproduction of the concept*, which never began, in its developed forms, 'from the very beginning', but took place as the *perfecting of already existing* concepts, as the transformation *of already accumulated* theoretical knowledge, as its 'increment'.
>
> ILYENKOV 2008A, 247

Before the actual unfolding of a phenomenon from its starting point – the Concept, the cell-form, unit of analysis, or project – there is a *prehistory* of development. If, for Marx, in "Capital" the commodity relation was the conceptual cell-form of the more advanced capital relation, this did not mean that there was no historical process leading up to the actual formation of capital. His conceptual investigation of the tendencies and logic of capital accumulation presumed the existence of capital as a historical fact. It was primarily a study of the *extended reproduction* of the capital relation. In the last part of Volume One of "Capital," Marx (1990) sketched the prehistory of capital formation by positing a process of *original* or *primitive accumulation*: the dispossession of public and petty-private means of production, bringing together the elements of real capital accumulation.

Transposing this insight to the domain of human activity, the development of a project into a more advanced and complex activity-system is its phase of extended reproduction, where actions breed more actions and develop the project as a whole. However, collaborations do not drop from the sky: they presuppose existing projects of which they appropriate elements – individual participants, motivations, concepts, ideal and material artifacts – that are turned into a new coherent and cohesive unit of activity, i.e., a project. This is the prehistoric phase of the original or primitive accumulation of a collective subject. The distinction between the original accumulation and extended reproduction of a project will help us to understand the actual dynamic of the 25 January Revolution (cf. Chapter 25).

Finally, a project also has a dimension that is projected outside the spatial and temporal boundaries of the existing collaboration (De Smet 2014b). A projection is an outward or inward *appearance* of a project. An outward projection appears to non-participants of the collaboration as an imaginary and can be considered an invite or interpellation to join or at least develop an attitude toward the project. As such it is the ideal form of a spatial extension of the activity-system. An inward projection, on the other hand, appears to the participants of the project and serves as a proleptic imaginary: the form of collaboration in a future, more advanced state, which stimulates its participants to develop the activity-system accordingly. As such it is the ideal form of a temporal development of the project.

PART 2

Subject and Struggle

∴

CHAPTER 5

Class as Subject

Whereas the previous chapters have elaborated a general framework for understanding subjectivity from the perspective of project collaboration, this part of the work engages with a theory of the emancipatory subject, with a strong emphasis on the 'making of' the working class. The following chapter discusses the implications of emancipation in the context of capitalism and the workers' movement as the archetypical object–subject of capitalist relations.

Political and Human Emancipation

Just as Hegel, Marx conceived of alienation as a fundamental predicament for humanity. Unlike Hegel, this alienation was not the estrangement of human culture and activity from 'pure' thought, but *the lack of collective subjectness*. Humankind did not recognize its own, ever-increasing agency in the course of history, and treated not only Nature, but also the ideal and material objects of its own activity and the organization of society, as *external* forces:

> The social power, i.e., the multiplied productive force, which arises through the co-operation of different individuals as it is determined by the division of labour, appears to these individuals, since their co-operation is not voluntary but has come about naturally, not as their own united power, but as an alien force existing outside them, of the origin and goal of which they are ignorant, which they thus cannot control [...].
> MARX AND ENGELS 1976, 48

In the terminology of Leontyev, the division of labor parceled the activity of the reproduction of human existence into a series of actions that each had a different goal than the motivation of the original, overarching activity. As soon as society, the whole of cooperative forms between individual human beings, emerged, its character and rationale became mystified. Without society organized as a collective subject, individuals were subjected to the division of labor which pushed the division of society into *classes*. The organization of production required the extraction, appropriation, and redistribution of economic surplus. From this amorphous 'economic' sphere the 'political' domain was differentiated: the *state* emerged as a structure that mediated and subsumed the productive and reproductive activity of society under its control. Marxist historian Ellen Meiksins Wood highlighted that the history of class society is the history of the differentiation between *class* and *state* power:

> The long historical process that ultimately issued in capitalism could be seen as an increasing – and uniquely well-developed – differentiation of class-power as something distinct from state-power, a power of surplus-extraction not directly grounded in the coercive apparatus of the state.
> WOOD 2012, 22

With the arrival of capitalist society, the precapitalist subsumption of the 'economic' under the 'political' – the direct appropriation of surplus by state power – is seemingly reversed. The system of wage labor embeds the process of surplus extraction in the sphere of production itself. Conversely, in contrast to the feudal lord, the capitalist appropriator relinquishes his *direct* political power over the workforce, which he can only control indirectly, through the state (Wood 2012, 26–27). However, the formal separation of the economic and the political spheres in bourgeois capitalist society veils the fact that the economic domain remains permeated by the political, i.e., relations of class and state power. Whereas the substance of the economic field is sharply political, its appearance is 'neutrally economic'. Gramsci observed that the division of labor between civil society and political community disguised their concrete unity as an 'integral' or 'extended' state: "[…] the entire complex of practical and theoretical activities with which the ruling class not only justifies and maintains its dominance, but manages to win the active consent of those over whom it rules […]" (Gramsci 1971, 244).

Marx argued that the Western European political emancipation from feudalism – i.e., the realization of politico-juridical equality between individual subjects within the state – was "certainly a big step forward" although it was not "the last form of general human emancipation" (Marx 1992, 221). Even 'human rights', as opposed to civil rights, which seemed to supersede the distinction between civil and political society, were still dependent on the political community to be enacted.

> Only when real, individual man resumes the abstract citizen into himself and as an individual man has become a *species-being* in his empirical life, his individual work and his individual relationships, only when man has recognized and organized his *forces propres* as *social forces* so that social force is no longer separated from him in the form of *political force*, only then will human emancipation be completed.
> MARX 1992, 234

Bourgeois political emancipation eliminated the political character of civil society and abolished the particularist nature of ancien régime politics, by separating the sphere of civil society from political society, and by differentiating the individual subject as a private person with particular interests from the individual subject as a citizen of the universal community. The abolition of distinctions between humans on the basis of "birth, drank, education, and occupation" (Marx 1992, 219) only took place in the political sphere – in fact, the necessity of their legal eradication acknowledged their continued existence in the civil sphere: "Far from abolishing these factual distinctions, the state presupposes them in order to exist, it only experiences itself as a political state and asserts its universality in opposition to these elements" (Marx 1992, 219).

Hegemony

The bourgeoisie had emancipated the whole feudal social formation, but from its particular perspective as a bourgeois class. Its particular condition – as a possessor of wealth but not of noble birth or privilege – was raised as the universal measure for all classes. Nevertheless, in its era of ascent, the bourgeoisie was able to present itself as a progressive force that advanced the common good of all society:

> No class of civil society can play this role without awakening a moment of enthusiasm in itself and in the masses; a moment in which this class fraternizes and fuses with society in general, becomes identified with it and is experienced and acknowledged as *its universal representative*; a moment in which its claims and rights are truly the rights and claims of society itself and in which it is in reality the heart and head of society. Only in the name of the universal rights of society can a particular class lay claim to universal domination.
>
> If the *revolution of a people* and the *emancipation of a particular class* of civil society are to coincide, if one class is to stand for the whole of society, then all the deficiencies of society must be concentrated in another class, one particular class must be the class which gives universal offence, the embodiment of a general limitation; one particular sphere of society must appear as the *notorious crime* of the whole of society, so that the liberation of this sphere appears as universal self-liberation.
>
> MARX 1992, 254

Here Marx anticipated Gramsci's concept of *hegemony*: the capacity of a class to lead other factions of civil society and to represent its rule as the general good. The Italian Marxist expanded Lenin's concept of hegemony, which had defined the relation between the proletariat and the peasantry in their alliance against Czarism as one where workers, because of their much more developed activity-system, played a directive role (Morton 2007, 88; Townshend 1996, 245). Whereas for Lenin the notion of hegemony served as a category in the study of proletarian strategy, for Gramsci it became a key concept in the theory of the state. Gramsci noticed that:

> [...] the supremacy of a social group manifests itself in two ways, as 'domination' and as 'intellectual and moral leadership'. [...] A social group can, and indeed must, already exercise 'leadership' before winning governmental power (this indeed is one of the principal conditions for the winning of such power); it subsequently becomes dominant when it exercises power, but even if it holds it firmly in its grasp, it must continue to 'lead' as well.
> GRAMSCI 1971, 57–58

While domination is 'naked' and 'top-down' class rule, whereby the ruled are the passive object of state policies, hegemony is the active acceptance of the bourgeoisie's class *leadership* by other social groups because of its prestige, its directive capacities, its cultural aura, its ability to 'manage' society and resolve societal problems, and so on. The ruling class has to take into account the "[...] interests and the tendencies of the groups over which hegemony is to be exercised, and that a certain compromise equilibrium should be formed [...]" (Gramsci 1971, 161). This political compromise requires sacrifices from the directive class, however:

> [...] there is also no doubt that such sacrifices and such a compromise cannot touch the essential; for though hegemony is ethical-political, it must also be economic, must necessarily be based on the decisive function exercised by the leading group in the decisive nucleus of economic activity.
> GRAMSCI 1971, 161

For the bourgeoisie, hegemony is its capacity to present itself as a progressive and leading force in society, to represent its own particular interests as the general good, and to "[absorb] the entire society, assimilating it to its own cultural and economic level" (Gramsci 1971, 260). During the ancien régime, the bourgeoisie had emerged as the class most capable of defeating the dominant aristocracy, and the need for its own emancipation coincided with that of society at large. However, if the political emancipation of any group of civil society systematically leads to its particularist domination under a universalist guise, is real, universal, human emancipation possible? And if so, why did Marx hail the proletariat as the collective subject to accomplish this feat?

The Proletariat as Subject

Marx discussed at length the contradictions of the capitalist mode of production. Capital accumulation developed the productive forces to an unprecedented level; the socialization of labor made cooperation at the point of production the norm instead of the exception, and the world market brought diverse individuals and cultures together through the exchange of commodities on a global scale. The different histories of human cultures become, for the first time, world history, and this history, in turn, creates the unified world of humanity. However, in capitalism the degree of the socialization of labor as cooperative production is directly proportional to the movement of the means of production in fewer and fewer hands. Due to the concentration-effect of capital accumulation, the capitalist class: "[…] absorbs all propertied classes it finds in existence […] in the measure to which all property found in existence is transformed into industrial or commercial capital" (Marx and Engels 1976, 77). At the other side of the class spectrum: "[…] the majority of the earlier propertyless and a part of the hitherto propertied classes are developed into a new class, the proletariat […]" (Marx and Engels 1976, 77). The process of original or primitive accumulation was (cf. Marx 1990) and is (cf. Perelman 2000, Harvey 2003) a process of *dispossession* and the creation of a population that was forced – not because of political coercion, but out of economic necessity – to sell its labor power in order to reproduce its existence.

In the capitalist mode of production the expanding class of wage laborers holds a unique position. Labor power is treated as an *object*: a commodity that can be exchanged and a means to produce surplus-value and realize profits on the market. Labor power is an element in the productive activity of the capitalist; an activity motivated by the generation of profit. Through his ownership and control of the tools that are used in the labor process, the capitalist organizes, disciplines, and mediates labor power. The state also intervenes directly and indirectly in the labor process, by the organization of coercion and consent at the point of production – the workplace – itself, and by its general institutional framework of legislation and education, respectively.

At the same time, labor power is inseparable from the labor population. "Of all the instruments of production, the greatest productive power is the revolutionary class itself," Marx (1976b, 211) commented in "The Poverty of Philosophy." Individuals who are legally free to dispose of their labor power, but who do not possess their own (sufficient) means of production, are economically forced into an activity-system of which the motivation (profit) and forms of mediation (discipline, division of labor, machines, and so on) are imposed on them. For them, the ultimate goal of their participation in the labor process is quite different: the reproduction of their natural and social life. The human emancipation of wage laborers necessitates the abolition of the selling and buying of labor power: of wage labor *tout court*. As the whole edifice of bourgeois society is based on the exploitation and commodification of labor power, it crumbles down when the population of labor power becomes a *collective subject* and revolts. As wage labor constitutes the kernel of the capitalist mode of production and surplus extraction, proletarian emancipation abolishes capitalism, freeing other subjugated groups in the process. In this sense, capitalism produces its own 'gravedigger': "[...] the formation of a class with radical chains [...] a sphere which cannot emancipate itself without emancipating itself from – and thereby emancipating – all other spheres of society [...]" (Marx 1992, 256). The *particular* position and suffering of the working class becomes the germ of the *universal* liberation of humanity from alienation.

However, Robert Cox correctly underlined that: "[...] if the production process creates the potentiality for classes, it does not *make* classes" (Cox 1987, 355). Whereas the process of formal and real subsumption of labor under capital – the subordination of labor power to the control of capital and the technical and social transformation of the labor process itself, respectively – creates a workforce, it does not constitute the working population as a collective subject. At this point, class only exists as the objective separation of a population from the condition of other classes, not as a subjective unit of social life, as Marx observed in the "Eighteenth Brumaire of Louis Bonaparte" (1979), but with regard to the small peasantry in France:

> Insofar as millions of families live under economic conditions of existence that separate their mode of life, their interests and their culture from those of the other classes, and put them in hostile opposition to the latter, they form a class. Insofar as there is merely a local interconnection among these small-holding peasants, and the identity of their interests begets no community, no national bond and no political organisation among them, they do not form a class.
>
> MARX 1979, 187

The Hungarian Marxist György Lukács (1885–1971) emphasized that the workers' subaltern position within the relations of production is not automatically and mysteriously 'reflected' in consciousness as proletarian subjectness (cf. Lukács

2000). The activity-system of the capitalist labor process, in which workers function as a mere means for capital accumulation, cannot be the substance, the subjectivity of a proletarian subject. The socialization of labor merely *collects* individual workers at the point of production, but it does not offer them the ideal and material means to develop themselves as a collective subject. From the perspective of proletarian subject formation, the alienating and exploitative capitalist labor process is a *predicament*. It is, in Vygotsky's vocabulary, the *social situation of development* of the worker subject: a restrictive condition from which it liberates itself by making an internal development.

Actual and Logical Development

Vygotsky observed that for each stage of child development one neoformation plays a central part in developing the entire mental structure. The maturation of this specific psychological function (e.g. 'voluntary attention') pushes forward the development of the whole mental structure, opening up a new social situation of development. After this phase, another neoformation takes over the leading developmental role (e.g. 'logical memory'), integrating the previously developed neoformations in a novel line of development. Although the developmental logic of ontogenesis (the formation of individual subjects) cannot be simply transposed to the domain of sociogenesis (the formation of collective subjects) Vygotsky's findings in the *particular* field of pedagogy substantiate a *general* understanding of 'dialectical' development. From a methodological perspective, Vygotsky invites us to investigate a subject genetically, as an actor-in-formation, and to discern the structural relation between its current 'situation', its developmental phase, and the central neoformation that steers the whole process. Such an analysis not only allows us to trace back the movement of the subject to its previous stages, but also, by means of rational speculation, enables us to plot its potential trajectories into the future. With regard to proletarian sociogenesis, this perspective was strongly worded by Marx and Engels in "The Holy Family":

> It is not a question of what this or that proletarian, or even the whole proletariat, at the moment *regards* as its aim. It is a question of *what the proletariat is*, and what, in accordance with this *being*, it will historically be compelled to do. Its aim and historical action is visibly and irrevocably foreshadowed in its own life situation as well as in the whole organization of bourgeois society today.
> MARX AND ENGELS 1975, 37

A superficial interpretation of this paragraph endows the proletariat with a historical 'mission', a view that has been all too common in deterministic accounts of the formation of class subjectness. Teleological perspectives assumed that wage laborers automatically and mechanically developed class consciousness in direct proportion to the growth of capitalist exploitation. Zachary Lockman, historian of the Egyptian workers' movement, mused that:

> Workers and working classes have [...] been made to play a set role within a narrative of historical process whereby capitalist development produces a growing and ever more conscious working class, which is ultimately destined to achieve the overthrow of capitalism and the establishment of a postcapitalist social order.
> LOCKMAN 1996a, XIX.

While I sympathize with the spirit of the anti-teleological critique, there is a danger of mixing up the notion of 'teleology' with 'immanence'. A teleological view perceives the development of a process from the perspective of its presupposed end point, while an immanent method speculates the potential trajectories and end point(s) of a process from the contradictions between its actual and logical development. This is what Marx and Engels meant when they claimed that: "Communism is for us not a state of affairs which is to be established, an ideal to which reality [will] have to adjust itself. We call communism the real movement which abolishes the present state of things. The conditions of this movement result from the premises now in existence" (Marx and Engels 1976, 49). And, again in the Communist Manifesto:

> The theoretical conclusions of the Communists are in no way based on ideas or principles that have been invented, or discovered, by this or that would-be universal reformer. They merely express, in general terms, actual relations springing from an existing class struggle, from a historical movement going on under our very eyes.
> MARX AND ENGELS 1998, 51

Whereas determinism only conceives of class formation in logical, necessary terms, empiricism merely reveals the different, accidental appearances of the subject in actuality. Both approaches mystify the developmental process of subject formation. Actual development – "the real dialectics of history" (Gramsci 1996a, 284) – has to be absorbed conceptually, comparable to the manner in which a literature or film critic logically extracts the *plot* (*syuzhet*)[1] from the

---

1 Syuzhet and fabula are terms from the narratology established by Russian Formalists Vladimir Propp (1895–1970) and Victor Shklovsky (1893–1984).

story (narrative, *fabula*). In order to make sense of the story, the reader or viewer needs to reconstruct its plot in thought. Even novels or films that present themselves as a dream-like sequence or a stream of consciousness, often encourage their interpreters to grasp for a plot or 'meaning' if they do not want to merely passively *undergo* the story, but actively *understand* it.

If history is the narrative in case, the necessity to understand instead of merely experiencing it becomes all the more pressing, because understanding allows for conscious intervention. When the unfolding of actuality is only observed in terms of contingency,[2] it is "[...] almost impossible for us to make predictions, to orient ourselves, to establish lines of action which have some likelihood of being accurate" (Gramsci 1996b, 286). Without a confrontation between the logical and actual development of the workers' movement, there can be no concept of progress and pathology in subject formation. From its inception, reformism as an ideology (instead of a mere practice), embraced empiricism as its political methodology. Its founder Eduard Bernstein (1850–1932), criticized Marx's method, arguing that "[...] actual development is forever bringing forth new arrangements and forces, forever new facts, in the light of which that exposition [...] seems inadequate and, to a corresponding extent, loses the ability to serve as a sketch of the development to come" (Bernstein in Townshend 2007, 51).

Against Bernstein, one could argue that, firstly, the fact of a contradiction between actual and 'expected' development is not a negation of the relevance of dialectical logic, but constitutes the beginning of a *problem* to be investigated. A recognition of the complexity, amorphousness, and fluidity of everyday reality does not preclude an attempt to make sense of the whole process. If the flow of history, i.e., the activity of humanity, is totally open-ended and accidental, collective agency is impossible. Without an educated guess of things to come, how can actors intervene in the historical process in any meaningful way?

---

2 For example, when in 1978 Foucault intervened in the political and public debate on the unfolding Iranian Revolution and celebrated the 'political will' of the Khomeini-led movement, the limits of his philosophy to act as an intellectual tool for emancipatory politics became painfully obvious. The main problem of his intervention was not that he misread the chain of events, which, to contemporary intellectuals such as Maxime Rodinson, was clearly heading for an authoritarian outcome (cf. Afary and Anderson 2005). Although Foucault correctly rejected a conception of the revolution as a predetermined and linear process, he bent the stick the other way, considering the situation as totally contingent, open-ended, and fluid: "I cannot write the history of the future, and I am also rather clumsy at foreseeing the past. However, I would like to grasp *what is happening*, because these days nothing is finished, and the dice are still being rolled" (Foucault in Afary and Anderson 2005, 220). His metaphor has to be completed with the insight that the dice are heavily loaded toward a certain outcome before they are rolled.

This brings us to a second point: *the conceptualization of the movement of the subject is not isolated from or external to its actual development* – quite the contrary: theoretically-grounded political practice is one of the important 'facts' in the 'arrangement of forces'. Philosophers and social scientists have been discussing the nature of the workers' class consciousness and their capacity to act collectively for the last two centuries, because something real and salient was happening that interpellated their intellectual activity. Conversely, workers have been able to develop forms of consciousness exactly because of theories that were organically connected to their struggles. An example of this reciprocal process is the 'discovery' of the Egyptian working class by the orientalist economist Jean Vallet in 1911 (Lockman 1996b, 98–99). Would the Egyptian workers have developed a notion of themselves as a class independent from these 'foreign' intellectuals? This is a moot point because the development of global capitalism and its forms of thought allowed Egyptian workers to use and appropriate such categorizations and theories as forms of mediation to understand their own globally induced predicament.

Returning to Vygotsky, the only way to study the behavior of a subject is by interacting with it, or, in Blunden's terminology, by participating in its 'project'. Evidently an immanent methodology contains an ethico-political dimension as the scientist-activist chooses which 'imaginations' are to be explored as lines of development. But this form of 'instruction' is appropriate for a practical-critical activity that does not see itself as external to its object of research, but chooses to be in collaboration with its development – as I argue in Chapter 7.

Workers or Working Class?

With regard to the study of the Egyptian working class, labor historian Joel Beinin engaged in self-criticism, claiming that in past writings (e.g. Beinin and Lockman 1987) he "[…] tended to homogenize and reify the working class as a historical subject and regard only those who engaged in collective struggle as real workers, despite our presentation of evidence that the historical experience of workers was diverse […]" (Beinin 1996, 267). Beinin also confessed that his focus on interviewing worker and leftist leaders "[…] led me even further away from understanding the experience, consciousness, and structural position of those workers who were not engaged in economic or political struggles in an organized framework over a protracted period of time" (Beinin 1996, 267–268).

Beinin's *mea culpa* reflected a 'revisionist' trend within the study of working classes, which, since the 1970s, began to shift the object of research from workers on the factory floor (the sphere of production) to their lives and subjectivities outside the workplace (the realm of reproduction) (Burke 1996, 306). The transformation of Italian *Operaismo* into autonomism is exemplary of this broader paradigmatic shift. *Operaismo* or 'workerism' was developed by Mario Tronti as a critique of the practice of Italian communism – especially the reformist interpretation of Gramsci – and trade unionism. The resurgence of the Italian workers' movement in the 1960s required a return of communist intellectuals to the struggles in the workplaces. The development of the strike dynamic in the factories would overcome the bureaucratization of the party and trade union structures, and reinvigorate the workers as a revolutionary subject. Conversely, the 'material' base of the rise of autonomism was the subsequent defeat of the mass strikes of the Italian workers' movement in the late 1970s. Whereas *Operaismo* conceived of the workplace and the 'mass worker' as the cell-form of the class struggle, Autonomism – demoralized by the workers' defeat in the factories – turned its attention to the 'social worker' and society at large as the locus of the fight against capital. Workers were 'discovered' as participants in wider entities such as the household, community, gender, cultural, ethnic, or religious group, and so on. Attention was diverted away from grand actions such as mass strikes and demonstrations, and reoriented towards 'everyday', 'invisible', or 'molecular' forms of resistance: "The class struggle is everywhere, therefore, and so too is the proletariat. Whoever in their conditions of life experiences the domination of capital is part of the working class" (Callinicos 2001, 43).

From a methodological point of view, the emergence of workplace subjectivities is a different object of study compared to the subjectivities that arise through participation in other activity-systems. Bayat argued that if "[...] class is perceived only in terms of an identity resting on a set of differentiations, then 'class' can easily be confused with and subsumed into other forms of identity, such as gender, nation, ethnicity, and so on" (Bayat 1996, 187). For example, women workers play an important role in the formation of a workers' movement, but when investigating class formation, the object of study is women as workers and not workers as women.[3] Studying workers without studying the collaborative struggles from which they emerge as collective subject, can produce valuable insights about workers as objects of capitalism, as members of their community, as religious believers, and so on, but it is *not* an analysis of class formation. Indeed, 'worker' is but one subjectivity within a modern wage laborer's composite person.

---

3 Koptiuch for example claimed that: "[...] the dominant labor history narrative is decidedly masculinist in that it privileges [...] explosive, virile forms of struggle (strikes, organized political parties) over 'feminine' subtler forms of resistance embedded in the practices of everyday life" (Koptiuch 1996: 64). I am very skeptical towards such a distinction between 'masculine' and 'feminine' forms of struggle. Without engaging in a profound debate about this dichotomous gender approach, I think it is conceptually dangerous to cast degrees of militancy or forms of struggle in a fixed gender mold.

Any person is a microcosm[4] of subjectivities. Yet, even though the researcher of class formation should pay attention to these other subjectivities and how they interact with a person's subjectivity as a wage worker, his object of study remains the development of worker subjectness.

From a political perspective, the 'autonomist turn' from the workplace to 'society' is all the more paradoxical since the neoliberal strategy for accumulation *increased* the exploitation of wage labor in the setting of the workplace (Moore 2011, 31–33). If anything, neoliberalism worsened both the objective (exploitation) and subjective (fragmentation) predicament of the global working class. Autonomist politics withdrew from the workplace at a time when leftist assistance was most needed.

Sam Moore argued that: "There is no clear evidence that work has been marginalised as a source of identification and collectivity. Social identities are materially rooted in changing capitalist relations of production, as manifested in the workplace [...]" (Moore 2011, 17). Moreover, the objective condition of wage labor is still expanding. Chris Harman (2002, 7) estimated that the global number of wage laborers in the mid-1990s was around 700 million, or almost one third of the entire labor force. When non-employed spouses, children, and unemployed and retired workers are added, this number increases to 1.5 to two billion 'members' of the modern working class. Whereas in European countries the number of 'traditional' industrial workers decreased, in the USA – often labeled the 'motor' of the world economy – their number increased from 26 million in 1971 to 31 million in 1998.

Regardless, a wage laborer does not have to produce commodities in order to be indispensable for production, profit, and the whole process of capital accumulation. Alex Callinicos commented that:

> Wage-labour is demanding more and more from people, whether they are privileged software designers or ultra-exploited migrant workers. If anything, the relationship between capital and wage-labour is becoming more pervasive economically and socially than it was in the past. Consequently the power that workers gain because capital depends on their exploitation remains of central strategic significance to anyone who wants to change the world.
>
> CALLINICOS 2004

Let us then conclude with Lockman that: "[...] to the question of whether Middle Eastern working classes constitute coherent historical subjects and legitimate objects of inquiry we can respond with a properly nuanced and contingent 'yes'" (Lockman 1996a, xxviii).

---

4 Cf. Chapter 2.

CHAPTER 6

The Modern Prince

In the preceding chapter, following Marx, I elucidated that the main challenge for human emancipation is class society and its contemporary form of the capital relation and its state. The collective subject best suited to emancipate society is the modern working class, as it liberates the other subaltern classes when emancipating itself from the capital relation. I also discussed the difference between a teleological and immanent view on subject formation. I ended with emphasizing the continued relevance of the proletariat – i.e., population of wage laborers – as a social force capable of societal transformation. The next chapter gives an overview of the archetypical development of the worker subject from its cell-form. As a unit of analysis I suggest the strike. From the strike develop forms of trade unionism, which point towards the limit of the workers' 'economic' line of development. From another point matures a 'political' line of development, which eventually intertwines with the worker project in the hegemonic structure of the Modern Prince.

The Strike as Cell-Form

Just as the formation of any other subject, the development of the workers' movement can be comprehended as a rational process. Its development is not driven by an externally preconceived scheme of stages, but by a logical trajectory of overcoming real predicaments. In its first stage as merely 'being' (Hegel), a 'class-in-itself' (Marx), the proletarian subject is dispersed as discrete workforces in the many individual workplaces of capitalist production. At this point, its *objective* social situation of development is determined by the conditions in the workplace: the degree of exploitation and coercion involved in surplus extraction and the lack of workers' control over the process of production. The workplace is a microcosm[1] of bourgeois-capitalist society (Cooper 2005, 203): "Each individual plant, a highly organised and integrated unity with its own hierarchy and structure of authority, contains within it the main sources of class-conflict" (Wood 2012, 28).

The general logic of capital accumulation and the relations of economic exploitation, political oppression, and ideological domination are folded and

---

1 Cf. Chapter 2.

compressed into the workplace. The essence of the objective social situation of the worker subject is the whole capitalist social formation, but this situation only presents itself indirectly, through the spatial division of capitalist enterprise and the actual social relations at the workplace. The *subjective* predicament of the worker subject is its social fragmentation: the division between individual workers in the same workplace and the division between workers in different workplaces (Wood 2012, 28–29). The individual predicament has to be recognized as the particular predicament of wage labor, and the particular predicament of wage labor has to be recognized as the general predicament of the capitalist mode of production. In order to become an emancipatory project, the cell-form of collective subjectivity, individual workers have to participate in a shared activity in which ideal and material tools are deployed that organize the collaboration.

Vygotsky observed that in ontogenesis the first step toward concept formation is the organization of "[...] a number of objects in *an unorganized congeries*, or 'heap' [...] consisting of disparate objects grouped together without any basis [...] a vague syncretic conglomeration of individual objects that have somehow or other coalesced [...]" (Vygotsky 2012, 117–118). Transposed to the domain of proletarian sociogenesis, this describes the lack of cohesion and coherence of a the collective subject in its primordial state. It is "[...] a tendency to compensate for the paucity of well-apprehended objective relations by an overabundance of subjective connections and to mistake these subjective bonds for real bonds between things" (Vygotsky 2012, 118). At first, proletarian workplace subjectivities are subsumed under other subjectivities and only acquire some stability in the shared space of the labor process. This represents the prehistory of class formation.

In "The Making of the English Working Class," the Marxist historian Edward P. Thompson (1924–1993) observed that:

> Class happens when some men, as a result of common experience (inherited or shared) feel and articulate the identity of their interests as between themselves, and as against other men whose interests are different from (and usually opposed to) theirs. The class experience is largely determined by the productive relations in which men are born – or enter involuntarily. Class-consciousness is the way in which those experiences are handled in cultural terms: embodied in traditions, value-systems, ideas, and institutional forms.
>
> THOMPSON 1963, 9

Thompson was correct to underline the importance of cultural tools in the formation of a worker subject: the means to express and to change the predicament workers face. However, in this paragraph he does not distinguish sufficiently between those experiences and cultural forms that mediate the position of the workers as *object* of the capitalist labor process, and those that represent *their own subjectivity*. Marx remarked in the "Poverty of Philosophy":

> Economic conditions had first transformed the mass of the people of the country into workers. The combination of capital has created for this mass a common situation, common interests. This mass is thus already a class as against capital, but not yet for itself. In the struggle, of which we have noted only a few phases, this mass becomes united, and constitutes itself as a class for itself.
> MARX 1976B, 211

The differentiation and opposition of the workers as a population from other classes – from which particular cultural forms emerge – is an insufficient condition for its formation as a 'class for itself'. What is needed is the appropriation of these cultural forms and their deployment in a *specific form* of collaboration: a shared activity of revolt, i.e., the 'class struggle'. Another 'definition' of Thompson's is much closer to this idea:

> [...] people find themselves in a society structured in determined ways (crucially, but not exclusively, in productive relations), they experience exploitation (or the need to maintain power over those whom they exploit), they identify points of antagonistic interest, they commence to struggle around these issues and in the process of struggling they discover themselves as classes, they come to know this discovery as class-consciousness.
> THOMPSON 1978, 149

Not the diffusion of proletarian cultural experiences but the "process of struggling" is the subjectivity of the collective worker subject. What then is the *Urphänomen* (Goethe), the Concept (Hegel), the cell-form (Marx), the unit of analysis (Vygotsky), or the project (Blunden) of proletarian subject formation? It is the *strike*.

Firstly, the strike, in its broadest sense of collective economic action, is the most primitive form of collaboration through which workers jointly confront their immediate predicament – by 'combining'[2] and refusing to participate in the capital relation. Obviously, the strike has a prehistory, a process of 'original accumulation' of 'everyday', 'molecular', or 'hidden' forms of resistance (cf. Cohen

---

2 Cf. Marx's 'combinations of workers' in "The Poverty of Philosophy" (1976b).

1980; Scott 1985). Bayat observed that: "Under repressive conditions, labor resistance may take the form of absenteeism, sabotage, disturbances, theft, religious practice, and poor quality production. Labor activism of this nature is not necessarily unplanned or purely 'spontaneous' [...]" (Bayat 1996, 180). We can add riots (Au 2007, 276), humor, and the carnavalesque[3] to this list of important 'prehistoric' forms of proletarian subjectivity. However, these forms are *elements* but not *units* of class formation. Actions that are merely survival strategies or coping mechanisms, are almost indiscernible from such everyday forms of resistance. Calling an individual or collective act of Luddite destruction, 'laziness', or sarcasm a form of organized resistance imputes a much too advanced consciousness and intentionality to the actor (cf. Abbink and van Walraven 2003, 1–10). Although the participants of such a collaboration may *objectively* destabilize the production process or undermine its legitimacy, often they are not conscious of their activity *as* resistance (Cohen 1980, 21). Moreover, they do not confront their predicament in terms of a struggle about the conditions of wage labor. There are, of course, important *historical* exceptions, but these specific cases underline the rule that 'everyday resistance' cannot function as a *logical* archetype for class formation.

Secondly, the strike *generates* forms of mediation that in turn expand the agency of the workers as a collective subject. From a Vygotskian perspective, the subject has to create those neoformations that allow it to develop and transcend its social situation of development. Naturally, with regard to the domain of proletarian sociogenesis, the neoformations of the strike are not inner psychological functions such as 'logical memory', 'will', 'voluntary attention', and so on, but the developing *social organs of the collective subject* such as committees and assemblies. In this regard, Lukács commented that: "The organisational forms of the proletariat [...] are real *forms of mediation*, in which and through which develops and is developed the consciousness that corresponds to the social being of the proletariat" (Lukács 2000, 79). Social neoformations are the product of struggle and once created they begin to restructure the whole activity of struggle itself, differentiating the social functions of 'organization', 'communication', 'deliberation', and so on, within the emerging project.

Thirdly, any strike contains in miniature, enveloped, and primitive form the more advanced neoformations of trade unionism, workers' control, and workers' democracy. For example, in Egypt, as I discuss further in the text, the first independent trade union since the Nasser era directly emerged

---

3 In the Bakhtinian sense of a brief moment of fantastic and utopian liberation in which the established order is mocked (cf. Bakhtin 1984).

from the struggle of the real estate tax workers. The organization of the Mahalla strikes between 2008 and 2010 created practices of democratic deliberation. And so on.

However, the struggle does not start with an explicit political character. Vygotsky observed that for each stage of ontogenetic development, one neoformation and one line of development play a central part in developing the entire mental structure. The central neoformation of the strike is the committee, assembly, or cell through which, on the one hand, the individual workers can recognize themselves as a united social force, overcoming their fragmentation – i.e., their subjective predicament – and, on the other, the organized and concentrated power of capital in the workplace – i.e., their objective predicament – can be challenged. The central line of development is a direct and spatially restricted (local) economic struggle around the conditions of wage labor (cf. Wood 2012, 28).

Trade Unionism

Although the activity of the strike is the starting point of proletarian class formation, it does not *necessarily* lead to further development. There are many causes of the collapse of the central neoformation, the strike committee, before it can evolve into something different. Firstly, there is a limit to the duration of any strike, which is by nature a temporary activity. Workers can be defeated by a lock-out or state repression, or they become simply exhausted, economically and morally, before they have been able to organize themselves adequately. Secondly, if the workers' demands have been met, their *immediate* predicament disappears. If the maturation of their central neoformation has not constituted a new social situation of development, a new ensemble of expectations, needs, motivations, and desires, the workers do not perceive the limits of their actual developmental stage as a collective subject – or they are content to remain within that phase. The central neoformation disintegrates, sinks into stasis, or deforms into a pathological structure – e.g. a bureaucracy without active rank and file.[4] Often a collapsed strike project hibernates within the workforce in the form of a collective historical memory that guards lessons drawn, practices learnt, tactics developed, and so on. These ideal forms of the project are time and time again reappropriated when a new strike activity develops.

---

4   Cf. Chapter 9.

With the successful development of the strike committee a new social situation of development opens up. The objective predicament is the competition, not between individual workers within the same workplace, but between workers of different workplaces within the same sector of production. This situation mirrors the subjective condition of the developing worker subject: its fragmentation and atomization over countless workplaces. The independent committee itself becomes an obstacle for further development. In order to become the general social body of workers, the movement has to subsume the various instances of the strike project under a new whole. With regard to concept formation in ontogenesis, Vygotsky observed that a major step in overcoming the syncretism of thought was the thinking in 'complexes': "In a complex, the bonds between its components are *concrete and factual* rather than abstract and logical [...]. The factual bonds are discovered through direct experience" (Vygotsky 2012, 120–121). "The principal function of complexes is to establish bonds and relations. Complex thinking begins the unification of scattered impressions; by organizing discrete elements of experience into groups, it creates a basis for later generalizations" (Vygotsky 2012, 144).

Transposed to the domain of proletarian sociogenesis, this development needs a new organizational form to structurally connect and unite the various committees, and a novel concept that grasps its particular form of collaboration. The central neoformation of this phase is the *trade union* and its concept is *trade unionism*. The central line of development of trade unionism is divided into two stages, as Gramsci posited:

> The first and most elementary of these is the economic-corporate level: a tradesman[5] feels *obliged* to stand by another tradesman, a manufacturer[6] by another manufacturer, etc., but the tradesman does not yet feel solidarity with the manufacturer; in other words, the members of the professional group are conscious of its unity and homogeneity, and of the need to organize it, but in the case of the wider social group this is not yet so. A second moment is that in which consciousness is reached of the solidarity of interests among all the members of a social class – but still in the purely economic field.
> GRAMSCI 1971, 181

In a first phase, labor committees unite in federations and organize joint negotiations and collective actions to defend the interests and conditions of

---

5 In the sense of a skilled worker.
6 In the sense of an industrial worker.

workers of a particular sector. Concomitantly, the problem of wage labor is *generalized* from its *individual* appearance in the workplace to its *particular* character in a branch of production. In a second phase, trade unions defending specific branches of workers unite in national and even international federations. This movement represents the generalization of the problem of wage labor from its *particular* appearance to its *universal* essence: capitalist exploitation.

Whereas in the activity of the strike organizational forms emerged from mobilization, trade unionism organizes and structures mobilizations (cf. Moore 2011, 25). The existence and further development of the trade union itself evolves from purely a means to defend particular economic interests to an end in itself (Gramsci 1971, 162). The individual strike continues to exist in the current stage, but loses its decisive role in the development of the whole subject. Individual strikes are subsumed under general trade union activity, which can – but, unfortunately, does not always – offer a shortcut to the organization of collective action. As both Gramsci and Luxemburg emphasized, the trade union is a neoformation that defends the workers' interests within the framework of capitalism, and does not constitute a transitional form to socialism (cf. Morton 2007, 82; Thatcher 2007, 32). The traditional trade union's division of the working class by industrial branch and economic sector reflects capitalism's organization of society (Lavalette 2001, 116). A new social situation of development opens up, in which the capitalist state constitutes the worker subject's objective predicament, and the restricted economism of trade unionism becomes its subjective condition:

> Already at this juncture the problem of the State is posed – but only in terms of winning politico-juridical equality with the ruling groups: the right is claimed to participate in legislation and administration, even to reform these – but within the existing fundamental structures.
>
> GRAMSCI 1971, 181

The Economic and the Political

Up until now I have only discussed the process of class formation flowing from the specific position of the proletariat in the capitalist economic structure. At this juncture, when the economic line of development, of which trade unionism is the motor, turns into a political one, it is time to take a step back and return to the beginning of the chapter, where I elucidated the differentiation between the 'economic' and the 'political' in bourgeois-capitalist society.

The essence of the economic line of development of the proletarian subject is that: "The struggle over appropriation appears not as a political struggle, but as a battle over the terms and conditions of work" (Wood 2012, 27). In order to politicize the economic line and organize the workers' movement as a political force, capital has to be confronted in its essentially political character. This transformation is difficult because of the differentiation between the economic and political spheres. As Wood commented:

> Class-conflict generally breaks into open war only when it goes outdoors, particularly since the coercive arm of capital is outside the wall of the productive unit. This means that when there are violent confrontations, they are usually not directly between capital and labour. It is not capital itself, but the state, that conducts class-conflict when it intermittently breaks outside the walls and takes a more violent form. The armed power of capital usually remains in the background; and, when class-domination makes itself felt as a direct and personal coercive force, it appears in the guise of an 'autonomous' and 'neutral' state.
>
> WOOD 2012, 28

At the very beginning of the economic line of development of the worker subject – the local, 'particularist' workplace strike – wage laborers already face the full political predicament of capitalist state power *in a direct and explicit form outside the workplace*. Whereas the general condition of wage labor appears to workers in a fragmented and apolitical manner, the political essence of capital is represented as the state, standing above them, as an entity divorced from their direct economic life. Therefore, workers do not automatically confront the state as capital, but as a purely political antagonist.

When revolting against state power, wage laborers participate in other projects than the proletarian subject, struggling alongside (or against) other subaltern actors such as farmers, slum dwellers, professional groups, and other 'petty bourgeois' elements and sometimes even with bourgeois actors. The political object of such emancipatory projects is the transformation of oppressive relations of race, gender, disability, ethnicity, religion, age, and so on. Most of these struggles already have a prehistory of activity before the emergence of the bourgeois-capitalist society. Irrespective of historical struggles, in the present subaltern actors pose their demands in the context of bourgeois-capitalist society. The rise of the modern integral state[7] entails a transformation of their project as they are confronted with the opportunity/obstacle

---

7 The differentiated unity of civil and political society, cf. Chapter 5.

of the apparently purely political domain. The differentiation of the economic domain from the political community means that their demands are mainly formulated in terms of civil and human *rights*, which have to be legally expressed, enacted, and safeguarded by mediation of the 'neutral' state. Because of the historical process of delinking between the functions of private surplus extraction and public coercion, the economic substance of the state as organized and concentrated capital remains largely hidden to the political struggle.

When workers engage in political protests, collaborating with other actors, they do not, at first, face the state as *wage workers*, but as 'the people', 'citizens', 'members of a minority group', 'members of a community', 'youth', and so on. Their proletarian project does not automatically and directly coincide with their political activity. In a developed, bourgeois-capitalist social formation, *the political line of development starts and develops, at first, independently from the economic one.*

In his analysis of the ontogenetic relation between human thinking and speech, Vygotsky offers us an insight into the logic of entwinement of two different lines of development. His studies showed that the development of human (and primate) speech and intellect began as two separate faculties. Speech has preintellectual emotional and social roots: "The child's babbling, crying, even his first words, are quite clearly stages of speech development that have nothing to do with the development of thinking" (Vygotsky 2012, 87). Conversely, the first forms of thought are prelinguistic: "thinking in terms of tools" (Bühler in Vygotsky 2012, 86), i.e., independent, consciously purposive actions mediated by material artifacts. These two functions develop autonomously, until: "[…] at a certain moment at about the age of two the curves of development of thought and speech, till then separate, meet and join to initiate a new form of behavior" (Vygotsky 2012, 87).

At this point a spiral, a 'double helix' of development emerges, in which the developmental lines of speech and thought become intertwined. Speech becomes 'intellectualized' and thought 'verbalized'. Externally, this is directly observable in the development of grammar and semantics. Internally, the double development of 'verbal thought'[8] goes through a transitional form of 'egocentric speech' followed by 'inner speech' (Vygotsky 2012, 100). Here it is

---

8 Vygotsky stressed that not all speech and thinking becomes verbal thought, however. Emotional-social forms of speech remain unintellectualized – e.g. exclamations of joy or anger, gesturing, and so on – and areas of thought remain unverbalized – e.g. tool-use and 'practical intellect' in general (Vygotsky 2012, 94).

sufficient to note that Vygotsky draws our attention to the fact that two lines of development mature independently until they reach a point where they begin to influence one another and in the process constitute an entirely new line of development. When translating this insight to the domain of proletarian sociogenesis it becomes clear that the challenge for proletarian class formation is to combine and unite the economic and political lines of development.

Demonstration and Party

Whereas workers are only treated objectively, i.e., as a concrete unit of labor power in the economic sphere, without a recognition of their subjectivity in the political domain, 'the citizenship' or 'the people' are immediately recognized as collective entity, but merely in abstract terms. The national-popular subject is endowed with a will and thus subjectness, but it has no real objective social body of its own that allows it to *act*. Bar the restricted and isolated space of parliament, it lacks organizational forms that connect its actual, heterogeneous conditions of life with the highly abstract and homogeneous principles it represents. Whereas the proletarian subject is a fragmented body struggling to attain, cohesion, coherence, and self-consciousness, the national-popular subject is from its inception a universal yet empty subjectness – a mere concept – that has to discover its substance by grounding itself in social reality. During the 18 Days, for example, the slogan of "The people want" expressed the transformation of 'the people' from an abstract concept into a real project. 'The people' created for itself a social body and activity.[9]

The political line of development of the national-popular subject begins with the critique that 'its' state misrepresents the 'general good', and ends in the understanding that the state represents all too correctly the interests of a particular class, repositioning 'the people' as a *class* against an alien state. The class content of the abstract equality between citizens before the law is discovered, as the French writer Anatole France (1844–1924) sarcastically remarked in his poem "Le Lys Rouge":

---

9 Cf. "[...] the living organism, however, did not originate through *the building up of parts into a whole* but, on the contrary through the beginning or origin, the *generation of parts* (organs) from an originally undifferentiated whole. Here the whole preceded its own parts, and functioned in relation to them as the purpose they all served" (Ilyenkov 2008a, 149).

> La majestueuse égalité des lois, qui interdit au riche comme au pauvre de coucher sous les ponts, de mendier dans les rues et de voler du pain.[10]

Whereas the development of the worker subject is a journey of *generalization* in which wage laborers discover themselves as a universal project of emancipation, the trajectory of the national-popular subject is led by a process of *differentiation* and *particularization*, through which the class content of its subjectivity (and that of its antagonist) is revealed.

If the *strike* is the cell-form of the proletarian subject, the *demonstration* is the unit of analysis of the national-popular subject, of which the substance – its subjectivity – is the active struggle for democracy and sovereignty. A political demonstration is literally a *showing* of discontent and collective subjectness: a message directed at those in power and a rallying call towards potential supporters. A 'modern'[11] demonstration starts from an already shared concept of a particular *right to*, which in turn flows from the universal popular sovereignty that the political community claims to represent. Yet a demonstration organizes citizens or 'individual people' inevitably as a *particular* group, a specific social body of demonstrators, separated from the state, but nevertheless demanding the application of *universal* rights.

Whether the actual demands of the demonstration are (partly) met or rejected by the state – both reactions can weaken or strengthen the movement depending on the concrete circumstances – the formulation of slogans, the coordination of the demonstration, the organization of internal communication and deliberation, the experienced confrontation with state power, and so on, renders the project more and more concrete. Temporal repetition and spatial expansion of the demonstration not only draws in new bodies into the project, but it also consolidates and systemizes its activity: the demonstration becomes a political *movement*. At this point, the national-popular subject has gained a body of its own and it no longer seeks to demonstrate its discontent and to petition the state, but it demands its rights *as* a political community by constituting a *mass party*[12] in civil society. In this sense, the party itself becomes

---

10 "The majestic equality of laws, which forbid rich and poor alike to sleep under bridges, beg in the streets, and steal bread" (Anatole France, 1894, Le Lys Rouge (The Red Lily)).

11 In an ancien régime context demonstrations could demand particular rights flowing from a corporate division of society. Here the conceptual development takes the existence of a fully-formed bourgeois-capitalist state as its premise.

12 Note that this not necessarily signifies a formal, electoral party, as Gramsci quipped: "Parties may present themselves the anti-party or the 'negation of the parties'; in reality, even the so-called 'individualists' are party men, only they would like to be 'party chiefs'

"[...] an embryonic State structure [...]" (Gramsci 1971, 226). Throughout the political struggle, universalist state power is discovered as particularist class power – "[...] Since every party is only the nomenclature for a class [...]" (Gramsci 1971, 152) – and civil and political society are revealed as merely the arena of the struggle for hegemony – i.e., class leadership.

Proletarian Hegemony

Summarizing the conceptual narrative: there are two lines of development at work in the constitution of the proletarian subject. The first one is an economic line of development, which develops the project of strike into the consolidated activity-system of trade unionism. The second one is a political line of development, which develops the project of demonstration into the consolidated activity-system of the party. The entwinement of these two lines of development takes place when the economic struggle of workers is organized as a political struggle, and when the popular political struggle becomes grounded in its economic – i.e., class – reality. A trade union organizes itself politically in order to safeguard its interests and a party takes up the economic plight of its political constituency.

The neoformation that leads the new 'political-economic' line of development is what Gramsci called, with a nod to Machiavelli, the 'Modern Prince': "[...] an organism, a complex element of society in which a collective will, which has already been recognized and has to some extent asserted itself in action, begins to take concrete form" (Gramsci 1971, 129). The rationale of the Modern Prince is the development of proletarian hegemony, which allows the worker subject to conquer, appropriate, transform, and eventually liquidate state power (Gramsci 1971, 59). Hegemony is secured through the development of a *hegemonic apparatus*: "[...] the wide-ranging series of articulated institutions (understood in the broadest sense) and practices – from newspapers to educational organizations to political parties – by means of which a class and its allies engage their opponents in a struggle for political power" (Thomas

---

by the grace of God or the idiocy of those who follow them." (Gramsci 1971: 146) Moreover: "Although every party is the expression of a social group, and of one social group only [...] the organic parties and fundamental parties have been compelled by the exigencies of the struggle or for other reasons to split into fractions – each one of which calls itself a 'party' and even an independent party." (Gramsci 1971: 148) He also adds that structures and functions of the 'organic party' often exist outside the narrow party organization, such as the press and the cultural world.

2009, 226). The Modern Prince is a party in its broad sense: a politically-organized faction in society that represents the interests of a class. Different, formally autonomous parties may represent the same class, or one party can contain multiple class projects. Independent media, intellectuals, civil society organizations, and so on, may belong to a party in its broad sense.

If the hegemonic apparatus is the concrete, organizational *form* of the political-economic line of development, proletarian hegemony is its *content*. The development of proletarian hegemony requires the development of political leadership in order to, firstly, compete on the same level with the bourgeoisie, and, secondly, to attract other subaltern projects to its activity-system:

> The metal worker, the carpenter, the builder, etc., must not only think as proletarians and no longer as metal worker, carpenter, builder, etc., but they have to take one more step forward: they have to think like workers who are members of a class that aims to lead the peasants and intellectuals. They have to think like a class which can win and build socialism only if it is helped and followed by the large majority of these social strata. If this is not achieved, the proletariat does not become the leading class [...].
> GRAMSCI 2005, 41

Unlike Michael Hardt and Antonio Negri's 'multitude' (2006), Gramsci's 'counterbloc' is not the dissolution of the working class into a loose collection of subaltern actors who resist the 'rule of capital' (Callinicos 2004). On the contrary, the formation of the counterbloc *affirms* the proletariat as the only counterhegemonic class able to defeat the bourgeoisie (Harman 2002). Moreover, it affirms the need to concentrate and centralize subaltern power to fight the historically developed institutions of state and capital.

However, whereas bourgeois hegemony is exercised 'from above' through repressive technocratic and bureaucratic methods and 'coercive consent',[13] proletarian hegemony is based on a *dialectical pedagogy* 'from above to below and back again': a continuous organic and dialogic exchange between leaders and the masses; between revolutionary theory and 'good sense'; and between workers and their subaltern allies (Thomas 2009, 437–438).

For Gramsci, the archetype of this dialectical pedagogy had been the praxis of the factory councils during the *Biennio Rosso* – the two years of intense class struggle in Italy after the First World War. Against the top-down bureaucratism of the trade unions, the intellectuals around *L'Ordine Nuovo* developed a concept of

---

13   Consent-creating policies backed up by (the threat of) violence.

grassroots and democratic worker participation, which emerged organically from their solidary assistance to the 'spontaneous' factory councils. The dissipation of the revolutionary movement in Italy, on the one hand, and the Stalinist Thermidor[14] on the other, convinced Gramsci that the immanent democratic dynamic of the workers' movement needed a directive center in order to be successful, and, conversely, that this directive center needed a continuous organic connection to the worker activity-system (Morton 2007, 82–85).

The Modern Prince is much more than the institutionalization and concentration of the workers' movement in a 'parliamentary' party or 'vanguard' organization. It is the formation of a directive 'collective intellectual', a hegemonic apparatus, and a system of political activity governed by a 'dialectic pedagogy'. In this sense, proletarian hegemony offers its subaltern allies the concrete means of their human emancipation instead of another form of veiled class rule. In the next chapter I discuss the notion of a political pedagogy in more detail.

---

14   Thermidor was the eleventh month of the revolutionary French calendar. As Robespierre was overthrown in the month Thermidor, the term came to denote the moment in which the development of a revolution halted, and reaction took the upper hand. In a 1931 essay in the first edition of "Class Struggle," Trotsky described the rise of Stalinism in Soviet Russia as the Thermidor of the Russian Revolution.

CHAPTER 7

A Pedagogy of Revolt

The previous chapter discussed the strike as the cell-form of the worker subject, the economic struggle as the central line of development, and the trade unionist activity-system as the ultimate neoformation of this line. Subsequently I explained the limits of the economic line and the process of entwinement between the economic and political line of development. The political line starts from a separate point of origin, in the abstract concept of the national-popular subject and the project of demonstration, which develops into the mass party. Finally, the economic and political are united in the Modern Prince. In the following chapter I argue that the Modern Prince, apart from playing an organizational function, has also a crucial educational role by developing a philosophy of praxis and conjoining 'organic' and 'traditional' intellectuals in a 'dialectical pedagogy' with the masses.

Learning and Instruction

Marx claimed that in order to transform the alienating capitalist society:

> [...] the alteration of men on a mass scale is, necessarily, an alteration which can only take place in a practical movement, a revolution; this revolution is necessary, therefore, not only because the ruling class cannot be overthrown in any other way, but also because the class overthrowing it can only in a revolution succeed in ridding itself of all the muck of ages and become fitted to found society anew.
> MARX AND ENGELS 1976, 53

In the previous chapters I discussed how from the activity of strike and demonstration neoformations emerge that guide the whole developmental process of the worker subject. The whole of outward-oriented performances and objectifications of the movement – the creation of organizational, deliberative, and communicative structures, signs, and leaders – are originally produced as external *weapons* in the struggle with capital organized in the workplace (management) and in civil and political society (the state). However, as Marx pointed out, the 'practical movement' is not only an instrumental activity; it also generates an 'alteration of men'. Workers do not become an emancipatory force because of some mystical, inner quality, but because their struggle develops new subjectivities. In this regard, Hal Draper (1914–90) wisely commented that:

> [...] emancipation is not a form of graduation ceremony [...] but rather it is a process of struggle by people who are not yet 'ready' for emancipation, and who can become ready for emancipation only by launching the struggle themselves, before anyone considers them ready for it.
>
> DRAPER 1971, 95

Returning to Vygotsky, it is clear that also in the domain of sociogenesis competence follows rather than constructs performance.[1] External performances are *interiorized*: "An operation that initially represents an external activity is *reconstructed* and begins to occur *internally*" (Vygotsky 1978, 56. Emphasis added.). The struggle of workers against company management produces the object of the strike or trade union committee, which is oriented externally, as a means to mediate the relations between workers and 'bosses'. But this instrument also turns inward, organizing and structuring the collective actor, turning a volatile and amorphous collaboration of wage workers into a stable system of activity.

As during ontogenesis, in proletarian sociogenesis every neoformation appears twice. Obviously here the developmental divide is not between intermentally and intramentally, but between objectively (external to the project) and subjectively (internal to the project). Whereas the local committee, trade union, party, and, ultimately the Modern Prince, function externally as a weapon against the capital relation, internally they are constituted as the political and cultural embryo of a new, authentically human – as opposed to alienated – society (socialism, communism).

The reciprocal relation between external and internal development elucidates class formation as, at its core, a process of *collective learning*. Similar to ontogenesis, instruction plays a crucial role in collective learning processes, as it leads development: it assists and stimulates the subject in creating those neoformations that allow it to overcome its social situation of development. There is a distance between the actual level of development and the potential developmental level that can be attained by means of instructive assistance – the zone of proximal development (ZPD).[2] Instruction only stimulates development – i.e.,

---

1   Cf. Chapter 4.
2   Similarly Lukács observed that: "There is a distance between the consciousness of their [the workers'] situation that they actually possesses and the consciousness that they could

those forms of learning that are central to the current developmental phase – when it is 'proleptic': when it anticipates or imagines competence through the representation of a future act or development as already existing. There are two forms of proleptic instruction: *autoprolepsis* and *heterolepsis*. Autoprolepsis is self-instruction, whereby the subject casts itself in the role of a future, more developed self. In the domain of proletarian sociogenesis, the actions and structures of the 'actually existing' worker subject anticipate a future moment within its potential development (Au 2007, 283). Wildcat strike committees imagine grassroots and independent trade unions; workers' control over factories illustrate their potential of running the economy without capitalists; and practices of participation, election, and discussion within the movement foreshadow forms of participative democracy. Moreover, politically 'advanced' workers show 'backward' layers the possible future and outcome of their current struggle. The process of autoprolepsis affirms the maxim of Marx and Engels that the emancipation of the proletariat must and can be the activity of the working class itself.

Heterolepsis, on the other hand, is the interpellation of a potential capacity of a subject by another actor. With regard to proletarian sociogenesis, heterolepsis offers a means to imagine the instructive relation between proletarian and non-proletarian actors. However, transferring the ontogenetic notion of heterolepsis to the domain of proletarian sociogenesis is a delicate exercise, as it should avoid paternalist and elitist interpretations of emancipation. Obviously, workers are not children and a political 'pedagogy' is qualitatively different from the typical teacher-student relation. How can the heteroleptic role of 'teachers' be reconciled with the principle of self-emancipation? I argue that Gramsci's concept of 'philosophy of praxis' and of 'intellectuals' offer a concrete solution to understand the technical division of labor within the worker subject and instructive assistance as a reciprocal process of 'educating the educator'.

Philosophy of Praxis

In "The German Ideology," Marx and Engels argued that the historical division of labor liberated knowledge from its immediate context and encouraged

---

have – given their class position" (Lukács 2000: 65–66). Au gives a similar example of Lenin's distinction between the consciousness of the 'economic struggle' and 'political consciousness' (Au 2007, 286). Arguably, Vygotsky's concept of ZPD is more elastic and dynamic, because it measures the relative distance between two points within a developmental phase, not between the abstract, absolute minimum level of objective class position and the maximum level of socialist consciousness.

abstract thinking (Marx and Engels 1976, 45; Ratner 1991, 98). This came at the price of a growing separation between practice and thought via the differentiation and consolidation of a category of professional 'ideologists', who became the bearers of 'advanced' or 'pure' thought:

> The division of labour, which we already saw above as one of the chief forces of history up till now, manifests itself also in the ruling class as the division of mental and material labour, so that inside this class one part appears as the thinkers of the class (its active, conceptive ideologists, who make the perfecting of the illusion of the class about itself their chief source of livelihood), while the others' attitude to these ideas and illusions is more passive and receptive, because they are in reality the active members of this class and have less time to make up illusions and ideas about themselves.
>
> MARX AND ENGELS 1976, 60

The layer of 'ideologists' had an important role in constituting the hegemony of the ruling class: "[…] it has to give its ideas the form of universality, and represent them as the only rational, universally valid ones" (Marx and Engels 1976, 60). After the Dreyfus affair at the end of the nineteenth century this social group was increasingly denoted as 'intellectuals' in political discourse (Thomas 2009, 407).

The separation between 'theory' and 'practice' was also reflected within the development of the workers' movement. Socialist theories were largely constructed by intellectuals who were sympathetic to the plight of the workers, but who stood, in general, outside the 'lifeworld' of the class (Lukács 2000, 82–83). Karl Kautsky, as chief theoretician of the Second International, claimed that the concept of socialism developed separately – in (petty-)bourgeois circles – and had to be introduced to the workers from without the movement:

> […] socialism and the class struggle arise side by side and not one out of the other; each arises under different conditions. *Modern socialist consciousness can arise only on the basis of profound scientific knowledge.* Indeed, modern economic science is as much a condition for socialist production as, say, modern technology, and the proletariat can create neither the one nor the other, no matter how much it may desire to do so; both arise out of the modern social process. *The vehicle of science is not the proletariat, but the bourgeois intelligentsia* [emphasis by Kautsky]: *it was in the minds of individual members of this stratum that modern socialism originated, and it was they who communicated it to the more intellectually developed proletarians* […]. Thus, socialist consciousness is something

introduced into the proletarian class struggle from without and not something that arose within it spontaneously.
KAUTSKY IN LENIN 1973, 37

However, Kautsky confused a crucial *predicament* of proletarian sociogenesis – the separation between 'theory' and 'practice' – for its *developmental logic*, encouraging paternalist and elitist ideas of emancipation. The development of the strike poses the problem of how workers can connect their direct and local struggle against the capital relation in the workplace (their economic line of development) with a national and global mobilization against the capital relation organized as state (their political line of development). Lukács recognized the issue as one of generalization, flowing from the economic line of development of the worker subject:

> [...] the social being of the proletariat places it *immediately* only in a relationship of struggle with the capitalists, while proletarian class consciousness becomes class consciousness proper when it incorporates a knowledge of the *totality* of bourgeois society.
> LUKÁCS 2000, 83

In order to arrive at a concrete understanding of capitalism and bourgeois society – and thus of themselves as a subject – workers had to develop a concept of society as a whole. Alongside the development of activities (forms of struggle) and neoformations (organizational structures) proletarian sociogenesis is also characterized by a development of concepts (theory). Similar to the economic and political lines of development, the formation of proletarian concepts begins from two separate points and developmental lines.

Gramsci famously claimed that: "[...] all men are philosophers [...]" (Gramsci 1971, 323), in the sense that everybody engages in what he called *spontaneous philosophy*; a mode of thought which is comprised of:

> 1. language itself, which is a totality of determined notions and concepts and not just of words grammatically devoid of content; 2. 'common sense' and 'good sense'; 3. popular religion and, therefore, also in the entire system of beliefs, superstitions, opinions, ways of seeing things and of acting, which are collectively bundled together under the name of 'folklore'.[3]
> GRAMSCI 1971, 323

---

3 Note that in Gramsci's writings these three subcategories often mediate and subsume each other in their relation to philosophy. Sometimes folklore is called a part of common sense, while sometimes common sense is called the folklore of philosophy (Cf. Colucci 1999).

Spontaneous philosophy is the real, living, organic base from which advanced forms of consciousness are developed. Every thought already contains a conception of the world, but in spontaneous philosophy this is a "[...] disjointed and episodic [...]" (Gramsci 1971, 323) awareness. Spontaneous philosophy is the gelatinous and ever-changing collection of everyday conceptions of social reality by that actor. Its flexibility allows for improvisation: "One's conception of the world is a response to certain specific problems posed by reality, which are quite specific and 'original' in their immediate relevance" (Gramsci 1971, 324). However, it also impedes coherence of thought. Spontaneous philosophy is an uncritical consciousness, but it is not a 'false' consciousness or 'self-deception'. Lukács explained that: "The direct forms of appearance of social being are not, however, subjective fantasies of the brain, but moments of the real forms of existence, the conditions of existence, of capitalist society" (Lukács 2000, 79).

Similar to Gramsci, Vygotsky developed the notion of an 'everyday' or 'spontaneous' line of conceptual development that embedded the formation of concepts within the direct experience and lifeworld of the child. A child first acquires everyday concepts within the setting of personal experience "[...] which is immediate, social, practical activity as against a context of instruction in a formal system of knowledge" (Daniels 2007, 31). There is an organic and experimental connection between thinking and activity (Vygotsky 2012, 205). Likewise, the Marxist linguist Valentin Voloshinov described the 'basic' sphere of 'behavioral ideology' as: "[...] the whole aggregate of life experiences and the outward expressions directly connected with it" (Voloshinov 1973, 91).

Opposed to 'spontaneous philosophy' Gramsci posited 'philosophy proper', and, in a similar vein, Vygotsky differentiated between 'everyday' and 'scientific' lines of development, and Voloshinov between 'behavioral ideology' and 'ideology proper'. For Gramsci, philosophy is the "criticism and the superseding" (Gramsci 1971, 326) of everyday modes of consciousness: "To criticize one's own conception of the world means therefore to make it a coherent unity and to raise it to the level reached by the most advanced thought in the world" (Gramsci 1971, 324). The key qualities of philosophy are 'homogeneity', 'coherence', and 'logicality'. Vygotsky, for his part, conceived of the 'scientific'[4] line of development, in which concepts are 'emancipated' from the "[...] unique spatiotemporal context in which they are used [...]" (Wertsch 1985, 33). Scientific concepts are acquired through explicit instruction; they are culturally

---

4 'Scientific' in this context means coherent and systematic knowledge, of which 'science' in the narrow sense is the most advanced form. For example, a rigorous theology is a 'scientific' form of knowledge.

transmitted, systematized, and consolidated 'everyday' concepts: "[...] the *absence of a system* is the cardinal psychological difference distinguishing spontaneous from scientific concepts" (Vygotsky 2012, 217). Voloshinov's notion of ideology is analogous.[5]

Gramsci, Vygotsky, and Voloshinov[6] argued that both modes of thinking were equally relevant and valuable. Vygotsky suggested that: "The strength of scientific concepts lies in their conscious and deliberate character. Spontaneous concepts, on the contrary, are strong in what concerns the situational, empirical, and practical" (Vygotsky 2012, 206).

Moreover, the relation between the two modes is characterized by a continuous exchange and interpenetration. Gramsci remarked that: "Common sense is not something rigid and immobile, but is continuously transforming itself, enriching it with scientific ideas and with philosophical opinions which have entered ordinary 'life'" (Gramsci 1971, 44; cf. Colucci 1999). Likewise, Voloshinov stressed the reciprocal 'sustenance' of the two spheres of knowledge:

> The established ideological systems of social ethics, science, art, and religion are crystallizations of behavioral ideology, and these crystallizations, in turn exert a powerful influence back upon behavioral ideology, normally setting its tone. At the same time, however, these already formalized ideological products constantly maintain the most vital organic contact with behavioral ideology and draw sustenance from it; otherwise, without that contact, they would be dead, just as any literary work or cognitive idea is dead without living, evaluative perception of it.
>
> VOLOSHINOV 1973, 91

---

5 The dichotomy between 'everyday' and 'scientific' forms of knowledge is not uncommon in developmental psychology. For example, Basil Bernstein made a distinction between 'horizontal' and 'vertical' discourse. Horizontal discourses arise from everyday experiences. They are fluid, amorphous, and prone to change. Vertical discourses, on the other hand, are produced by explicit instruction and are (more) coherent, systematic and stable (Bernstein 1999).

6 Voloshinov probably developed Bukharin's distinction between 'social psychology' and 'ideology', who was, in turn, influenced by Plekhanov (cf. Tihanov 1998). It is highly probable that the ideas of Plekhanov and Bukharin, known and criticized by all three authors (Gramsci, Vygotsky, and Voloshinov) are at the root of their shared understanding of the relation between 'practical' and 'pure' theory. Au (2007) also points to the parallel between, on the one hand, Lenin's concept of 'spontaneous' and 'conscious' awareness, and, on the other, Vygotsky's 'everyday' and 'scientific' concepts.

From an ontogenetic perspective, Vygotsky revealed that:

> In working its slow way upward, an everyday concept clears a path for the scientific concept and its downward development. It creates a series of structures necessary for the evolution of a concept's more primitive, elementary aspects, which give it body and vitality. Scientific concepts, in turn, supply structures for the upward development of the child's spontaneous concepts toward consciousness and deliberate use. Scientific concepts grow downward through spontaneous concepts; spontaneous concepts grow upward through scientific concepts.
> VYGOTSKY 2012, 205

Vygotsky's research disclosed that the interpenetration of the everyday and scientific lines of development stimulates the development of *true concepts*.[7] In ontogenesis, true concepts develop in adolescence, through social practice, formal instruction, and participation in society. Everyday concepts can become true concepts when integrated with those learned at school or another instructive environment, and, vice versa, scientific concepts gain substance when integrated with everyday concepts (Blunden 2010, 162). However, in class society, the organic process of reciprocal appropriation between everyday and scientific modes of thinking is *distorted*. Gramsci concluded that the individual worker has:

> [...] two theoretical consciousnesses (or one contradictory consciousness): one which is implicit in his activity and which in reality unites him with all his fellow-workers in the practical transformation of the real world; and one, superficially explicit or verbal, which he has inherited from the past and uncritically absorbed.
> GRAMSCI 1971, 333

There is a contradiction between both *forms* of consciousness, flowing from a disturbed organic relation between the everyday and scientific *modes* of thinking. The philosophical conception of the world, which is already implicit in the real activity of the worker subject, has to become explicit and articulated. Within the 'common sense' of the proletarian project there is already a 'healthy

---

7 In Vygotsky's theory the 'truth' of concepts is not their correspondence to 'objective reality'. A concept is true when it represents an organic connection between everyday and scientific modes of thinking.

nucleus', a *good sense*: "[...] a form of practical activity or will in which the philosophy is contained as an implicit theoretical 'premiss'" (Gramsci 1971, 328). Good sense is the cell-form of a philosophy of praxis:

> [...] it is consciousness full of contradictions, in which the philosopher himself, understood both individually and as an entire social group, not only grasps the contradictions, but posits himself as an element of the contradiction and elevates this element to a principle of knowledge and therefore of action.
> GRAMSCI 1971, 405

The philosophy of praxis has to be a complete and thorough criticism of common sense, while, at the same moment, it has to connect with existing forms of spontaneous philosophy, because "[...] it is not a question of introducing from scratch a scientific form of thought into everyone's individual life, but of renovating and making 'critical' an already existing activity" (Gramsci 1971, 331).

In summary, the creation of a philosophy of praxis requires the development of the good sense that arises spontaneously and organically from the activity of class struggle. This conceptual line of development is the outcome of, on the one hand, the theoretical generalization of the activity itself – the 'upward' growth of everyday into scientific concepts – and, on the other hand, the appropriation and instrumentalization of existing critical theories – the 'downward' growth of scientific into everyday concepts. The central neoformation that steers the development of a philosophy of praxis is the Modern Prince. Apart from a directive and organizational center, the hegemonic apparatus of the worker subject is also a *pedagogic* mechanism. The Modern Prince inspires and leads class formation by the spatial generalization and unification of local experiences of struggle, the forging of hegemonic alliances with non-proletarian actors, and the integration of the 'economic' and 'political', 'everyday' and 'scientific', lines of development.

Intellectuals and Assistance

Gramsci stressed that every human activity requires a degree of intellect and that pure practice or theory do not exist. In that sense, every human is an intellectual and a philosopher (Gramsci 1971, 347). However, just as the division of labor made some men into farmers, it consolidated others as intellectuals. Similar to Marx and Engels in "The German Ideology," Gramsci posited that intellectuals do not constitute an autonomous social group of their own,[8] but that each class produces specialists who fulfill a function in the realm of production, culture or politics. Gramsci distinguished between organic and traditional intellectuals. *Organic* intellectuals are those ideologists and leaders whose sociogenesis is interwoven with the historical formation of the class they represent:

> Every social group, coming into existence on the original terrain of an essential function in the world of economic production, creates together with itself, organically, one or more strata of intellectuals which give it homogeneity and an awareness of its own function not only in the economic but also in the social and political fields.
> GRAMSCI 1971, 5

Conversely, those specialists whom a rising class finds already existing, as relics from a previous social form, are *traditional* intellectuals:

> [...] every 'essential' social group which emerges into history out of the preceding economic structure, and as an expression of a development of this structure, has found (at least in all of history up to the present) categories of intellectuals already in existence and which seemed indeed to represent an historical continuity uninterrupted even by the most complicated and radical changes in political and social form.
> GRAMSCI 1971, 6–7

Traditional intellectuals often perceive themselves as autonomous and independent from the current ruling classes because they 'survived' the social form from which they emerged. For example, investigating the complex Italian transition from an ancien régime to a bourgeois-capitalist social formation, Gramsci discussed the continuing role of rural intellectuals who were historically rooted in the precapitalist landowning classes. The terms 'organic' and 'traditional' are not used in an absolute, but in a relative sense, in accordance with the perspective of a specific class. From the point of view of the working class, the organic intellectuals of the bourgeoisie are traditional intellectuals.

---

8 Other approaches conceptualized intellectuals as a separate 'class' (e.g. Julien Benda) or class fraction (e.g. Pierre Bourdieu) with its own distinct interests; or as class-less (e.g. Karl Mannheim), and able to transcend their group of origin. For a discussion: Kurzman and Owens 2002.

Organic intellectuals of the proletarian subject emerge from the working class population within the developing proletarian project. They represent the self-emancipatory drive of class formation. Their instruction is autoproleptic, pushing forward the development of the whole worker subject by moving 'one step ahead' of their peers and the actual developmental level of the project. Loosely following Gramsci we could distinguish three archetypical forms of instruction that lead development. Firstly, *directive* instruction mediates the formation of relations of leadership and consent. Individual strike, demonstration, trade union, and party leaders are given a mandate and are endowed with authority to make decisions representing the interests of the whole subject. These leaders embody the spatial generalization of the proletarian project as their individual person mediates the movement of the whole collective. Secondly, *cultural* instruction mediates the interpenetration of the 'everyday' and 'scientific', 'political' and 'economic' lines of development. Artists, educators, philosophers, writers, and so on, articulate the worldview and aesthetics of the subject. They integrate everyday meanings and concepts with historical traditions, texts, and signs, and through art and literature they imagine future lines of development.[9] Thirdly, *technical* instruction mediates the procedural and organizational production and reproduction of the workers' activity as a cohesive system. Organizers set up strike funds and editors publish newspapers and journals. In actuality, different persons may embody different instructive functions, and their instructive position may change over time.

The developing project of organic intellectuals is facilitated by the assistance of traditional intellectuals.[10] As Marx and Engels already observed: "[...] communist consciousness [...] may, of course, arise among the other classes too through the contemplation of the situation of this class" (Marx and Engels 1976, 52). Non-proletarian intellectuals – politicians, journalists, lawyers, artists, and academics – may be drawn into the activity-system of the working class as 'democratic philosophers': "[...] a philosopher convinced that his personality is not limited to himself as a physical individual but is an active social relationship of modification of the cultural environment" (Gramsci 1971, 350).

---

9   In the case study of the Mahalla strike movement I discuss three subforms of cultural assistance: connective, projective, and integrative instruction (cf. Chapter 21).

10 Gramsci's distinction between 'organic' and 'traditional' intellectuals and the recognition of a role for both 'internal' and 'external' instructors reinforces Au's interpretation of Lenin's concept of political leadership, articulated in "What Is to Be Done?" that leaders come "[...] both from among the enlightened workers and from among the intellectuals [...]" (Lenin cited in Au 2007, 288).

Due to their position and activity within civil and political society, they have developed directive, cultural, and technical capacities to assist the developing worker subject and are able to offer heteroleptic instruction. Through the media progressive journalists share particular class experiences with the whole workers' community and other subaltern groups. Labor lawyers defend specific cases, which become precedents for the struggle of other workers. Artists, cartoonists and writers universalize class subjectivities in an aesthetic form. Philosophers and academics combine disjointed stories of worker protests into a coherent narrative of class struggle.

Different class projects require different modes of assistance to organize and secure their hegemony and domination. Bourgeois pedagogy, based on 'coercive consent', is qualitatively distinct from proletarian pedagogy (Thomas 2009, 416). Gramsci proposed that the workers' hegemony, i.e., class leadership, was realized through a *dialectical pedagogy*: a reciprocal process of learning and instruction between intellectuals and masses, the workers' movement and its subaltern allies. Gramsci's notion of a dialectical pedagogy was influenced by Marx's third Thesis on Feuerbach (Thomas 2009, 436), which stressed that "the educator must himself be educated" (Marx 1976a, 7). Within a healthy and authentic development of the worker subject there is no stable, unilateral, top-down relation between 'teachers' and 'students'. Rather, there is a continuous reciprocity and mutual proleptic instruction between participants within the proletarian activity-system and between different subaltern projects. I use Blunden's typology of relations between projects,[11] to understand the modes of collaboration between the worker subject and other collective actors.

Domination, enslavement, or *colonization* represents an asymmetrical collaboration between a dominant and submissive subject. While the servant is subjectively dependent on the master, the colonizer is objectively dependent on the activity of the colonized for his existence as a subject. Both subjects find the means of mediation in each other, and are able to recognize themselves as subjects, but in a distorted way. This is the basic condition of wage labor. In the labor process, the worker has to subject himself to the activity of the capitalist (production), who realizes her goal (profit) through the objectifications (products) of his labor power. However, this mode of collaboration is also applicable to the typically paternalist attitude of (petty-)bourgeois actors who want to 'emancipate' and 'enlighten' the wretched working class by subsuming it under their subjectivity.

---

11   Cf. Chapter 4.

Commodification, exchange, or trade, happens when two subjects meet on formally equal terms and need something from each other. The other remains only a means to an end, instead of an end in itself. This collaboration designates relations between the worker subject and other forces that try to benefit themselves from its activity: political activism that recognizes the proletarian project as a field for recruiting and journalism that perceives of strikes merely as a news item.

A third mode of interaction between two projects is *solidarity*. Blunden defines solidarity as a collaboration between different subjects that strengthens the subjectness of the shared project and of each participant. Solidarity entails the freely offered submission of the provider of assistance to the beneficiary, in order to increase the agency of the other. Solidarity is the mode of collaboration that leads internal class formation and forges alliances between subaltern actors. Arguably, a distinction could be made between *directive* and *directed* solidarity. Whereas directive solidarity is the assistance of a stronger actor to a weaker one, directed solidarity is a recognition by the weaker party of the leadership of the stronger one, and that its own emancipation can only be completed as part of the emancipation of the other.[12] The hegemonic capacity of the proletarian subject can be measured by the degree in which the solidarity of other actors towards it is directive or directed.

---

12 'Strong' and 'weak' with regard to internal coherence and cohesion: their capacity to act as a collective subject, i.e., their subjectness. Moreover, these adjectives denote the relative strength and weakness of subjects at a certain level in their sociogenesis and within their specific social situation of development.

CHAPTER 8

Revolution

In the previous chapter I sketched the pedagogic dynamic of the Modern Prince, paying attention to the formation of a 'philosophy of praxis' and the role of 'intellectuals' in the process of subject formation. The next chapter distinguishes between a gradual and stable mode of development and development characterized by rapid changes and crises. Revolution and the mass strike are understood as intensified and punctuated phases of emancipatory development, and linked to the concepts of 'war of movement' and 'war of position'.

Growth and Crisis

According to Vygotsky, during 'stable' periods of development, the capacities of the subject gradually mature, slowly opening up a new social situation of development. However, there may emerge an ontogenetic 'crisis', which signifies a rupture with the existing social condition, calling into being 'transitional neoformations', and abruptly creating a new social situation of development (Vygotsky 1987b, 194–198). Likewise, in the process of its sociogenesis, the gradual development of the worker subject is punctuated by moments of rapid transformation. These transformations may involve a sudden spatial generalization of the worker subject, the skipping of developmental phases, and/or a prompt integration of lines of development. The occupation of a workplace, for example, and the establishment of workers' control, immediately politicizes the economic line of the strike. By its very nature, occupation *directly* addresses the question of property rights in bourgeois-capitalist society, confronting class power as state power, and revealing the particular class substance of seemingly universalist state interests. Moreover, when turned inward, occupation accelerates the development of structures of self-governance, as workers are forced to organize the production process, both technically and politically, thus demonstrating themselves as a force capable of leading society.

Nevertheless, it is important to distinguish political-economic neoformations that are created as *supporting* structures within a primarily economic or political developmental line, from a political-economic neoformation that *leads* the *whole* development of the class. For example, a demonstration can be part of a strike, and, conversely, a strike can be part of a demonstration. In the first case the action of demonstrating is subsumed under the economic project of a strike; in the second instance the strike action is subsumed under the political collaboration of a demonstration. The function, character, and understanding of the action is determined by its position within the whole activity. A strike that deploys a demonstration in order to demand economic rights can reveal the universality of the capital relation by its confrontation with the state and can urge workers to organize politically – as happened during the strike waves leading up to the 25 January Revolution. Likewise, workers who strike and disorganize state power in support of a demonstration are able to show the connection between the economic and the political base of state power – as happened during the 18 Days of insurrection against the Mubarak régime. The aftermath of the 25 January showed a limited interpenetration of strike committees and popular revolutionary committees, and their unity represented an embryo of a proletarian hegemonic apparatus.

Finally, it appears that, in order to lead the whole developmental process of class formation, any form of rapid transformation should take place within a spatial generalization of the worker project. An individual occupation that rapidly develops the political-economic line of its spatially bounded project remains ineffective as a proleptic instructive force for the whole movement if it remains isolated: if it cannot share its specific activity and experience with other workplaces. What is needed for a *general* rapid, qualitative transformation of proletarian lines of development is a *massification* (cf. Tronti 2005) of the class struggle: a critical mass of strikes and demonstrations that develop simultaneously – i.e., a *revolution*.

Revolution

Seeing that little had changed over the course of two years after the fall of Mubarak, labor historian Joel Beinin claimed that: "The January 25 Revolution is not over. Rather, it has not yet occurred" (Beinin 2013a). The authoritarian state apparatus was largely untouched by the mass protests and there was no fundamental transformation of the political and economic relations of power in Egypt. Beinin was right to point out that revolutions are:

> [...] social, political, and economic transformations involving social movements and political mobilizations, one or more moments of popular uprising, and a longer-term process of reconstructing a new socio-political order involving the replacement of the former ruling coalition with new forces of a substantially different social character and interests.
> BEININ 2013A

The popular uprising of 25 January did not represent the whole process of revolution and the palace coup by the Supreme Council of armed forces (SCAF) was all but the end of the reconstruction of a new order. As the *outcomes* of the uprising at the level of state power were not (yet) revolutionary, Beinin refrained from categorizing the whole process as a revolution. This outcome-centered approach echoed the works of Theda Skocpol (1979) and Samuel Huntington (2006), who emphasized rapid transformations in the structure of societies as a key element of defining a process as a revolution.

However, such an outcome-centered or consequentialist approach turns a particular *outcome* of the revolutionary process into a primary determinant of its categorization, rendering the notion of a *failed* revolution problematic, as its *success* – i.e., the conquest, break-up, and transformation of state power (c.f. Lenin 1964b) – becomes a precondition of its definition.[1] Thus, in the case of Egypt, the success of the counterrevolution after the fall of Mubarak could be interpreted as evidence that there was, in fact, no authentic revolution taking place. This, in turn, would mean that the protagonists of the 25 January uprising fell victim to a cruel self-deception when they called their own mass activity during the 18 Days a 'revolution'.

It is more productive to think of insurrection and the conquest and transformation of state power as salient *moments* in an ongoing revolutionary *process*. As Beinin himself emphasized, the mass uprising of 25 January was but one moment within a chain of diverse protests that preceded it. It was, however, a crucial moment because that what had been there already, in an undeveloped, implicit, and hidden form, was rendered explicit and salient. The 18 Days represented a sapling of which both its past, as a seed, and its potential future, as a tree, were hidden from immediate observation. Nevertheless, these moments are part of the same developmental process of subject formation. A project approach allows us to recognize within the 25 January uprising the development of collaborations that existed before 2011 and, conversely, to recognize the undeveloped form of 'revolution' within collaborations that paved the way for the insurrection. The Egyptian uprising was not simply initiated by the Tunisian protests that started in December 2012, but it constituted a development of earlier projects of revolt, such as pro-democracy sit-ins and strikes for higher wages. The famous occupation of Midan Tahrir had been anticipated by

---

1 Achcar tries to solve this conundrum by distinguishing between a 'revolutionary dynamic' as the process of revolution and 'revolution' as its proper outcome (Achcar 2013, 15). In this case we simply use different words to denote the same processes: my 'revolution' is his 'revolutionary dynamic' and my 'revolutionary conquest and transformation of state power' is his 'revolution'.

a large demonstration in the square in 2001 and a brief occupation in March 2003, when 20,000 protesters protested against the U.S. military intervention in Iraq (Howeidy 2005). The strike wave that started from 8 February 2011 – and which continued unabated after Mubarak's resignation – was foreshadowed by the upturn of workers' struggles since the mid-2000s (Zemni, De Smet, and Bogaert 2013). What the uprising represented was a moment in which this molecular accumulation of economic strikes and protests, and political sit-ins and demonstrations was forged into a meaningful, salient, and explicit whole – into a quantitatively and qualitatively new project of revolutionary change.

Instead of conceiving of revolution as an *object* produced by mass political activity, it should be understood *as the activity itself*, from which a new collective subject emerges: al-sha'b, 'the people'. Jack Goldstone's definition of revolution as "[…] an effort to transform the political institutions and the justifications for political authority in society […]" (Goldstone 2001, 142) points in the right direction: revolution is the formation and mobilization of a collective will. Apart from an expression of desire (Gribbon and Hawas 2012, 119), the slogan of "the people want" underlines the process of active massification and democratization of the normally isolated and elevated sphere of politics. As Trotsky underlined:

> The most indubitable feature of a revolution is the direct interference of the masses in historic events […] the masses […] break over the barriers excluding them from the political arena, sweep aside their traditional representatives, and create by their own interference the initial groundwork for a new régime. The history of a revolution is for us first of all a history of the forcible entrance of the masses into the realm of rulership over their own destiny.
> TROTSKY 2001, 17–18

Revolution is the accelerated development of the demonstration as cell-form of the national-popular subject. Instead of a gradual spatial expansion there is an explosion of demonstrations, sit-ins, and political strikes. Instead of a slow and stable integration of different lines of development, political consciousness develops with leaps and bounds. The struggle against the *capitalist* state also opens up a new social situation of development for the worker subject.

The Mass Strike

In her 1906 pamphlet 'The Mass Strike', Luxemburg explained the rapid entwinement of the economic and political lines of development throughout the activity of revolution. As a process the dynamic of revolution was dictated by the ebb and flow of mass political and economic protests. The leading activity of the worker subject within the revolution was the 'mass strike': "[...] the method of motion of the proletarian mass, the phenomenal form of the proletarian struggle in the revolution" (Luxemburg 1970, 182). The local and particular character of the strike was forcefully transformed in a general context of mass political activity: "Only in the sultry air of the period of revolution can any partial little conflict between labor and capital grow into a general explosion" (Luxemburg 1970, 186). Astutely Luxemburg recognized the intertwining of the 'economic' and 'political' lines of development of the proletarian subject within the mass strike:

> In a word: the economic struggle is the transmitter from one political center to another; the political struggle is the periodic fertilization of the soil for the economic struggle. Cause and effect here continually change places [...].
> LUXEMBURG 1970, 185

The activity of the proletarian subject feeds and reinforces the activity of the national-popular subject and vice versa. For the national-popular subject "[...] the mass strike appears as the natural means of recruiting the widest proletarian layers for the struggle" (Luxemburg 1970, 202) against state power, while the worker project recognizes in the national-popular will a means to end capitalist exploitation. In other words, there is a real collaboration between the two subjects, which, depending on the relative strength of their subjectness, may take on the mode of colonization, commodification, or solidarity.[2]

The temporal coincidence of real labor struggles allows the worker subject to recognize itself as a concrete, cohesive collective actor (instead of an abstractly coherent subject in the heads of its intellectuals) and overcome the predicament of its spatial fragmentation. Moreover, the generalization of the worker subject and the dialectic of political and economic struggle stimulates the growth of a hegemonic proletarian neoformation that guides the whole revolutionary process.

Surprisingly, unlike Trotsky, Luxemburg did not recognize the unique hegemonic apparatus that developed organically during the 1905 Russian Revolution: the soviets. Through these soldiers' and workers' councils the Russian proletariat exercised leadership over the whole revolution, subsuming

---

2 Cf. Chapters 4 and 7.

the national-popular movement under their direction, as Alan Shandro aptly analyzed:

> Organizing themselves into soviets, the workers spontaneously reorganized the space of political life: opening the process of political decision-making to the scrutiny of the popular masses, they encouraged the masses to enter politics; merging the social, economic and cultural demands and grievances of the people in the assault upon the autocratic régime, they palpably expanded the range of political struggle; dispensing with formalities that barred the path to participation in the struggle, they facilitated the confluence of popular forces in all their contradictory diversity.
> SHANDRO 2007, 18

As the cell-form of the Modern Prince, the soviets revealed in their practice the class content of the national-popular subjectivity; the political substance of 'the people'. The soviets realized the abstract political community as a concrete activity-system, in which participants united their abstract subjectness as 'the people' with their real subjectivity as subaltern actors in society.

The powerful developmental dynamic of revolution and the mass strike brought the Italian 'workerist' Mario Tronti to claim that: "There is no possible process of class massification without first having reached a mass level of struggle. In other words, there is no true class growth of the workers without mass labor struggle" (Tronti 2005). However, if this is the case, the question emerges if proletarian class formation is only possible in revolutionary conditions, and if so, what the limits are of development within a non-revolutionary social situation. Facing social-democratic reformism on the one hand, and the rise of fascism on the other, Gramsci differentiated between a war of movement, war of position, and guerrilla warfare as different *modes* of proletarian sociogenesis and instruction relevant to different *social situations of development*.

Movement, Position, Underground

Gramsci distinguished between three broad modes of struggle against the bourgeois-capitalist state: war of movement, war of position, and 'underground' warfare: "Boycotts are a form of war of position, strikes of war of movement, the secret preparation of weapons and combat troops belong to underground warfare" (Gramsci 1971, 229–230). Although the struggle of the workers' movement contains elements of all three modes of political warfare, at any time one way of struggling is dominant or leading. Whereas the war of movement represented a frontal attack on state power, a "concentrated and instantaneous form of insurrection" (revolution and the mass strike)[3]; the war of position is a more "'diffused' and capillary form of indirect pressure" (Gramsci 1971, 110), a deliberate and steadfast siege of the state.[4] Neither of these modes are voluntary strategies (Gramsci 1971, 234), but they are part of the social situation of development of the proletarian project.

The Italian Marxist famously mused about the different trajectories of the Russian and West-European worker subject that "In Russia the State was everything, civil society was primordial and gelatinous; in the West, there was a proper relation between State and civil society, and when the State trembled a sturdy structure of civil society was at once revealed" (Gramsci 1971, 238). The uneven and combined development of capitalism created a situation where advanced capitalist forms co-existed with a feudal rural economy and an absolutist state in Russia (cf. Trotsky 2001). The state had not yet emancipated itself as an abstract entity from the economic sphere and direct coercion remained an important means of surplus extraction. Unlike in the Western liberal democracies, the political line of development was not fully differentiated from the economic one, immediately integrating, in a primordial form, the political and economic struggle. Because capital was more primitively (and thus explicitly) organized as the state, the state "[...] as a more visibly centralized and universal class-enemy, has served as a focus for mass-struggle" (Wood 2012, 29). Labor relations were mediated by state coercion rather than hegemonic consent, creating a situation "[...] in which every form and expression of the labor movement is forbidden, in which the simplest strike is a political crime [...]" (Luxemburg 1970, 190). In these standard conditions the growth of the worker subject took on the form of a trajectory punctuated by crises and sudden developmental jumps, instantaneously connecting the fragmented workplace-bound activity, and frontally attacking the state as class because "[...] it must logically follow that every economic struggle will become a political one" (Luxemburg 1970, 190).

---

3   Gramsci commented on Luxemburg's pamphlet on the mass strike "[...] this little book [...] is one of the most significant documents theorizing the war of manoeuvre in relation to political science." (Gramsci 1971, 233).

4   For the working class, underground warfare is not a realistic option as a leading activity, because: "[...] a class which has to work fixed hours every day cannot have permanent and specialised assault organisations – as can a class which has ample financial resources and all of whose members are not tied down by fixed work" (Gramsci 1971, 232).

Nevertheless, it would be wrong to draw the conclusion that the war of movement was only the mode of struggle of 'backward' capitalist countries such as Russia in 1905 and 1917, whereas the working class in 'advanced' or 'core' capitalist countries was locked in a perpetual war of position against the much more sophisticated class-state. Both modes are always present within the development of the worker subject. However, if at any one moment one mode of struggle functions as an overall *strategy*, it subsumes the other mode as a *tactic* (cf. Gramsci 1971, 235). If the war of position is *leading* the pace and character of development, this mode does not preclude sudden and sharp 'attacks' – assertive (mass) strikes and demonstrations – that reinforce the 'position' of the class vis-à-vis the capitalist state: "[...] they render merely 'partial' the element of movement which before used to be 'the whole' of war, etc." (Gramsci 1971, 243). Conversely, when the war of movement is the dominant strategy, this does not absolve the fast developing project from a "[...] long ideological and political preparation, organically devised in advance to reawaken popular passions and enable them to be concentrated and brought simultaneously to detonation point" (Gramsci 1971, 110). Moreover, accidental factors such as war and foreign intervention and cyclical forces such as economic upturns and crises may destabilize "the massive structures of the modern democracies" (Gramsci 1971, 243), transform the proletarian social situation of development, and change the leading mode of struggle from a war of position to a 'war of maneuver' – and vice versa (cf. Gramsci 1971, 110).

CHAPTER 9

Pathologies

In the preceding chapters I presented the ideal typical development of the proletarian subject, reconstructing the 'plot' behind the historical 'story' of the workers' movement. In actuality, however, this trajectory has all but been a smooth and 'healthy' process, from the normative perspective of authentic subject formation.[1] Below I briefly sketch some of the developmental pathologies that may arise – and have risen historically – during the formation of the worker activity-system.

Iron Law of Oligarchy?

A first pathology is the historical tendency of the participants of a developed and complex activity-system to lose democratic control once its organizational structures are formed. Seeing how social-democratic trade unions and parties fell prone to the rule of small elites and cliques at the turn of the nineteenth century, the German sociologist Robert Michels (1876–1936), a student of Max Weber's (1864–1920), fatalistically claimed that: "Who says organization, says oligarchy" (Michels 1968, 365). Hard empirical evidence of the systematic exclusion of the rank and file from the decision process in the German Socialist Party brought Michels to the theoretical conclusion that, throughout history, there was an 'iron law of oligarchy' at work that transformed originally democratic activity-systems into bureaucratic structures. As an explanation for this recurrent phenomenon the German sociologist invoked – in line with the rationalization thesis of his mentor Weber – the logic of class organization and mobilization, which necessitated a division of labor and relations of hierarchy and authority, and the social psychology of the masses, who desired to delegate the responsibilities of power to a group of revered leaders. Instead of a means (*Mittel*) to an end (*Zweck*), social-democratic structures became an end in themselves (*Selbstzweck*) for the leaders to accumulate personal power. Michels's pessimistic perspective led him straight to elite theories as elaborated by

---

[1] As Vygotsky pointed out, the conception of the 'normative' development is constructed through the appearance of the pathological, and vice versa: "Pathology is the key to understanding development and development is the key to understand pathological changes." (Vygotsky 1998, 152).

Vilfredo Pareto (1848–1923) and Gaetano Mosca (1858–1941), eventually joining Mussoloni's Fascist Party.

From an emancipatory perspective, there is little to gain from the determinist and fatalistic *interpretation* of the empirical facts of bureaucratization and elite formation. Nevertheless, Michels's notion of *Selbstzweck* and the pitfalls of organization and representative politics highlights a concern shared with anarchist, Marxist, and contemporary alterglobalization thinkers. Returning to Hegel and Marx, the concept of alienation formulates the essence of the problem: the inert object of activity that is disconnected from living praxis and confronts it as something external and alien. In his densely written "Critique of Dialectical Reason," Sartre took up the issue as the problem of the 'anti-dialectic' of the 'practico-inert'. As the basic unit of human subjectness Sartre posited the 'fused group', an undifferentiated totality constituted by an immediate activity or praxis shared by its individual participants. Sartre conceived of the 'fused group' as but a fleeting, temporary force: "The fused group should [...] be characterised as an irreversible and limited process: the reshaping of human relations by man had temporalised itself in the practical context of a particular aim and as such would not survive its objectification" (Sartre 2004, 390).

Praxis, the 'constituent dialectic', creates a domain of worked inertia: the 'practico-inert', which is equivalent to Hegel's objectification of human subjectivity. The 'practico-inert' represents an 'anti-dialectic', a 'dialectic of passivity', because it resists the active 'constituent dialectic'. Whereas Blunden's notion of project already presupposes forms of mediation (either appropriated from other activities or produced by the collaboration itself), the 'fused group' is primordial, undifferentiated, unmediated activity. Sartre considered tools, signs, and organizational forms as 'worked' activity, the 'practico-inert', which "comes to man from outside" (Sartre 2004, 471). When the 'fused group' becomes mediated it turns into an organization or institution, becoming alienated from the vitality of its 'constituent dialectic': "It is in the concrete and synthetic relation of the agent of the other through the mediation of the thing, and to the thing through the mediation of the other, that we shall be able to discover the foundations of all possible alienation" (Sartre 2004, 66f27).

The problem with Sartre's approach is that his notion of alienation is derived from Hegel instead of Marx. As discussed in Chapters 3 and 5 Marx had criticized Hegel's conflation of objectification, which was part of the human condition, with alienation. Alienation was the outcome of the historically-immanent, involuntary, and undirected cooperation between human beings who did not recognize the products of this spatially, temporally, and socially fragmented collaboration as the objectifications of their own activity. The 'mediation of the thing' is, in fact, a necessary element in subject constitution, because it is through the historical development and actual use of material tools and ideal signs (cultural universals), that human beings are able to be 'active' at all. The 'practico-inert' is always already present within the 'fused group', for example when protesters shout slogans, throw bricks, and tend their wounded in the 'primordial' activity of a 'spontaneous' demonstration. In conclusion, Sartre's concept of the 'practico-inert' helps us to understand the passive, inert side of human activity, but it does not offer a solution to comprehend the process of bureaucratization and authoritarianism of previously dynamic and democratic activity-systems.

The idea that a project is an active, transformative force, which is succeeded by an inert, conservative obstacle, has also been explored by social movement studies, for example in the work of Ron Eyerman and Andrew Jamison (1991). They conceive of a social movement as the creative, dynamic, and vital form of collective activity, which they *oppose* to the ossified, bureaucratic, and hierarchical institutions such as trade unions and parties that are often its products. The emergence of *structure* (practico-inert) appears to spell the end of *agency* (praxis). However, instead of excluding each other, movement mobilization and organizational institutionalization are entwined and presuppose each other (Beinin and Vairel 2011, 9). Blunden argued that "[...] it is far more productive if, instead of viewing an institution as something alien to social movements in general, we see them as a project at a specific stage of its development, different from the social movement it used to be" (Blunden 2012b). The fundamental relation between movement and institution is not one of mutually excluding entities, but one of contradictory *moments of one and the same process*. Movements are continuously organized into institutions and institutions are mobilized as movements – praxis is constantly transformed into 'practico-inert' matter, and these coagulated cultural artifacts metamorphose back into living activity.[2] Thus, the problem is not the process of institutionalization *an*

---

2 There is a strong similarity between Sartre's 'practico-inert' and Ilyenkov's notion of 'fetishization': "Fetishisation registers the results of human activity but not man's activity itself, so that it embraces not the ideal itself but only its estrangement in external objects or in language, i.e., congealed products. That is not surprising; the ideal as a form of human activity exists only in that activity, and not in its results, because the activity is a constant, continuing negation of the existing, sensuously perceived form of things, is their change and sublation into new forms, taking place in accordance with general patterns expressed in ideal forms" (Ilyenkov 2008a, 275). Arguably, for Ilyenkov the pathology does not arise at the moment of objectification, but when this objectification is not reappropriated by an activity that transforms it anew.

sich – to which the eternal perpetuation of the moment of the movement appears the solution – but the bureaucratic, hierarchical, and authoritarian *form* that institutionalization often takes.

Especially the centralization and concentration of subaltern power, the consolidation of its ad hoc actions into everyday practices, and the emergence of a technical division labor, which differentiates the amorphous activity of revolt and renders its subjectivity concrete, are perceived as inevitably alienating the vital subject from its inert objectifications. The concentration of power and "the logic of representation" (Nigam 2012, 174) lead to authoritarianism and elite formation and a differentiation of functions within the project ends up in bureaucratization and hierarchism. This is a concern shared by contemporary autonomist, anarchist, and other alterglobalist tendencies who promote 'direct action', 'horizontalism', 'prefiguration', and 'network politics' as an alternative to the traditional forms of institutionalized contestation, especially the 'party-form'.[3] In general, these political agendas tend to encourage a diversity of goals among participants in a project and a plurality of outcomes, rather than a shared platform and objective, or even common adversary, which are seen as *threats* to the authenticity and health of the movement (Maeckelbergh 2013, 35).

Unfortunately here the historically well-founded suspicion against authoritarianism and bureaucratism leads to a diminished subjectness and a stunted development of the project. Within any activity-system, the *technical* division of labor, which, admittedly, might evolve into a *social* division of labor, is a necessary solution for the de facto unevenness of individual capacities within the subject (cf. Johnson 2001, 113). Rejecting a distinction between leaders and led is an admirable mission, but in itself it does not solve the real problem of the uneven development of competence, experience, and consciousness within a project, which cannot be transcended by simply declaring it undesirable. What is needed is the demanding work of a dialectical pedagogy that brings together the 'educators' and 'educated' in a reciprocal, dialogical relation – as I elaborated in Chapter 7. Furthermore, in order to successfully challenge "the organised opposition of the adversary" (Johnson 2001, 113) the building of a cohesive and coherent hegemonic apparatus, the articulation of a shared concept of the state as class, and the concentration of power is required. If this emancipatory development is blocked, the subject is trapped

---

3   Cf. "To the party-form belongs the hijacking of popular initiative and will (or may we say, desire?), such as is expressed either in mass revolts or in elections. To this form belongs the history of 20th century totalitarianisms." (Nigam 2012: 173–174).

in a fragmented, incoherent, and powerless condition, which constitutes another pathology – that of self-liquidation.[4]

Gramsci recognized the danger of political organizations "to become mummified and anachronistic" (Gramsci 1971, 211). Instead of an 'iron law', *Selbstzweck* was an empirically-identifiable historical tendency in which the necessary centralism of worker neoformations lost its organic and democratic character "[...] because of a lack of initiative and responsibility at the bottom [...]" (Gramsci 1971, 189). The democratic-pedagogic role of centralism is to encourage the formation of organic intellectuals 'from below' and to embed these specialists within the 'masses' in a continuous reciprocal practice of learning and instruction. This requires an active rank and file, the creation of structures that stimulate, reinforce, and concentrate this activity, and a capable leadership that is organically connected to the 'masses', that is conscious about the pitfalls of centralism, and engages in a dialectical pedagogic practice. Both internal forces – e.g., factional infighting and personal power games – and external forces – e.g., defeat and repression – can hamper the healthy formation of a hegemonic apparatus. Such accidental – because not part of the developmental logic – yet often dominant factors can create powerful pathologies – of which the unfortunate degeneration of the Soviet Communist Party is the most famous case (cf. Trotsky 1991).

Revolution-Restoration

The development of the worker subject does not unfold in a societal vacuum; on the contrary, the strength and weakness of the ruling class and the state, the general level of culture, the structural and conjunctural stage of capitalism, the country's position in the international state system and the global economy,

---

4   Self-liquidation is the opposite of bureaucratic centralism. Under its label could be grouped those tendencies within the worker subject itself that actively suppress the formation of a necessary neoformation in the developmental trajectory of the project. For example revolutionary syndicalists who reject the necessity of building an explicitly *political* organization; 'economists' who only stimulate the maturation of an economic line of development; 'spontaneists' who reject the necessity of leadership, stable organizational structures, and the intertwining of everyday and scientific lines of development; 'democrats' who argue that the worker subject should not play a leading role in a class alliance; and so on. Moreover, at a certain point 'old' neoformations (such as trade unions or social-democratic parties) may stand in the way of the development of the proletarian project and should be subsumed under new structures or even destroyed because they only express a partial emancipation.

and war and peace constitute its social situation of development. The political and economic intervention of the ruling classes in the proletariat's social situation has a profound impact on the developmental trajectory of the working class. In his study of the *Risorgimento* – the modern process of unification and state formation of Italy – Gramsci discussed the process of 'revolution-restoration' or *passive revolution*: the exercise of political leadership by the bourgeoisie through molecular reforms and the fragmentation of its civildemocratic and proletarian opponents. Unlike its French counterparts, the Italian bourgeoisie had not been able to develop itself as a coherent and cohesive political force. Socially locked in an economic-corporate state and spatially divided between north and south, it was unable to rally popular forces behind a revolutionary project of nation state building and industrial-capitalist transformation. Eventually, Italian unification was forcefully realized by military conquest of Piedmont 'from above', and not by a mass movement 'from below' (cf. Versieren and De Smet 2014). Hegemony over the popular classes was exercised through a limited *social extension* of the ruling class and the Italian state, instead of being achieved by political leadership and cultural prestige. This extension was realized by a politics of *transformism*: the gradual absorption into the dominating class and state apparatus of, in a first phase, the individual cadres of the popular parties, and then, in a second phase, whole political factions: "[...] the absorption of the enemies' *élites* means their decapitation, and annihilation often for a very long time" (Gramsci 1971, 59). Obviously, the attraction and integration of subaltern intellectuals in the capitalist class project directly halts, damages, or even liquidates the formation of national-popular and proletarian subjects. This is a form of the 'colonization' relation as described in Chapters 4 and 7.

A second aspect of passive revolution has a much more subtle and ambiguous impact on proletarian development. Gramsci suggested that there was a strong connection between the war of position as a mode of political struggle and passive revolution (Gramsci 1971, 108). The siege warfare between the developed integral state and subaltern forces could induce a politics of piecemeal and gradual reforms, "relatively far-reaching modifications" to the economic structure, regulation and control of profits, and concessions towards political rights (Gramsci 1971, 120). This reformism stabilized the social situation of the subaltern classes *objectively* because it lessened its direct predicament, and *subjectively* because it was possible "[...] to avoid the popular masses going through a period of political experience such as occurred in France in the years of Jacobinism, in 1831, and in 1848" (Gramsci 1971, 119). In this regard the reformism of an era characterized by passive revolution reinforces the war of position mode of struggle, and vice versa.

From the perspective of the well-being of individual workers political and economic reforms of the capitalist state and improvements to their working conditions are unquestionably a step forward. However, from the point of view of subject formation the influence of reforms is more complex. As Vygotsky emphasized, development takes place when there is a will to overcome a predicament that prompts the growth of the necessary means to overcome the obstacle. Put simply, when the proletariat does not conceive of its situation as a predicament, it will not develop the neoformations that constitute it as a subject. Nevertheless, it would be politically immoral and tactically unsound to reject the pursuit of reforms within capitalism. In "Reform or Revolution?" (1970) Luxemburg highlighted that the struggle for immediate reforms was a necessary activity in developing the worker subject. From the struggle emerge the neoformations and lines of development that eventually defeat the capitalist state and plant the seed for a new, classless society. Small, partial victories grant workers confidence and experience to continue their movement and the fulfillment of direct needs creates new needs and expectations. The important distinction, then, is not between reform and revolution as modes of struggle, but between reforms that are the outcome of a victorious struggle 'from below', and 'top-down' reforms that preempt the further development of the worker subject and have a pathological effect. Furthermore, from a long-term perspective any reform within capitalism is just a provisional and partial victory or concession for the working class, and only temporarily stabilizes its social situation of development.

Inadequate Instruction

Vygotsky stressed that instructive assistance leads development, but only when it operates within the 'zone of proximal development' (ZPD) of the subject: the distance between its actual and potential developmental level at a precise moment in its formative process. Instruction that addresses capacities 'below' or 'above' the ZPD does not encourage development. This insight has important consequences for proletarian sociogenesis. First of all, there is a hard limit on how fast and far a project can develop in a specific phase of its existence. This limit is not absolute, but depends on its social situation of development. For example, the distance between actual and potential levels of development increases exponentially during a 'war of maneuver' mode of struggle:

> During a revolution millions and tens of millions of people learn in a week more than they do in a year of ordinary, somnolent life. For at the

> time of a sharp turn in the life of an entire people it becomes particularly clear what aims the various classes of the people are pursuing, what strength they possess, and what methods they use.
> LENIN 1977, 227

Conversely, in periods of general defeat or passive revolution the developmental horizon may be quite modest. The difficulty for a democratic and organic political pedagogy is to recognize the lower and upper boundaries of proleptic assistance, and avoid the extremes of *voluntarism* (ignoring the upper limits of the ZPD) and *pessimism* (ignoring the lower limits of the ZPD). This is probably the crux of any serious leftist politics: how to recognize, support, and improve those structures and concepts within the worker subject that push its development to its most advanced level. There is no general formula of "always be one step ahead of the masses"; sometimes it is necessary to be two, three or four steps ahead. Instructive assistance should not reflect the actual developmental level – let alone a previous stage – but carefully move ahead along the current line of development. Voluntarist assistance, exceeding the upper limit of the ZPD, leads to a *vanguardism* that loses its organic connection with the everyday line of development and alienates itself from the proletarian activity-system. Instruction that exceeds the developmental level of the entire worker subject may only interpellate small sections of the project, which may become impatient and move too much ahead of the class, losing their organic connection with the whole. Alternatively, the form and content of instruction may be so distant from the actual consciousness that it becomes an *absurdity* in the eyes of the class it wishes to interpellate – consider the 'propaganda of the (violent) deed' by some anarchists. Pessimist assistance, on the other hand, merely echoes the actual or previous developmental level, and results in *tail-ending* the movement of the working class, and a subsumption of the domain of the 'scientific' under the 'everyday'. Voluntarist and pessimist forms of assistance are found among both organic and traditional intellectuals. The demands formulated by strike leaders may be too weak or too strong for the rank and file. Middle-class leftist activists may underestimate or overrate the capacity of the working class to lead a protest movement. And so on.

With regard to *adequate* assistance, Vygotsky's method of 'double stimulation'[5] should be recalled: [...] the problem is put to the subject from the start and remains the same throughout, but the clues to solution are introduced stepwise [...] (Vygotsky 2012, 112). Likewise, workers face their predicament as

---

5 Cf. Chapter 4.

a whole, but they cannot immediately jump to a solution, they have to work their way through the problem. This pedagogic method has a strong resemblance to Trotsky's concept of 'successive approximations' during a revolutionary movement: "The fundamental political process of the revolution thus consists in the gradual comprehension by a class of the problems arising from the social crisis – the active orientation of the masses by a method of successive approximations" (Trotsky 2001, 18–19). As Trotsky remarked, the capacity of learning and development of the masses within a certain phase of the revolution is not absolute. Every phase of the revolution has its own ZPD. The failure, at a certain point in its trajectory, to develop a suitable neoformation to deal with a specific situation limits its entire development.

The political pedagogy of adequate, proleptic instruction reveals itself perhaps most explicitly in its concentrated, conceptual form as *transitional demands*. Whereas the *content* of a transitional program is conjunctural – articulating the specific circumstances of the worker subject – unlike the mechanical separation between a minimum (reforms) and maximum (socialism) program, its *form* has a direct pedagogical function: "It is necessary to help the masses in the process of daily struggle to find a bridge between present demands and the socialist program of the revolution" (Trotsky 1996, 275). Not only do transitional demands connect the everyday and the scientific lines of development, but they express the limits of the potential developmental level. These boundaries are not to be understood as repellants, but, on the contrary, as attractors of the movement. In the process of reaching for these demands, the limits of (the current form of) capitalism are exposed in practice and the proletarian subject develops neoformations that open up a new social situation of development, which, in turn, expands its ZPD.

Substitutionism

A final pathology sketched here is the tendency for an internal or external force to substitute its own agency for that of the working class. Internally, there may emerge a bureaucratic-centralist clique, as discussed above, which cannibalizes from within the proletarian project. This bureaucratic substitutionism is different from the formation of a politicized faction within the worker subject, which desires to act or understands the conjunctural necessity to act in a situation where the actual developmental level or the general passivity of the whole class restricts such a mobilization. The formation of the worker subject may move too slow to adequately follow rapid changes in its social situation. When a developmental crisis erupts, the class may not be able to forge the necessary neoformations and take a developmental leap in a timely manner. It misses the 'moment'.[6]

Anxiety or frustration to 'miss the moment' may force a group within the worker subject to *act in the place of* the whole class instead of *leading* it. The result is a political faction that "[...] *thinks for* the proletariat, which *substitutes itself* politically for it [...]" instead of a leadership that "[...] politically *educates* and *mobilises* the proletariat to exercise rational pressure on the will of all political groups and parties" (Trotsky 1904). By substituting its own activity for that of the working class no process of collective learning is allowed to take place and subject formation as self-emancipation is blocked.

Externally, the weakness of proletarian subjectness may attract other forces to colonize[7] its activity-system and replace its subjectivity with that of their own. In "The Principle of Self-Emancipation in Marx and Engels" (1971), Draper dispelled the illusion that a force – e.g., the state as 'Savior-Ruler', the philanthropic intelligentsia or the 'enlightened' bourgeoisie – could emancipate the subaltern 'from above'. Only the proletariat could emancipate itself through an independent, collective learning process: "One learns to revolutionize society even as one revolutionizes oneself; one learns to revolutionize oneself by trying to revolutionize society" (Draper 1971, 96). However, the 'emancipatory' interventions of other forces 'from above' may induce profound pathologies in the sociogenesis of the working class, for example in the form of *Bonapartism* or *Caesarism*.

In the "Eighteenth Brumaire of Louis Bonaparte" (1979), Marx discussed a societal crisis in which a state or state faction dispossessed the ruling classes of their direct and formal political power. The French state appeared to balance between the classes and gain a level of autonomy vis-à-vis its constituent class. However, it still articulated the interests of the ruling class and acted as its diligent guardian. Gramsci elaborated upon the concept of 'Bonapartism' through his concept of 'Caesarism', which "[...] can be said to express a situation in

---

6 "A situation whose duration may be longer of shorter, but which is distinguished from the process that leads up to it in that it forces together the essential tendencies of that process, and demands that a decision be taken over the future direction of the process. That is to say the tendencies reach a sort of zenith, and depending on how the situation concerned is handled, the process takes on a different direction after the 'moment'. Development does not occur, then, as a continuous intensification, in which development is favourable to the proletariat, and the day after tomorrow the situation must be even more favourable than it is tomorrow, and so on. It means rather that at a particular point, the situation demands that a decision be taken and the day after tomorrow might be too late to make that decision" (Lukács 2000, 55).

7 Cf. Chapters 4 and 7.

which the forces in conflict balance each other in a catastrophic manner; that is to say, they balance each other in such a way that continuation of the conflict can only terminate in their reciprocal destruction" (Gramsci 1971, 219). The stalemate is solved by the intervention of "[...] a third force [...] from outside, subjugating what is left [...]" (Gramsci 1971, 219). To the common interpretation of Bonapartism as an essentially right wing phenomenon, Gramsci added that there were 'progressive' and 'reactionary', 'military' and 'civil', 'quantitative' and 'qualitative' forms (cf. De Smet 2014a). A progressive and qualitative Caesarist régime may implement far-reaching reforms from above, creating a sustained illusion among subaltern actors that their predicament could be solved by mediation of an external force. Until it runs into objective obstacles, the 'octroyal socialism'[8] of this type of régime turns top-down reforms into political hegemony. As we will see in the historical excursus, in Egypt this was the case with Nasserism.

---

8 The handing down of social reforms from above (Draper 1971).

PART 3

Historical Lineages

CHAPTER 10

Roots of the 25 January Uprising

Surprised by the Expected

The Tunisian and Egyptian uprising took many observers, scholars, and politicians by surprise, as I remarked in the introduction. However, for those activists and researchers who had been working in Egypt 'on the ground', among the discontented masses, the revolution was only a *surprise of the expected*. They were surprised by the moment and mass scale of the uprising, but not by the fact that, finally, something happened (cf. Khalil 2012, 121). In 2008 journalist John Bradley aptly named his book: "Inside Egypt: The Land of the Pharaohs on the Brink of a Revolution." In 2009 interview I conducted with Hassanein, cartoonist of the socialist *al-Ahali* (The People) newspaper, he prophesized that: "The situation is growing worse, sooner or later there will be a revolution."[1] Senior journalist and editor Medhat al-Zahed of *al-Badil* (The Alternative) claimed that:

> Within three or four years Egypt will change, one way or another, the official structure will collapse as social conflict looks for a way to express itself beyond the limited pseudo-democracy. People don't like to go on the streets and protest, but they do it out of necessity. Anger will continue and accumulate. Through the struggle they will find a way to unify and the movement will gain a political dimension."[2]

Leftist activist Wael Tawfiq suggested to me that "Even in the next year there could be a revolution: we should be ready and start organizing right now, or we won't have a successful revolution."[3]

Through the character Busayna in his novel "The Yacoubian Building" (2006) Egyptian writer Alaa al-Aswany had denounced sharply the poverty, intimidation, and harassment that ordinary Egyptians – and especially young women – faced on a daily basis in Mubarak's Egypt:

> When you've stood for two hours at the bus stop or taken three different buses and had to go through hell every day just to get home, when your

---

1   Interview with Hassanein, Cairo, 14 April 2009.
2   Interview with Medhat al-Zahed, Cairo, 8 April 2009.
3   Interview with Wael Tawfiq, Cairo, 20 October 2010.

house has collapsed and the government has left you sitting with your children in a tent on the street, when the police officer has insulted you and beaten you just because you're on a minibus at night, when you've spent the whole day going around the shops looking for work and there isn't any, when you're a fine sturdy young man with an education and all you have in your pockets is a pound, or sometimes nothing at all, then you'll know why we hate Egypt.

ASWANY 2006, 138

Two months before the revolution, and in the middle of the parliamentary elections, I conducted an interview with al-Aswany. With regard to the violence surrounding the elections he declared that: "[…] what is significant is that the régime has reached the point where it finds itself obliged to shoot the people – the citizens. This is a very significant sign that we are close to a real change in the country."[4]

In "The Collapse of the Second International" (1974), Lenin had outlined three symptoms of a revolutionary situation: (1) a crisis of the régime and a conflict between factions of the ruling class; (2) an increase in the suffering of the subaltern classes; (3) when (1) and (2) lead to "a considerable increase in the activity of the masses." In other words, a revolutionary situation emerges when the social situation of development of the subaltern classes takes on the character of a crisis, transforming their mode of struggle from a war of position to a war of movement. The popular uprising of 25 January did not represent the whole process of revolution, but constituted the salient explication and massification of a whole range of projects of revolt that were slowly building up toward open insurrection. As I discuss further in the text these movements were definitely a reaction against a hegemonic crisis of the régime, growing discontent among ruling and subaltern classes, and a worsening of the living conditions of the masses. These revolutionary anticipations made some organic and traditional intellectuals contemplate the necessity and possibility of revolution, years before 25 January 2011.

Original Accumulation and Extended Reproduction

Whereas Alan Shandro suggested that: "The forces of revolution are assembled only on the field of battle, in the course of hostilities, from whatever elements present themselves, drawn often from the ranks of opposing forces" (Shandro

---

4 Interview with Alaa al-Aswany, Cairo, 26 November 2010.

2007, 21), Trotsky observed with regard to the Russian Revolution of 1917: "The dynamic of revolutionary events is *directly* determined by swift, intense and passionate changes in the psychology of classes *which have already formed themselves before the revolution*" (Trotsky 2001, 18. Emphasis added.). When studying the revolutionary process, both authors appear to be right. On the one hand, the development of the 25 January protests as a project can only be understood through an investigation of the real forces and confrontations 'on the ground', because: "The uprising was forged in the heat of street fighting, unanticipated both by its hopeful strategists and its watchful adversaries" (al-Ghobashy 2012, 27). On the other, mass protests do not drop from the sky, they presuppose existing projects.

When considering the development of the 25 January Revolution as a project, a separation should be made between 'revolution' as the explicit, salient, and self-referential process from 25 January 2011 onward, and the molecular accumulation of subject formations that led up to the explosion. Analogous to Marx's treatment of the original or primitive accumulation and extended reproduction of capital, I suggest that projects also have a *prehistory* of collaborations – their original accumulation – and a developmental process through which they develop into a more advanced and complex activity-system – their extended reproduction.[5]

Labor activist Fatma Ramadan commented that she was "[...] not measuring the revolution since 25 January, but since the year 2000, since the anti-imperialist movements and the social movements and the strikes [which] were a prelude to the revolution."[6] Since the 2000s there emerged a diversity of collaborations among human and civil rights activists, pro-democracy forces, workers, farmers, the urban poor, and so on. Workers moved against their crumbling purchasing power, the rise of unemployment, and precarious working conditions. Together with experienced militants from every ideological pedigree – communist, liberal, nationalist, Islamist – a new generation of young activists organized demonstrations in solidarity with the Second Palestinian Intifada of 2000, and protests against the wars in Afghanistan, Iraq, and Lebanon. From these collaborations emerged new projects such as the democratic movement *Kefaya* (Enough). This democratic movement was supported and stimulated by the advent of 'virtual' political activism by bloggers, Facebook users, and tweeters. In the countryside, petty farmers struggled against increasing land rents and the dispossession of their lands by occupying their holdings and organizing cooperatives. Villagers cut off roads, railways, and canals to protest a lack of potable water or electricity. And so on (De Smet 2014b).

---

5   Cf. Chapter 4.
6   Interview with Fatma Ramadan, Cairo, 15 March 2011.

Despite this complex image of protests that preceded the 25 January insurrection, Austin Mackell observed that the popular uprising was rooted in the original accumulation of two political subjects:

> In the decade leading up to 2011, the baton of rebellion was passed back and forth repeatedly between two distinct categories of political actors. One category is that of the bourgeois groups, led by intellectuals and activists, focussed in Cairo and Alexandria, and focussing on political rights and broad systematic changes. [...] As Kifaya faltered and fell by the way side, the second category – working class groups – organised around economic demands, often quite local, and strongest in the industrial cities of the Nile Delta and along the Suez Canal, began to rise. These in turn inspired more bourgeois activists, and an increasingly intense feedback loop was created.
> MACKELL 2012, 21

The twin pillars of the revolution were a developing civildemocratic[7] and a workers' subject, who represented the leading forces within a broad field of subaltern actors.

It would be wrong, however, to content ourselves with an investigation of subject formation since the 2000s. As "the actuality of capitalism encompasses a burden of the past as well as of the present,"[8] it is necessary to return all the way back to the historical moment of modern nation state formation and the penetration of the capital relation in Egypt. The legacy of colonialism, underdevelopment, Nasserism, and so on, is still present within the contemporary predicament of the Egyptian subaltern classes. Both the strike and the demonstration have a protracted, non-linear trajectory within the Egyptian social formation. The political and economic lines of development and the formation of proletarian and national-popular subjects have a complex history that becomes intelligible only when discussed within the context of changing social situations of development.

Uneven and Combined Development

At this point it is time to bring the abstraction of the sequence of real events back into the orbit of its subject matter. Before the conceptual exercise, history

---

7 Austin's designation of this movement as "bourgeois" is problematic because its members hailed mostly from the petty bourgeoisie and salaried professionals instead of the commercial, industrial, financial or landholding capitalist classes.
8 Cf. "Introduction."

appeared as an amorphous and unintelligible whole of contingent events; a chronology without meaning. Conceptual development, as I sketched out in parts I and II, highlighted political subject formation from the perspective of logical necessity. During my research in Egypt, and before, the formulation of this logic has been in a constant dialogue with the investigation of history, of *real* development, which functioned as the narrative from which the 'plot' has been distilled. This 'prehistory' of the conception of history is not treated here, as it would necessarily assume the form of a biographical and bibliographical narrative.

Gramsci explained that the study of the formation of subaltern classes in general, and the proletariat in particular, required two dimensions. Firstly, the transformations in the objective and subjective social situation of the worker subject – the class 'in-itself' – should be investigated: both the changing position of workers within the economic structure and their attitudes toward the capitalist classes. Secondly, the neoformations that emerge from the working class should be studied in their capacity as movements toward self-determination (Morton 2007, 62).

With regard to the objective predicament of the working class the conceptual starting point of a labor process fully subsumed under the capital relation has to be confronted with the actual process of subsumption. Capitalists did not simply find a population of willing wage workers, but such a group was created and is still being created through policies of economic and political coercion. Proletarianization, commodity production, and capital accumulation have not been an *instantaneous event*, but a *protracted process* that met with the resistance of precapitalist subaltern actors. Moreover, it has not been a *synchronous* but *asynchronous* process, as its cell-form was spatially restricted to Western-Europe and Great Britain more specifically (cf. Wood 2002). The capitalist mode of production came into being at a certain time, and in a certain place, and it did not immediately absorb or subjugate other modes of production. The creation of the world market, however, went much faster than the expansion of wage labor and the capital relation in different social formations.

In order to understand this complex process of capitalist 'transition', some approaches have focused on the nation state as the primary unit of analysis for capitalist transformation, while others have taken the global as their conceptual point of departure. The chief methodological problem of both the 'nation state' and 'world-system' approaches was that they *reduced* the development of the whole to the movement of the particular parts, or vice versa (Allinson and Anievas 2009, 47–48). Trotsky's concept of 'uneven and combined development' (Trotsky 2001), critically appropriated by Gramsci (Morton 2007), elaborated upon by Mandel (1976) and more recently by authors such as Rosenberg (2009, 2010), allows for a more dialectic view of the interrelation between capitalism's whole and parts.

Although some elements of 'uneven and combined development' had already been expressed by Marx, Rudolf Hilferding (1877–1941), and Anton Pannekoek (1873–1960) (Van der Linden 2007, 146), Trotsky (2001) was the first to elaborate these notions as a coherent concept in the introductory chapter of his "History of the Russian Revolution." He emphasized that the qualitative difference between the productive forces that capitalism unleashed and their precapitalist counterparts created a deep dichotomy – 'unevenness' – between 'advanced' and 'backward' forms. Unevenness does not only become a relation *between* social formations, but also a dynamic *within* one and the same society. Nations, institutions, people, and so on, do not exist in isolation from each other; on the contrary, through the world market capitalism universalizes itself, connecting different national, regional, and local activity-systems with each other. Advanced and backward social forms and modes of production are found 'in combination'; they become part of the same totality without losing their separate identity.

The combined character of capitalist development means that nations cannot repeat in isolation the historical trajectory of the first countries where the capitalist mode of production became dominant. A superficial reading of Marx had led to the belief that capitalism, interpreted in terms of a purely *national* economic 'stage', could not be skipped: "The country that is more developed industrially only shows, to the less developed, the image of its own future [...]. One nation can and should learn from others [...] society [...] can neither leap over the natural phases of its development nor remove them by decree" (Marx 1990, 91–92). Marxist stage theories claimed that non-capitalist countries should go through a transition that repeated the historical experience of the West – consisting of a national-democratic revolution that would destroy feudalism, establish a parliamentary democracy, promote free trade and markets, defend private property and civil rights, and protect the nation's sovereignty. As the historical agent of the national-democratic revolution had been the industrial bourgeoisie, consequently, in precapitalist social formations, subaltern classes had to support 'their' nascent ruling class against imperialism, colonialism, and feudalism.[9]

---

9 Stage theory became the dominant 'transitology' for the Second International and the Comintern (cf. Attewel 1984, 215–216; Townshend 1996, 143). Ironically this view echoed capitalist modernization theory, which, especially through the works of Walt Rostow (1960) and Samuel Huntington (1991) conceived of 'development' as a gradual and linear transition from a 'traditional' to a 'modern' society. Backward states had to emulate the historical development of capitalism in Western European countries in order to develop their economies. Some Marxist authors such as Bill Warren (1973) even claimed that imperialism and colonialism were progressive forces that emancipated the so-called Third World countries from their precapitalist and traditional social formations.

Conversely, the perspective of 'uneven and combined development' encourages the view that capitalist development is an organic process of both the whole – the world market, the internationalization of capital, the global division of labor – and its parts – nation states, regions, and specific modes of production. Through their relation with the world market, backward nations can directly appropriate advanced forms without going through all the historical steps that the advanced country experienced to get there. However, this 'privilege of backwardness' is only a potentiality; sometimes more advanced forms are debased when they are embedded in a backward context, which paradoxically leads to a strengthening of these backwards conditions instead of revolutionizing them (Trotsky 2001, 25–37).

In some specific historical cases, for example the development of Germany and the USA, backwardness proved to be an advantage indeed. Most non-industrialized societies, however, missed the advent of the capitalist mode of production and were confronted with strong capitalist nations. Against the backdrop of the decolonization movements in the 1950s, 1960s, and 1970s, Marxist scholars discussed the nature of development – or rather the lack thereof – in colonial and postcolonial states. Roughly two explanations were offered. A first trend of thought moved that Third World countries suffered a 'blocked transition' toward (full) capitalism because of the dominance of domestic elites, such as merchant capitalists and landlords, who were unwilling and/or unable to industrialize their economies. The concept of 'blocked transition' enabled a critique of colonialism and imperialism – which supported domestic precapitalist forces – while, at the same time, it reinforced the 'stagist' idea that the fundamental problem of underdevelopment was 'too little' capitalism, in national terms.

The dependency school reacted against this perspective and initiated a paradigm shift by conceiving of the world capitalist system, and not the nation state, as the primary unit of analysis. One should not look for the causes of underdevelopment and backwardness at the level of the nation state, but by analyzing instead the structural position of underdeveloped nations in the world capitalist system.[10] While dependency theory and world-system analysis

---

10   Raul Prebisch and Hans Singer laid the foundations of 'dependency theory', which was elaborated upon by authors such as Paul Baran (1957). Samir Amin (1976) saw the distorted development of the Third World as a form of capitalism in its own right: a peripheral capitalism that differed fundamentally from the capitalism found in the core countries. Andre Gunder Frank (1969) rejected the notion of one type of capitalism in the periphery and another in the core; according to him there was only one capitalist system, which dominated the globe and which determined all social forms and modes of production as 'capitalist'. Immanuel Wallerstein (1974) developed Frank's concept of a single system determining the nature of its parts into world-system analysis.

paid attention to the dynamics of capitalism as a totality, they reduced the movement of the parts as mere functions of the whole. The role of local and national class struggles, modes of production, and non-capitalist structures in defining the capitalist totality was neglected (Chilcote 1981, 4–5). The integration of non-capitalist spaces into the capitalist totality furthered the development of the whole – the expansion of the world market and the global accumulation of capital. But it did not automatically develop the parts 'from above' evenly. The economic trajectories of the 'periphery' are not merely 'blocked' by its structural relations with the 'core' capitalist countries. Underdevelopment is the concrete outcome of global and local relations of power, transformations, and struggles, resulting in specific 'combinations' (Gramsci 1971, 182).

Despite an emphasis on the interpenetration of local, national, and global scales, as a framework for analysis, uneven and combined development takes the nation state as its 'nodal point' (cf. Morton 2007), not in the least because:

> It is altogether self-evident that, to be able to fight at all, the working class must organize itself at home as a class and that its own country is the immediate arena of its struggle – insofar as its class struggle is national, not in substance, but, as the Communist Manifesto says, 'in form'.
> MARX 2008, 30

Intra-national, inter-national, and trans-national social forms and forces are concentrated and crystallized into a meaningful whole, which Gramsci called a 'historical bloc'. Morton lucidly explained that Gramsci's concept of historical bloc entails two dimensions. Firstly, it points to a certain 'vertical' cohesive and coherent ensemble, a totality of base and superstructures (cf. Gramsci 1971, 366, 377): the "[...] necessary reciprocity between the social relations of production and ideas within the realm of state-civil society relations [...]" (Morton 2007, 96) For example, post-Second World War 'Fordism' could be conceived of as a historical bloc as it expressed a capitalist accumulation strategy[11] (e.g. by capital-intensive investments), the totality of social and technical relations in the workplace (e.g. assembly line production), and ideological (e.g. Keynesianism), legal (e.g. state corporatism) and political (e.g. reformism) expressions.

Secondly, the concept of historical bloc represents 'horizontal' alliances between class actors: "[...] various social-class forces with competing and heterogeneous

---

11   "An accumulation strategy defines a specific economic 'growth model', including the various extra-economic preconditions and general strategies appropriate for its realisation" (Morton 2007, 153).

interests had to be fused to bring about at least some kind of unity in aims and beliefs. A historical bloc therefore indicates the integration of a variety of different class interests and forms of identity within a 'national-popular' alliance" (Morton 2007, 96–97). In other words, the historical bloc is the way in which certain, historically developed and often contradictory relations of production, political forces, and cultural forms are united in a coherent and cohesive whole (*Gestalt*).

The historical blocs that emerged in the Global South – in the sense of both the articulations between infrastructures and superstructures, and the shapes of the class alliances – also refracted the uneven and combined development of global capitalism, containing 'advanced' and 'backward' – from the perspective of capitalism – production relations and techniques; colonial and indigenous actors; bourgeois and traditional state structures; Western and local forms of culture. As we shall see further in the text, this hybridity also determined the nature of political subject formations in Egypt.

As a cohesive and coherent unity of economic base, superstructures, and class alliances, a historical bloc contains the centrifugal forces of nationally and internationally contradictory class interests and the possibilities and limitations of the economic structure, glued together by the hegemony and domination of the ruling class. When internal or external dynamics disturb the equilibrium, centrifugal forces may become stronger than the centripetal power and a crisis ensues. Gramsci distinguished between conjunctural and organic crises. A conjunctural crisis appears "as occasional, immediate, almost accidental" and does "not have any very far-reaching historical significance" (Gramsci 1971, 177). Conversely, an organic crisis is a long-term, structural instability of the system. The methodological difficulty is that organic crises always express themselves in conjunctural terms. For example, the crisis of the Nasserist historical bloc came to the surface through the Six Day War defeat in 1967, and the disintegration of the Western 'Fordist' bloc was articulated through the conjunctural 'oil crisis' of the 1970s.

Permanent Revolution

The uneven and combined character of capitalist development created historical blocs that contained elements of both capitalist and precapitalist social formations. This resulted in a peculiar situation whereby workers employed in advanced capitalist industries were already contesting modern relations of capitalist exploitation and state domination, while peasants were still struggling to overthrow forms of tributary[12] surplus extraction and the power of the absolutist state. In Russia urban pockets of industry, generalized commodity production, and capitalist accumulation existed within the larger framework of an agrarian ancien régime absolutist state. In Italy combination was expressed in spatial unevenness, with a capitalist, industrial north existing in an uncomfortable unity with an economically 'backward' south, dominated by landlords. In the colonial and semi-colonial countries, colonialism and imperialism both introduced and fettered capitalist development. The subaltern classes of these nations faced the entwined predicament of precapitalist and capitalist exploitation and domination.

Communist stage theorists suggested that the solution should be phased: first a national-democratic revolution, led by the 'native', progressive bourgeoisie against both the remnants of the precapitalist order and the imperialist powers; then, when capitalism and bourgeois society had been sufficiently developed, a socialist revolution, led by the working class. Trotsky criticized this strategy because it did not take into account the effect of the combined development of capitalism. The alliance between international finance capital and national ancien régime forces had blocked the emergence of a powerful and independent industrial bourgeoisie in these countries. Domestic industrial capital was subjugated to the interests of foreign capital, the absolutist state, and local landed and commercial elites. In the absence of an indigenous 'progressive' bourgeoisie, a subaltern alliance of workers and peasants had to confront the double predicament of capitalist/imperialist and precapitalist exploitation and domination. In other words, the 'national-democratic' revolution had to be waged by workers and peasants instead of a 'progressive' bourgeoisie (Trotsky, 1962).

So far, Trotsky's critique ran parallel to Lenin's formula of the 'dictatorship[13] of workers and peasants' in the context of the Russian Revolution. Trotsky, however, pointed out that the working class, however small, could and should play a directive role within the class coalition, because of its superior cohesion (organization) and coherence (consciousness) as an emancipatory subject compared to the peasantry and petty bourgeoisie. Within the subaltern alliance

---

12   Cf. Haldon 1993; Wood 2002.
13   The notion of dictatorship is used here not as a method of rule, but as a clarification of which class dominates and leads society. Bourgeois democracy, for example, is the dictatorship of the capitalist class. After the rise of the Fascist and Stalinist dictatorships, Trotsky preferred to use the less tainted concept of 'workers' democracy' over Marx's original slogan of the 'dictatorship of the proletariat', although they denote essentially the same: the rule of the working class (cf. Townshend 1996).

the proletariat should be the hegemonic force: "The 'democratic dictatorship of the proletariat and peasantry' is only conceivable as a dictatorship of the proletariat that leads the peasant masses behind it" (Trotsky 1962, 154). This required the development of the 'subjective factor': i.e., the building of a proletarian Modern Prince that could articulate the working class as the universal emancipator.

When the proletariat became the leading class in the national-democratic revolution against precapitalist, colonial, and imperialist forces, it would not content itself with installing a 'pure' bourgeois, capitalist order, but, on the contrary, it would challenge the exploitative capital relation, private property, and the limits of bourgeois democracy as well. A 'democratic' revolution led by the working class would immediately put the demands of the socialist revolution on the agenda: "The democratic revolution grows over directly into the socialist revolution and thereby becomes a *permanent* revolution" (Trotsky 1962, 154).

The 'permanence' of the revolution did not only consist of the programmatic coincidence of the national-democratic and socialist struggle, but also of the enduring aftermath of the conquest of power. As the socialist transformation of society only really began after the proletariat had taken power, the class struggle against internal and external antagonists continued as well. In Gramscian terms, the transformation of the historical bloc that started at the national level required a confrontation with local, national, and international actors. The international division of labor, the world market, and the geopolitical relations of power rendered 'socialism in one country' impossible. Therefore, the permanence of the revolution also denoted its spatial expansion within the global capitalist order.

Gramsci, however, criticized the concept of permanent revolution for only articulating the war of movement mode of struggle in the context of colonial and semi-colonial countries (Gramsci 1971, 236). Moreover, he attacked the theory for being too abstract and too general: "[...] permanent revolution, which is nothing but a generic forecast presented as dogma, and which demolishes itself by not in fact coming true" (Gramsci 1971, 241). Indeed, in many nations of the Global South the industrial working class did not play a *leading* role in the national-democratic revolution or decolonization struggle, and socialism was not implemented. Trotsky himself had warned that: "A backward colonial or semi-colonial country, the proletariat of which is insufficiently prepared to unite the peasantry and take power, is thereby incapable of bringing the democratic revolution to its conclusion" (Trotsky 1962, 155). A quarter of a century later, Tony Cliff argued that: "While the conservative, cowardly nature of a late-developing bourgeoisie [...] is an absolute law, the revolutionary character of the young working class [...] is neither absolute nor inevitable"

(Cliff 2000, 44). The building of a proletarian Modern Prince was fettered by the amorphousness of the working class, the dependence on non-proletarian directive intellectuals, corporatist attitudes by the state, and a lack of political organizations that offered adequate instruction. This led to a *deflection* of the process of permanent revolution and the substitutionist, colonizing, or Caesarist appropriation of proletarian agency by petty bourgeois forces such as the intelligentsia or state actors such as the military: "It is one of the tricks of history that when an historical task faces society, and the class that traditionally carries it out is absent, some other group of people, quite often a state power implements it" (Cliff 2000, 45). Unfortunately, this process of deflection became a recurrent theme in Egypt's revolutionary history.

CHAPTER 11

Colonial Subjects

In the previous chapter I explained 'uneven and combined development' and 'historical bloc' as methodological instruments that allow for a conceptual appropriation of the complex historical process. In the next chapter I begin the historical investigation with a brief overview of the Egyptian historical bloc before and during the colonial era, and an outline of the development of modern proletarian and national-popular subjectivities.

At the Doorstep of Capitalism

The social formation in the Ottoman Empire until the nineteenth century can be roughly defined as a tributary system with feudalistic trends (Chaichian 1988, 25). Agricultural production was, in general, organized by the *çift-hane* system: a peasant household gained the usufruct[1] of state-owned lands and the surplus was appropriated outside of the actual production process, enforced by a land tax as a percentage of the crops (Beinin 2001, 13). Surpluses were not reinvested in agricultural production, but flowed directly to the cities, which became rich centers of trade, guild handicrafts, and state administration (Richards and Waterbury, 2008, 39). By the eighteenth century the establishment of large farms and the weakening of Ottoman state power reinforced the power of landlords and regional governors (Mamluks) in Egypt (Cuno 2005, 197).

The increase of large landholdings, low agricultural prices, and the expansion of European markets between the 1740s and 1815 intensified trade relations between the Ottoman Empire and the West, incorporating Egypt in the developing world capitalist market. The blossoming world trade created large profits for the rural elites, encouraging a new urban financial sphere of credit, loans, and giving rise to a commercial capitalist class in the cities (Richards and Waterbury 2008, 38–40). The urban workforce was classified and organized according to the specific handicraft, commercial activity, service, or trade in which the laborers were employed. Analogous to Western feudal guilds, their organization was the *ta'ifa* (plural: *tawa'if*), which 'vertically' gathered the productive forces relevant to a particular profession. Alongside these professional

---

[1] The right to use someone else's property and enjoy the profits thereof.

groups existed a "[...] stratum of more or less unskilled, propertyless workers who took whatever short-term jobs were available and were not identified with any specific craft" (Lockman 1996b, 78). However, these sub-proletarians were subsumed as a social group under the category of the 'poor' or the 'needy'.

Aside from the expansion of the world market, modern geopolitics stimulated the penetration of capitalist forms in non-capitalist countries. Military confrontations with the rising European powers forced the Ottoman Empire and its provincial rulers to raise revenues in order to modernize and expand their armies. At the end of the eighteenth century the Mamluk chief Murad Bey imposed a state monopoly on customs collection and the government purchased and resold a large part of the wheat crop to pay for its military expenditures. This move anticipated the policies of Muhammad Ali (1769–1849) who defeated the French (who had occupied Egypt between 1798–1801), the Ottomans, and the old Mamluk elite. As the new Pasha was beleaguered by both the West and his former Ottoman suzerain, he continued Murad Bey's attempt at building a modern army, while pursuing a mercantilist policy. In order to gain fiscal autonomy from the landed elite, he partly adopted the reform program of the French who had seized tax farms, nationalized agricultural lands, and brought the *tawa'if* under state supervision. In 1814 tax farming was abolished. Peasants kept the usufruct of their lands, but were obliged to sell their crops directly to the state at low set prices. This monopsony allowed the government to trade agricultural produce with a large profit margin on both local and international markets. Protectionist measures safeguarded the weak Egyptian industries – primarily textile and weapon manufacturing – against competition with Western capitalist countries. Attempts were made at substituting Western commodities with Egyptian products, anticipating the import substitution industrialization (ISI) policies of the later neo-colonial and post-colonial state. Through forced conscription wage laborers were recruited among the peasants and guild artisans (Owen 2005, 114–115; Tucker 2005, 234–235).

Muhammad Ali's centralized fiscal, mercantilist, and industrial policies were primarily oriented toward the needs of the military and the bureaucracy, curtailing the power of urban guilds and merchant capital. Rather than a development toward some form of 'indigenous capitalism', Ali's policies closely resembled the political economy of European absolutism (al-Khafaji 2004, 43). Although there was a development of *manufacturing*, no significant *industrialization* emerged. The Egyptian manufactures lacked mechanization, division of labor, and new energy resources (Beinin 2001, 42–43). There was neither a formal nor a real subsumption of labor under capital: laborers were drawn into the production process by means of extra-economic coercion (corvée) and not through a labor contract; and the new production methods did not transform precapitalist relations of production and exploitation into capitalist ones.

Muhammad Ali's military expansionism and economic protectionism brought him into a showdown with the European powers – especially Great Britain – which sought to stabilize the Ottoman Empire. Through the Anglo-Ottoman Commercial Convention (1838) and the Treaties of London (1840, 1841) the military power and economic sovereignty of Ali's Egypt was curtailed. The reduction of Egypt's domestic and regional markets and the imposition of a free trade régime created, until the 1930s, external obstacles for an indigenous road to industrial and capitalist development. Between 1850 and 1880 Egypt became fully integrated into the capitalist world market on the basis of raw cotton production (Chaichian 1988, 28).

European military power ended the absolutism of Muhammad Ali. The Egyptian state now found itself scraping for financial resources. Foreign intervention strengthened the resistance of precapitalist structures and social forces against political centralization and economic modernization (Cuno 2005, 221; Issawi 2005, 189; Tucker 2005, 232). The Pasha's family, military officers, and other sections of the ruling classes were able to appropriate state lands as their own private property. By 1844–8, 53 percent of lands (often the most fertile ones) were in private hands (Beinin 2001, 52). Concentration of private lands was driven by the cultivation of long staple cotton – introduced in 1821 – which was capital and labor-intensive, required new production methods, and was best cultivated on large plots. Tax farming, the delegation of state power to local landlords, and the debt bondage system reinforced feudalistic relations in the countryside (al-Khafaji 2004, 19–20). From 'below', the central state was weakened by peasant struggles against conscription and heavy taxation, which led to a shortage of labor and a decline of state revenues.

During the reign of Muhammad Ali's successors, Egypt's 'feudal turn'[2] was reinforced. The building of the Suez Canal (1854–63) generated more debts than revenues for the Egyptian state. This was compensated, at first, by the American Civil War (1861–1865), which heightened the demand for Egyptian cotton. The bulk of new revenue was used for the modernization of the military,

---

2   Although agricultural products, especially cotton, were sold as commodities to the world market, and despite the presence of cash-crop farming, markets, and money, there was no capitalist accumulation in the Egyptian countryside: "[...] there was little investment, even by wealthy landowners, in either mechanization or in other means of raising productivity" (Beinin and Lockman 1987, 9). Moreover, rural social relations remained definitely precapitalist.

urban prestige projects, and as a guarantee for further loans. When the Civil War ended, American cotton flowed back into the world market and global cotton prices dropped, causing a fiscal crisis in Egypt. Between 1865 and 1868 taxes were raised by 70 percent, which indebted many peasants and led to a further concentration of agricultural lands (Beinin 2001, 52). In 1871 new tax reforms made small landholders lose their lands and become an "unpaid, bonded workforce" (Mitchell 2002, 73). Peasants were converted into laborers who received a small plot of land for themselves or who were paid in kind (Owen 2005, 119).

The economic depression of 1873–96 led to a global decline of prices for agricultural produce, which caused the bankruptcy of several Ottoman provinces. Their inability to pay debts instigated European intervention in their internal financial affairs. In 1876 the *Caisse de la Dette Publique* was established to oversee Egypt's treasury. In order to secure its financial grip, Great Britain had to intervene directly in Egypt's politics. In 1882 British troops occupied Egypt to quell the revolt of Colonel Urabi against foreign domination. This marked the beginning of the explicitly colonial era.

A Colonial Historical Bloc

The British colonial intervention encouraged the uneven and combined development of Egypt's economy. Cultivating cotton required large estates and stimulated bimodalism[3] in the countryside. Agriculture was politically and economically controlled by domestic large-scale landowners with connections to urban centers of trade and petty commodity production (Bush 2007, 1601). The colonial state did not abolish feudalism in the countryside because farming out the production of cotton to domestic landlords was more profitable for foreign capital. In this manner, the colonial state reinforced the unevenness and 'backwardness' of Egypt's economy vis-à-vis the European powers.

On the other hand, through the instrument of the colonial state, foreign industrial and finance capital forcefully introduced the capitalist mode of production in Egypt (Clawson 1978). In the early 1870s Khedive (viceroy) Ismail had implemented a modest industrialization program, establishing some 40 state owned enterprises. The state bankruptcy of 1876 led to either their destruction or sale to foreign firms. From then onward the initiative of industrialization shifted

---

3 "[…] a land-tenure system that combines a small number of owners holding very large estates with a large number of owners holding very small farms" (Richards and Waterbury 2008, 177).

to foreign corporations and the *mutamassirun*: foreign capitalists living in Egypt (Beinin 2001, 68). Egypt under colonialism[4] was not only the product of uneven development, but its social formation also combined precapitalist social and economic structures with modern capitalist sectors and relations of production. Foreign capital introduced the capitalist mode of production, but de-industrialized most of the indigenous manufactures, preparing the Egyptian markets for an influx of European commodities (al-Khafaji 2004, 41). The industrializing role of the colonial state was restricted to the creation of large-scale transport, communication, service and (some) manufacturing enterprises.

Rural landlords, urban merchants, and colonial capitalists were melded into the ruling stratum, as they all shared an interest in providing agricultural goods to international markets. Hence, domestic merchant capitalists and landlords who were allied to foreign capital kept their positions as local and national ruling classes in the Egyptian social formation (Chaichian 1988, 30). The colonial intervention had created the first modern historical bloc in Egypt, which was a combination of precapitalist and capitalist social forms, presided by an alliance between foreign capital and domestic landed and commercial forces.

During the economic crisis of 1906–8 global prices of cotton dropped. Some large landowners realized that monoculture production posed risks and that the base of their wealth should be diversified with other economic activities. As merchant capitalists became engaged in loan activities, real estate speculation, and intermediary trade, landowners attracted by the large profit margin began to invest in these activities. Both classes became aware that foreign capital appropriated a large part of 'their' surplus and this became the focus of a conflict of interests. Domestic commercial and landed elites aimed to renegotiate their position within the colonial historical bloc. Their struggle led to a confrontation with the colonial state and to the formation of a nationalist movement, led by large landlords and supported by the emerging modern middle classes and the urban proletariat (Beinin 2001, 46–47, 72; Farah 2009, 28).

The colonial mode of production and its state produced their own layer of organic intellectuals: the *effendiyya*, a group of modern middle-class professionals, engineers, journalists, lawyers, teachers, and bureaucrats with often a nationalist and Western outlook. Many effendiyya became fellow travelers of the nationalist movement, which revolted against the colonial bloc. The nationalist 'counterbloc' counted among its ranks such diverse forces as discontented

---

4 In this work I do not discuss the differences between 'colonialism' and 'imperialism'. I simply use the term 'colonial bloc' to denote the Egyptian historical bloc that became structured by the historical dynamic between foreign capitalist actors, domestic class forces, and the internationalization of capital. For a more profound analysis of imperialism: Hanieh 2013.

social-conservative landlords and peasants, urban *ta'wifa* and commercial capitalists, radicalized layers of the effendiyya and modern wage laborers. The development of the strike in Egypt increasingly illustrated the capacity of workers to mobilize and organize themselves collectively. For nationalists, the emerging worker subject constituted a powerful potential constituency for their own political project.

Development of the Strike

Muhammad Ali's push for 'manufacturization' was based on extra-economic corvée labor and did not initiate a process of proletarianization (Beinin 1981, 14). Farmers and artisans who had constituted the temporary workforce of the manufactures moved effortlessly back to their original occupations. The port, railway, urban, and canal construction during the reign of the Pashas in the second half of the nineteenth century was also based on corvée and did not constitute a collection of wage laborers that could develop into a modern working class (Lockman 1996b, 80).

The British occupation and the beginning of the colonial era coincided with the legal and actual abandonment of corvée labor and the formal recognition of private property in land. As advanced irrigation techniques had removed the dead season, landlords wanted full control over the labor of their farmers. The process of feudalization and dispossession bereft many peasants from their lands and drove them to Egypt's first industries: "[...] they could now be recruited not by physical coercion through the bureaucratic and repressive mechanisms of the state [...] but rather through the less obviously coercive mechanism of the market, which just as effectively kept wages low and working conditions inhuman" (Lockman 1996, 83).

In the 1880s, the Egyptian industrial workforce stood at the threshold of a transformation in the direction of a modern working class. The Port Said coal heavers' strike of April 1882 revealed a fledgling worker subjectivity within an ensemble of predominating precapitalist subjectivities. The coal heavers were peasants turned laborers from Upper Egypt and were paid by piece rate. When their demand for a higher rate was not met, they went on strike, blocking coal operations on the canal. The Urabi government intervened on behalf of the laborers and put the British coaling companies under pressure to accede to the strikers' demands. However, when the British occupied Egypt, they restored the previous piece rate (Lockman 1996b, 84).

This episode entailed two forms of struggle that expressed the dual predicament that the Port Said workforce faced. Firstly, the coal heavers "[...] can thus be understood as wage workers subject to an essentially capitalist system of labor contracting, hence comprehensible within a narrative of modern labor activism" (Lockman 1996b, 84). Their economic struggle was oriented against the exploitation of a foreign, capitalist industrial company. As such it was both the first stirring of a nascent modern workers' movement, and the earliest and implicit form of the future *political* alliance between workers and the national liberation movement. Secondly, at the moment of the strike the organization of 'coal heaver laborers' was still much a precapitalist formation; a unity of "[…] exploitative labor contractors against […] exploited contracted wage workers" (Lockman 1996b, 85). From this perspective, the coal heaver strike was also representative of the final pangs of the precapitalist 'guild' organization that, by then, had degenerated into a labor contracting instrument (Chalcraft 2001, 114). Even though throughout the nineteenth century the organic *tawa'if* were slowly replaced by state institutions: "[…] the discourse of occupational identity still remained powerful" (Lockman 1996b, 80).

The transformation of the strike from a precapitalist 'economic-corporate' subjectivity to a modern class subjectivity reached a next phase in 1896, when the coal heaver laborers presented a petition to Lord Cromer, demanding fair treatment from their 'own' labor contractors or *shuyukh* (singular: *shaykh*) (Lockman 1996b, 85–86). This episode reflected a horizontal class cleavage in the vertical structure of the coal heavers' organization. Nevertheless, the systematic use of the word *'amil* (plural: *'ummal*) to denote a modern wage worker emerged in Egypt only at the beginning of the twentieth century (Lockman 1996b, 77–78).

At the end of the nineteenth century, an estimated 37 percent of the rural workforce had become wage laborers (Chaichian 1988, 33). Moreover, the concentration and dispossession of landed property drove farmers to the cities where they engaged in petty commodity production, as there were few jobs to be found in the modern, privately owned colonial industries (Koptiuch 1996, 47): "There were only 15 modern European style factories employing 30–35,000 workers in Egypt in 1916" (Beinin 1981, 15). Urban wage laborers ended up chiefly in the transport, communication, and services sector of the colonial state. In 1907 489,296 wage laborers worked in the colonial production and transport industries. By 1917 this number increased to 639,929 (Ismael and al-Sa'id 1990, 15). The colonial industries generated a modern urban working class that existed side by side with the traditional *tawa'if* craftsmen.[5]

---

5   Ironically, in this way, colonialism extended and reinvigorated the existence of precapitalist social forms. Kristin Koptiuch defined this process as "paradoxical preservation" which is "[…] essentially the subsumption of a new, modern form of petty commodity production […] to colonial capital by virtue of this new form's inability to realize its own reproduction except insofar as that reproduction was tied to the expanded reproduction circuits of peripheral capitalism" (Koptiuch 1996, 62).

Although there were many strikes throughout the 1880s and 1890s, most of them expressed a dual, transitory character, as exemplified in the Port Said coal heaver strike. The first 'modern' strike that initiated a process of development of the Egyptian worker subject was probably the collective action of the cigarette rollers between December 1899 and February 1900. Lockman summarized its significance as follows: "It involved several thousand skilled workers from many different workplaces, some of them quite large, who went on strike simultaneously and remained out for two months, suggesting a strong sense of solidarity and a capacity for effective organization" (Lockman 1996b, 88). The strike of the cigarette rollers spawned a short-lived trade union formation, and was followed by many other collective actions of Egyptian workers, who, in turn, constituted their own trade unionist neoformations. Just as the English 'trade' union suggested a gathering of people on the basis of their 'trade' or occupation, the first Egyptian trade union – the Manual Trades Workers' Union (MTWU) established in 1909 – was called *niqaba*, which referred to the position of the *naqib* (custodian) in the precapitalist *ta'ifa* (Lockman 1996b, 90–91).

However, the colonial historical bloc constituted a peculiar predicament for the development of the working class as a cohesive subject. Many workers who were employed in the colonial industries were foreigners, living in their own, separate communities. For example, most cigarette rollers were Greek laborers, employed by Greek capitalists. Therefore, from everyday conditions, the strike of the cigarette rollers could be understood as a particular, intracommunal conflict instead of an exponent of the general struggle between labor and capital. Furthermore, the colonial economic structure reinforced a divide between: (1) the large-scale, capitalist companies that employed averagely skilled (and mostly foreign) wage workers; (2) an industrial periphery of unskilled Egyptian laborers employed in such activities as coal heaving; and (3) precapitalistic centers of petty commodity production and services that often employed highly skilled workers (Lockman 1996b, 88). From the perspective of an emerging national worker subject, each of these divisions was further intersected by 'vertical' interests and communal subjectivities.

Modern corporatism emerged in the Egyptian workers' movement as the organic answer to the combined nature of the colonial economic structure. Trade unions such as the MTWU still embodied many precapitalist characteristics, such as the inclusion of non-wage laborers, property owners, and employers. Some trade unions refused members on the basis of their religion, nationality, or specific position within the occupational hierarchy. Other worker organizations, such as the Cairo Tramway Workers' Union (CTWU) established in 1909, were more 'universally proletarian' and accepted all employees of the company as members on the basis that they were all wage laborers working for the same employer.

Revolution

Similar to other colonial countries such as India and China, the First World War enabled the Egyptian nationalist counterhegemonic forces to rally popular dissatisfaction for the cause of independence. After the war, an Egyptian delegation (*wafd*) led by the nationalist Saad Zaghlul, supported by a popular campaign of civil disobedience and petitions, demanded independence for the country. British repression of the movement in 1919 provoked a mass revolution, which forced the colonial masters to grant Egypt conditional independence in 1922. Whereas the revolution expressed the slumbering agency of the subaltern subjects involved, its trajectory also reflected their mutual separation.

First, in March 1919, the peasantry rose in a rural insurrection, which was violently quelled by British military intervention (cf. Al-Shakry 2012). In the end, however, the Wafdist national-popular counterbloc was unable to rally the peasants behind its nationalist project, because their primary predicament was feudalism rather than imperialism. The absence of peasants as a social force within the counterbloc would remain a weakness of the nationalist opposition up until the Free Officers' coup. From April onward began a drawn-out stage of the revolt, led by urban proletarian and middle-class groups – students, lawyers, and professionals. The political system was transformed into a constitutional monarchy based on the Belgian model, but, reflecting the revolution in general, it fell short of fully transforming Egypt into a bourgeois, civil democracy. Instead of overthrowing and transforming the colonial historical bloc, the 1919 revolution only fortified the position of domestic elites vis-à-vis foreign forces in the existing power configuration. British capital relinquished its grip over the colonial state, but remained in control over the Suez Canal and Egypt's defense, foreign affairs, and minority policies. Colonialism was not defeated, but its partial retreat opened up opportunities for domestic capitalists to embark on a project of 'indigenous' industrialization. Their strategy of accumulation, however, was blocked by the powerful feudal lords and the British-supported King Fuad, who appeared as the most powerful political actor. The colonial historical bloc was thus reconstituted as a semi-colonial historical bloc, in which the colonial relations of power were renegotiated but not abolished. From the perspective of the national-popular subject that emerged as a real force in the streets during the 1919 revolution, the project of Egypt's national liberation had just begun. Effendiyya played a key role in the formation of the first counterhegemonic apparatuses, such as the National Party and the Wafd Party.

The rise of nationalist politics also coincided with the emergence of a strong trade unionist movement. The war caused food shortages and rising inflation, which decreased real wages in 1917–8. Cigarette workers in Alexandria and Cairo organized the first wartime strikes, demanding higher wages. In their wake other groups of workers began to protest declining wages and worsening working conditions. With the help of the National Party, the MTWU was revived, and other, new trade unions emerged from the struggle. The revolution of 1919 incited the 'mass strike': "The popular uprising, spontaneous and massive, incorporated and sustained this new social movement, and made possible its rapid growth and quick victories" (Beinin and Lockman 1987, 90). Conversely, economic strikes were often perceived by non-proletarian actors as a form of support for the nationalist activity-system of resistance – principally because most striking workers were employed by the colonial industries and its state.

The workers' war of movement and their partisan participation in the anti-colonial bloc forged new links between their own organic intellectuals and the nationalist effendiyya. The effendiyya assisted workers to set up new trade unions, consolidating the mass strikes into more or less stable proletarian neo-formations. However, their mode of assistance was largely colonial, as worker struggles were subsumed under the nationalist project. The nationalists sought to emancipate themselves from political and economic domination through the activity of the workers, and aimed to overwrite the emerging class consciousness with a nationalist narrative of anti-colonialism. This colonization of emerging class subjectivities was not a one-way street: the main antagonist of the Egyptian workers was *Western* capital in the direct, political appearance of the *colonial* state and the economic reality of *foreign*-owned factories; and, as a result, the workers' struggles against exploitation were easily subsumed under a nationalist and anti-imperialist subject. In general, the emergent trade unions recognized themselves economically and politically through the mediation of non-proletarian class forces such as bourgeois nationalists.

CHAPTER 12

Colonial Crisis

The preceding chapter described the formation of a 'combined' colonial historical bloc and equally hybrid subjects. The next chapter discusses how the economic line of proletarian sociogenesis is developed into trade unionism and how the double predicament of capitalist exploitation and colonial domination politicizes the movement. However, inadequate assistance, fickle class allies, and the failure to establish proletarian hegemony over the subaltern classes, are found to block the formation of a Modern Prince and the successful conquest of state power.

Dependent Development

In 1920 nationalist landowners provided the capital for the establishment of an independent Egyptian bank with the explicit goal of creating an indigenous industrial sector (Deeb 1976). Industry would diversify the landholders' sources of income and break the domination of foreign finance capital within the ruling classes. Bank Misr (Egypt) concentrated its funds on low value-added cotton production, establishing industries such as the Misr Spinning and Weaving Company in Mahalla al-Kubra, which became the largest industrial complex of the Middle East at the end of the Second World War. Political developments such as the 1936 Anglo-Egyptian Treaty and the abolition of capitulations in 1937 allowed the Egyptian state to implement protectionist measures to protect its budding national industry. The crisis of the 1930s reduced European commodity exports to the Middle East and expanded the market for domestic firms (Beinin and Lockman 1987, 257). At the same time, the crisis increased Western capital exports, as British and French capitalists were more inclined to invest outside Europe because of falling profits in their domestic markets (Clawson 1978, 19).

At this juncture, it seemed as if Egypt's 'privilege of backwardness'[1] could have catapulted the country's economy into the era of advanced capitalism. However, Misr Industries was unable to transform the Egyptian economy. Firstly, the 'privilege of backwardness' only applies when a society is able to use

---

1 Cf. Chapter 10.

the most advanced forms available in order to skip the intermediate stages of development. In Egypt the imported machines were outdated, which rendered its industry *less* productive and *more* labor intensive than its international competitors. Moreover, low labor costs did not raise incentives to increase efficiency. The subordination of workers to the authority of management was deemed more important than their productivity (Versieren and De Smet 2014). Secondly, Bank Misr was not strong enough to compete with foreign capital. Even though 'indigenous' Egyptian capitalists played an important role in the industrialization process of the 1930s and 1940s, foreign and *mutamassir* capital remained the chief protagonists of capitalist development. Their industries were better established and they often controlled monopolies and semi-monopolies. Misr Industries was not profitable enough and declined sharply. In the late 1930s Bank Misr entered into joint ventures with British enterprises, as they possessed the keys to the world market (Clawson 1978, 20). Consequently, Bank Misr's 'national character' was subordinated to foreign capital (Deeb 1976, 79). The largest share of Egyptian capital remained controlled by feudal landlords and directed toward the foreign and *mutamassir*-dominated cotton market. Thirdly, the Second World War encouraged industrial production while it reoriented industries toward the needs and demands of foreign markets. The end of the war lowered foreign demand and plunged Egyptian industries into crisis causing high rates of unemployment and raising the cost of living. The crisis increased the centralization of land ownership (Ansari 1986, 26). Landlords were even more inclined to invest in their profitable landholdings than industrial production.

The Egyptian ruling stratum continued to be composed of landowners, *mutamassirun*, 'indigenous' commercial and industrial capitalists, the Palace, foreign capital, and the British state. Domestic capitalists began to consolidate their own hegemonic project in a contradictory relationship of both competition and alliance with international capital. The path to the formation of an Egyptian 'integral state' was obstructed by the stubborn remains of precapitalist social forms and the dependency on foreign capital. Civil society remained underdeveloped and the constant use of coercive state power was the gambit of a weak indigenous ruling class wishing to superimpose itself on the subaltern classes.

The Road to Trade Unionism

Between 1920 and 1924 economic conditions worsened for the working class as unemployment was on the rise and real wages remained low. However, the workers' movement had emerged stronger out of the revolutionary year of 1919, encompassing 89 formal trade unions in Cairo, Alexandria, and the Suez Canal Zone. Whereas the MTWU was on the decline, public service unions in tramway, gas, electric, and water companies became the leading neoformations of the whole class struggle (Beinin and Lockman 1987, 124).

Before and during the First World War socialist ideas and methods of struggle had seeped into Egypt, especially through Egyptian students who returned from Europe (Ismael and al-Sa'id 1990, 1), but only in 1921 was the Egyptian Socialist Party (ESP) formally established. The leaders of the ESP were Egyptian and foreign intellectuals who were strongly influenced by both the spirit of the Russian Revolution of 1917 and the reformist strategy of European social democracy. Within a year the party moved to the left, embraced Bolshevism, and, reborn as the Communist Party of Egypt (CPE), became a member of the Comintern.

Between 1918 and 1924 the young socialist movement entered the trade unions and even though its directive role was limited, it played an important instructive part: "It projected conceptions of Egyptian society and of working class identity that challenged those of the Wafd whose bourgeois nationalism the left criticized" (Beinin and Lockman 1987, 138). Initially the CPE was principally anti-capitalist, and rejected an alliance with bourgeois nationalist forces such as the Wafd, but at the Fourth Congress of the Comintern in 1923 communist parties in colonial countries were encouraged to participate in the national liberation movements – even if they were dominated by bourgeois class fractions. For Egypt, this marked the embrace of the two-stage theory[2] of socialism by the communist movement: first communists had to cooperate with nationalists in order to get rid of foreign domination, and only then could they fight for socialism. Nevertheless, the first communists were able to give the workers a self-concept as a class "[…] independent of other class forces and oriented toward social transformation through political and industrial power […]" (Beinin and Lockman 1987, 154).

Despite the presence of leftist activists in some of the trade unions, the Wafd maintained a strong influence over the workers' movement. Moreover, the 'first wave of communism' was short lived. In 1924 a spontaneous strike movement in Alexandria, supported but not organized by the fading National Party and the young CPE, was crushed by the Wafd government. CPE leaders were arrested and the communist movement collapsed. Attempts were made to revive the communist movement but, due to the liquidation of its vanguard and the continued state repression of its activists, communism as a political force only resurfaced during the Second World War.

---

2 Cf. Chapter 10.

When the Wafd won the parliamentary elections in 1924 it aimed to subsume the existing movements under its direct paternalistic control in a General Federation of Labor Unions (GFLU) (Ismael and al Sa'id 1990, 28–29). Workers accepted the Wafd's hegemony as long as the party would be able to alleviate their immediate economic problems. Moreover, they principally accepted the Wafd's claim that Britain's continued domination was the nation's priority, as it was mostly British troops who quelled strikes and labor protests (Beinin and Lockman 1987, 135–137). The Wafd appeared as the uncontested hegemonic leader of the popular anti-colonial counterbloc.

Egyptian trade unionism in the interwar years suffered from a pathological development. The GFLU overcame the economic-corporate predicament of the workers in an artificial and colonizing way: the workers' suffering was decreased by the top-down external intervention and mediation of the Wafd, which, at the same time, denied the workers the development of self-determining neoformations such as independent trade unions. The Wafd appropriated the economic line of protest activities of the workers, and subsumed them under its own political battle of the 'nation' against 'foreign domination'. The nationalists' concept of the 'worker' and 'capitalism' was amorphous and undeveloped, reflecting the still gelatinous composition of the Egyptian working class and the lack of large-scale private industries owned by Egyptians. Workers were still conceived of as a collection of precapitalist and capitalist *manual* laborers instead of a cohesive class of *wage* laborers. Not the *social position* within the ensemble of production relations, but the *material form* of labor determined if a person was considered a worker or not. Likewise, a critique of capitalism was reduced to a critique of foreign domination, because the nationalists themselves had little experience with the capitalist mode of production and its far-reaching social transformations (Beinin and Lockman 1987, 162). The corporatist ambitions of the Wafd anticipated the future hegemonic politics of Nasser, who successfully integrated the workers' movement into the state.

Between 1930 and 1935 the Wafd was replaced as the 'Savior-Ruler'[3] of the workers' movement by Prince Abbas Ibrahim Halim, who was a great-grandson of Muhammad Ali and a cousin of King Fuad. Halim sided with the Wafd against the King and gained the patronage over the trade unions, which were now gathered in the National Federation of Trade Unions in Egypt (NFTUE). To counterbalance the influence of the Wafd and secure the NFTUE as a personal base of power, the prince encouraged workers instead of non-proletarian elements to lead the movement, and sponsored the structure with his own money.

---

3 Cf. Chapter 9.

Even though the concept of a workers' movement governed by workers themselves was a step in the direction of self-determination, in reality the NFTUE remained under strict control of its princely patron (Beinin and Lockman 1987, 162). In 1935 the Wafd aimed to retake direct control over the trade unions. Because of a rise in political protests in 1936 and the Wafd's leadership of the national-popular anti-colonial bloc, Halim's federation lost prestige and disintegrated. However, the unions that had constituted the NFTUE remained in existence and continued to struggle without the patronage of their Prince. For them, Abbas Halim's rule had been a transition toward autonomy from the Wafd (Beinin and Lockman 1987, 210–215).

In 1936 King Fuad died and was succeeded by his son Faruq. The Wafd returned to power and negotiated the Anglo-Egyptian Treaty, which granted Egypt increased independence – except for a continued presence of British troops in the Suez Canal Zone. This episode was both the high point and the beginning of the end for the Wafd as a counterhegemonic force. Not only did Britain and the King systematically undermine its rule, from 1936 onward its leadership over the national-popular counterbloc was eroded from within by the emergence of an independent workers' movement, of the Muslim Brotherhood, and extreme nationalist or fascist groups such as Young Egypt.[4] Workers could and would no longer wait to address their economic problems until the colonial question was resolved. Inspired by mass strikes in Europe, they began to strike themselves. In Naguib Mahfouz's "Sugar Street," part of the trilogy that sketches Egypt's political history between 1919 and 1944, the character Adli Karim aptly observed:

> The Wafd Party has crystallized and purified Egyptian nationalism. It has also been a school for nationalism and democracy. But the point is that the nation is not and must not be content with this school. We want a further stage of development. We desire a school for socialism. Independence is not the ultimate goal. It's a way to obtain the people's constitutional, economic, and human rights.
>
> MAHFOUZ 2001, 80

No longer able to simply *colonize* the workers' movement, the Wafd tried to *commodify* it,[5] promising workers concessions if they went back to work. There

---

4   The attraction of fascism – which was perceived as a 'strong' version of nationalism – among effendiyya who were disappointed with the Wafd's 'imperialist compromise' was all the more understandable when Italy and Germany emerged as enemies of Britain in the geopolitical arena (Beinin and Lockman 1987, 287).

5   Cf. Chapters 4 and 7.

was a clear shift in the discourse of the Wafd vis-à-vis the workers: its hegemony "[...] was based not on patriotism or the need for national unity but on purely pragmatic grounds" (Beinin and Lockman 1987, 224). According to the Wafd, workers did not have the political capacity to solve society's problems, so they should support the Wafd in this task, and in return the Wafd would, step by step, concede to their economic demands. The position of workers within the national-popular bloc was reconfigured as they now appeared as a more or less independent ally of the bourgeois leading class.

From 1937 onward, autonomous trade unions aimed to create a new, legal, and independent federation. They established the General Federation of Labor Unions in the Kingdom of Egypt (GFLUKE), which was the first fully independent trade union federation in Egyptian history. Trade unionism finally began to overcome the economic-corporate condition of the Egyptian working class. From the spontaneous activity of the workers' struggle a self-concept of wage laborers as a class emerged – even though many of its members were still artisans and petty producers. Ironically, at this point trade unionism already showed signs of becoming a future obstacle for the further development of the worker subject. Governed by pragmatism, trade union leaders were not interested in politics as such, and were ready to strike a deal with any party as long as it suited their short-term goals. The GFLUKE was never legalized. The outbreak of the Second World War granted the state the opportunity to repress the federation (Beinin and Lockman 1987, 234–241).

The Muslim Brotherhood

In 1928 Hassan al-Banna, a young teacher, established the Society of Muslim Brothers or *al-Ikhwan al-Muslimun*. At this historical stage, the rise and success of the Brotherhood can be seen as both an expression of and a reaction against Egypt's colonial historical bloc. The class base of the Society consisted of 'traditional', precapitalist, urban artisans and petty merchants, as well as 'modern' white collar workers, civil servants, teachers, and other layers of effendiyya that had been produced by colonialism (Ayubi 1991, 171). The hybridity of its social constituency revealed itself in the ideological mobilization of modern notions of corporatism, organicism,[6] and paternalism, which expressed the combined

---

[6] A holistic but hierarchical vision of society which parallels the human body: e.g. the ruling classes as the head; the professional groups and soldiers as the hands; and the manual workers as the feet.

nature of the Egyptian social form. The activity-system of the Ikhwan structured and totalized a whole range of activities in which these groups participated: education; charity; the building of mosques; sports; the organization of healthcare and welfare; media; and politics. The primary object of Islamist 'pillarization' was the prevention of the disintegration and alienation of Egypt's precapitalist social forms by foreign capitalism. For the Muslim Brothers, cultural and religious 'foreignness', rather than the political economy of dependent capitalism, constituted Egypt's predicament. A utopian vision of the Islamic past, rather than Western modernity was the analeptic[7] ideal to which the Brotherhood aspired (al-Ghobashy 2005, 376).

Yet, despite its precapitalist ideological appearance and rigid master-disciple relations, the Society's activity-system was organized and structured along modern lines with elections, debate, membership and meritocracy (Lia 1998, 60–71, 98–104). Unlike its ideology, its political *practice* was less oriented toward a utopian notion of the past than a modernist view of the future. The militancy of its anti-colonial discourse surpassed that of the secular Wafd, which was held back by its leadership of large landholders.

Although the Brotherhood advanced social demands that aimed to alleviate modern forms of exploitation, domination, and alienation, it did not assist in the development of the self-determination of subaltern subjects such as the working class and the peasantry. The Ikhwan rejected the autonomy of the workers' movement and only supported strikes in foreign owned companies. Like the nationalists, the Brothers assisted the workers' movement in a colonizing way blocking its development as an immanent project. The workers' predicament had to be solved through the tripartite corporatism of state, employers, and employees (Ayubi 1991, 174). This stance toward organized labor combined both a traditional 'guild' outlook of vertical integration of the interests of 'masters' and 'craftsmen' and a modern notion of the defense of the 'national good'.

As a political force, the Ikhwan articulated some of the classic 'tasks' of the national-democratic revolution. The political program of the Brotherhood demanded a state-led economy, nationalization of key industries, an 'Islamic' financial system – which would guarantee interest-free loans for Egypt's budding industrial development – and social reforms, such as a minimum wage for civil servants and unemployment benefits (Mitchell 1993, 7–19).

However, the Brotherhood was all but a revolutionary Islamist force bent on the conquest and transformation of state power. Not the establishment of an Islamic state, but 'change and reform' – the Islamization of society and the expansion of

---

7   The opposite of proleptic: instruction by imagining *a past* instead of *a future*.

Sharia law – was the priority of the movement (al-Ghobashy 2005, 376). A practice of incremental reform and compromise with the current rulers characterized Ikhwan politics. As such, the Society seemed to be caught in a perpetual war of position strategy, which advanced the movement in periods of relative societal stability, but challenged its political premises in periods of crisis. For example, even though al-Banna participated in the elections of 1942 and 1945, parliamentary agitation was seen as a means to expand influence and achieve certain concrete demands, instead of a strategy of conquering state power (al-Ghobashy 2005, 377).

The Second Wave of Communism

The Second World War stimulated industrial production in Egypt to sustain the British war effort. In 1942 British troops intervened against King Faruq – who behaved increasingly sympathetic to Nazi Germany to counterbalance British influence in Egypt – and, ironically, brought a Wafd government to power. As the war economy needed a stable and docile workforce, Britain favored a (temporary) politics of cooptation and concession toward 'its' overseas workers' movements.[8] In 1942, for the first time in Egyptian history, trade unions were legalized. Trade union federations, however, remained outlawed, crippling the capacity of workers to overcome their fragmentation into different workplaces and industrial sectors. Circumventing the law, the Wafd organized its own 'Clubs' and 'Fronts', which gathered unions from various companies. However, after the Wafd left power in 1944, its direct directive and technical role in the workers' movement ended for good. Trade unionists began to experiment with their own political neoformations, such as the Workers' Committee for National Liberation (WCNL) in 1945 (cf. Beinin and Lockman 1987).

The emergence of a fully independent workers' movement coincided with the rebirth of communism in Egypt. In fact, there was a reciprocal assistance between workers and communists in the development of their respective economic and political lines of development: "Communist influence was partly the result of, and in turn accelerated, the decline of patron-client association and corporatist ideology in the workers' movement" (Beinin and Lockman 1987, 310). In the second half of the 1930s, communist ideas had been reintroduced by Italian and Greek migrants and Jewish intellectuals (Ismael and al-Sa'id 1990, 32–33).

---

[8] However, wealthy Egyptian landowners and capitalists resisted any substantial concessions to the workers' movement (Beinin and Lockman 1987, 304–305).

From the 1940s onward, the 'second wave of communism' granted the proletarian struggle a political perspective and bridged the gap between a layer of radicalized effendiyya and workers. It also interpellated a leftist wing in the Wafd around the 'Wafdist Vanguard' tendency (Beinin and Lockman 1987, 311).

Between 1942 and 1952, the political 'party' of the workers, in its broad sense, was represented by various organizations, of which the most influential were: the Communist Party of Egypt, the People's Liberation Group, *Iskra*,[9] the Egyptian Movement for National Liberation (EMNL), and New Dawn. Apart from personal and sectarian infighting, there were important organizational, tactical, and strategic differences with regard to the degree of centralization of the movement, the role of students and intellectuals, and the nature of the Egyptian working class and bourgeoisie.[10]

Organic Crisis

By 1948, more than half a million workers were employed in the new industries (Chaichian 1988, 33).[11] However, after the Second World War, industrial unemployment decreased, not only due to the end of wartime demand, but also because of the increased mechanization of industries and the concentration of the workforce in a few large factories. The industries could not absorb the exodus of rural laborers, who ended up in the service and petty trading sectors (Chaichian 1988, 33).[12] The uneven and combined character of Egypt's economy was expressed in the composition of the working class:

---

9   Russian for 'Spark' – used in reference to Lenin's newspaper of 1901–5.
10 Only in 1958 was a unitary Communist Party of Egypt founded – and by then Nasserist hegemony over the workers' movement was firmly established.
11 Half of them were employed in the British military production centers (Beinin and Lockman 1987, 260). Estimating the evolution of the position and weight of wage labor in the total workforce is difficult. Firstly, before the Second World War, statistical sources are almost non-existent. Secondly, the primary source – the census of 1907, 1917, 1927, 1937, and 1947 – presents a sectoral composition of the workforce, which does not allow for an investigation into the character of the relations of production. Nevertheless, the tripling of workers in mining and manufacturing between 1907 and 1947 points toward a qualitative transformation of the economic structure. Around 1947–48 industrial wage laborers composed 28 percent of the total workforce of more than 16 million (calculated on the basis of Beinin and Lockman 1987, 38).
12 In 1907 the rural workforce composed 69 percent of Egypt's total labor force. In 1947 this fell to 58 percent (Beinin and Lockman 1987, 38).

> The working class of the postwar period therefore included, at one end of the spectrum, a large number of workers employed in very small enterprises producing in labor intensive and capital-poor conditions where the distinction between employer and employee was often not very sharp, and at the other end, a large, and what is more important, growing number of workers in large-scale mass production industries.
> BEININ AND LOCKMAN 1987, 265

The salient rise of industrial capitalism and the type of workforce it produced as its object, reinforced the concept of the worker as an industrial wage laborer vis-à-vis precapitalist notions of the 'artisan'. The industrial worker was a proletarian, not only in the historical-conceptual sense of belonging to a category of working people bereft of their means of production, but also in its hyperbolic moral meaning of having nothing to lose except for his or her chains. Just as their European counterparts in the second half of the nineteenth century, the Egyptian proletariat suffered malnutrition, disease, overcrowded housing, unhygienic living conditions, illiteracy, and so on. For the industrial proletariat, capitalism was a predicament that did not offer them any means of liberation. They had to find the means of overcoming their condition in themselves: in the development of the strike. Industrial textile workers replaced workers in public services sectors such as communication and transport as the vanguard of the Egyptian workers' movement (cf. Beinin and Lockman 1987).

The failure of domestic capitalists to independently industrialize and develop the economy, and the consolidation of the power of commercial capitalists, large estate holders, the Palace and foreign financial capital, revealed that Egypt in the first half of the twentieth century was not a social formation moving gradually toward 'full' capitalism, but a historical bloc of which the *combinations* increasingly became *contradictions*. British colonial intervention had continuously reinforced the position of feudalistic landowners and commercial capitalists vis-à-vis fledgling domestic industrial capitalists. Instead of simply 'dissolving' precapitalist relations, capitalism added a new layer of social contradictions to Egyptian society. Up until the early 1950s, powerful landlords were still able to block any attempt at land distribution among the small peasants. In general, landlords were reluctant to free capital from agriculture, especially the profitable production of cotton, and channel it into risky industrial initiatives that could not compete with Western manufacturing. Some of them did engage, hesitantly, in the building of an Egyptian industrial base, and could be perceived as a kind of 'native' bourgeoisie, but, in the end, there was no fundamental differentiation between landed, financial, commercial, and industrial interests, nor was there a clear break with foreign and mutamassir capital (Clawson 1978, 21). The Egyptian industrial bourgeoisie had not developed itself as a class-for-itself, but remained a fragmented, amorphous collection of economic actors, subjugated to domestic landlords and international capital groups, and thus incapable of leading a national-popular bloc (Farah 2009, 31).

The effendiyya, for their part, longed for national sovereignty and economic modernization,[13] but they did not constitute a social force on their own. Because of the subsumption of the Egyptian bourgeoisie under the interests of foreign capital, they turned increasingly to other potential subjects, such as the emerging workers' movement, as a means to emancipate themselves from colonialism.[14] Especially after the Second World War workers, supported by communists, left-nationalists, and, sometimes, Muslim Brothers engaged in a war of movement against the colonial bloc, organizing a series of economic and political strikes and protests, which spawned nationwide neoformations such as the National Committee for Workers and Students (NCWS) and the Congress of Egyptian Trade Unions (CETU). The coalescence of the workers' and nationalist movement constructed a new national-popular counterbloc with the trade unions, the communist and left-nationalist effendiyya, and the Muslim Brotherhood as its 'hard core'.

The pragmatic stance of the Brotherhood leadership toward the semi-colonial state led to a growing dissatisfaction among its younger and more radical members who engaged in guerrilla warfare as opposed to the movement's war of position.[15] Ikhwan members organized attacks on British administrators, military personnel, Egyptian police stations, and, after 1948, Jewish targets. Even though al-Banna openly condemned these acts of terrorism, the Brotherhood leader was assassinated by government agents in 1949. The Society was declared illegal and four thousand of its members were arrested and detained. With the election of Hassan al-Hudaybi as the new Supreme Guide of the organization,

---

13 However, they did not have a conception of capitalism as a transformative mode of production, but only as a technical means of 'catching up' with the West.

14 "Thus, the full co-operation between purely Egyptian and local foreign elements of the local bourgeoisie was not accompanied by a similar co-operation between the Egyptian urban middle class and the petty bourgeoisie and their local foreign counterparts. On the contrary, they remained at loggerheads, and perhaps the antagonism at those levels even increased" (Deeb 1976, 82).

15 For example, in 1942 Hassan al-Banna decided to withdraw from parliamentary elections in exchange for tougher legislation against prostitution and alcohol (Mitchell 1993, 19–22).

the divisions between reformists and radicals within the movement escalated. Al-Hudaybi supported the pro-British King and denounced the idea of a revolutionary overthrow of the semi-colonial state, while rank and file Brothers joined the war of movement of the newly emerging national-popular counterbloc (cf. Lia 1998, Mitchell 1993).

However, the counterbloc was not able to defeat the coalition between the Palace and Britain. Even in the early 1950s, the Egyptian working class *in general* – despite the emergence of independent trade unionism since the 1940s – was still relatively inexperienced and unorganized in comparison with its vanguard of textile workers. Workers were not able to develop a unitary, coherent, cohesive, and centralized trade union movement, let alone a political hegemonic apparatus, in less than a decade. Moreover, the workers' movement remained isolated from the peasantry[16] and lacked a unified leadership with a clear class analysis (Beinin and Lockman 1987, 455). Furthermore, the vacillating support of the Muslim Brotherhood for the emancipation of the subaltern classes, undermined the cohesion and coherence of the national-popular counterbloc. Lastly, the Egyptian communist movement failed to constitute a genuine and systematic dialectical pedagogy between workers and other subaltern forces (such as farmers) and between organic and traditional intellectuals. Because of Stalinist dogmatism there was a tendency to subjugate the class struggle to the national liberation movement, as Beinin explained:

> Although historically the Marxist intelligentsia encouraged the formation of trade unions and other forms of working class organization and struggle, it also imposed its own agenda on the working class and consistently subordinated class struggle to the anti-imperialist national struggle [...] the immediate significance of the working class as a historical and political subject was considered to be its potential contribution as the vanguard of a national united front whose objective was to free Egypt

---

16   In the context of Italy – with its dichotomy between an industrial North and an agricultural South – Gramsci had emphasized that the only way of overcoming both the capitalist exploitation and precapitalist 'backwardness' of the Italian social formation was through a united front between Northern workers and Southern peasants (Gramsci 2005, 28). Despite, obviously, many important differences, there are some striking similarities between Italy's uneven and combined character in the early twentieth century, and the nature of the Egyptian social formation after the Second World War. As a hegemonic strategy, the construction of a counterbloc which incorporated the peasant masses under the direction of the urban proletariat was imperative in both cases.

> from military occupation by Great Britain and economic domination by
> Europe and its local 'feudalist' allies.
>
> BEININ 1996, 254

The counterbloc imagined by the communist movement was based on a leftist-nationalist hegemony, rooted in a class alliance between workers and the 'progressive national bourgeoisie', their domination of foreign financial and domestic rural capital, and a strategy of accumulation based on 'productive', 'national' capitalism. Just as the nationalists before them, the communist intelligentsia assisted the emerging worker subject in a colonizing way, appropriating its particular forms of activity, organization, and mobilization for its own goal of national liberation. Beinin argued that by bereaving the workers' movement of its own immanent project: "[...] the Marxist Left inadvertently contributed to the disorganization and disorientation of the labor movement during the régime of Abdel Nasser" (Beinin 1996, 255).

Up to 1952 strikes, protests, riots, and insurrections – i.e., the subaltern war of movement – destabilized the colonial historical bloc. It disorganized the state, but it was not able to offer an alternative of its own. As the counterbloc was not able to achieve civil and political hegemony, let alone conquer state power, the societal stalemate was forcefully resolved by mediation of a third force: the army, led by the 'Free Officers'.

CHAPTER 13

Nasserism

In the previous chapter I explained the development of trade unionism, the rising organic crisis of the colonial bloc, and the emergence of a national-popular alliance that challenged its rule. In the following chapter, I consider the Free Officer's coup, the popular yet authoritarian historical bloc it produced, and the Caesarist pathology it entailed for the formation of a proletarian subject.

The Nasserist Intervention

A spontaneous popular insurrection on 25 January 1952 in Cairo led to a mass repression of trade union and communist leaders. Whereas the state's violent coercion successfully weakened the proletarian vanguard of the national-popular bloc, it also revealed its own feeble grasp over Egypt's gelatinous civil society. Lacking any significant ethico-political dimension to their rule, the dominant classes had to rely increasingly on coercion to control the population. However, sections of the Egyptian police and armed forces had also joined the counter-hegemonic mobilization, weakening the domination by the colonial bloc. After the 25 January insurrection, the rule of the Palace had ended, but the national-popular bloc was not able to fill the power vacuum. Central state power was disorganized, but not replaced. The political void lasted for six months until the Free Officers of the Revolutionary Command Council (RCC), led by Colonel Gamal Abd al-Nasser, organized a coup on 23 July 1952, deflecting[1] the revolutionary process.

The Free Officers appeared on the political scene as a *deus ex machina*, promising to forcefully solve Egypt's Gordian knot. Most members of the RCC came from a petty-bourgeois background (Richards and Waterbury 2008, 127) and their demands expressed the goals of the national-popular bloc.[2] Once in

---

1 Cf. Chapter 10.
2 Gramsci commented that: "In a whole series of countries, therefore, military influence in national life means not only the influence and weight of the military in the technical sense, but the influence and weight of the social stratum from which the latter (especially the junior officers) mostly derives its origin" (Gramsci 1971, 214).

power they improvised a 'classic' program of national-democratic demands: democracy; social justice; abolition of feudalism; establishment of a strong, national army; and full independence and sovereignty for Egypt (al-Khafaji 2004, 199). The main predicament for the nation's development was understood as the twin evils of imperialism and feudalism, and the military clique around Nasser sought to create a new historical bloc that subjugated these social and political forces to their rule.

The Muslim Brotherhood's Supreme Guide al-Hudaybi had condemned the spontaneous popular uprising in Cairo on 25 January 1952, although individual members were active within the mass movement. The coup of the Free Officers was welcomed by the Supreme Guide as a means to solve the social chaos, while rank and file Ikhwan saw the RCC as the harbinger of decolonization.

After the coup a power struggle within the military clique ensued, which was expressed in terms of the character of the new national-popular bloc. General Muhammad Naguib, who was chosen by the RCC as head of state because of his seniority and prestige, aimed to reduce the military intervention to a minimum and advocated a return to civil rule. Nasser, however, claimed that this withdrawal represented a return to the societal stalemate. Only the transformation of the national-popular project into a strong, homogeneous, and centralized state could overcome Egypt's predicaments. In 1953 the new government banned all parties except for the Brotherhood, which remained loyal to the RCC. The Ikhwan were asked to join the Nasser-led 'Liberation Rally', and as a token of goodwill al-Hudaybi dissolved the Society's paramilitary 'Secret Apparatus' and kicked its leaders out of the organization. During the open power struggle between Nasser and Naguib in late 1953 and 1954, the Brotherhood first sided with Naguib, but then switched to the Nasser camp. In exchange for its support, the Brotherhood demanded an Islamic constitution, democratic institutions, freedom of press, and an end to emergency law. As Nasser was not inclined to share power a number of Ikhwan members secretively founded a new paramilitary cell which tried to assassinate the president on 26 October 1954. The attempt failed, but it gave Nasser a perfect alibi to eliminate the Muslim Brotherhood as a competitor for power (cf. Beinin and Lockman 1987; Burgat 1995; Mitchell 1993).[3]

---

3 During the wave of repression that began in 1954 the Society broke up into four parts. A first group consisted of Ikhwan militants who were imprisoned. Their main leader and ideologue was Sayyid Qutb, who translated the experiences of torture and abuse in the camps in a radicalization of the Brotherhood's worldview. For him, the inhumanity and violence of the prison keepers signified that they were no longer Muslims, but idolizers of the Nasserist state. According to Qutb, contemporary Muslim societies, even though they claimed to be Islamic,

As the ruling stratum in the 1950s and 1960s, the military became a 'state within a state'. The armed forces consisted of various contending power structures – the army, air defense, air force, navy, intelligence services, Republican Guard, ministry of defense, and so on – which were each ruled by their generals as small fiefdoms. Nasser himself tried to limit and counterbalance the autonomous power of the military – embodied in such independent figures as Chief-of-Staff Abd al-Hakim Amer – within the ensemble of state structures through the formation of 'civil' forces of coercion and consent. Especially after the Six Day War in 1967, Nasser began to sidetrack the role and position of the armed forces in political society, moving towards a dictatorship of the police rather than the military.[4]

Escaping Colonialism

The ideology of the Nasserist bloc was to a large extent a continuation and expansion of the theory of the grassroots national-popular counterbloc.

---

were (still) in a state of *jahiliyya*: religious ignorance. The traditional reformist strategy of the Brotherhood was doomed to fail in a context of jahiliyya and had to be replaced by an intellectual and a collective *jihad*: a moral, intellectual and political project of personal and societal Islamization. A vanguard of righteous Islamists should educate the masses until the majority of Muslims participated in the Islamic project (cf. Mitchell 1993; Kepel 1985). A second group was comprised of Muslim Brothers who were not detained but nonetheless remained in Egypt. They were led by Zaynab al-Ghazali and Abd al-Fattah Ismail, who reorganized the movement according to the reformist ideals of Hassan al-Banna. A third faction, under the guidance of Shukri Mustafa, founded the *takfir wa-l-hijra* group whose members advocated either a physical or ideological escape from *jahiliyya*; either they withdrew from their community, or they continued to participate while hiding their nature as 'true' Muslims. A fourth group migrated to the Gulf countries, where they were strongly influenced by the social conservatism of Wahhabism. Those who became successful businessmen returned to Sadat's Egypt in the 1970s, constituting the backbone of the Islamic bourgeoisie. The inability and unwillingness of Nasser to integrate the Muslim Brotherhood into his authoritarian historical bloc would lead to its resurgence, almost *ex nihilo*, under President Sadat in the 1970s. The repression and sundering of the Brotherhood in the 1950s and 1960s laid the foundation of the three 'modern' forms of Islamism in Egypt: Qutb's radical Islamism mutated into jihadism; the apolitical reformism of *takfir wa-l-hijra* transformed into puritanical salafism; and petro-Islam grew into bourgeois Islamism, which remained the core of the contemporary Muslim Brotherhood. Lastly, the civildemocratic movement of the 2000s and the 25 January Revolution of 2011 rallied a fourth and almost forgotten form of 'social movement' Islamism that had its historical roots in the pre-Nasserist national-popular bloc.

4 I discuss this shift in the following chapters.

The twin problems of imperialism and feudalism were understood as the consequences of geopolitical subordination and economic underdevelopment. In order to overcome feudalism, Egypt had to be industrialized. In order to industrialize, the nation had to be able to overcome its subaltern position within the world economy. Full national sovereignty was the key to overcoming Egypt's predicament.

Although an agreement in 1954 between Egypt and Britain, to demilitarize and evacuate the Suez Canal region and revert control of the canal to the Egyptian state, stipulated a phased and conditional withdrawal of troops and personnel, Nasser had to achieve national sovereignty much quicker, if he wanted to consolidate his prestige as leader of the national-popular bloc. In addition, the creation of Israel in 1948 and its consolidation as a nation state were perceived as a direct threat against Egyptian and Arab sovereignty. As a directive force, the Free Officers had to prove that they were able to defend the country against British and Israeli imperialist forces. The emerging bipolar world order offered Nasser a road to achieve these goals. Both the USA and the USSR sought strong allies in the region against each other. Nasser aimed to balance between the two superpowers, creating the necessary geopolitical space for national sovereignty (Gaddis 1997, 167–172).

Concerning the 'problem' of Israel, Nasser hoped to buy arms from the USA. However, his strong anti-Zionist stance blocked any possibility of US Congress approving a sell of military material to Egypt. Nasser then turned to the USSR, which sold him weapons through the Czech arms deal in 1955. The following year the USA retaliated by withdrawing its financial support for the Aswan Dam project. Nasser immediately reacted with the nationalization of the Suez Canal. A tripartite of British, French, and Israeli forces invaded Egypt in October 1956 to neutralize what they had come to perceive as a fundamental danger to their interests in the region. However, diplomatic and financial pressure by the USA, along with military threats by the Soviet Union, forced the tripartite to withdraw their forces (Alteras 1993). Even though the Egyptian military had been defeated, Nasser emerged victorious from the conflict, strengthening national sovereignty, the prestige of Egypt in the Arab world, and his own position within the new historical bloc.

The Nasserist bloc aimed to overcome 'feudalism' by industrial development and agricultural reforms. As early as September 1952 the new régime undertook a number of important rural reforms in its war against feudalism. Land size was capped to 200 feddans[5] per owner and 300 feddans per family. Subsequent land reforms in 1961, 1963, and 1969 redistributed some twelve percent

---

5 One feddan is 1.038 acres or 0.42 hectares (Bush 2007, 1601).

of cultivable lands among landless and near landless farmers. Rents were limited to seven times the land tax (Bush 2007, 1601). An agricultural minimum wage was implemented. Peasants gained the right of perpetual tenancy at controlled rents, which severely restricted the ownership rights of the feudal landlords. The position of landlords in the agricultural credit cooperatives – which supervised "[…] cropping patters, input supplies, credit provision and marketing […]" (Bush 2007, 1601) – was replaced by state employees. This measure restricted the political influence of the landlords and formally excluded them as participants in the newly emerging Nasserist historical bloc (Aoude 1994).

For the Free Officers, expropriation, land reform, and rent control served three interconnected goals: (1) weakening the economic power base of the monarchy and the feudal landlords[6]; (2) increasing productivity in agriculture and freeing capital for industrial development (Chaichian 1988, 35; Mitchell 2002, 226); (3) gathering support from peasants for its own political project. The land reforms did not eradicate the political and economic role of landlords in the Egyptian social formation, however: "Dispossessed landowners received compensation, private property persisted, large landowners found ways of retaining their land: there was ultimately very little fundamental shift in the balance of political and economic power" (Bush 2007, 1601).

The rationale of industrial development was purely political and served to strengthen national sovereignty – an economic means to catch up with the Western nations (Chaichian 1988, 35). At first the state merely acted as the midwife of 'spontaneous' industrial development by private domestic and foreign actors. Roughly from 1954 until 1960 the state diligently defended the interests of the Egyptian industrial bourgeoisie (Johnson 1973, 4). The government encouraged domestic and foreign industrial investments by lowering corporate taxes and relaxing protectionist measures. By establishing public-private committees – such as the Permanent Council for the Development of National Production – that guided national development, the state cast itself in the role of impartial facilitator (Aoude 1994). However, neither domestic nor foreign capitalists were interested in industrialization. Between 1950 and 1956 private investments dropped by 300 percent (Farah 2009, 33). Step by step the state itself was forced to take the economic initiative: "In 1952–1953, 72 percent of gross capital formation took place in the private sector. By 1959–1960, the state was responsible for 74 percent of gross capital formation" (Beinin 1989, 79).

---

6 However, the process was firmly controlled 'from above' and spontaneous attempts of the peasantry to seize lands of large landholders were violently suppressed (cf. Marfleet 2011).

Geopolitically motivated foreign aid and economic assistance on the one hand, and the contingent sequestration of private assets on the other, allocated capital and expertise necessary for industrialization to the state, which ultimalety became the primary economic actor.[7] In 1959 the First Five-Year Plan for the whole economy was formulated. The Plan acknowledged an already existing reality as it established the public sector as the dominant industrial producer and investor. The Egyptian textile sector spearheaded a project of Import Substitution Industrialization (ISI), which was expected to create a domestic demand for spinning and weaving machinery, which, in turn, needed locally produced iron and steel. Between 1952 and 1960 the number of wage laborers working in manufacture increased with 23.5 percent – more than half of which were employed in the textile industry (Beinin 1989, 77).

The rationale of Nasserist 'state capitalism'[8] was the inverse of the historical logic of capital in Western Europe. In Egypt, the goal of national development was pursued through the means of state-led capital accumulation, whereas in Western Europe the development of the productive forces was a by-product of profit-driven private accumulation. Nasser's 'Arab socialism' proved to be the most efficient way to transform precapitalist social forms into capitalist relations of production.[9] State-led industrialization, construction, and land reclamation projects absorbed the surplus population from the countryside and turned peasants into modern wage laborers. Between 1961 and 1967 the propertyless workforce increased from 6 to 7.3 million (Chaichian

---

7 The building of the Aswan High Dam illustrated the logic of expanding state intervention in the economy. At first, the Free Officers encouraged domestic private actors to invest in the project through public-private committees. The reluctance of the 'indigenous' industrial capitalists to invest in a long-term project with a low rate of profit forced the state to turn to foreign capital. When a World Bank loan was blocked by the USA because of the Egyptian-Czechoslovakian arms deal in 1955, the state looked for other sources of revenue and expertise, which eventually led to the Suez Crisis of 1956–1957 and a rapprochement with the Soviet Union. The sequestration of foreign assets after the Suez Crisis enabled the state to embark on an industrial plan that aimed to build a basic industry. In 1957 and 1958 Egypt received loans and technical know-how from the Soviet Union to build the High Dam (Farah 2009, 33–35).
8 "Thus, Nasser's 'socialism' was nothing more than state capitalism, and as such was an attempt to concentrate and direct investment toward nonagricultural capitalist production" (Chaichian 1988, 36).
9 The existence of a large public sector and state ownership are not in contradiction with the dominance of the capitalist mode of production: "The simple fact of public ownership does not mean that the profit motive disappears or that the workers gain control of the surplus value of their own labor" (Richards and Waterbury 2008, 207).

1988, 39). This process of formal subsumption of labor under capital (the expansion of wage labor) was complemented with a real subsumption of labor under capital: the transformation and modernization of the labor process and the methods of production themselves thanks to the influx of new sources of capital and technical expertise. Soviet technical assistance reinforced the prestige of 'socialism from above' as a means to overcome problems of development and colonialism.

An anti-Nasserist bourgeois revolt in Syria and the disinclination of the private sector to support the Five-Year Plan led to the socialist decrees of 1961, through which, at once, large-scale industry, banking, insurance, foreign trade, utilities, marine transport, airlines, many hotels and department stores were nationalized (Aoude 1994). Instead of a preconceived plan, the increasing role of the state and the expansion of the public sector was an unintended, but logical, outcome of the reluctance of domestic capital groups to support Nasser's industrialization project and the restructuring of geopolitics after the Second World War. The 'socialist' decrees qualitatively deepened the intervention and direction of the political state in the economic structure, and explicitly connected this policy to that of the Soviet geopolitical bloc. Moreover, the 'socialist' turn of the Nasserist bloc also entailed a more profound integration of subaltern subjects, especially industrial workers, into the authoritarian-turned national-popular project. This integration was expressed in the key régime concept of 'democratic cooperative socialism', which represented first and foremost Egyptian and Arab *unity*, from which all other political and economic ideological notions, such as egalitarianism and social justice, were derived (Akhavi 1975).

Officers and Workers

Against the popular mass demonstrations of his political opponent Naguib, Nasser had mobilized loyal trade union leaders, whom he integrated in the new state machine. The strike of the Cairo transport workers "[...] was a decisive contribution to the RCC's ability to turn back the tide of popular opinion, consolidate the power of 'Abd al-Nasir, and confirm the continuation of military rule" (Beinin and Lockman 1987, 440). Nevertheless, despite their adherence to the national-popular project, the Free Officers forcefully blocked the independent development of its supporting subaltern subjects. Less than a month in power, the RCC government violently repressed a strike at Kafr al-Dawwar, hanging two worker leaders (Beinin and Lockman 1987, 418). The worker subject was integrated into the Nasserist bloc, but, under the slogan of

'Unity, Order, and Labor', in a colonizing way that obliterated its autonomous trade unionist organizations. Nasserist hegemony over the workers' movement was secured by coercive consent: through a combination of unilateral and far-reaching social reforms, repression of organic intellectuals, and state-led corporatism, grassroots proletarian subjectivities were subsumed under the top-down nationalist subject of the state's project. Strikes and independent worker actions were prohibited,[10] but proletarian bargaining power – previously defended by the organically developed independent trade unions – was from 1957 on secured by the state-controlled General Federation of Egyptian Trade Unions (GFETU). Historian Anne Alexander summarized the dual hegemonic role of the Nasserist unions in civil and political society:

> [...] as organs of social control they channelled benefits such as access to workplace-based social welfare schemes to workers and worked hand in glove with state employers to enforce 'social peace' within the workplace. As organs of political control they acted as an electoral machine for the ruling party, controlling nominations for the 50 percent of seats in parliament which were reserved for 'workers and peasants', and a mechanism for mobilising a stage army of apparently loyal régime supporters whenever the régime felt it needed to make a show of its 'mass base'. Consistent with both of these roles the trade union bureaucracy acted ruthlessly in concert with the repressive apparatus of the state to crush workers' attempts to organise collective action and build their own independent organisations.
>
> ALEXANDER 2012, 111

Unilateral concessions toward the workers' social conditions softened class contradictions in the industrial sphere. In exchange for syndical and political passivity, the workers gained social reforms and rights such as a 42-hour working week, higher wages, social security, free healthcare, protection against arbitrary dismissal, and education (Clément 2009, 103). Even in the private sector, the government enforced minimum wage standards and protective laws (Posusney 1996, 218). In the public sector, the introduction of workers' participation or co-management

---

10 This does not mean that there were no worker protests under Nasserism – on the contrary, strike actions increased in comparison to the pre-1952 period (Beinin 1989, 77). However, without the directive and organizational framework of independent trade unions, these actions remained fragmented and isolated. After the 1956 Suez crisis, leftist trade union leaders tried to "counter-colonize" Nasserism by presenting "[...] the working class as the vanguard of the national united front against imperialism" (Beinin 1989, 83).

had the objective of integrating the working class in the national project, softening class contradictions, and raising productivity. In reality it was participation without the right to debate or disagree. Industrial power relations did not change and the trade union leadership and the workers' representatives were integrated into the state bureaucracy (Bayat 1993, 68–74). The Nasserist hegemonic strategy of coercive consent vis-à-vis the working class would remain more or less in place until Mubarak's neoliberal offensive in the 1990s. Marsha Posusney argued that:

> Although moving quickly to suppress workers' protests with force, Egyptian authorities have almost always given in to some or all of the workers' demands. At the same time, only the largest incidents are ever covered in the official press, and these are customarily blamed on outside agitators. Preventing any escalation of the protest and maintaining an image of national harmony and worker satisfaction seem to be far more important to Egypt's rulers than minimizing financial concessions.
> POSUSNEY 1996, 216

The reluctance of the bourgeoisie to play its part in the industrialization process and the rapprochement with the Soviet Union strengthened corporatist structures and inspired an increasingly radicalizing anti-imperialist and socialistic rhetoric. The agent of 'Arab socialism' was, in theory, the 'alliance of working forces', consisting of peasants, wage workers, urban intellectuals and professionals, national capitalists, and the military. However, in practice the popular masses were the object of authoritarian régime policies instead of an independent political subject. Despite the improved living conditions and social status of 'the industrial worker' in Egyptian society, the proletarian subject was reduced to an economic-corporate state and a position of subalternity in the Nasserist bloc.

The Concept of Nasserism

As a new and unexpected phenomenon, the Nasserist coup and the formation of an authoritarian national-popular bloc sowed confusion among the Egyptian Left. The largest communist organization, the Democratic Movement for National Liberation (DMNL) supported the Free Officers in 1952, as it saw them as an anti-imperialist force (Beinin and Lockman 1987, 427). The government's subsequent violent crackdown on communist activists pushed the movement into the opposition camp. Unilaterally declared labor reforms in December 1952, and the subsumption of trade unionist leaderships under the Liberation Rally, however, weakened the class base of communist and leftist nationalist political activists, which had united in the National Democratic Front (NDF). Nasser used the subsumed trade unions as a social force in the streets against the popular demonstrations that called for a democratization of the régime. This episode clearly demonstrated the distorted class base of the new Nasserist bloc.

By 1956 the Nasserist régime had distanced itself from the USA and was moving toward a position of 'non-alignment'. All communist factions agreed to support Nasser's project. There was a clear tendency among communists to subordinate the struggle for democracy and socialism to the formation of a 'popular front' against imperialism. The only substantial political difference between nationalists and communists was the latter's emphasis on the vanguard role of the working class. However, a conflict between Nasser and the Iraqi communists in 1958 created a divide within the Egyptian communist movement, with a majority taking the side of their Iraqi comrades (Beinin and Lockman 1987, 580–581).

The 'socialist turn' from 1960 onward, was devised by Nasser as a political instrument to counterbalance the right, especially the influence of the old elites. Even though the old elites were bereft of formal political power and direct control over the state apparatus, the military clique had not completely destroyed the economic base of their class power. Private capital withdrew itself in the economic domains of landed property, real estate, internal trade, and construction. Their grip over the countryside, as well as new alliances with high-ranked officers and bureaucrats, enabled the old ruling classes to influence the political decision making process through informal networks and channels. Changes in the internal political make-up of the régime, such as the formation of the Arab Socialist Union (ASU) in 1962, the foundation of a Marxist cadre school (Egyptian Socialist Youth) in 1965, and the removal of pro-capitalist ministers from government, accompanied socialistic economic initiatives and improved relations with the Soviet Union (Johnson 1973, 4). When in 1964 communist prisoners were released, the two biggest communist organizations voluntarily dissolved themselves into the ASU (Beinin and Lockman 1987, 583–584).

Through its salient and convincing leadership of the Egyptian nation, the prestige of its vanguard role within the 'non-aligned' world, social and economic reforms that integrated subaltern groups such as workers, farmers, students, women, and so on, and violent state repression, the rule of Nasser was based on a strong hegemony. Today, leftist activists are still wrestling with the political heritage of Nasserism, for the régime appeared as both a revolutionary and a reactionary force. Personally, I remember a discussion with a group of young leftist activists in May 2009 during a gathering in the *Afaaq Ishtirakiyya* (Socialist Horizons) center, the NGO-type front organization of the illegal Egyptian Communist Party. Some youth, both socialists and left-nationalists, defended Nasser because of his welfare and anti-imperialist politics. For them, Nasser remained a mobilizing symbol of socialism and liberation, and this iconicity was physically present in the offices of *Afaaq Ishtirakiyya*. In fact, our debate had started because of the saliency of his picture on the wall. The intellectual roots of this 'positive' historical reception of Nasser's rule could be traced back to 1960s and 1970s narratives of Nasserism and similar 'interventions' in the region that, in general, presented the military as a progressive and transformative force (cf. Hurewitz 1969, Vatikiotis 1972). In the absence of a strong, progressive, national bourgeoisie the 'modern' military – and its petty-bourgeois class base (cf. Halpern 1963) – was the only social force that could and would substitute itself for the national-democratic and anti-colonial subject. Conversely, other leftists in *Afaaq Ishtirakiyya* claimed that Nasser laid the foundations of the authoritarianism of Sadat and Mubarak, and that he was a tyrant rather than a liberator. Yet in their denouncing of Nasserism they unintentionally shared with the intellectuals from the liberal tradition a utopian vision of the pre-Nasserist constitutional monarchy, which was presented as a period of civil rights, freedom, and democracy. Their arguments were derived from the political and academic critiques of the developmental, military, and democratic failures of the 'Arab socialist' states that emerged from the 1970s onward (cf. Picard 1990, 198–199).[11]

Lastly, a few militants advanced a more circumspect image of Nasserism, pointing toward the dual character of the authoritarian popular bloc. In my conversation with the novelist Alaa al-Aswany, he echoed this ambiguity vis-à-vis the Nasserist heritage:

> I do not think it was a coup, rather a coup supported by a real revolution. Nasser was a great leader [...] many Egyptians had for the first time the opportunity to enjoy a good education, healthcare, food, because of Nasser's revolution. So I don't think it's fair to forget this. But also we shouldn't forget that the current dictatorship and régime is based on Nasser. The security state, the control system, the elections [...] everything is based on this régime. The irony is that he established a dictatorship

---

11   Others conceived of the military coups as forms of premodern continuity rather than modernist change. For example, Perlmutter (1974) argued that Egypt had always been a 'praetorian state' in which elites constructed their rule 'on top of' the existing society.

while he didn't need it. Nasser was supported to the extent that in any free elections he would have easily gained a majority. That was not the case with the presidents who came after him. He was the one who built the dictatorship machine. And the problem with this machine is that everyone can use it. Everything is ready for the dictatorship: the security, the torture. If you are in the driving seat you just push the button and the régime will keep on running.[12]

Al-Aswany offered us a glimpse of the contradictions that were at the core of the Nasserist bloc: 'a coup supported by a real revolution'.

A Caesarist Pathology

With regard to the Nasserist intervention, neither coup nor revolution appear as sufficient and adequate concepts to understand the contradictory phenomenon. Gramsci's understanding of Caesarism[13] helps to elucidate the ambiguous and contradictory character of Nasserism (cf. De Smet 2014a). The Free Officers' intervention was an act of Caesarism because, as a semi-independent, 'external' force, it was able to end the protracted power struggle between the national-popular and the colonial bloc – a fight that remained undecided in the decade after the Second World War. The Free Officers' coup was anticipated by years of social and political upheaval and the building of mass movements. The coup captured central state power before the masses had matured into a political subject that could conquer state power. Whatever the intentions or motives of the RCC, noble or opportunistic, the Caesarist intervention 'deflected' the revolutionary process, and substituted its own authoritarian direction for the embryonic hegemony of the subaltern alliance.

In Caesarist terms, the coup was relatively progressive, because the RCC took the side of the popular masses against feudalist and imperialist forces. This was reflected in the 'national-democratic' program of the Free Officers' and their subsequent policies of land reform, welfare, and education, which favored the subaltern classes. Nasserism also brought about a qualitative change, as it transformed the Egyptian social formation in a revolutionary way. Industrialization went hand in hand with the massification of education and political mobilization. Although the Free Officers had delivered the death blow to the old

---

12   Interview with Alaa al-Aswany, Cairo, 26 November 2010.
13   Cf. Chapter 9.

colonial bloc by using military force, they could and would not base their rule solely on coercion. In order to subsume the population into its authoritarian nationalist project, the state first had to create the terrain of a modern civil society. The absorption of the existing, underdeveloped modern civil society, together with lingering premodern social forms into an expanding and developing political society also entailed the massification of these structures and practices. The political state created mass trade unions, professional syndicates, public companies, universities and schools, women, youth, and children organizations, cultural clubs, peasant associations, and so on; drawing, for the first time in Egypt's history, the majority of the population into the activity of a – tightly state-controlled – mass civil society. Just as the colonial era had produced the effendiyya, the expansion of modern education under Nasserism created a fresh layer of intellectuals who were embedded within the nationalist project. The rule of the military clique was not only based upon coercion, but also on its prestige and its economic and political direction of the Egyptian social formation. The Nasserist project contained an ethico-political dimension, expressed in its populist, nationalist, 'tiermondist' and eventually 'Arab socialist' ideology, which mobilized and inspired the masses.

Despite its relatively progressive and qualitative character, from the perspective of proletarian class formation, the Nasserist era was a pathological throwback. On the one hand, the 'octroyal socialism'[14] of the state softened the economic predicament in the workplace by improving the immediate living conditions of Egyptian wage workers. The expanding public sector confronted workers in the production process directly as the state and not as capital, thereby transforming the political-economic relation between workers and management into a moral-economic patron-client relation. As long as the state's political, economic, and cultural leadership was recognized by the workers and as long as it succeeded in improving their direct living conditions, this 'objective' social situation of development fettered any movement toward subject formation.

On the other hand, the neoformations of the working class were colonized by the Nasserist state, which destroyed the independent social organs of the proletarian subject and obstructed its economic and political lines of development. Recalcitrant worker leaders and communists were detained, independent political and trade union organizations outlawed. Much like the process of transformism that Gramsci described with regard to the Italian *Risorgimento*,[15] organic subaltern intellectuals were absorbed by 'extending' the state. This created a 'subjective' social situation of development that was unsatisfactory to

---

14　Cf. Chapter 9.
15　Cf. Chapter 9.

the workers. As the state claimed to be the expression of the 'alliance of working forces' workers became frustrated when, with the best of intentions, they tried to appropriate and mobilize its bureaucratic organs (cf. Bayat 1993). Suddenly they realized that there was not identity, but opposition between their goals and the means of mediation the state provided.

Nasser did not at all represent a Modern Prince, but his rise to power on the waves of revolution and mass strikes necessarily transformed him into a pharaonic 'Savior-Ruler'.[16] While the subaltern classes were politically subordinated to the military dictatorship, the régime itself was heir to the class forces that generated it. Nasserism was a product of revolutionary, popular mobilization and the dictatorship could not easily abandon its subaltern clients without, at the same time, forfeiting its hegemonic base.

---

16   Cf. Chapter 9.

PART 4

Neoliberal Capitalism

∴

CHAPTER 14

Sadat's *Infitah*

The Caesarist intervention of the Free Officers had transformed the anti-colonial, national-popular movement of the late 1940s and early 1950s into a subaltern-supported yet authoritarian-led historical bloc. In the following chapter I discuss the reconfiguration of this historical bloc along neoliberal lines, the re-emergence of worker and national-popular subjects, and the 1977 uprising as a missed moment of revolutionary transformation.

Crisis of Nasserism

The popular-authoritarian historical bloc that Nasser wrought, was an inherently unstable and contradictory ensemble. Firstly, there was a contradiction between the class nature of the régime and its state capitalist logic of accumulation. The state had to carry out a difficult balancing act between, on the one hand, securing political consent from its popular base through its 'octroyal socialism', and, on the other, allocating sufficient resources for its project of modernization: the state's expansive "populist consumption policy" stood in contradiction to the "investment demands of developmentalism" (Cooper 1979, 482–483). The industrializing ambitions of the régime required an economic rationale of labor discipline, high productivity, and low wages. This logic conflicted with the interests of its subaltern base of which the workers demanded workers' control (or at least real participation), reductions in working hours, and high wages. The socialistic rhetoric of the régime perversely exacerbated this contradiction, as it encouraged the popular masses to defend their social rights (Bayat 1993, 70–74). While the First Five-Year Plan was a success, growth rates almost halved during the Second Five-Year Plan (1965–70) (Farah 1986, 98). As the corporatist consensus put job security and full employment high on the agenda, industrial productivity was fettered by a high ratio of variable capital, rising fixed costs, and under-capacity. From 1965 onward, it became obvious that the system could not sustain both capital-intensive industrialization and high levels of consumption (Beinin and Lockman 1987, 459). The régime was reluctant to cut consumption after a brief and much contested experiment in 1965 (Farah 1986, 98–99). Nasser then briefly turned to the 'left' to counterbalance rightist layers of the state bureaucracy and their bourgeois allies who called for economic liberalization. However, the defeat of

Egypt in the Six Day War in 1967 weakened Nasser's position and halted the leftist turn: prices and taxes were increased; the workweek was increased from 42 to 48 hours without compensation; forced savings were deducted from monthly wages, and paid holidays were cancelled (Posusney 1996, 219).

Secondly, the partial and authoritarian statization of the economy generated a tendency toward *private* capital accumulation and a 'self-privatization' of the public sector. Egypt's economy was never fully nationalized, and pockets of private accumulation continued to exist in agriculture, trade, and some industrial sectors. Although the rural ruling class had lost lands, it was able to continue its domination of the countryside through traditional networks and the new government cooperatives. Because domestic trade was left relatively free and prices of consumer goods were only influenced through subsidies, commercial capitalists flourished (Cooper 1979, 499). The industrial bourgeoisie developed new activities to accumulate capital, especially as subcontractors for the government. Without the full liquidation of the private sector, the growth of the public sector stimulated a proportional expansion of the subcontracting companies (al-Khafaji 2004, 247). State capitalism strengthened private capitalists within its protective womb (cf. Marfleet 2011), who, ironically, favored more liberal economic policies (cf. Cox 1987, 243).

Thirdly, without any democratic supervision over the economy, the powerful state bureaucracy gained ever more the subjectness of an independent ruling class, treating the 'public' sector as its own property (Farah 2009, 36, 76). However, as a bureaucracy cannot reproduce itself legally as a private class it has to find footholds outside the 'public' sphere to safeguard its private interests (Richards and Waterbury 2008, 207–209). Nasserist state capitalism was unstable because in the long run it had "[...] an inherent tendency to divert resources to private hands [...] and therefore it paved the road for economic liberalization irrespective of the intentions of its political leaders" (al-Khafaji 2004, 241). This tendency was reinforced by the appointment of former owners of private companies, such as construction mogul Osman Ahmed Osman, as managers of public companies. State capitalism drove the state bureaucracy to develop into some type of private capitalist class, and it encouraged existing private capitalists to (re)capture state power.

Lastly, these endogenous contradictions were exacerbated by the war in Yemen (1963–7) and the disastrous Six Day War with Israel (1967) (Cooper 1979, 484). The Nasserist bloc barely survived the defeat, probably more due to the fragmentation of its discontents than the strength of the postwar consensus. The national-popular project was in shambles, and the Nasserist bloc fell back on its core actors: the state apparatus; the bureaucratic and technocratic middle classes; and the army. To secure their support, the import policy was changed, granting these groups expanded access to luxury consumer goods. Moreover, the first denationalizations were carried through in mid-1968, and licenses for private production quadrupled between 1967 and 1969. Incentives were given to the rural bourgeoisie to increase agricultural production (Cooper 1979, 484–488).

After the Six Day War the political optimism of the Nasserist epoch was transformed into cynicism. The dream of 'Arab socialism' was shattered and the state had lost its ethico-political dimension. The war and subsequent organic crisis forced the leading stratum within the Nasserist bloc to change its accumulation strategy and the composition of its class alliances. Without the wholesale abolition of the private sector, the full liquidation of the old ruling classes, and the implementation of popular democracy, Nasserism would remain caught between the logic of accumulation and the interests of its class base.

Even though a democratization of the state was out of the question for the ruling clique, at the end of the 1960s there was a debate on the manner in which the economic crisis had to be solved. One faction proposed to reinforce the authoritarian national-popular bloc by a further radicalization of the 'socialist' aspect of the régime; i.e., the full nationalization and statization of the economy. This strategy of accumulation was opposed by classes and social groups who wished to strengthen private actors through the liberalization of trade, the privatization of public companies, and the attraction of foreign investment (Beattie 2000, 12): wealthy landlords; industrial capitalists who had become managers of public companies; bureaucratic state elites that had emerged during the Nasserist era; high-ranking army officers; and commercial capitalists who wanted to expand their activities.

Capitalist Offensive

When in 1970 Sadat became president, he supported the market-oriented strategy of private capital accumulation and continued the process of economic liberalization and privatization that had already begun under Nasser in the late 1960s. Unlike Nasser, however, Sadat leaned heavily on private capital groups in order to 'solve' the problems that the Egyptian economy faced. Sadat's new historical bloc would become an alliance between military generals, state bureaucrats, public sector managers, powerful landlords, subcontractors, new layers of private commercial and financial bourgeoisie, Islamic students, foreign capitalist investors, and the USA. This required a reconfiguration of the class alliances within the authoritarian national-popular bloc. The Nasserist political superstructure had become an obstacle for Sadat's policies and during the top-down 'Corrective Revolution' of 1971–1972 the state apparatus was cleansed from the influence of Marxists and Nasserists such as Ali Sabry and Sharawy Gomaa. Because of the weakness of the 'socialist' faction in the state apparatus and the economic-corporate state of the working class, the right obtained a swift victory over the bureaucratic Nasserist left, which was uncomfortable with mobilizing the masses (Aoude 1994; Farah 1986, 27). In 1976 the ASU was hacked up in a 'left', 'center', and 'right' platform, which became independent parties: the National Progressive Unionist Party or Rally Party (*Tagammu*); the Egyptian Arab Socialist Party (EASP); and the al-Ahrar party. In 1977–8 Sadat created the National Democratic Party (NDP), which became, after its forced merger with EASP, the de facto ruling party of Egypt. The new course was presented as a democratic revolution: "supremacy of law, the state of institutions, the establishment of freedoms, and respect for the constitution" (Tucker 1978, 6). However, the multi-party system was but a democratic façade for Sadat's civil dictatorship (Aoude 1994). Despite Sadat's attempts to replace or undermine 'Arab socialism' with Islam and bourgeois democracy as new ideological forms, the state lost its ethico-political dimension. A cynical epoch began in which the hegemony of the ruling classes became less and less constituted by their leadership and prestige, but more and more by the capacity of the régime to fragment, repress, and pacify subaltern subjects.

The 'democratic revolution' also legitimized the reduction and reconfiguration of the position of the military in the historical bloc. Nasser had already attempted to decrease the power base of the military within the authoritarian national-popular bloc by strengthening the position of the interior ministry and expanding its tasks and responsibilities (cf. Kandil 2012). However, through the influential and charismatic figure of Field Marshal Amer, the military was able to continue its domination of domestic security until the Six Day War of 1967. Nasser used Amer's fall and the tainted prestige of the armed forces to reduce the army's authority to purely military matters. From 1967 onward, the balance of power shifted from the ministry of defense to the ministry of interior. To compensate for the military's retreat to the barracks and to counterbalance its power, the president created *Al-Amn al-Markazi*, the (General Security and) Central Security Forces (CSF) (Springborg 2009, 10). The CSF became a 'civil army' of some 300,000 conscripted troops. In addition, the civil *Amn al-Dawla*, the General Investigations Department, was charged with internal repression. Whereas the CSF was established as a direct and straightforward coercive state instrument to beat up and fragment mass protests and strikes, General Investigations engaged in the selective detainment and torture of activists and political leaders. Sadat expanded these civil apparatuses and developed them into the coercive tools of the new historical bloc (cf. Kandil 2012).

After the Camp David negotiations of 1978, the armed forces not only lost their political, but also their military function within the new bloc. To appease the officers, Sadat granted them economic concessions, as Paul Amar explained:

> [...] the military has been marginalized since Egyptian president Anwar Sadat signed the Camp David Accords with Israel and the United States. Since 1977, the military has not been allowed to fight anyone. Instead, the generals have been given huge aid payoffs by the USA. They have been granted concessions to run shopping malls in Egypt, develop gated cities in the desert and beach resorts on the coasts. And they are encouraged to sit around in cheap social clubs.
> AMAR 2012, 85

From Caesarist overlords, the generals were transformed into petty capitalists, whose mediocre surpluses were artificially shielded from private and public competition. Military Caesarism turned into a largely civil dictatorship.

Whereas the position of the military in Sadat's historical bloc weakened, other class fractions were strengthened. Large landowners were able to reclaim some of their sequestered lands and agricultural rents were raised for the first time since 1952 (Bush 2007, 1603). Private companies were legally protected against nationalization, public-private enterprises were regulated as private instead of public companies, and a number of 'free economic zones' were created that offered beneficial labor and tax conditions to foreign investors. In 1974 the president announced the *Infitah* (Open Door Policy), a program of economic and political liberalization and reintegration in the capitalist world market, aimed at attracting foreign investment. The Infitah was accompanied by huge loans from the Arab oil states and the USA, and the International Monetary Fund (IMF) demanded that the Egyptian state devalued the pound and cut subsidies on basic consumer goods. The Infitah constituted an explicit declaration of a new strategy of accumulation that reoriented Egypt's domestic economic structure along a neoliberal path, anticipating changes in the global economy (cf. Cox 1987, 219–244). Together with Pinochet's Chile, Sadat's Egypt pioneered the worldwide neoliberal shift in the Global South (Beinin 1999, 21; Callinicos 2011).[1]

---

1 In the West, a post-war 'Fordist' historical bloc had emerged. At the level of the economic structure, this capitalist ensemble consisted of an accumulation strategy based on "[...] high rates of labour productivity, based on a strict division of labour and the utilization of technology that was mechanised to an unprecedented extent" (Kiely 2009, 51). Capital-intensive production was driven by the export of capital from the USA and structured around the gold-dollar standard. At the level of class relations, strong trade unions and a militant working class were able to enforce a limited redistribution of wealth, social reforms, and often a further

Sadat's counter-reforms convinced many Muslim Brothers who had migrated to the Gulf countries to return to Egypt, bringing with them petrodollars and social conservative values. The Infitah also directly benefitted Ikhwan merchants, petty-traders, artisans, rich peasants, and landlords who had stayed in Egypt (Ates 2005, 137–139). The Brotherhood of the 1970 differed fundamentally from its predecessor in the colonial era. Despite its anticommunism and sometime alliance with the Palace, the Society of the 1940s was a popular mass movement of approximately half a million members that advanced revolutionary national-democratic demands such as land reforms, state-led development, and nationalization of the Suez Canal. In the 1970s the Brotherhood had become an elite organization of a few hundred activists with strong ties to Saudi Arabia – the emerging regional power.

The Islamic bourgeoisie was sympathetic to an economically liberal, but socially conservative interpretation of al-Banna's original project. Their ideology rejected Western moral and cultural values, but defended a free market capitalist economy, and contained elements of anti-Semitism, anti-communism, and anti-secularism. Brothers active in the liberalized financial and service sectors became a rising 'Islamic' business class. They lent money to new private companies, encouraging patron-client relations between Islamic bankers, entrepreneurs, and state bureaucrats (Beinin 2005a, 120–123). By the 1980s the rising private sector was controlled by eighteen families, of which eight had ties to the Brotherhood. About 40 percent of all private economic ventures were connected with Ikhwan interests (Naguib 2009, 163). Omar Tilmisani became the new leader of the Society and published its views in the monthly *al-Da'wa* (the Call) paper. Because of its support for the Infitah and its enmity toward the Left, the new Brotherhood gained the tacit approval of the Sadat

---

democratization of the state (along bourgeois lines). On the other hand, corporatist policies partly absorbed and neutralized these institution into the 'extended' state. Ideologically, Keynesian theories affirmed the necessity of deficit spending and regulating prices and markets to stabilize capitalist production cycles and guard the social peace. Post-colonial states in the Global South in the 1950s and 1960s constructed historical blocs along similar lines (Amin 2011, 101–102). However, a globally unequal distribution of capital, unequal exchange, and unequal geopolitical power relations remained major obstacles for development (Kiely 2009, 57–58). Once Fordist mass production systems that raised productivity had been put in place, the rate of productivity and profit began to fall (Kiely 2009, 62). Already in the second half of the 1960s, the strong bargaining position of the working class appeared to fetter the rate of profit. Neoliberal policies such as the deregulation of prices and markets and the internationalization of finance capital would tear open the 'Fordist' historical bloc by weakening the bargaining position of nationally organized trade unions and increasing exploitation at the level of the workplace.

régime. Together with state bureaucrats, military officers, and Infitah nouveaux riches the Brotherhood became a crucial vassal of Sadat's new hegemonic project (Naguib 2009, 162–163).

As the Egyptian bourgeoisie was too weak to force an Israeli retreat from the Sinai, Sadat had to court the United States in order to solve the important question of the occupied lands. A reorientation of foreign policy, away from the Soviet Union and toward the USA, was a crucial addition to Sadat's domestic political realignment. The October War of 1973 improved Sadat's nationalist credentials and prestige in the short term, and allowed him in the long term to negotiate a separate peace with Israel, switch sides in the bipolar world order, and become a loyal client state of the USA.

Strikes and Demonstrations

The roots of the 'third wave of communism' can be traced back to 1967, to the wake of the Six Day War. The military defeat of Egypt is often perceived as the harbinger of the downfall of Arab nationalism and its subsequent substitution by Islamist subjectivities and practices. Indeed, the 1967 war did provoke an ideological crisis, but not the sudden rise of religiosity and Islamism. On the contrary, it led to a huge popular mass movement, which lasted until the general uprising in 1977 (Farah 1986, 22–24). "It was the best era for the Left," [2] leftist activist Wael Tawfiq claimed.

Already from the second half of the 1960s discontent among workers and students was fomenting over the lack of democracy and failing development goals. In February 1968 workers in Helwan went on strike against the light sentences of the Egyptian officers who were considered responsible for the defeat in 1967. Workers from other workplaces and students from all of Cairo's universities joined their protest (Anderson 2011). In November, students organized actions against education reform plans and in favor of an expansion of political freedoms, occupying Alexandria University. News of the Western student and workers revolts reached the movement and stimulated the formation of a leftist counterculture: a semiotics that contained both global and local elements, combining the emancipative icon of Che Guevara with the authenticity of songs and poems by Ahmad Fuad Negm and al-Shaykh Imam (Anderson 2011; Booth 2009). In 1969 mass meetings organized by leftists in Helwan gathered some 4,000 to 5,000 workers discussing political and economic issues (Posusney 1996, 220).

---

2 Interview with Wael Tawfiq, Cairo, 20 October 2010.

Sadat's capitalist offensive also interpellated a war of movement from the part of the subaltern forces, especially the workers' and students' movements. From 1968 to 1973 the student movement formed the nucleus of the leftist movement, reflecting the global wave of revolt of May 1968. After the October War and the implementation of the Infitah general living conditions deteriorated, and as universities struggled to function normally, political student activities collapsed (Anderson 2011). Economic malaise and labor unrest shifted the center of gravity of the protests to the factories and workers' communities. Due to the success of Nasserist hegemony, workers had remained relatively passive during the 1950s and 1960s, but in the 1970s they started to move when their economic predicament worsened and the national-popular bloc collapsed. A first wave of labor protests took place in 1971 and in 1972, primarily directed against the slow erosion of wages. The restoration of wage levels in 1972 and the October War in 1973 temporarily halted the strike activities, which were resumed in the fall of 1974. Between 1975 and 1977 workers protested against the Infitah, which they perceived as an assault on the rights and concessions they had gained under Nasser (Posusney 1996, 220–222). In 1975 a series of clashes took place between workers and the police in urban areas and between evicted peasants and the security forces in the countryside. Students joined in the protests and marched on the People's Council, demanding democracy and the right to assembly, strike, demonstrate and organize political parties (Lachine 1977, 4–5). Social and economic issues were raised together with demands for political reform opening up a possibility of uniting the largely separated 'economic' and 'political' lines of development of the struggle.

The transformation of the objective social situation of development of the workers into a predicament, highlighted the subjective condition of the working class as a subject without its own, independent means of mediation. As protesting workers did not receive any support from the existing trade union structures or political figures, they had to develop new grassroots networks and forms of organization. After lying dormant for more than a decade, the economic line of development was rekindled. Labor activist Sabr Barakat recalled that:

> In Abd al-Nasser's days we tried to complain to the government and we directed our complaints to him, Abd al-Nasser. We thought he was protecting us against capitalism and we discovered that this was wrong. In the Sadat era we were working against Sadat himself and capitalism directly [...]. By law we were prevented from participating in the unions,

and we were cut off from the candidate lists in the elections. And we were arrested and jailed.[3]

In the public sector workers had conserved their old leaders and collective memories of the struggles of the 1940s and 1950s, which meant that they did not have to build their movement entirely from scratch. These organic intellectuals played an important role in reviving the proletarian activity-system that was rendered 'practico-inert' during the Nasser years. In general, workers of the public sector exercised a proleptic influence over the whole class and led the development of the economic struggle, as Beinin observed: "Their social relations of production, above average level of skill and education, concentration in industries perceived as vital to the national economy, and relatively privileged conditions gave them the greatest capacity to organize themselves outside formal trade union structures or transform local trade union committees into organs of struggle" (Beinin 1996, 259). The struggle of the public sector not only drew private sector workers into the strike, but also students, the unemployed, and other urban subaltern groups were interpellated by their 'bottom-up' pedagogy of revolt.

Meanwhile, the Egyptian Left was reorganizing itself as a political force. At the beginning of the 1970s the Left consisted of various tendencies, differing in ideology, social origin and/or generation. A first group were the radical elements in the Nasserist political establishment, especially among the mid-cadre of the ASU and the Organization of Socialist Youth, but also amid high-ranked officials and RCC members such as Khaled Mohieddin. A second layer was composed of the old guard of the Communist Party and the DMNL from the 1950s. Thirdly, a new generation of leftist students, intellectuals, trade unionists, and young workers became politically active, their loyalties divided between different shades of Marxism and leftist Nasserism. Groups identifying with Nasserism defined themselves as anti-imperialist and defended the public sector and the social and economic reforms gained under Nasser (Lachine 1977, 4)

During the second half of the 1970s and throughout the 1980s two parties encompassed the majority of leftist activists: Tagammu and the Egyptian Communist Party (ECP). From its inception, Tagammu had been a construct of the régime. Moving toward a controlled multi-party system in 1975, Tagammu was established as the left wing of the ASU and turned into a full party in 1976. Headed by the leftist Free Officer Khaled Mohieddin, the party was a heterogeneous leftist front, including "Nasserists, Marxists, the enlightened religious trend[4]

---

3 Interview with Sabr Barakat, Cairo, 16 October 2010.
4 Mohieddin himself was, despite his Marxist leanings, a devout Muslim and hoped to enrich the Tagammu platform with a religious left (cf. Sid-Ahmed 2005).

that is democratic and socialist, and Arab nationalists" (Seeking a New Style 1995). Through, on the one hand, a broad ideological consensus based on anti-imperialism, anti-Zionism and the struggle for democratic rights, freedoms, and a socialist society free of exploitation, and, on the other, an organizational flexibility, the party was able, to a large extent, to contain its internal centrifugal forces. Although Tagammu had been pragmatic since its foundation, accepting the conditions set out by Sadat for its existence as a legal party,[5] it tried to make the best out of a bad situation, often transgressing the political limits that the régime imposed (Sami 2005). When Tagammu sided with the mass movement after the January riots of 1975, issuing declarations in favor of the right to strike and political freedoms, it was accused by Sadat of being a cover for illegal communists.[6] Some 200 of its members were arrested (Lachine 1977, 5).

In the same year when the Tagammu 'platform' was created, communists of various backgrounds closed ranks and founded the underground Egyptian Communist Party (ECP). The relation of the ECP with Tagammu was complex, both on an organizational and ideological level, and evolved strongly throughout the last three decades. In the years after the ECP was established, its members succeeded in acquiring influential positions within the Tagammu apparatus. The communist Salah Adli recalled that:

> In the seventies the ECP realized that the most powerful leftist party at that time was Tagammu. And of course there were a lot of communists then in Tagammu, Marxists, but they would not declare it, because the party law bans this kind of ideology, and we could not mention that some of the ECP's members were in Tagammu. But it was widely known. The relation in the seventies and eighties between the ECP and Tagammu was good. We played a main role in developing the direction of Tagammu.[7]

---

5 Sadat allowed Mohieddin to set up Tagammu, on the condition that the party would not call itself a workers' party, would not support strikes, or hinder the régime in any other way.
6 As the only legal left-wing opposition party, Tagammu quickly became a political arena for leftist organizations that deployed entryist strategies, such as the Egyptian Communist Party, the Labor Communist Party, the Revolutionary Tendency, the 12th of January Organization Movement, and the Revolutionary Egyptian Communist Party – parties with a small but active membership (Tucker 1978, 7).
7 Interview with Salah Adli, Cairo, 13 November 2010. Husayn Abd al-Razek recalled that: "The Communist Party played a very important role in building Tagammu. Rifaat Said and myself and many others of the leadership were members of the Communist Party. And the Communist Party decided that we, many of us, had to play a role in building this party. At that time comrade Nabil al-Hilali who was the most important leader of the Communist

The ECP was itself a heterogeneous organization with various tendencies expressing the unresolved discussions that dominated the Egyptian communist movement since the Second World War. Its membership consisted of the old cadres from the 1940s and 1950s and young militants, who had emerged from the post-1967 student movements (Farag 1999).

In conclusion, the 1970s represented a war of movement in the development of both the strike and demonstration. New trade union and political structures expressed the increasing coherence and cohesion of proletarian and national-popular subjects. Successful state repression, fierce opposition by Islamist forces in the streets, inadequate leftist assistance, and the shift from the neoliberal offensive to a war of position would roll back the movement in the subsequent decade, however.

Islamic Fascism?

The Islamic bourgeoisie could not have become a social force without the mass support of Islamist students who came from rural areas and small towns (Farah 1986, 34–35). Independently of *al-Da'wa*, groups of Islamist students started to provide services to their peers organizing summer camps, study circles, physical training, selling cheap study books, and so on (Meijjer 2009b, 192). Thanks to state support,[8] clientelism, violence, intimidation, a strong ethico-political vision, and the failure of the Left to offer an attractive alternative, the Islamist student movement grew quickly (Beinin 2005a, 119). At the end of the 1970s *al-Gama'at al-Islamiyyat* (lit. "The Islamist Associations") – had taken over the domination of the Left on university campuses (Naguib 2009, 163–164).[9]

Party had a meeting with Khaled Mohi Al-Din and he gave them the names of the members of the Communist Party who would leave their posts in the Communist Party and become members in Tagammu, including of course Rifaat Said and others; many of the members of the Communist Party from Alexandria to Aswan became members of Tagammu" (Interview with Husayn Abd al-Razek, Cairo, 25 October 2010).

8 Already in 1971 Sadat saw the potential of the Islamist student associations and, together with Colonel Qaddafi, he erected the transnational youth organization *al-Jam'a al-Shari'yya* to combat leftist hegemony in the universities (Tucker 1978, 6).

9 Al-Gama'at al-Islamiyyat were divided along sociological and ideological lines. Peasants from Upper Egypt, who migrated to the Gulf countries during the 1970s, often returned wealthy. They were able to buy land, establish markets, and set up charity organizations at the local level, gaining both economic benefits and social prestige. Their children became cadres in al-Gama'at al-Islamiyyat (Beinin 2005a, 128). These layers were much more radical than the Lower Egypt student leaders, who had stronger ties to the reformist and moderate Muslim

The merger of the largest and most successful Lower Egypt Islamic student association, led by Essam al-Erian and Abd al-Moneim Abu al-Fotouh, with the *al-Da'wa* group supplied the newly emerging Brotherhood project with fresh cadres and a new social base (Naguib 2009, 164). The withdrawal of the state from public services opened up new possibilities for the Islamists to expand their influence among the urban poor and impoverished middle classes. Rich Ikhwan patrons established their own charity organizations. Through the patron-client relations of these foundations the Islamic bourgeoisie was able to mobilize layers of the lower-middle classes, the 'lumpenintelligentsia',[10] and the subproletariat. Due to their exclusion from Sadat's emerging bloc, students and professionals from the South in particular were attracted to radical forms of Islamism. Once they had benefited from Nasser's land reform and free education, and now, when they migrated to the cities, they lacked employment and social networks (Ates 2005, 137). Ironically, petrodollars and Infitah money financed the private Islamic welfare policies that had become necessary due to Sadat's privatization and liberalization politics of which the Brotherhood bourgeoisie was the main beneficiary. As Beinin remarked: "[…] Islamism appeals to both the losers and the winners of global neo-liberal economic restructuring" (Beinin 2005a, 113). Islamism came to represent the ideology of both those who were included and excluded from Sadat's new hegemonic bloc.

Politicized Islam became a powerful weapon in the arsenal of Sadat's capitalist offensive that sought to dismantle the Leftist opposition and redirect the entire social formation toward free market capitalism (Farah 1986, 25). The use of 'Islam' as a political concept had many benefits. Firstly, it subsumed everyday and deep-rooted religious and cultural signs and practices that were immediately recognizable to the masses under an ideological, 'scientific'[11] concept. Secondly, as a 'floating signifier' or abstract concept, 'Islam' was sufficiently vague to represent different and even contradictory class platforms. Thirdly, the deliberate confusion between political and religious uses of Islam delegitimized the *political* criticisms of the secular Left as *cultural* attacks of an alienated and Westernized Other (cf. Farah 1986, 28).

The defeat of leftist student movements in the universities left a lasting imprint on the communists of the 'third wave'. When I asked Fakhry Labib, an

---

Brotherhood (Meijjer 2009b, 195–196). In 1978 many Lower Egypt student leaders declared their allegiance to the Brotherhood, while Upper Egypt Islamists established their own *al-Gama'a al-Islamiyya* – the Islamic Group.

10 During the seventies the public sector failed to absorb the increasing number of graduates who were turned into a group of frustrated unemployed with a university degree.

11 In the Vygotskian sense, cf. Chapter 7.

elderly Marxist and senior leader of the African-Asian Peoples' Solidarity Organization (AAPSO), in 2008 whether the Muslim Brothers constituted a danger or a potential ally to the left, he answered that:

> They are very dangerous. They are enemy number one, because they are fascists. Not because they are religious, but because they are the most rightist stratum in capitalism. [...] it is a problem of conflicting class interests. They are primarily an anti-revolutionary force. [...] I sense that they are greater enemies than Mubarak. Not Mubarak as a man, but as a system, as a régime. [...] You see what they are doing in Sudan: destruction. Or in Iraq. Or what they have done in Palestine: they have divided Palestine. Anywhere they divide and destroy. Whereas we [as leftists] want to go forward and the right wants to keep the status quo, they want to take you back. But back to where? To when? [...] there are some on the left, some communists, who are making alliances with them. This is a very bad thing. And they are trying to tell us that our situation is comparable to South America where you find the liberation theology of the priests and so on [...]. But this is a completely different situation.[12]

The understanding of the *contemporary* Islamist phenomenon among many elderly activists of the 'third wave' is informed by their experience of the Egyptian religious right in the 1970s and the outcome of the Iranian Revolution of 1979. The movements that were mobilized under the flag of a politicized Islam were perceived as a reactionary force, bent on destroying the leftist student and worker movements while serving the interests of the ruling classes – much like the historical experience of European fascism in the interwar years.

At first sight the Islamist movements of the 1970s had a lot in common with European fascism.[13] As Gilbert Achcar and Samir Amin explained (Naguib

---

12   Interview with Fakhry Labib, Cairo, 17 February 2008.
13   Nadia Farah (1986) pointed toward the similarities between Islamist and fascist ideologies: (1) a cult of the state or the community embedded within an organicist worldview; (2) nationalism; (3) respect for private property and capitalist economy and a resistance against international finance and monopoly capital; (4) corporatism. Following Nicos Poulantzas, she analyzed fascism and Islamism as the ideological articulations of a weak middle class that desires to emancipate itself through the state, balancing between the interests of the proletariat and the bourgeoisie. However, she also acknowledged that the nature of a social movement is not determined by its abstract ideology, but strongly shaped by its particular activities. Rather than an ideology, Leon Trotsky (1969) defined fascism as a spontaneous mass movement with the downtrodden petty bourgeoisie at its core. When both bourgeois democracy and classic military dictatorships failed as stable

2009 156–157), Sadat and the Infitah bourgeoisie wished to settle accounts with the Nasserist national-popular bloc and mobilized the spontaneous movement of the Islamist petty bourgeoisie – students, professionals, shopkeepers, and so on – against the organized left. Ismail Sabri Abd Allah remarked at the beginning of the 1980s: "[...] the social base of the Islamic movement is essentially a revolutionary base which was stolen from the revolution. The social position and interest of the members of the Islamic movement should have made of it a progressive force" (Farah 1986, 40).

However, Islamism does not exist as a stable and homogeneous movement. Politicized Islam can express a grassroots protest movement, an instrument to suppress or mediate the class struggle, and a cultural framework for capital accumulation. Various classes are able to express their interests through the abstract concept of Islam: "Islam has always been present in the array of cultural elements available to define local identities. And in the modern era it has been mobilized for a wide range of contradictory political purposes" (Beinin 2005a, 116). Nazih Ayubi concurred that religious interpretations "[...] may range anywhere from being on the one hand a tool of legitimation and preservation of the status quo, to being a vehicle for protest and a spearhead for revolution on the other" (Ayubi 1991, 61). Therefore, the similarity between European fascism in the interwar years and Egyptian Islamism in the 1970s is the political integration of potentially progressive middle-class forces in a reactionary bourgeois dominated historical bloc, as Gramsci argued with regard to the historical cases of Italian state formation, Fascism, and Fordism.[14]

Despite, or because of, its fascistic potential, Sadat was wary of any powerful independent Islamist movement. Unlike European fascism, the government did not use the Islamic student associations as a battering ram against the working class, but fell back on its classic agents – the police and the army – to suppress strikes. Furthermore, at moments of profound class confrontations, the government found itself facing a spontaneous alliance of working and

---

state forms during the economic and political crises of the interwar years, the ruling classes employed the fascist movement as a battering ram against the organized working class. The rule of fascism was first established in the streets through the destruction of workers' organizations. The conquest of political society followed the fascists' de facto domination of civil society, as Gramsci also observed. The fascist state then continued with the liquidation of the workers' movement and the atomization of the working class, which prevented the development and crystallization of new class organizations.

14   Cf. Chapter 9.

middle classes. Nonetheless, it is clear that the Islamist movements of the 1970s played a reactionary role in aiding the state to suppress the first post-Nasserist popular mass movements of students and workers. The cadres of the 'third wave of communism' personally experienced 'Islamism as fascism'. For many members of this generation, the politicization of Islam became entwined with a counterrevolutionary practice and they remained suspicious of the ulterior motives of Islamic political agents, casting the different appearances of the Ikhwan in the mold of 1970s Islamism.

Crisis and Defeat

Sadat's neoliberal recipes failed to live up to their expectations. Despite a high economic growth of eight percent between 1975–82, foreign investment was little and almost solely directed toward the development of tourism and the new private financial sector. Privatization and liberalization of state companies, coupled with high inflation rates – an average of 25 to 30 percent per annum – led to deindustrialization, an increase of unemployment – from 2.2 percent in 1960 to 11 percent in 1986 – and a decrease of real wages (Farah 2009, 39–41). The implementation of IMF austerity measures resulted in price hikes, which provoked the spontaneous 'bread riots' of January 18–19 in Cairo in 1977 – the joint zenith of the neoliberal and subaltern war of movement. Industrial workers in Helwan struck and demonstrated in Tahrir Square. Leftist students joined workers in their protests, which quickly spread through the whole country, from Aswan to Alexandria. Even though the movement started as a protest about everyday economic grievances:

> [...] the demonstrators advanced beyond declaring disapproval of the specific economic policies that had prompted the demonstrations to challenge the legitimacy of the entire régime and its restructuring of Egyptian society as embodied in the open door policy. The slogans raised by the demonstrators began to articulate a vision of an alternative social order.
> BEININ 1996, 250

However, the 1977 uprising became Egypt's icon of 'missing' the revolutionary moment, and the political pathologies it generated.[15] Sadat's régime was shocked by the uprising and quickly restored the subsidies on basic consumer goods in order to disperse the spontaneous protests. The government denied

---

15   Cf. Chapter 7.

the spontaneous nature of the insurrection and blamed 'secret communist organizations' for organizing the 'riots'. Sadat mobilized the police, security forces, and the army on the streets to stem the pre-revolutionary tide. Once the masses were demobilized, the state implemented a zero tolerance policy for street politics. Leftist newspapers were shut down and socialist, communist, and Nasserist leaders – especially those active in the workers' movement – were imprisoned (Posusney 1996, 237). New laws restricted mass political action and gave life sentences for participation in demonstrations (Farag 2007).

That the masses could be quickly demobilized was due to the organizational and ideological weakness of the proletarian and national-popular projects. Even though there was an almost feverish political activity among workers and leftist activists during this decade, it was impossible for the working class to immediately develop itself, on its own, from its shattered, economic-corporate position into an independent hegemonic force in such a short period (Beinin 1996, 261). The autonomous political expression of the working class had been eradicated during the Nasserist era and had to be forged in the struggle itself. Perhaps the heteroleptic assistance of leftist activists and a *structural* entwinement of 'economic' and 'political' struggles could have created a counterhegemonic force before 1977, but the left failed to engage in a dialectical pedagogy with the workers' movement. At the beginning of Sadat's reign, many leftists believed that his coming to power signaled a leftist shift in Egyptian politics. Even after the president's 'Corrective Revolution', communists still had illusions in Sadat's continuation of Nasser's national-popular bloc and only hesitantly supported (if at all) the workers' emerging strike projects in 1971 and 1972 (Beinin 1996, 256–257). The October War of 1973 postponed any critical reflection of the Marxist intelligentsia on the rightwing reconfiguration of the Nasserist historical bloc until the declaration of Infitah in late 1974. The left was shocked by Sadat's 'betrayal' of the Nasserist project and started to organize political opposition against the president. In the next few years, worker actions were supported, but: "Once again, workers' struggles were represented by the Left as a component of the nationalist project, a front in the battle for economic self-determination" (Beinin 1996, 258). The left's organizational weakness, colonial attitude toward the working class, and political myopia left it unprepared to take a leading role in either the strike movements of 1975 and 1976 or the insurrection of 1977. Leftist activist Wael Tawfiq explained:

> [...] the national question could not point the way to revolution and only in 1977 this was discovered. The leftists were surprised with the uprising on 18 and 19 January. Their main activity was working among the students and there was little engagement with the workers' movement. There were

no movements that could profit from this moment, because the absence of a strong organization and the weakness of political consciousness kept the workers from making a connection between their own social problems and the nature of the system. So they were not working against the system, they had reformist demands. Whenever the government accepted [these demands], the protest was finished. The parties could not lead their supporters. The leftist organizations were also too closed. They had a huge number of members but they were not effective among the base of society. And the parties only discovered their weakness and little effectiveness during their actions. And it was easy for the system to find and destroy them after encouraging the Islamic groups in the universities. These were the two reasons of the failing of 1977.[16]

There was separation in activity and thought between workers and 'their' leftist intellectuals. Leftists were primarily occupied with the 'abstract' issues of imperialism, Zionism, and national development, while the consciousness of workers began with their everyday economic grievances and worries. The fact that most leftists courted the illusive 'national bourgeoisie' as allies in their anti-imperialist struggle did not help their rapprochement with the workers (Tucker 1978, 7). Socialism and self-determination were not recognized by leftists as part of the ZPD of the worker subject. Leftists were active in their campuses, parties, and urban street protests, and did not focus on establishing a solidary system of activity with the spontaneous workers' movement (Farah 1986, 25–27). In short, the lack of a collaborative project between leftists and workers blocked the organic formation of a counterhegemonic alliance, and of a genuine philosophy of praxis that offered solutions for the emancipation of workers and other subaltern classes.

Objective changes in the social situation of the proletariat reinforced its subjective weakness. The régime's fear for a repetition of the 'bread riots' slowed down the process of liberalization and privatization (Bayat 1993, 76–78). Although the spontaneous opposition had not been able to present itself as a counterhegemonic force and transform the neoliberal bloc, it succeeded in turning Sadat's capitalist offensive into a war of position. Contingent changes in the Egyptian economic structure because of regional developments – especially the influx of rents and migration of labor to the Gulf countries – created room for a more molecular process of counter-reform. The restoration of real wages combined with a precision-repression of worker leaders, prevented major industrial action between 1977 and 1981 (Posusney 1996, 222).

---

16   Interview with Wael Tawfiq, Cairo, 20 October 2010.

Meanwhile, the repression of the 1977 insurrection and the Camp David negotiations with Israel increasingly alienated the radical Islamists from their patron, the Sadat state (Farah 1986, 126). Conversely, Sadat distanced himself from his erstwhile Islamic discourse and claimed that the Islamist student associations were funded and supported from abroad. Between 1979 and 1980 the Islamic Group fused with the radical *al-Jihad* organization (Meijer 2009b, 197). The increasing confrontation between the state and the radical Islamist groups, on the one hand, and the powerful example of the Iranian Revolution of 1979 on the other, led key figures such as Abd al-Salam Farag to a Blanquist interpretation of political jihad – arguing that a small minority of righteous believers should overthrow and capture the state in a direct, paramilitary way. A preemptive detainment of 1,536 Islamic activists in 1981 forced the hand of *al-Gama'a* and *al-Jihad*, which plotted then to assassinate the president before their organizations were completely destroyed. In 1981, at the yearly October War parade that commemorated the 1973 war against Israel, four of their military sympathizers opened fire on Sadat, killing him.

CHAPTER 15

Mubarak's Détente

While the 1970s were characterized by a capitalist offensive and the concomitant resurgence of national-popular and worker subjects, in the 1980s the pace and intensity of neoliberal counter-reform decelerated considerably. The next chapter investigates how, during the first decade of Mubarak's rule, a transformist politics successfully absorbed leftist and Muslim Brother opposition forces within the historical bloc. As a consequence the worker subject remained stuck in its economic-corporate predicament.

Politics of a Rentier Economy

From a purely economic perspective, Sadat's Infitah was meant to move the main burden of industrial development from the state to the private sector by activating domestic capital groups and attracting foreign investments. However, the privatization and liberalization process did not reinforce the position of industrial capital, but of domestic and foreign commercial and financial capitalists. In 1982 only twenty percent of total investments went into manufacturing activities (al-Khafaji 2004, 278). Commercial capitalists were not interested in revolutionizing production, but followed the principle of 'buying cheap, selling dear' through trade and speculation, and by controlling local markets, real estate, and petty production units. They were able to function as mediators between foreign capital and local selling places. Together with commercial capitalists, large landowners engaged in speculative activities, as the combination of high rental income and real estate property granted higher revenues. Due to their monopoly position and because of their high amount of constant capital – which led to a more efficient production process and a lower value of produced commodities – foreign industries were more competitive than their Egyptian counterparts. In the emerging free trade régime their advantage increased. Due to a lack of labor-saving techniques and technological investments, along with the undesirability of a higher rate of exploitation, Egypt's industries became even more dependent on foreign capital.

Despite the failure of the ISI-model, the end of state-led industrialization, and the collapse of the Nasserist consensus, the public sector continued to expand until the mid-1980s and the régime was able to sustain its redistributive polices (Richards and Waterbury 2008, 190). State capitalism had given up its industrializing ambitions, but it was able to prolong its life-form through an accumulation of non-productive revenues or rents.[1] From the second half of the 1970s, a steady stream of revenues from migrant workers' remittances from the Gulf region, foreign loans and aid, tariffs of the Suez Canal, oil, and tourism, compensated the loss of income from the productive sectors. In practice, not the 'liberated' capital accumulation of the private sector, but state-controlled rent accumulation and distribution constituted the economic backbone of Sadat's historical bloc. This 'rentier capitalism' served the interests of both 'public' bureaucrats and private capitalists: rents were accumulated and distributed centrally through the state on the basis of patron-client relations, while private capital entered the rent distribution process through subcontracting and the black market (Farah 1986, 115). In addition, a sizeable part of rents that escaped direct state control were absorbed by the Islamic banks and investment companies, fuelling the economic activities of the rising Islamic bourgeoisie (Mitchell 2002, 278).

In the 1960s the economic structure of the state had played a relatively progressive role in developing the means of production. The political society had subsumed the capitalist classes under its developmentalist project. From the 1970s onward, the form of state capitalism remained, but its content was turned inside out. The state bureaucracy and Infitah bourgeoisie subsumed the state under their project of private rent accumulation. Neoliberal policies did not 'roll back' the state in favor of the market, but they instrumentalized the state according to the interests of the new ruling alliance. The cynical, direct patronage of the 'postpopulist'[2] state replaced Nasserist leadership and prestige as the main pillar of the rulers' hegemony.

After the assassination of Sadat in 1981, his successor, Hosni Mubarak, leaned on the rentier economic structure for a transformist[3] politics toward

---

[1] Richards and Waterbury defined economic rent as: "[...] the difference between the market price of a good or a factor of production and its opportunity cost (the price needed to produce the good or to keep the factor of production in its current use)" (Richards and Waterbury 2008, 15). Marx perceived capitalist rent – as opposed to feudal rent – rather as a social relation: "[...] reflective and derivative of historically specific property relations in the dominant mode of production [...]" (Yates 1996, 19). For a discussion on the concept of 'rentier state' and 'rentier economy': Yates 1996.

[2] Here understood as a state form that keeps (to an extent) the economic redistributive character of its populist predecessor, but without the same political legitimacy or popular mobilization capacity.

[3] Cf. Chapter 9.

the political opposition. Political prisoners were released, civil rights such as freedom of press and of association were restored – to a degree – and in 1984 parliamentary elections were held. Relations with the Arabic nations, which had soured over the separate peace with Israel, were improved. The political 'détente' was *not* a process of 'democratization from above', but a tactical retreat of the dictatorship, leaving limited spaces open in civil and political society for contentious politics that remained subordinated to régime interests. Egypt's parliamentary democracy was but a façade behind which the authoritarianism of the régime was carefully hidden (cf. Abdelrahman 2004). Via the prolongation of emergency law, the state held civil society in a tight grip: banning strikes, demonstrations, and critical newspapers; and introducing military courts to deal with recalcitrant political opposition (cf. Marfleet 2011). The rules of the new democratic game were set by the government and the NDP. Elections were manipulated and voters were systematically bought or intimidated, as the Egyptian novelist Alaa al-Aswany claimed:

> Well, I do not think we have elections. When you say elections you are using a term from political science and this has specific criteria which do not exist here. What we have is a miserable form of theater which is repeated over and over again for thirty years. The results of these so-called elections are in the desk of the generals and the interior ministry.[4]

Mass demonstrations, street politics, and political strikes were out of the question. The Political Party Committee systematically blocked the legalization of important political trends such as the Muslim Brothers, and it monitored and supervised parties even after their recognition. However, as long as the legal and illegal, secular and Islamist oppositions played along, they were tolerated.

Absorption of the Brotherhood

Whereas the left failed to appropriate Mubarak's détente for its own development – and was, consequently, completely domesticated by it – the Brotherhood made good use of the 'pores' of Egypt's restricted civil and political society (Al-Ghobashy 2005, 374). Firstly, the resurrected Society was able to gain a foothold in the professional syndicates. The Nasserist massification of education in

---

4 Interview with Alaa al-Aswany, Cairo, 26 November 2010.

the 1960s and the guaranteed employment of graduates in the public sector produced a mass of middle-class professionals in the 1970s and 1980s. The expansion of university education transformed professional associations from elite clubs into mass organizations of white collar workers. Because of their recent massification and their lack of a militant tradition, these labor organizations were less controlled by political society than the industrial trade unions. The Brotherhood's presence in the professional syndicates flowed organically from its influence over the graduates who came from the Islamist student associations. Islamist student leaders became doctors, engineers, lawyers, and journalists.[5] As the only organized oppositional force within the professional syndicates, the Brotherhood quickly dominated these associations. In 1984 the Ikhwan controlled seven of the 25 seats of the board of the Physician Syndicate: by 1990 twenty of the 25 seats were in the hands of their members (Naguib 2009, 165). By the beginning of the 1990s they also gained majorities in the engineering, dentistry, pharmacology, agricultural and even bar and journalist syndicates, which had traditionally been strongholds of the left.

Secondly, the decrease of state-led welfare and housing projects led to a growing number of urban poor in the *ashwaiyyat*: informal neighborhoods "[...] where buildings have no permits, where streets have no formal names, where men wear the traditional galabia, where women sit and socialize in front of their homes in the alleyways [...]" (Bayat and Denis 2000, 197). The social intervention of aid organizations connected to the Muslim Brotherhood transformed these 'declassed' layers into the beneficiaries and clients of private Islamist charity (Naguib 2009, 165–166).[6]

Thirdly, the Society was able to mobilize its local bases of grassroots support in the professional syndicates and *ashwaiyyat* to strengthen its position in the 'national' field of political society. As the Brotherhood was still an illegal organization it could not openly put forward its candidates in elections. This problem was solved through electoral coalitions. In the parliamentary elections of 1984 the Brothers forged an alliance with the right-wing nationalist Wafd party, which was the only opposition front that put out a respectable score of 15.1 percent. The 'Islamic Alliance' of 1987 saw the Brotherhood absorbing the

---

5 ...or not: between 1975 and 1985 university graduates tripled, yet the state budget for public sector employment was cut, creating a layer of unemployed and impoverished middle-class youth. This dissatisfied 'lumpen intelligentsia' constituted the primary social base of Islamists who were more radical than the Brotherhood (Beinin 2005a, 144).

6 However, the Brotherhood's presence in the *ashwaiyyat* was challenged by more radical groups such as *al-Gama'a al-Islamiyya* (Meijer 2009b, 199).

socialist *Amal* (Labor) party and the liberal al-Ahrar, and successfully obtaining seventeen percent of the vote (Al-Ghobashy 2005, 379).[7]

Throughout their interventions in civil and political society the Ikhwan were careful not to step too hard on the state's toes. The Brothers realized that they were tolerated rather than recognized as a political force by the government. Their interpellations in parliament were first and foremost political performances oriented toward their own rank and file and potential sympathizers. Despite enjoying majorities in many of the professional syndicates, the Brothers always left the chair to a member of the NDP. In this manner the régime was able to maintain its dominance, while the Ikhwan could always shift the blame of unpopular decisions to the NDP (Al-Ghobashy 2005, 380). Behind the screens the Brotherhood and the government negotiated the margins of opposition. The presence of the Ikhwan in these associations and in parliament was used to increase its political bargaining power in the negotiated consensus between the government and the opposition. There was a symbiotic relation between the Mubarak state and the Brotherhood, which continued as long as the Ikhwan did not grow too powerful or outspoken. This reformist strategy of the Brotherhood and its preference for recruiting members of the educated middle classes alienated radical students, industrial workers, and slum dwellers, particularly those who migrated from poor Upper Egypt to metropolitan Cairo. These groups were attracted to more radical and/or puritanical forms of Islamic activism.

Absorption of the Left

Between 1976 and 1981, Tagammu had waged a fierce opposition against the Sadat state, building a membership of 125,000 to 160,000 members (Tucker

---

[7] The absorption of the Amal party in 1987 may give the impression that the Brotherhood began to move to the left at the end of the 1980s. Adil Husayn, general-secretary of the Amal party and chief editor of the *al-Sha'b* (the People) newspaper re-imagined a socialist discourse on social-Islamic lines, arguing for a corporatist society. Notwithstanding these corporatist voices, the election program of the Ikhwan in 1987 articulated a clear neoliberal economic view. It defended cuts in the public sector, an increase of productivity, and the stimulation of the private sector as the backbone of the economy. Apart from an Islamic touch – Islamic banking and *zakat* were seen as the primary tools for social justice and distribution of wealth – the social-economic recommendations of the Brotherhood paralleled those of the government. Criticisms of rampant corruption, bureaucratization, and inefficiency were not directed at the nature of Egypt's political economy, but at the stalled execution of neoliberal policies by the Mubarak clique (Ates 2005, 138).

1978, 7). Its policy was one of mobilization and engagement with the struggle of workers and students. Although Tagammu and the Egyptian left in general intervened in the 1977 insurrectionary movement, it was not able to organize, structure, and direct the masses against the power of the state. Some leftist leaders drew pessimistic conclusions about the potential of street politics to change the status quo. In 2009 I asked Rifaat al-Said, historian of the Egyptian Communist movement and chairman of Tagammu, if the mass democratic and worker protests of the 2000s constituted a force of societal change. The elderly man waved his hand in a disdainful gesture and answered:

> What happened in Mahalla al-Kubra [...] even if it accumulated a thousand times, it cannot change the régime. In 1977 we had an insurrection and moved thousands, millions of people, from Alexandria and Aswan. The régime didn't feel the emotions of the people. It is the same in Europe, when millions went on the streets to contest the war in Iraq. Did the British government accept this revolution? No. So what happened? We demonstrated and suddenly in the morning we found the army in the streets. So we stopped. The Egyptians used to respect the army, not to be afraid of the army, to respect it. Secondly, we didn't want the return of the army as an influential force in politics. So, in my imagination it needs a patient accumulation of protests, oppositional actions, and sit-ins, and then, perhaps, the régime will retreat. [...] We have changed a lot in this régime. If you were here twenty years ago and if we had such a conversation, we were both imprisoned and all the people here would be in prison. We have vaccinated the régime to accept what we are saying. And we have vaccinated the people to be more courageous. What has happened historically should change historically. If you imagined a revolution or something like that, it is too far-fetched, in my imagination. Poor people don't make revolutions, believe me. Poor people need to return in the afternoon with some pieces of bread to their family. They are too afraid. And if the poor don't find a way out, they usually return to God. And that is the main influence of Islamism today.[8]

Al-Said entered Tagammu as a member of the illegal Communist Party at the beginning of the 1980s. He began to advocate a nonconfrontational policy toward the Mubarak régime. The failed uprising had shown the impossibility of revolutionary street politics and, in order to survive state repression, Tagammu had to refrain from challenging the state directly, by striking a balance

---

8   Interview with Rifaat al-Said, Cairo, 12 April 2009.

between criticism and accommodation. Under al-Said's and other Communist leaders' influence, Tagammu slowly turned away from its historical engagement with the mass movement, instead focusing on activities within the boundaries of Egypt's restricted civil and political society. His disregard for self-determining politics from below would eventually lead him to denounce the January 25 mass mobilizations, which further marginalized his already much contested position in the party.

When I visited Mansura in the same year, I met with Hamdi Qenawi, a middle-aged Tagammu activist. Walid Ali and Muhammad Taher, both young members of Tagammu and journalists of the leftist al-Badil journal, were present as well. Proudly Qenawi showed me the still scarred location of a bullet that had penetrated his arm during the 1977 uprising and had not been removed since. He vehemently disagreed with al-Said's disengagement with grassroots politics: "During the seventies, Tagammu was very strong because it sided with the workers against the government. When Sadat moved to the right and toward the USA, there were many protests and demonstrations,"[9] he recalled. Repression by the Sadat régime weakened the left, but this was not the real cause of its crisis in the 1980s:

> Even in 1980 there were still demonstrations and actions by Tagammu, for example during the student movement of 1980. The real turning point was the new presidential régime in 1981 and the idea within the ranks of Tagammu that the situation would change [...] When in 1981 Mubarak replaced Sadat, he continued his policies, but disguised his intentions better in the beginning. At first he made a lot of promises; he promised to be fair and just, and he released 1,400 activists whom Sadat imprisoned. Some people in Tagammu, like Rifaat al-Said, believed that the presidential administration of Mubarak differed from Sadat. He believed that Tagammu should give the régime a chance to change Sadat's system. This was the starting point of our current weakness. We cut the relation between the party and the people [...]. From that moment onward there were good relations between the party and the régime; which is logical as it needed a license from the régime to exist.[10]

From 1984 onward Tagammu participated in parliamentary elections, which did not prove very productive, as this once mass party of the left with strong ties to the industrial working class only got a few percent of the national vote.

---

9   Interview with Hamdi Qenawi, Mansura, 17 April 2009.
10   Interview with Hamdi Qenawi, Mansura, 17 April 2009.

Government rigging was only one cause of the electoral defeat. Tagammu had acquired the right to compete in elections and to operate freely in the national political sphere in exchange for a moratorium on street politics. Without the ability to mobilize its traditional mass base, the party was cut off from its organic electorate. At the end of the 1980s, its membership had dropped to 25,000 members (Aoude 1994). Tagammu activists remained active within farmers' and workers' organizations, but there was an increasing gap between the real 'politics from below', embedded in local, everyday struggles, and the abstract 'politics from above', articulated in the Cairo HQ and performed in the virtual spheres of parliament and media. The growing discrepancy between local practices and national discourses and the cordial relations of the party's leadership with the government, made workers suspicious toward Tagammu (al-Khashab 2007). Ironically, whereas the absence of mass street politics convinced the leftist leadership that democratization had to come through negotiations with the régime, its reluctance to mobilize subaltern actors bereft them of any substantial bargaining tool vis-à-vis the state (Howeidy 2006).

The trauma of 1977, the aftermath of the Iranian Revolution, the détente of the early Mubarak years, and the triumphant trajectory of Islamism frustrated and confused the Egyptian left. Was the main enemy imperialism and Zionism, the Mubarak régime, or Islamic fascism? With what political forces should the enfeebled left ally itself? When Abd al-Rahman al-Sharqawi advocated a national front between all political forces, including the government, against externally sponsored Islamist groups, Husayn Abd al-Raziq, then chief editor of *al-Ahali*, answered that any national front should be directed against the USA, Israel, and Egypt's own parasitic government. Militant Islamism was only a secondary danger in comparison with imperialism and its domestic agents. Throughout the 1980s Tagammu and other opposition parties refused to side with the government against the Muslim Brotherhood (Flores 1993, 37).

When during the 1987 elections the Muslim Brotherhood effectively took over the Amal party, and when Communist candidates openly featured on Tagammu lists, the government put pressure on Tagammu to get back in line. The discourse of al-Ahali became one of 'relative moderation', which is still the paper's line today.[11] In the same year Fouad Zakariyya argued that even if both the Islamists and the régime were enemies, the fight against the Islamists had absolute priority:

> Once the governing body comes to speak in the name of the Shari'a, opposition turns to unbelief, any difference becomes an insolence in the

---

11   Interview with Farida Na'ash, Cairo, 27 October 2010.

face of God's law or an apostasy that has to be punished applying the appropriate law. The conditions of political and social struggle will become much worse and much more difficult. I am not exaggerating if I say that the idea of the struggle itself will then be thoroughly uprooted. Therefore the interest of the left, and with it all nationalist forces, in maintaining the proper conditions for a legitimate political struggle imposes on all the duty to close ranks and stand against a tendency threatening to eradicate the principle of struggle itself.

FLORES 1993, 37

Zakariyya's position, published in al-Ahali, sparked off a debate in Tagammu on the nature and role of Islamism, which was a repetition of the discussions on the 'nature' of Islamism since the 1970s. Of the eleven replies appearing in al-Ahali, only one argued in favor of a front with the government. Yunan Labib Rizq made the comparison between Islamism and fascism and called for a struggle against political Islam akin to the European fight against fascism in the interwar years. Most saw the Muslim Brotherhood as a fraction of the big bourgeoisie, which should be fought, while others saw the radical wing of the Ikhwan as a potential ally against the government (Flores 1993, 37–38). At the end of the 1980s the intellectual debate on Islamism and the relation between secular leftists and anti-government Islamists had been thoroughly conducted. The main different views that crystallized out of the discussion are similar to those of today: Islamism as (1) a form of fascism (e.g. among Tagammu's rightwing); (2) representing a faction of the bourgeoisie (e.g. among ECP leaders); (3) a potential ally in the anti-imperialist and anti-Zionist struggle (e.g. the line of the Revolutionary Socialists vis-à-vis non-bourgeois Islamist youth).

Absorption of the Workers

A combination of state repression, relative wage stability, migration of workers to the Gulf and distribution of economic and strategic rents had kept the industrial peace between 1978 and 1981. Mubarak's détente encouraged new, small-scale labor protests in 1982 and 1983. The drop in oil prices from 1984 forced the government to enter negotiations with the IMF. A section within the Egyptian ruling class called for a far-reaching process of liberalization and privatization to fight rising inflation and to restore the rate of profit. Due to the fall of real wages and the threat of neoliberal reform, workers increased their collective actions from 1984 onward (Posusney 1996, 222–223). They were led by organic worker intellectuals and often supported by local leftist activists. Beinin noted that just like in the 1970s: "Once again, unionized workers in large-scale public sector enterprises, especially those located in major industrial centers, were most prominent in this upsurge of workers' collective action" (Beinin 1996, 263). Since workers in the newly privatized companies were less organized, and because their situation was more precarious than those employed by the state, they were less inclined to participate in strikes.

The actions of the workers movement in this decade were primarily defensive and apolitical, aimed at achieving particular economic demands and restoring the strong bargaining position of the working class toward the postpopulist régime (Beinin 2009, 23–24). These struggles often ended in the violent repression of the movement and/or concessions from the state. The GFETU was caught between its loyalty to the Mubarak régime and its role as guardian of the Nasserist social reforms (Bayat 1993, 77–78). Nevertheless, the obstinacy of the labor bureaucracy, combined with grassroots working class actions, slowed down the process of neoliberal counter-reform, which was rekindled in the second half of the 1980s (Abdelrahman 2004, 107).

Posusney claimed that, despite the sometimes very militant labor actions, the proletarian economic line of development remained embedded within the Nasserist 'moral economy': "[...] the nature of labor protest in Egypt suggests that workers did adopt the Nasserist ideology of the 1960s, stressing reciprocal rights and obligations. Workers see their responsibility lying in production, to contribute to the postcolonial modernization and development of their country" (Posusney 1996, 223). The postpopulist social situation of proletarian development relegated the meaning of collective worker actions to symbolic tools, which ritualistically renegotiated the position of particular groups of factory workers within the ensemble of corporatist social and political relations. The activity of labor protest had as its goal the affirmation and reintegration of workers within the moral-economic system. The main form of struggle of protesting workers at this point was not the classic 'work-stoppage', but the 'work-in': workers stayed at the workplace after hours, asserting their role as productive and loyal actors within the patronage activity-system (al-Mahdi 2011c). Posusney observed that: "[...] workers themselves have eschewed actual work stoppages, using them only as a last resort. The most common alternative to strikes is the in-plant sit-in, during which management is ejected or ignored but workers continue running the factory on their own" (Posusney 1996, 223).

Workers continued to confront factory management as 'their' state, instead of a statist form of private capital. Although their 'work-ins' reflected a 'good sense' – the everyday concept that the factory was theirs and that they were responsible for its operation – it did not reflect the changing relations of power within the historical bloc. As long as the state was able to fulfill its paternalist obligations, the illusion of populist politics could continue. The strike remained entangled in the economic-corporate moment, unable to transcend its spatio-temporal particularity and economic 'parochialism'. Because of direct, 'vertical' state mediations – and violent repressions – of labor conflicts through the GFETU and the police, there was little solidarity between factories in the same sector, let alone between different sections of the working class (Alexander 2012). Even though there was important support from the urban communities in which these public companies were historically embedded, such forms of solidarity ironically undermined the development of *class* subjectivities by drawing workers into a shared yet amorphous activity-system of communal subalternity (cf. Beinin 2011).

Within the left, the experience of 1977 had created a divide between those leaders, intellectuals, and activists who advocated a disengagement with street politics in favor of participation in the régime-controlled political community on the one hand, and those who tried to maintain relations with grassroots movements on the other. Leftists who withdrew from mass politics and who collaborated to various degrees with the state were either demoralized by the 1977 defeat, frightened by the specter of 'Islamic fascism', or genuinely believed in a gradual democratization process led by president Mubarak. Fadi Bardawil observed that:

> Those thinkers and journalists have moved from an idealization of the revolutionary potential of the masses in their youth to a diametrically opposite view in their old age, locating the inherent 'problems' plaguing the region in the culture of these same masses. What remained a constant in this interpretive and political inversion is the distance separating the militant then, intellectual now, from the masses adulated then and despised now.
> BARDAWIL 2011

Due to their colonial mode of assistance these leftist intellectuals had never developed a dialectical pedagogy with the everyday struggles of 'their' subaltern subjects, which they only recognized in abstract and mystifying terms. Their distance from the class struggle obstructed a conceptualization of the subjective economic-corporate predicament of the working class, and led them to 'objectivist' explanations of the workers 'passivity': variations on the European left's post-1960s 'embourgeoisement'[12] thesis.

---

12   The idea that the economic gains by workers via collective bargaining and political reform within capitalism embed their consciousness in a 'bourgeois' or 'middle-class' lifestyle – thus

Among those leftists who remained engaged with street politics and the class struggle, a renewed interest in the workers as a potential political subject emerged. Many leftists and trade unionists rejected the colonial mode of assistance that had plagued the communist movement since its inception. However, some of them exchanged their previous colonialist attitudes for a total liquidation of the role of the left in the development of the worker subject. This liquidationism suggested that "[...] the working class is capable of organization and action without the assistance of the Left intelligentsia and need not be bound by its agenda or its disabilities [...]" (Beinin 1996, 264). This call for a withdrawal of leftist assistance went hand in hand with the gradual liquidation of the instructive role of communist and left-nationalist institutions. For example, Tagammu cartoonist Hassanein recalled that:

> Rose al-Yusuf was a school of cartoonists who were drawing for causes, not only for money, they were communists. Drawing was a cause in itself, not a way to make money. And then they made a school which teaches to draw caricatures for money [...]. Cartoons changed from being a cause in itself, a universal language, to draw just to make money and to distribute ideas which move the society backwards.[13]

The collapse of the Soviet Union spelled the end of many institutions and practices that depended on its financial and cultural sponsorship. The feeble and distorted promise of a 'proletarian Prince' – a hegemonic apparatus of and for the working class – which had emerged in the 1970s slowly fell apart in the second half of the 1980s and the 1990s. How could a genuine philosophy of praxis develop when there was no real, dialogical collaboration through which a proletarian 'good sense' could be entwined with critical theory? With nostalgia, Hassanein recalled that:

> It was a tradition in Tagammu to educate the workers, helping them to understand present issues, how to solve problems and stand for their rights, and how to write, draw, and so on. But the reality is that the party

---

constituting a material brake on the formation of class consciousness. However, 'consumerism' is, arguably, a subjectivity that exists next to and in contradiction with class subjectivity. Ironically, in Egypt, for example, it was often the most organized and affluent workers – e.g. the cigarette rollers in the colonial era; the public sector workers in the 1990s; who engaged in strikes. *Relative* deprivation or affluence does not appear to constitute an *absolute* hurdle or springboard for the development of class consciousness.

13 Interview with Hassanein, Cairo, 13 October 2010.

is empty now. There were workers in Tagammu in the past, but now there aren't as many workers We are not in the factories as we were in the seventies or the eighties, we are away from them. I try to gather children and to teach them, but there is no money for this. So I get the colors and the pens from my own salary. Even when the children draw a gallery the party does not encourage me in this task.[14]

---

[14] Interview with Hassanein, Cairo, 13 October 2010.

CHAPTER 16

Neoliberal War of Movement

The 1980s saw a transformation of the economic structure of Egypt's historical bloc toward rentier state capitalism, which stabilized class relations and allowed the Mubarak régime to absorb and disarm political opponents. The following chapter reveals how a fall in rentier income encouraged the régime to move back to a neoliberal war of movement against the subaltern classes, engaging in a new and aggressive strategy of accumulation by dispossession and ending the 'postpopulist' consensus.

Neoliberal Counter-Reform

The rentier economy of the decade between 1975 and 1985 had supplied the ruling classes with enough financial leeway to appease the popular classes that were dominated in the postpopulist bloc. However, from the second half of the 1980s onward, rental income decreased and the 'steady state' economy showed signs of exhaustion. The global fall of oil prices diminished the influx of petrodollars from the Gulf region, and high inflation depressed real wages. National debt rose to more than 38 billion USD in foreign obligation and the budgetary deficit increased to over twenty percent (Richards and Waterbury 2008, 225). The Gulf War of 1991 led to the return of many migrant workers to Egypt, who flooded the domestic labor market. It also resulted in the collapse of tourism, compounding the state's fiscal crisis, which was induced by the régime's inability to pay back its military debts (Mitchell 2002, 276). Lastly, for the USA, the collapse of Stalinism decreased the value of Egypt's 'geopolitical rent': i.e., the price in loans and financial and military aid for its alliance with the Western bloc. The dry spell in traditional sources of rent income, combined with the reluctance of the state and private capital groups to invest in the productivity of agriculture and industry, left the régime with only three options: finding new sources of external rent; increasing the rate of exploitation of labor (absolute surplus extraction); and the dispossession of public assets. The fiscal crisis forced the Mubarak régime to turn to the IMF and World Bank to save the economy from bankruptcy (Farah 2009, 41). In 1991 Egypt accepted an Economic Reform and Structural Adjustment Program (ERSAP) inspired by the neoliberal paradigm of the 'Washington consensus' (Bush 2007, 1599). The IMF loan allowed the government to 'solve' the financial crisis of 1990–91 with a massive capital injection in the banking sector of 5.5 percent of GDP and an additional fiscal exemption worth ten percent of GDP (Mitchell 2002, 279). In exchange, the ERSAP aimed to contain and decrease foreign debt and inflation, by cutting state subsidies on consumer goods, privatizing public companies, liberalizing markets and prices, freezing wages, commercializing agricultural lands and implementing a flat tax. Thus, neoliberal, 'market-oriented' reform became the logical instrumentality of a crony-capitalist rentier state.

The liberalization of agricultural prices and markets had already began in 1987. The Egyptian government promoted "[…] a US farm-type model of extensive capital-intensive agriculture driven by market liberalisation, export-led growth and tenure reform" (Bush 2007, 1604) The underlying rationale of liberalization was that rising prices of agricultural produce would attract capital to invest in rural production. The state regarded landowners as willing allies in the realization of the free trade policies of the IMF, which promoted cash crop production. Similar to the colonial era, the economic interests of large-scale landholders were tied to those of foreign capital groups.

As a declaration of war against land tenants, Mubarak's Law 96 of 1992 abrogated Nasser's Agrarian Reform Law of 1952, granting former landowners the right to reclaim the lands that their families had lost during the redistribution policies of the 1950s and 1960s. In addition, the prices of land rents were to be governed fully by market forces instead of determined by law.[1] After a five year transition period, the New Tenancy Law came into effect in 1997: from then onward, land rents were governed by market prices instead of the former fixed rent system. Rents increased by as much as 400 percent (Bush 2007, 1606). In addition, landowners started to drive tenants from their land (Beinin 2001, 164). A majority of lands became fully owned by the landed elite and embedded in a modern capitalist system of cash paid tenancies, allowing the landlords to accumulate capital at an accelerated speed (Bush 2009, 88–90). The livelihoods of some five million Egyptians were endangered by the New Tenancy Law as neoliberal reform in the countryside brought about a rise in land rents, the concentration of landholdings, and rural violence; landowners sent police troops and thugs to chase farmers from their lands.[2] The fragmented

---

[1] In Nasserist and post-Nasserist Egypt tenants had to pay an amount of legally fixed capitalist rent. Law 96 removed the ceiling on the amount of rent. Increasing land rents was a necessary step to maintain the rate of profit for landowners, as the concentration of land had caused a fall in productivity (Dyer 1997).

[2] Ironically, the introduction of market-oriented production and price formation in the countryside reinforced the dominating rentier logic, strengthening low productivity and increasing the prices of agricultural goods.

forms of resistance against the neoliberal land reforms organized by landless or small landholding farmers were violently repressed (Bush 2000, 239). By the mid-1990s, half of the rural population lived in poverty, an increase of ten percent in comparison to 1990 (Mitchell 1999, 463). By 2007 the neoliberal offensive in the countryside had resulted in "119 deaths, 846 injuries and 1409 arrests" (Bush 2007, 1606).

In the industrial sector, state companies were deliberately put at a disadvantage vis-à-vis private enterprises in order to force their bankruptcy and subsequent privatization. A new 'ministry of investments' was established, which became the primary executor of the privatization process. Selling shares of state-owned enterprises on the Cairo stock market created an economic mini-boom in 1996–7. The state earned 1.5 billion USD from these privatizations. Public holding companies remained the largest shareholders in many of the privatized enterprises. Some privatized firms were sold to public banks. State holding companies set up private corporations or joint ventures. State elites became investors in large private sector enterprises or used state power to favor their friends and families in the subcontracting sector, realizing huge profits (Mitchell 2002, 280–281). Between 1993 and 1999 over 100 factories passed into private hands (Beinin 2005b). By 2002 half of the public enterprises were privatized or liquidated (Richards and Waterbury 2008, 251). After 2004, a new cabinet headed by prime minister Ahmed Nazif stepped up the privatization and liberalization process. Corporate taxes were halved in 2005, from 40 to twenty percent of earnings, whereas personal taxes were raised, especially those on housing. Private firms enjoyed the flat tax of twenty percent while the public sector had to pay double (Farah 2009, 49–50). These aggressive policies resulted in an economic growth of five to seven percent (Beinin 2009, 30).

Economic growth, however, did not reflect a development of 'extended reproduction', but a rapid 'accumulation by dispossession'.[3] State factories such as the Qalyub Spinning Factory were sold far beneath their actual value (Farah 2009, 49–50). It had been a myth that public sector companies were unprofitable: "In 1989/90, on the eve of the reforms, 260 out of 314 non-financial state-owned enterprises were profitable and only 54 were making losses" (Mitchell 1999, 458). Selling these valuable productive assets, however, resulted in quick and easy (yet unsustainable) profits, both for private actors and the state. The rate of exploitation in the industrial public sector was driven up, as real wages dropped by eight percent between 1990 and 1996 (Mitchell 2002, 280; 286). Privatization often led to mass firing of workers, with the aim of increasing

---

3 Cf. Chapter 4.

productivity. As in the countryside, neoliberal reform in the industries did not encourage investments. The process of dispossession did not enhance the rate of capital accumulation, but increased surplus extraction in the form of rents. Capital was directed to the construction of real estate, the production of luxury goods, and grand schemes such as the *Toshka* irrigation project, rather than invested in export-oriented industrial production (Mitchell 1999, 457). Cutting back on subsidies and wages decreased the purchasing power of the workforce. In 1998 it was estimated that 70 percent of the workers in the private sector lived in poverty (cf. Farah 2009, 44). The destruction of employment in the public sector was not compensated by new jobs in the private sector. In general, unemployment between 1998 and 2006 did not increase, as people either engaged in subsistence production, or joined the informal sector. Between 1998 and 2006 the share of the workforce employed in the informal economy increased from 57 to 60 percent (Assaad 2009, 2).

Sameh Naguib remarked that: "[...] the policies of neoliberalism were never about dismantling or even reducing the role of the state in the economy, but rather about increasing the role of the state as a facilitator of capitalist profit-making at the expense of the working class" (Naguib 2011). Neoliberal reform in Egypt did not at all entail a 'retreat' of the state from the 'economic field', but a redirection of state power and resources toward an increased accretion of private rents via an aggressive policy of dispossession, which only benefitted a small clique within the ruling classes. The state lost its function and position as 'universal capitalist'[4] and became the obedient tool of a particular and select group of oligarchs around Mubarak who were closely connected to sources of foreign financial capital.

Subordinating the Subalterns

The neoliberal strategy of accumulation by dispossession initiated a new era of intensified class confrontation and increased authoritarianism, as it required not only changes in the economic structure, but also a corresponding political reconfiguration of the postpopulist bloc: i.e., the exclusion of subaltern forces and the subduing of subordinate fractions of the capitalist class. Standing squarely behind private capitalists and landlords, the Mubarak clique finally

---

4 An evolution from protecting the interests of capitalism *in general* – e.g. by handling the workers' movement; by creating legal frameworks that favor and safeguard capital accumulation (for example via private property laws); by guaranteeing security and stability in civil society; and so on – to the defense of the interests of a *specific* group of capitalists.

pulled the plug out of the postpopulist consensus. The state forfeited its obligations in the moral economy, thereby undermining the patron-client relations between the subaltern classes and the ruling classes. As a true cynic, the state revealed the shallowness of its 1980s democratic and corporatist commitments by the increased use of coercion against its class opponents: opposition parties, Islamist movements, workers, peasants, slum-dwellers, and so on (Maher 2011).

In political society, direct state control over elections and parliament was increased. The electoral law was changed to the disadvantage of the Ikhwan, which, together with most other opposition parties, boycotted the 1990 parliamentary elections. Tagammu, however, participated in the sham elections, as the 'legal Left' was offered positions in parliament in exchange for a moderate political discourse and a hard stance against the Brotherhood (Down to Earth 2000).

The state tightened its grip over civil society as well. When the Brotherhood obtained majorities in the doctors', journalists', and bar associations, the government put all professional syndicates under direct state supervision (Abdalla 1993). From 1995 onward, Ikhwan activists, student leaders, and members of parliament were systematically arrested, intimidated, detained, and tortured. In addition, journalists and human rights activists were increasingly brought before court and trialed. In 1999 government passed a law that decreed that all NGO-type organizations had to reapply for a license to operate legally in Egypt. NGOs that engaged in political activities were banned (Mitchell 1999, 456).

The ruling stratum presented its coercive political project as an anti-Islamist alliance in order to: firstly, incorporate Western governments and enfeebled domestic nationalist, liberal, and leftist intellectuals in its hegemony; and secondly, restrict the capacity of the Muslim Brotherhood and radical Islamists to wage opposition. Jihadist organizations such as al-Gama'a al-Islamiyya had clear political goals. From the 1990s onward, the Islamic Group opposed "[...] the rise in land rents, political corruption, the extension of the state of emergency and infringement of human rights" (Meijer 2009b, 207). In order to fight and weaken the state, the organization mainly targeted military personnel, civil servants, police, and tourists. From 1992 to 1997 al-Gama'a and the state were involved in a small civil war in Middle Egypt that claimed 1,500 lives (Meijer 2009b, 207).[5]

---

5 During this decade, 'domestic' jihadist movements such as al-Gama'a al-Islamiyya became estranged from the 'global' jihadist organizations such as al-Jihad. The failure of overthrowing their own national governments led global jihadists to attack foreign targets such as the World Trade Center in 1993. Attacking imperialism 'directly' was seen as a shortcut to the fall of the 'comprador' régimes in their homelands. The emergence of global jihadism allowed the Mubarak régime to connect its own struggle against the Islamists with the national and geopolitical security concerns of Western states.

The terrorist acts of the Islamic Group provoked and provided a justification for a violent and authoritarian reaction of the state, which extended far beyond the repression of jihadist cells. The Egyptian 'war on terror' granted Mubarak's neoliberal policies a solid foundation from which to go on the offensive and restrict the civil and the political rights of the whole population (Khalil 2012, 24). In the cities, the ashwaiyyat were overrun by the CSF and brought back under control of the state, e.g. Imbaba and Ayn Shams in 1992 and 1998.[6]

The anti-Islamist[7] transformism of the régime was built around the concept of the 'lesser evil', and only absorbed fractions of the political opposition, especially leaders of Tagammu and the ECP. The rationale behind the liberal and socialist anti-Islamist stance was that, despite their sometime 'civil' and 'democratic' rhetoric, the Ikhwan were, because of their essential nature as 'Islamic fascists', fundamentally opposed to a genuine secular, liberal democratic system. The Brotherhood's pro-democratic stance was an element of a 'double discourse' that hid a real agenda of the establishment of a theocratic state (Al-Ghobashy 2005, 374). Even more so than the Mubarak régime, which at least preserved some elements of a secular and civil state, Islamism was a reactionary force, as the historical experiences of Saudi Arabia, Sudan, and Iran clearly illustrated. The intimidation and censorship of secular and leftist intellectuals by Islamists, and the assassination of Farag Foda in 1992, reinforced the perception that secularism itself was under siege by Islamism. Because the left was weak, it could not stand up against Islamism but in an alliance with the régime – an idea that had been a minority position within the left throughout the 1980s (Flores 1993, 38).

This line of thought produced a 'secular alliance' against the Ikhwan between, on the one hand, some Tagammu, Communist, liberal, and nationalist leaders and intellectuals, and, on the other, the Mubarak state (Naguib 2009, 170). For example, secular leftists supported the repressive 1993 Unified Law that granted government the power to intervene in the elections of the professional associations in order to curb the power of the Ikhwan (Abdelrahman 2009, 41–42). The government, for its part, integrated secular intellectuals into its project by (re)building and (re)financing cultural institutions such as the Cairo

---

6 By the late 1990s, Islamist guerrillaism was defeated. Despite the spectacular 'event' of 9/11, as a movement, jihadism was on the retreat in Egypt in the 2000s. Terrorist organizations such as al-Gama'a al-Islamiyya laid down their arms, renounced the use of violence, turned to reformism, and tried to set up a political party (Bayat 2011).

7 To complicate matters, the régime also continued to deploy a politics of attraction and repulsion, of inclusion and exclusion, vis-à-vis the Brotherhood. For example, in the 2000s, Brotherhood victories in the parliamentary elections of 2000 and 2005 were a mediated outcome of the Society's real electoral strength and the régime's maneuvering to portray itself as the only real 'secular' alternative to Islamist rule (Springborg 2009, 14).

Book Fair,[8] the Cairo Opera, and the Alexandria Library, and by opening up new money streams and platforms for writers and artists: "Thus, within a decade, the state went from being one of the chief obstacles to cultural production, to one of its chief protectors and subsidizers" (Colla 2011). The 'real' war against the Islamists was articulated in the domain of cultural politics, with secular intellectuals and parties playing the part of the state's enlightened allies against the dark forces of religious reaction. This alliance between régime and 'secular' forces against Islamism would resurface during Muhammad Morsi's bid for presidency in 2012.

Subordinating the Elites

Since the 1970s, the political autonomy, power, and influence of the armed forces within the Egyptian historical bloc had decreased. Through military aid, the USA helped to transform the armed forces in a docile, stable, and reliable state structure that functioned as its own guardian of the status quo.[9] However, even though the generals were financially and militarily tied to the USA, their historical consciousness was that of a 'national capitalist' class, which turned the rentier relation of dependence into a feeling of deep resentment towards their foreign donors (Amar 2012, Kandil 2011).

Moreover, the position of the military in Egyptian society was crumbling, while the NDP and the interior ministry emerged as the primary sources of state power (Kandil 2011).[10] In contradistinction to the armed forces, the CSF and its plainclothes counterpart were an apolitical, disloyal, and undisciplined force. Because

---

8   During the 1993 Cairo Book Fair, president Mubarak claimed that he aimed "to spare Egypt the fate of Algeria," where a civil war raged between the secular military forces and militants of the Front Islamique du Salut (FIS) (in Abdalla 1993, 29).
9   Interview with Sabry Zaky, Cairo, 10 March 2011.
10 At the eve of the 25 January Revolution, the interior ministry controlled all aspects of law enforcement, criminal investigations and repression through its various departments: State Security Investigations Service (SSI), Public Security, Municipal Police, Special Police, General Security and Central Security Forces (CSF), Traffic Police, Tourism and Antiquities Police, and so on. The hated SSI or Amn al-Dawla, counting some 3,000 officers (Kandil 2011), infiltrated, controlled, and terrorized political opposition groups and thus constituted the first line of defense of the state, preventing protest movements rather than containing them. When political or social protest did emerge, the CSF was mobilized to quickly and brutally subdue it. After the assassination of Sadat the number of CSF troops grew to 100,000 consisting mostly of conscripts who failed the standards for military conscription. The CSF uprising of 1986 called the armed forces back into the streets, showing that the military pillar of al-nizam was not completely eroded. Yet by the 2000s the number of CSF

of its low morale and morality, this blunt instrument was only effective if it could be mobilized in great numbers, surrounding and overrunning any opposition (Khalil 2012, 39). Failure to execute this simple tactic would result in demoralization and retreat, as would happen on 28 January 2011 during the uprising. Apart from the direct and centrally coordinated repression by the SSI and CSF, the terror through which the state governed was also rooted in everyday, decentralized, and local forms of violence. Police forces engaged in independent activities of exploitation, oppression, and domination of ordinary civilians, drug running, the organizing of protection rackets and other criminal activities (Amar 2012).

The armed forces were appalled by the shameful brutality and violence of the police forces, which had superseded the military as the main coercive force in Egyptian society. Moreover, in the 1990s and 2000s their economic power was overshadowed by the rise of the neoliberal capitalists surrounding the president's son Gamal Mubarak, who were perceived by the generals as 'crony capitalists' and greedy plunderers of the nation's wealth. Hazem Kandil emphasized that the economic profits of the armed forces were modest compared to those of the 'civil' state elites:

> [...] they were given projects that would provide profits which could fund a decent life for officers: a car, a flat, a vacation house, and so on. But this is no economic empire on the scale the Turkish army has built up, for example. It is a much more modest enterprise. Military facilities are quite shabby compared with what is on offer in the wealthy districts of Cairo. Officers have not grossly enriched themselves. What you gain in the army or air force pales in comparison to what you can get as a senior police officer or member of the ruling party. Under Mubarak, the Minister of the Interior stashed over $1 billion in his bank account. The Minister of Defence could not dream of that kind of money.
> KANDIL 2011

In the end the exclusion and subordination of traditional ruling class fractions, the increasing reliance on direct domination instead of political, cultural, or economic leadership, and only a limited transformism of political opposition forces, provoked a growing resistance from subaltern subjects.

---

conscripts had increased to 300,000 à 350,000, rivaling the number of military troops, and acting as Mubarak's private army (Amar 2012). The *Amn al-Markazi* was equipped with APCs, rubber bullets, water cannons, and tear gas canisters. From the end of the 1980s onwards, the CSF enjoyed the back-up of informal plainclothes police, or *baltageyya*: "[...] *a million and a half* [...] *hired thugs or informers without uniform or ranks, often people with a criminal record who had cut deals with the authorities*" (Kandil 2011).

CHAPTER 17

The Civildemocratic Project

The neoliberal war of movement of the 1990s and 2000s forcefully reconfigured the economic structure and class alliances of the post populist bloc along even stronger authoritarian lines. In the next chapter I discuss the gradual emergence of a new left, the resurgence of street politics, and the complex relation between leftists and Muslim Brothers.

Crisis of the 'Legal Left'

The fall of the Soviet Union and the associated discrediting of socialist thought in general encouraged the Tagammu leadership to translate their tactical 'secular-democratic' turn and alliance with the régime into a new ideological framework. For the elections of 1995 the traditional Tagammu slogan of 'Freedom, Socialism, and Unity' was replaced by 'Justice, Progress, and Democracy'. The 1998 party congress stated that socialism was no longer on the agenda, and that Egypt should strive toward 'democracy' and 'independent development' (Down to Earth 2000). How 'independent development' differed from 'normal' capitalist accumulation was not clear, as the party no longer resisted privatization in principle (Seeking a New Style 1995). Rifaat al-Said cynically asked how one could defend socialism in an age of liberalization:

> Of course, we have changed – there is no party that can remain the same. For example, our first platform spoke of the consolidation and support of the public sector, then reality changed and we had to adapt, so we changed that to 'protection of the public sector'. Then we called for the 'defence' of the public sector and now that the public sector has been practically sold, we call for 'the preservation of organizations and institutions of national importance'.
> *Opposition is not About Loud Voices* 2000

State repression and the demobilization of the masses after the uprising of 1977 made Tagammu leaders look for shortcuts toward successful leftist politics. The détente during the first years of the Mubarak régime created illusions in the potential and autonomy of democratic politics on the national level. In order to operate within the boundaries of the restricted political community, the 'legal left' cut its relations with its traditional social base of workers, peasants, and students – thereby further weakening its position vis-à-vis the régime. Communist leader Salah Adli explained that:

> At the end of the eighties a number of Marxists claimed that the direction of Tagammu, which opposed the government and took the side of the poor people and workers, led to a loss of support from the middle class and the industrial productive capitalists. They claimed that Tagammu had to diminish its class policies and represent a more moderate policy, and to diminish its opposition toward the régime, so that it can use the media in a better way. But the results were devastating for Tagammu. Tagammu lost MPs, members, and support in civil society.[1]

The rise of the Islamist movements and a reluctance to 'go back to the streets', drove the leaders of Tagammu and the ECP even more into the arms of the régime. After the repression of the 1977 insurrection the prospect of mass mobilization had been greeted with cynicism from party leaders. In the 1990s and 2000s, with Islamism on the rise, it was anticipated with dread: Rifaat al-Said claimed that the Brotherhood was the only organization capable of 'controlling' a mass movement (in Farag 2007) – which revealed a lot about al-Said's paternalist pedagogy toward the masses. In 1999, for the first time, Tagammu MPs did not vote against another term for president Mubarak (Down to Earth 2000). By the year 2000, the legal left, and especially Tagammu, was but the historical remnant of the failed Prince of the second half of the 1970s. Once it had been a party of some 200,000 members, but the integration of its leaders and politics in the Mubarak postpopulist and neoliberal bloc had reduced its active cadre to a few hundreds. In 2003 an internal report admitted that the party had lost its traditional influence in the universities, professionals syndicates, and trade unions (Tagammu Gets Tougher 2003). When, in 2009, I spoke with Husayn Abd al-Razek, a leader of the old guard in Tagammu, he admitted that: "[...] for years, Tagammu took no initiatives whatsoever, people only sat in the party's headquarters and in the offices of the newspaper, discussing, not taking any action to the streets."[2]

A New Left

In a 2007 article for MERIP Egyptian blogger and leftist activist Hossam al-Hamalawy distinguished between an 'old' and a 'new' left. Egypt's new left

---

[1] Interview with Salah Adli, Cairo, 13 November 2010.
[2] Interview with Husayn Abd al-Razik, Cairo, 12 April 2009.

represented an organizational, ideological, and generational renewal.[3] From an organizational perspective, the new left was rooted in the emergence of groups such as the Revolutionary Socialists (RS) and of a leftist human rights' community. Ideologically, the new left rejected the strategy of the 'secular front' and the principal enmity of Tagammu and the ECP toward Islamism. Lastly, the new left attracted a new generation of young militants to radical politics, overcoming the gerontocracy of the fossilized parties of the 'third wave'. The roots of the new left can be traced back to the 1980s, when activists became dissatisfied with the policies of Tagammu and the ECP. For example, the disengagement of Tagammu from grassroots politics and its rapprochement with the régime led the Revolutionary Current (RC) of Michel Kamal, one of the most influential wings of the ECP, to claim that the legal left was a means for the régime to corrupt the communist movement, integrating the radical left in the democratic façade of the state consensus. The RC defected from the ECP in 1989 to form the small People's Socialist Party.

A more important force on the Left were the RS. At the end of the 1980s a group of young Marxists set up a reading group, criticizing the Stalinist traditions of the Egyptian communist movement. This informal political circle was in 1991 formally established as the RS, using the trade union elections as a jump board.[4] In 1995 they established the Center for Socialist Studies in Giza, which became their legal front.[5] In the same period there was a discussion and subsequently a split in the organization, regarding the question of open work. A part of the RS argued that it was not yet the time for open work in the streets and that the group should focus on propaganda and producing its newspaper. This faction split and established itself as *Tahrir al-'Umal* (Workers' Liberation) around the paper *Sharara* (Spark).[6]

In an interview I conducted in 2009 with Baho Abdul, a member of the RS and of the *Tadamon* workers' solidarity group, she claimed that the politics of the RS differed from those of the old left on three fundamental issues: "First: our position toward the Muslim Brothers and [...] our view on anti-imperialist and anti-Zionist struggle, and the whole religion debate. Second: the question of reform or revolution, trying to push for change from below or above. Third:

---

3 The Egyptian new left should not be confused with the New Left of the 1960s and 1970s. Here the category merely serves as a marker to distinguish a variety of movements, individuals, methods, and ideas from older traditions and parties.
4 Interview with Mustafa Bassiouny, Giza, 12 October 2010; Interview with Gihan Shabeen, Cairo, 16 March 2011.
5 Interview with Mustafa Bassiouny, Giza, 12 October 2010.
6 Interview with Wael Tawfiq, Cairo, 7 October 2010; Interview with Gihan Shabeen, Cario, 16 March 2011.

the question of how to pursue development."[7] The ideology, tactics, and strategy of the RS constituted a critique of the Stalinist traditions of the Egyptian communist movement – a critique that was strongly influenced by the ideas of the British Socialist Workers' Party (SWP). Firstly, they rejected a stagist perspective on the (post)colonial revolution in favor of Trotsky's concept of permanent revolution.[8] Secondly, against the 'dead mass parties' of the legal left, they advanced the Leninist notion of an active and vibrant vanguard party that played a directive role vis-à-vis the subaltern classes. Thirdly, from the reading of Chris Harman's (1994) "The Prophet and the Proletariat," they derived the idea that the cultural and regional context of Egypt necessitated a tactical alliance with Islamist youth around a shared anti-imperialism, in order to win these layers for the socialist project.

The rapprochement between Tagammu leaders and the Mubarak régime also alienated Nasserists and leftist nationalists from the legal Left. In 1992 they split from Tagammu and founded the Arab Democratic Nasserist Party (ADNP). In 1996 a group led by Hamdeen Sabahi left the ADNP, establishing the *Karama* (Dignity) party. In contradistinction to the ADNP, al-Karama explicitly and unambiguously advocated political pluralism and civil democracy: "We are socialist but we also believe in democracy."[9] Al-Karama oriented itself to street politics and participated in alliances with other political forces against the government.

Other communists and leftists withdrew from the political arena altogether and engaged with movements from below through NGO-type organizations. Yussef Darwish and Kamal Abbas, for example, established in 1991 the Helwan-based Centre for Trade Union and Workers' Services (CTUWS), focusing on offering services, solidarity campaigns and education to workers (Beinin and Hamalawy 2007b). Within a few years the CTUWS was also active in other industrial areas, such as 10 Ramadan City, Mahalla, and Nag Hammadi. The foundation of the CTUWS anticipated the rise of civildemocratic NGOs and human rights centers in the 1990s, of which the Hisham Mubarak Law Center (HMLC) was one of the most influential. HMLC was established in 1999 to defend the rights of workers and political activists. The center offered legal advice, contacts with the media and support in court cases, as well as organizing seminars to raise awareness among workers of their labor rights. In the 2000s the center's Cairo offices would host meetings of political committees,

---

7 Interview with Baho Abdul, Cairo 10 May 2009.
8 Cf. Chapter 10.
9 Interview with Tareq Said, Cairo, 11 November 2010.

movements and parties, such as 6 April and Tadamon, thereby becoming a hub of the democratic opposition in the next decade.[10]

In Hossam al-Hamalawy's narrative, the novelty of the new left resided in its innovative ideas, fresh generation, and new organizations. While this is certainly true, one should be careful not to simply equate the membership of the relatively new organizations – such as the RS and HMLC – with the new left, and the rank and file of traditional parties – such as Tagammu and the ECP – with the old left. Throughout my fieldwork I met with young and revolutionary militants of Tagammu and the ECP who were highly critical of their leaders. Conversely, new parties, such as the 'Democratic Left', and many of the human rights organizations, defended a clear reformist and liberal-democratic agenda. Although the RS drew upon a new generation of leftist students from the 1980s and 1990s to form the core of their organization, they also forged alliances with workers and independent leftists from the 'older' generation of the 1960s and 1970s. Conversely, Tagammu and the ECP – parties where power was firmly in the hands of a pro-régime gerontocracy – still attracted layers of youth who engaged with the emerging street politics of the 2000s. Simply put, there was also a (limited) new left in the old left. What ultimately separated the 'new leftists' from the 'old leftists' was an engagement with street politics. The reconfiguration of small leftist forces in the 1990s planted the seeds for a new left, but activists remained largely isolated from the subaltern masses. The real turning point for a resurgence of Egyptian 'politics from below' came with the Second Palestinian Intifada in the fall of 2000.

Rise of Street Politics

In 2000 students organized massive demonstrations in Cairo in support of the plight of the Palestinians – collective actions 'from below' that ended two decades of political demobilization. Independent activists and some twenty NGOs established the Egyptian Popular Committee in Solidarity with the Palestinian Intifada (EPCSPI) (Howeidy 2005). Even though the foundation of the EPCSPI was a leftist initiative, it attracted Nasserist and Islamist activists who joined as individuals or as representatives from parties, syndicates, or NGOs. The second half of the 1990s had seen an increasing cooperation between leftist, Nasserist and Islamist groups at a grassroots level, especially in the Cairo and Ayn Shams universities. This cooperation tended to arise around

---

10   Interview with Khaled Ali, Cairo, 13 October 2010; Interview with Osama Muhammad Khalil, Cairo 13 October 2010.

a shared anti-imperialist and anti-Zionist agenda (Abdelrahman 2009, 42; Schewdler and Clark 2006, 10). This experience led a majority of RS leaders to advocate a broad front of 'anti-imperialist' forces, involving not only socialists and communists, but also Nasserists and Islamists. A minority supported a united front that was only composed of leftist forces, excluding the Ikhwan and other Islamist groups.[11]

The EPCSPI organized solidarity demonstrations in Cairo and all major universities, convoys and relief campaigns, and a boycott of Israeli and Western commodities. The EPCSPI became a social and political network that, under pressure of international and domestic events, spawned new movements. It also became a platform for political discussion, coordination and cooperation between leftist, Nasserist, and Islamist activists (Abdelrahman 2009, 42–44). From March to September 2001 the EPCSPI organized sit-ins and hunger strikes in support of the Intifada and a demonstration in Tahrir Square to condemn USA support for Israel. Atrocities against Palestinians in April and May 2002 triggered new student demonstrations in Egyptian universities and a large rally was held in front of Cairo University. When students marched to the Israeli embassy, Central Security Forces (CSF) violently intervened. On 14 October Muhammad Hassanein Heikal openly condemned the 'dynastic succession' that was being prepared, grooming Mubarak's son Gamal for the presidency (Howeidy 2005).

The war in Afghanistan in 2001 and the looming intervention in Iraq gave a new impetus to the development of the existing solidarity collaborations. On 18 and 19 December the first conference against imperialist war and Zionist occupation was held in Cairo; an event that gathered a broad coalition of leftists, nationalists, and Islamists. In January and February 2003 small rallies in Cairo and other cities protested against the preparations for war against Iraq. The military intervention in Iraq was greeted on 20 and 21 March with 20,000 Egyptians occupying Tahrir Square, giving birth to the 20 March Movement (Schwedler and Clark 2006, 10). This rally saliently signaled the return of mass politics in Egypt (Abdelrahman 2009, 43).

Over the course of the following months, the anti-war and Palestinian solidarity movement began to tackle domestic issues. The third anniversary of the Second Palestinian Intifada on 27 and 28 September was transformed into a protest against the government (Howeidy 2005). The Second Cairo Conference in December emphasized the connection between the Mubarak government, US imperialism, and Zionism. For the first time the Brotherhood formally participated as an organization (Abdelrahman 2009, 43–44). In September 2004,

---

11   Interview with Wael Tawfiq, Cairo, 7 October 2010.

the 20 March Movement, the Muslim Brotherhood, the ECP, al-Karama, HMLC, and other organizations established the Popular Movement for Change with the slogan of free and democratic presidential elections. On 12 December the Popular Movement organized the first explicit anti-Mubarak demonstration with the central slogan of free and democratic presidential elections. Although it mobilized only 300 to 400 activists, at the time the event constituted a landmark in Egyptian street politics for its bold criticism of the president (Howeidy 2005).[12]

On 21 February 2005 Kefaya (Enough) was established as a unitary movement of existing committees and campaigns. During the Cairo International Book Fair a second anti-Mubarak demonstration took place. In March the Muslim Brotherhood organized a separate rally demanding political reform. In April judges and university professors followed suit. The month of May saw the emergence of the Youth for Change and Workers for Change – Kefaya offshoots that addressed social issues such as unemployment, housing and the need for independent trade unions. In June, the Writers for Change, Journalists for Change and Doctors for Change followed (Howeidy 2005).

Meanwhile, the Mubarak régime began to take the movement seriously. At the beginning of the 2000s the government had cautiously supported the Palestinian solidarity campaign and attempted to co-opt the movement. As the protests grew in numbers and their goal shifted toward a criticism of domestic policies and the 'dynastic succession' issue, the régime felt increasingly threatened by the movement which, because of its spontaneity and hybrid political constituency, appeared as a "vague multi-headed monster" (Abdelrahman 2009, 50–51). CSF arrested hundreds of protesters and Muslim Brotherhood members and violently repressed the peaceful Kefaya demonstration of 25 May. On 4 June, former ministers and public figures close to the régime established the National Coalition for Democratic Change as a means to create a 'bridge' between the régime and the opposition movement and absorb its most moderate elements. These diversionary tactics did not pacify the movement: on the contrary, on 8 June Kefaya organized a 2000 strong demonstration in memory of Saad Zaghlul, founder of the Wafd and symbol of the 1919 revolution (Howeidy 2005).

The new left played a crucial role in the building and direction of the emerging movement. Gihan Shabeen remembered that: "We were noticeable, we were young [...] we are not so young now, but we were young, compared to other leftists, and we were active. We loved to work in the streets."[13] However,

---

12 Interview with Ahmed Shabeen, Cairo, 13 March 2008.
13 Interview with Gihan Shabeen, Cairo, 16 March 2011.

the scale and spontaneous dimension of the movement on the one hand and the participation of liberal, nationalist, and Islamist forces on the other, implied that the activity of 'street politics' constituted a space for political collaboration, rather than a simple instrument of leftist politics. Moreover, the new left not only shaped the movement, but it was itself transformed by the developing activity of demonstration.

In Tagammu, for example, there emerged a clear divide between, on the one hand, the politics of the national leadership, which did not engage in grassroots politics, but instead dominated Tagammu's representation in the media and in Parliament; and, on the other, the leaders of local branches, who often participated in the struggles and movements from below. Within the branches the political authority of directive intellectuals was not determined by their formal party position, but by their level of militancy and engagement in local struggles. Furthermore, much like in the Muslim Brotherhood and other organizations, generational conflict was added to the ideological and organizational disagreements. The Tagammu and ECP party leadership consisted of mostly elderly cadres who had led the communist movement in the 1950s, 1960s and, at best, the 1970s, and now blocked the youth's access to functions and positions within the party.[14] For grassroots activists and leaders in Tagammu, the main strategic question was whether to remain in the party and fight the 'formal' leadership of 'deep entryist'[15] ECP[16] members for control over the party's apparatus or leave the legal left and support the creation of an alternative, organic counterhegemonic apparatus. Throughout the 1990s and 2000s many capable leaders, such as Mustafa Bassiouny and Saud Omar, left the party to join other leftist formations. They argued that they better invested their energy and time in a new political project that was actively engaged with grassroots struggles, than in endless factional infighting in the dusty offices of Tagammu. Other militants argued that, despite its bureaucratic pathology, Tagammu still retained important traditions of struggle, a position within the collective memory of the workers' movement as the 'house of the left', a structure as a national leftist party with branches in the whole country, a material legacy of offices, meeting rooms, and so on. For these activists, the rise of the

---

14   Conversation with Ahmed Belal, Mahalla, 20 May, 2009; interview with Abd al-Nasser Ibrahim, Cairo, 22 May 2009; interview with Ahmed Belal, Cairo, 9 October 2010.
15   'Deep entryism' is the secret entry of a political faction into another party, as opposed to 'open' entryism.
16   Interview with Ahmed Belal, Cairo, 9 October 2010; interview with Husayn Abd al-Razik, Cairo, 25 October 2010.

civildemocratic and workers' movement was an opportunity to reactivate a 'practico-inert' field of the left.[17]

Brothers and Comrades

Even though secular leftists played an important role in initiating the first Palestinian solidarity campaigns, anti-war rallies, and Kefaya protests, it was the Muslim Brotherhood that was willing and able to mobilize thousands of people in the streets (Naguib 2009, 155). The Society mobilized support for the Palestinian Intifada, boasting strong ties with Hamas, and against the Gulf War of 1991. These actions indicated a growing political independence of the Brotherhood's leaders from Saudi Arabia and the Gulf States.

The state's offensive against Islamism forced the Brotherhood to start building a coalition of its own. In 1994 Ikhwan members visited the 82-year-old Nobel Prize winner Naguib Mahfouz after he was brutally stabbed by radical Islamists. This signaled the beginning of a rapprochement between Brothers and non-Islamist opposition forces. The political basis for a front between Islamists and Leftists was anti-imperialism – even though they often had a different view on the content of the concept – and the struggle for civil and human rights. The 'anti-imperialism' of the Ikhwan was not framed as a political-economic critique, but as a cultural-religious clash of civilizations between Islam and the West. Moreover, in order to evade a confrontation with the régime, the complicity of the Egyptian government in the Palestinian and Iraqi cases was often downplayed (Naguib 2009, 169). After the invasion of Iraq, the Brotherhood even organized a joint rally of 'national unity' with the NDP against foreign aggression (al-Ghobashy 2005, 389).

Repression of its activists and politicians moved the demand for democracy and civil rights to the forefront of the Society's political agenda (Naguib 2009, 170). The Brothers' participation in collaborative opposition politics transformed

---

17   Interview with Abd al-Nasser Ibrahim, Cairo, 22 May 2009; Interview with Ahmed Belal, Cairo, 9 October 2010; Interview with Wael Tawfiq, Cairo, 20 October 2010. The discussion among Tagammu activists about whether to stay and fight in the party in order to transform its historical capital into a counterhegemonic apparatus, or leave the sinking ship, still endured after the 25 January Revolution. The revolution immediately prompted a sizeable group of labor activists and youth, led by Alexandria MP Abu al-Ezz al-Hariry, to leave the party and join the Socialist Popular Alliance Party (SPAP), whereas other activists such as Ahmed Belal remained in Tagammu, where they established the small radical Union for Egyptian Socialist Youth (UESY) in opposition to the leadership-dominated Union of Progressive Youth (UPY).

the moderate, 'reformist' wing of the movement into a civildemocratic actor. Reformists such as Essam al-Erian and Abd al-Moneim Abu al-Fotouh embraced a discourse of democracy, civil liberties, and human rights, and engaged in practices of cooperation and negotiation with other civil society groups and political tendencies. This process led Mona al-Ghobashy to the claim that: "Over the past quarter-century, the Society of Muslim Brothers (Ikhwan) has morphed from a highly secretive, hierarchical, antidemocratic organization led by anointed elders into a modern, multivocal political association steered by educated, savvy professionals not unlike activists of the same age in rival Egyptian parties" (Al-Ghobashy 2005, 373).[18]

Whereas the leaders of the old left saw the presence of the Muslim Brothers in the civildemocratic movement as a threat, new left activists cautiously welcomed their participation. They argued that the detained, intimidated, and tortured Ikhwan activists and leaders were as much victims of the dictatorship as their leftist, liberal, and Nasserist counterparts. Instead of being determined by an ideological essence of Islamist fascism, the political activity and consciousness of rank and file Brothers were constituted through their lived experience of, on the one hand, arbitrary state repression, and, on the other, cooperation and negotiation with other trends (al-Ghobashy 2005, 373).

Jillian Schwedler and Janine Clark distinguished between three levels of cooperation between leftists and Islamists: tactical, strategic, and ideational. Their analysis is compatible with a project approach. *Tactics* represents basic cooperation in the sense of "[...] joint activities on an issue-by-issue and short-term basis" (Schwedler and Clark 2006, 10). Tactical cooperation does not require ideological justification. Cooperation happens purely on the level of mobilization: it is the collaboration of two distinct subjects. In this sense, the demonstration, as the cell-form of the national-popular subject, starts as a 'tactical' project. *Strategic* cooperation, on the other hand, necessitates a political rationale. The "[...] engagement is sustained and encompassing of multiple issues" (Schwedler and Clark 2006, 10), but this does not mean that there is a shared worldview or concept of their joint activity. Cooperation shifts to the domain of more or less stable, shared, organizational forms, such as committees.

---

18 However, the reformists faced stiff competition from the traditionalist, conservative factions. Whereas the reformists occupied the 'external' positions of the movement as members of parliament, spokesmen, leaders in the professional syndicates, negotiators with other factions of the civildemocratic movement, and so on, the conservatives continued to dominate most 'internal' positions of power, especially the Guidance Bureau. In the wake of the 25 January Revolution reformist figures such as Abd al-Moneim Abu al-Fotouh came into conflict with the conservative leaders, and split from the Brotherhood.

Shared participation in demonstrations becomes a movement. The collaboration between subjects becomes stabilized and structured. Joint activity becomes a *system* of activity. Finally, *ideational* or high-level cooperation "[...] is when groups remain distinct entities but strive to develop a collective vision for political, social, and economic reform" (Schwedler and Clark 2006, 10). Ideational cooperation takes place when the activity-system develops its own immanent goals and a shared concept of its joint activity. Collaboration between subjects becomes a subject in its own right.

Tactical and strategic forms of collaboration between Ikhwan and leftists could be found among all participants in the civildemocratic movement, even within the ranks of the 'secular' old left. For example, the Tagammu offices in Cairo hosted the meetings of a 'trans-party' labor committee, in which Muslim Brothers such as Yosri Bayumi participated.[19] Of all leftist forces, the RS developed the most profound engagement with Islamism and especially the Muslim Brotherhood. The RS condemned the 'sectarian attitude' of the 'anti-religious left', and accused Tagammu and ECP leaders of alienating the radicalizing Muslim youth by its principal stand on secularism – thus driving them into the arms of the Brotherhood. Contrariwise to the old left, the RS did not see Islamism as an inherently fascist force, but as a confused anti-imperialist movement that could be reoriented to a project of socialism. The left had to side with the Islamists when their democratic rights were attacked by the capitalist state. Following Chris Harman, this tactical stance was summarized in the slogan: "With the Islamists sometimes, with the state never" (cf. Harman 1994).

Harman had advanced leftist-Islamist collaboration in a decade when the left in the Islamic world – and in the global community at large – was on the retreat. "The Prophet and the Proletariat" was written for leftists who were looking for ways to connect with militant youth in conditions that were unfavorable for socialist thought. In Egyptian civil society, the weak Egyptian left was confronted with a formidable Islamic movement that constituted an obstacle for its own development. Leftists could not simply ignore politicized Islam, but they were too feeble to overcome the obstacle on their own: they either had to rally the support of other forces – such as progressive liberals or the state – in order to vanquish it; or engage with it in a collaborative way in order to absorb it. Furthermore, Harman devised leftist-Islamist collaboration primarily in terms of a 'united front from below'[20]: as a rapprochement between leftists and radicalized Islamic youth.

---

19 Interview with Talal Shukr, Cairo, 21 April 2009.
20 The concept of the "united front" has a long history in Marxist politics. In general, it points towards the tactical or strategic alliance between workers and other subaltern

The orientation of the RS towards the Islamic youth was realized in terms of a united 'anti-imperialist' and 'democratic' front from below *and* above. The united front 'from below' was achieved by struggling together: by supporting solidarity campaigns against the detainment and torture of Islamist activists by the state; by sharing prison cells with Muslim Brothers; and by encouraging individual Brotherhood members to participate in demonstrations, strikes, and other forms of collective action and street protest. Throughout the 2000s, the united front 'from above' with the Muslim Brotherhood and the Amal party was established through 'tactical' and 'strategic' forms of cooperation: jointly organized demonstrations; the Cairo Conferences; and the establishment of the Free Student Unions, which consisted of members of the RS, Muslim Brother students and independent leftists.

In their fervor to correct the sectarian attitude of the 'anti-religious' Left, the RS seemed to have bent the stick too much to the other side, focusing on the united front 'from above' instead of 'from below'. Baho Abdul of the RS admitted: "[...] The original idea was to join the Muslim Brothers in their actions and criticize them. In practice, however, there has been too little criticism."[21] Harman's 'defensive' strategy of leftist-Islamist collaboration was applied most vigorously by the RS in a decade that finally saw the resurrection of grassroots politics in which leftist ideas and modes of struggle could thrive. To the consternation of other leftist forces and rank and file revolutionary socialists, the RS leadership would even continue its 'critical support' for the Brotherhood in the post-25 January presidential elections of 2012 during the run-off between the Ikhwan candidate Muhammad Morsi and establishment favorite Ahmed Shafiq. The RS called for leftist support for the conservative bourgeois leadership of the Ikhwan against the 'bigger evil' of 'anti-bourgeois military dictatorship' (cf. Revolutionary Socialists' Statement 2012). Likewise, Tagammu leaders continued their 'secular front' to the extreme of supporting the former régime presidential candidate Ahmed Shafiq against the 'bigger' evil of reactionary Islamism.

There was a political paradox in the attitudes of both the old and new left toward the Muslim Brotherhood. The negative stance of traditional 'third wave' leftists toward the Muslim Brothers was a cynical self-fulfilling prophecy. By condemning the entire Islamist movement as Islamofascist or reactionary,

---

groups, and the attitude of the proletarian vanguard vis-à-vis reformist class organizations and their members. A 'united front from below' is the creation of alliances and connections with members of a subaltern group at the grassroots level, ignoring the formal structures which already organize it. A 'united front from above' entails a formal coalition between organizations.

21 Interview with Baho Abdul, Cairo, 10 May 2009.

they weakened the legitimacy of Ikhwan reformist tendencies and strengthened the position of the conservatives and radicals. At the same time, the political and economic demands and ideology of the legal left and the Brotherhood much more resembled one another than those of the Brotherhood and the RS. Both the old left and the Ikhwan were in favor of 'honest' privatizations, a merely guiding role for the state in a free market economy, improved labor and civil rights, and liberal democracy. Tagammu's 'secular front' was of great service for the state as it prevented the coalescence of two opposition movements that shared a surprisingly similar political and economic outlook.

Unlike the 'third wave' leftists, the Revolutionary Socialists radically rejected the notion of a 'progressive bourgeoisie' and stage theory in a colonial or postcolonial context. Educated in the perspective of permanent revolution, they stressed the capacity of the working class to lead the Egyptian masses in its struggle against imperialism. Because of the class nature of the workers' movement, a fight for democracy and national sovereignty conducted under proletarian hegemony would take on socialistic aspects.

However, up until the Mahalla strikes, the united front tactics of the RS were *not* primarily oriented towards the existing workers' movement. Priority was given to the building of anti-imperialist and subsequently civildemocratic coalitions. The collaborations between the RS and the Brotherhood were not based on the class interests and mobilization of the workers' movement, but on civildemocratic demands – which were shared by secular rightwing parties such as Wafd or *Ghad*. Furthermore, through a focus on the defense of civil, human, and cultural rights – e.g., via solidarity campaigns against torture and in favor of the right to wear the headscarf on university campuses – the RS instructed the Islamic youth it sought to attract not as a solidary ally of the workers' movement, but as a culturally embedded civildemocratic subject.

In a way, from the 1990s onward, both the old and new left sought ways to develop forms of political activity in the context of a more or less passive, economic-corporate working class and a restricted civil society. Because of the relative strength of Islamism – and especially the Ikhwan – as an oppositional force in civil society and grassroots politics, the ideological and tactical attitude of leftists towards the Brotherhood became a central point in the development of leftist politics and subjectivities. Islamism mediated the politics of both the old and the new left. Even though leftists differed in their analyses of the nature of the régime, of the role of the party, of strategy, of imperialism, of the working class, and so on, throughout the 2000s they shared an engagement with the Islamist problematic. The two tendencies equally established fronts with bourgeois forces in order to expand their influence. The 'secular' as well as the 'anti-imperialist' fronts derived their rationale from non-class politics, and primarily revolved around civildemocratic rights. They were *popular* rather than *united* fronts.²² Leftist struggles only fortified the political line of development and did not sufficiently stimulate its entwinement with the economic field. Nevertheless, whereas, in general the old left leaders turned away from grassroots movements, pursuing a front 'from above' with the state and liberal secular parties, the new left engaged with street politics, planting the seeds of a national-popular movement.

The End of the Political Line

Kefaya had galvanized layers of the urban youth and created a momentum for contentious politics. Young and militant members of the Muslim Brotherhood were increasingly engaged with the civildemocratic movement, collaborating with activists from the new left, dissidents from Tagammu and the ECP, and progressive journalists from al-Badil, al-Shorouk, al-Dostour, al-Masry Al-Yawm, and so on. The rise of internet activism further encouraged political discussion, the dissemination of information, and the mobilization of protest groups (Hirschkind 2011b).

The development of Egyptian street politics saliently illustrates the formation of the national-popular subject from the activity of the demonstration. Even though the initial goal of the demonstrations was the recognition of and solidarity toward the Palestinians by the Egyptian people, the experience of real collaboration of ordinary Egyptians in the streets and of the violent confrontation with 'their' state, turned this exteriorly-oriented subjectivity inward, revealing the concrete content of the abstract concept of the 'people'. The demonstration developed along its political line into a broad oppositional project that emphasized democracy and civil and human rights. The activists and networks that emerged from this civildemocratic movement would eventually become the organizers of the first, small-scale demonstrations on 25 January 2011, which turned into a nationwide popular revolution (Joya 2011, 369). The poet Abd al-Rahman Yussef, son of the preacher Yussef al-Qaradawi and campaign leader of Muhammad al-Baradei,²³ claimed that the civildemocratic

---

22 As the popular fronts between communists, nationalists, and liberals in France and Spain during the 1930s.

23 The Egyptian lawyer and diplomat Muhammad al-Baradei served as the Director of the International Atomic Energy Agency (IAEA) from 1997 to 2009. In February 2010 he founded the National Association for Change (NAC), a campaign that attracted especially young urban middle-class activists, and which continued the demands of the Kefaya movement.

movement of the 2000s also laid the spiritual and intellectual foundations of the 25 January Revolution:

> We are talking about the spirit of the revolution. In the revolution a lot of different forces and ideas came together. It was not only a political issue, but also a humanist and ideological protest. The words of writers and poets had a big role in charging people with emotions and ideological ideas. The Egyptian revolution is the result of a long struggle, prepared by writers, poets and political activists. The revolution is about rejection, how to learn to say no. This rejection has been part of organized writers' opposition since the formation of Kefaya. This helped the political and trade union movements.[24]

Yet in 2006 Kefaya appeared to be far from the spiritual and activist spark that would ignite a revolution some five years later. Firstly, the régime itself changed the constitution so that the president could be elected directly, preempting one of the chief demands of the civildemocratic movement. At the same time, it made sure that Mubarak would succeed himself as president. Political cartoonist Salah Abd al-Azim recalled that: "After the presidential elections, when Mubarak succeeded, the movement suffered a setback and was convinced that Gamal Mubarak would become the new president."[25] This episode in the struggle demoralized him and he became politically inactive during the following years, just as many other activists. Secondly, as a loose movement, Kefaya lacked a real directional center. It was scattered over bickering political families and prone to sectarian infighting. Thirdly, because it only expressed *political* demands, Kefaya remained largely confined to the social circles of students, intellectuals (in the classic sense), urban professionals, and other middle-class groups (Mackell 2012, 21; Naguib 2011). The project did not succeed in connecting its explicitly political, anti-Mubarak rhetoric with the economic woes of the working class, the poor, and the peasantry.[26] Kefaya spawned a number of more or less class-oriented groups, such as the 9 March Movement, the Coalition for the Defense of Health, Teachers Without a Trade Union and Doctors Without Rights; but these grassroots committees were scattered and often focused on their own particular projects. There was no concept of the historical bloc that united political and economic critiques, nor was there a reciprocal relation between the political and economic struggling that brought

---

24 Interview with Abd al-Rahman Yusuf, Cairo, 21 March 2011.
25 Interview with Salah Abd al-Azim, Cairo, 22 March 2011.
26 Interview with Medhat al-Zahed, Cairo, 8 April 2009.

the developing national-popular and proletarian subjects together in a real collaborative process. Finally, collaboration between leftists, Nasserists and Islamists, often entailed clashes, tensions and sometimes even violence (Abdelrahman 2009, 43–44). The idealized relations between 'equal partners' during the negotiation phase of the activity of political cooperation differed from the real relations of power that materialized in the concrete performance of a jointly organized demonstration, committee, or conference.

Nevertheless, the régime did not have time to rejoice in the collapse of the civildemocratic movement, as the demise of Kefaya was intersected by the rise of the workers' movement, which would pose an even greater challenge. The acceleration of the privatization and liberalization process since 2004 under PM Nazif inspired a resurgence of proletarian projects, which became the main vehicle for anti-régime protests after the collapse of Kefaya. Workers' strikes and collective actions interpellated and mobilized sections of the political Left, transforming their political practices and discourses, and creating new divides among leftists according to their attitudes toward the workers' movement.

PART 5

The Workers' Movement

CHAPTER 18

The Mahalla Strikes

The previous part investigated the emergence of a civildemocratic movement, developing the political line of the demonstration and the national-popular subject, which constituted the first pillar of the 25 January Revolution. This section engages with the second pillar: the workers' movement and the maturation of the strike into independent trade unionism. It discusses in detail the developmental dynamics, the role of intellectuals and forms of assistance, and the limits and pathologies of the movement. This chapter narrates the events of the Mahalla strikes, which played a central part in rebuilding the Egyptian workers' movement.

Ghazl al-Mahalla

The strikes of the textile workers of Ghazl al-Mahalla – the Misr Spinning and Weaving Company in the Nile Delta city of Mahalla al-Kubra – can be seen as a turning point in the sociogenesis and emancipatory struggle of the Egyptian working class since the 1980s, because of the scale, the intensity, the success, and the impact of the protests. The industrial complex in Mahalla is of economic and symbolic importance to the whole Egyptian workers movement. Ghazl al-Mahalla is the biggest factory in the whole of the Middle East, occupying 1,000 acres of land and employing some 27,000 workers. Here the 'point of production' physically coincides with the reproductive unit of labor: within the factory walls thrives a community of workers and their families, which is embedded within the town of Mahalla.

Mahalla al-Kubra was the birthplace of Egypt's modern industry, as well as its industrial working class. The national capitalist Talat Harb founded the factory in 1927 in a location close to the Delta cotton fields and near to a large reservoir of 'proletarianizable' labor, using 'indigenous' capital drawn from the newly established Bank Misr (Beinin and Lockman 1987, 275). In the 1930s it accounted for twenty percent of all Egypt's exports (Revolution Through Arab Eyes 2012). Since its foundation, Ghazl al-Mahalla has often acted as the vanguard of the working class initiating important strikes and articulating the interests of the whole Egyptian working class (Beinin and Hamalawy 2007a). Whenever Mahalla workers won an industrial victory, this led to a general upturn of industrial action in the whole of Egypt. The first real strike took place in 1938, when workers demanded a change in their work pattern from two shifts of twelve hours to three shifts of eight hours. Their actions were still framed within a nationalist subjectivity of resistance against British domination, and they tried to negotiate their rights within the boundaries of productivity and profitability of their 'national' factory (Revolution Through Arab Eyes 2012).

In 1947 workers held another strike, demanding the reinstatement of worker leaders who had demanded better working conditions. Tanks entered Mahalla to suppress the strike movement. Three workers were killed, and seventeen injured (Revolution Through Arab Eyes 2012). Even though the strike was indicative of a growing sense of solidarity among workers, its defeat paralyzed worker actions in Mahalla until 1952. Emboldened by the Free Officers coup, workers organized a strike against factory management. The strike was, however, brutally repressed by the new régime. In exchange for economic concessions, the trade union movement pledged its loyalty to Nasser, effectively preventing itself from becoming an independent political force. The colonization of the workers' movement by the Nasserist régime prevented industrial actions until 1967.[1]

After the Six Day War, the régime began to abandon its 'octroyal socialist'[2] policies. Sadat's Infitah prompted new industrial actions in Ghazl al-Mahalla. In 1975 workers returning to the factory after the October War led a strike for better working conditions: "[…] workers took over the factory […] demanding overtime pay, extension of the employment reforms to industrial workers, and improved health conditions" (Posusney 1996, 229). Worker leader Hamdi Husayn explained that the nationalist subjectivity of the previous decades was transforming into forms of class consciousness and activity:

> The most important thing about the strike of 1975 was that it was poor workers against capitalism. They entered the luxurious apartments of the engineers and they took food from the fridge. They tied the food to ropes and started waving it from the balcony to incite the other demonstrators. That's how the famous quote started: "they eat pigeons and chickens, we are tired of eating beans. And the beans are tired of us!"
>
> Revolution through Arab Eyes 2012

Mubarak continued Sadat's program of liberalization and privatization, but at a skulking pace. In 1985 and 1986 Mahalla workers protested demanding that they be paid for Fridays – their weekly day off (Posusney 1996, 225). Factory

---

[1] Cf. Chapter 13.
[2] Cf. Chapter 9.

management gave in and granted them a 30 day monthly wage (Revolution Through Arab Eyes 2012). Two years later they were back at the barricades. Mubarak had cancelled the educational allowances to workers, which prompted, within hours, some 20,000 Mahalla workers to take to the streets in order to contest the decision. Since the decision was taken at the highest political level, the workers' mode of protest was increasingly politicized as well. Hamdi Husayn recalled that: "We made a coffin draped in black cloth and with Mubarak's picture on it. We walked out on 21 September and that was the first time we shouted: 'Down with Hosni Mubarak'. That was the first time people clearly stated it" (Revolution Through Arab Eyes 2012). The strike was brutally repressed by security forces. Worker leaders were detained and lost their jobs, and/or were relocated to workplaces away from Ghazl al-Mahalla and their families. The defeat of the 1988 strike paralyzed the Mahalla workers' actions throughout the 1990s. Only in 2006 did the Mahalla workers move again in force.

On the Offensive

On 3 March 2006 Prime Minister Nazif promised all public sector manufacturing workers a raise of their annual bonus equal to a two-month wage. But in December the bonus was nowhere to be seen on the Mahalla workers' paycheck. The Ghazl al-Mahalla management and the minister of labor refused to pay out the promised bonus. Mahalla worker Amal al-Said remembered that:

> We complained to the syndicate and to the factory management. But all to no avail, so we decided to strike. We wanted increased production incentives, more food allowance, better working conditions, and the two month bonus. We closed all the mills to go on strike in Talaat Harb Square. We stayed there.
> *Revolution Through Arab Eyes* 2012

They refused their salaries and on 7 December at least 10,000 workers protested in front of the factory gates. Women workers initiated the strike:

> The men tried to convince us to go on strike. But when we walked out into the streets, they lagged behind. So I asked them why they weren't joining us in the street. They replied that they would join us after we went out first. Then a colleague shouted: where are the men? Here are the women! This irritated many men. But they laughed. The word spread and the women continued to repeat this refrain.
> *Revolution through Arab Eyes* 2012

When the security forces tried to shut down the factory the next morning, some 20,000 workers demonstrated. Their rally was joined by students and women from the urban community (Beinin and Hamalawy 2007a). After four days the strikers were victorious, gaining a 45-day bonus and a promise that the factory would not be privatized. Because the union committee delegates had attempted to thwart the strike,[3] the organic workers' leaders demanded their resignation from the General Union of Textile Workers and fair trade union elections. Between 13,000 and 15,000[4] workers from Mahalla signed the petition. When their request was ignored, some 6,000 workers quit from the GFETU (Beinin and Hamalawy 2007a).

In the last week of September 2007 the workers of Mahalla went on strike again demanding a further increase of their bonuses and food allowances, a rise of the national minimum wage to 1,200 EGP, and the resignation of the management – and they were victorious (Mackell 2012, 23). As the strike was organized in Ramadan, the workers stayed in the factory and people brought them food in the afternoon.[5] Drawing on the experience of December 2006, workers occupied the factory and established their own security force to protect the factory from a lock-out. They organized committees responsible for security and health issues, along with food provision for the strikers. Worker leader Muhammad al-Attar recollected that the strike had changed from a simple protest at the factory gate to a protracted siege with factory management and the security forces: "We set up tents and proved to the government that we could hold to our cause longer than they could to theirs" (Revolution Through Arab Eyes 2012). Much of the organization of the strike was now coordinated by Kamal Fayumi and Sayyid Habib of the Textile Workers' League, an independent trade union committee that had played a secondary role in the previous strike and which was close to the RS.[6] The strike lasted for six days and ended in a victory for the Mahalla workers, who gained a two month bonus along with extra bonuses in January and June 2008 and January 2009. Additionally, they succeeded in impeaching the trade union leaders who were too close to the régime, and in reducing factory debt by one billion EGP (Revolution Through Arab Eyes 2012).

The strike spirit also got a hold over workers in various other sectors and governorates, such as the cement industry in Tura and Helwan, Cairo subway

---

3   They were perceived as illegitimate, because of massive fraud and the exclusion of candidates during the trade union elections of 2006 (Mackell 2012, 23).
4   Or 60 percent of the Mahalla workforce, according to Kamal al-Fayumi (Mackell 2012, 23).
5   Interview with Sayyid Habib, Mahalla, 12 November 2010.
6   Interview with Hossam al-Hamalawy, Cairo, 14 May 2009.

drivers, bakers, and so on (Beinin and Hamalawy 2007a).[7] In contrast to the 1980s and 1990s, the strikes were not restricted to public sector employees, but also encouraged workers in private companies, such as Arab Polvara Spinning and Weaving in Alexandria, to struggle for their rights (Beinin 2009, 38–39).

In February 2008, once more, some 20,000 workers and citizens took the streets of Mahalla. The factory had claimed a loss of 45 million EGP, despite a capital injection of 450 million EGP. Amal al-Said angrily recalled that "It was a joke. We needed to protest [...]. We wanted to know the reason for the loss" (Revolution Through Arab Eyes 2012). The February demonstration was jointly organized by worker leaders such as Kamal Fayumi and Sayyid Habib and political activists from the new left. Protesters demanded a national minimum wage, improved living conditions, and also raised political slogans against the president and his son (al-Hamalawy 2008).

Insurrection

On 6 April 2008, leftist worker leaders and activists planned a new strike. Some political groups, bloggers and intellectuals seized the event to call for a political 'general strike' against the régime, without, however, organizing anything on the ground. Sayyid Habib recalled that:

> We invited all workers for the strike on 6 April, but some Islamic and political trends invited the people to make a general strike on this day. The biggest mistake was that they called people for strikes and they could not organize the people. In Ghazl al-Mahalla we decided to stop our strike. When people outside the factory organized an action we participated as people and not as workers. So it was a big mistake that political trends called the people to strike and at the same time not organizing the people.[8]

The Mahalla movement was not ready to challenge the state in a politicized way. The régime, for its part, was well prepared for the confrontation. Six days before the strike, worker leaders were intimidated by GFETU chairman Husayn Megawer to stop their preparations or be arrested (Mackell 2012, 25). Four days later, plainclothes policemen were called into the police station of Mahalla: they were given walkie-talkies and instructions for wreaking havoc

---

7 Interview with Muhammad Abd al-Azim, Mahalla, 12 November 2010.
8 Interview with Sayyid Habib, Mahalla, 12 November 2010.

in the city.⁹ The security forces acted with a pre-emptive lock-out, arriving in the factory before the first workers and taking over the machines (al-Hamalawy 2008). Ahmed Belal recalled that:

> [...] the violence started after Haisam al-Shami, a policeman, beat an old woman. People became angry, began to fight and threw stones at the hated Central Security troops, who retaliated with tear gas. For two days Mahalla became the arena of a violent clash between police and citizens. Three youths were killed and shops, houses, hospitals and schools were destroyed.¹⁰

The combination of repression and co-optation – the régime pledged to accede to some of the workers' demands – put pressure on the strike committee to cancel the strike. In the end, Mahalla workers and their families participated in street protests as citizens, shifting their demands to the high price of bread (Beinin 2011, 199). They were met by violence and the insurrection was quelled. While there were some symbolic solidarity actions in other cities, in general the adventurist call for a 'mass strike' was not heeded and the Mahalla uprising remained isolated.¹¹ Mahalla worker Faysal Lakusha bitterly remembered that: "When Mahalla citizens had their demonstrations on 6 April, no one in the country had a strike, no one supported them, no village or town had a strike."¹²

After the botched revolt the Mahalla movement disintegrated. Although there was much talk of the necessity of creating an independent trade union, this neoformation did not develop beyond the level of the strike committee. Concessions from factory management and the state and the threat of police repression divided the leaders and rank and file workers of Ghazl al-Mahalla over the further development of their movement (Beinin 2011, 200).¹³ Labor activist Fatma Ramadan explained that:

> The violence of 6 April only lasted for a few days, five or six, and after this the movement rose again. A lot of strikes happened. So it wasn't the violence that made the workers afraid, but it made them more organized and it gave them the knowledge of how the government would react. But the government and the labor union created new pressures through

---

9   Interview with Ahmed Belal, Cairo, 6 April 2009.
10 Interview with Ahmed Belal, Cairo, 6 April 2009.
11 Interview with Sayyid Habib, Mahalla, 12 November 2010.
12 Interview with Faysal Lakusha, Cairo, 20 October 2010.
13 Interview with Wael Tawfiq, Cairo, 16 October 2010.

firing the workers, especially the leaders. The workers see that the leaders who were in the streets have been fired now and don't have money or food and they think twice before they join a strike. That's the new system. Additionally, the economic crisis had an impact on the labor movement.[14]

With the defeat of the Mahalla uprising the whole proletarian movement lost its center and its vanguard. However, the Mahalla protests had initiated a new wave of workers' actions that did not simply subside after 6 April 2008, but it engulfed other workplaces and sectors, stimulating new demands and organizational forms. Now the shared demand of the minimum wage united the Egyptian workers' movement – at least conceptually. Moreover, the movement found a new model for struggle and organization in the form of the Real Estate Tax Authority Union (RETAU), which inspired, even before the 25 January Revolution, other movements to create their own independent trade unions.

---

14   Interview with Fatma Ramadan, Cairo, 11 October 2010.

CHAPTER 19

Development of the Strike

In the previous chapter I narrated the story of the Mahalla strikes and how it evolved from a simple sit-in to a community wide insurrection against the Mubarak régime. The next chapter analyzes the strike movement in detail, revealing the developmental logic of class formation behind the movement. Attention is paid to the systematization, interiorization, and projection of the strikes, the limits of the Mahalla movement, and the emergence of independent trade unionism.

Systematization

During the eras of the Nasserist and postpopulist historical blocs, worker actions had been guided by a moral-economic understanding of their predicament, which was expressed in a subaltern subjectivity of support for the state-led nationalist project. Workers rarely went on strike, in the classic sense of a protracted work stoppage, but instead stayed at the workplace after hours, reinforcing their symbolic position of fidelity within the patronage system. In fact, production often increased during these episodes, and it was the state that cut off electricity, water, or gas to halt the 'work-in'. In general, these protests: "[...] lasted less than 24 hours [...] The very short duration of protests curtailed opportunities for the movement to develop workers' consciousness and organisation, as well as preventing them from triggering a solidarity movement or copycat strikes in other workplaces" (Bassiouny and Omar 2008).

However, because of the neoliberal breakdown of corporatist patron-client relations, the 'work-in' tactic had become an anachronism. Neither the management nor the government was interested in working class displays of loyalty. Sabr Barakat summarized that:

> In the beginning of the work of the labor movement, the movement was infected by the paternalist control of the government: the Abd al-Nasser state was a state that granted us social rights, but blocked our freedom. After this came Sadat, who blocked our social rights *and* our freedom. Then came Mubarak, who introduced us to global capitalism.[1]

---

1 Interview with Sabr Barakat, Cairo, 16 October 2010.

The Mahalla strike of December 2006 started as a simple *action* – a sit-in in front of the factory gates – and a straightforward objective: obtaining the promised bonus. Because the management did not immediately give in to the demand, the sit-in became a work-stoppage that lasted for three days. The simple action became a prolonged activity, a project interpellated by a shared goal.[2] The realities of a protracted strike necessitated the development of new directive, technical, and discursive competences (Bassiouny and Omar 2008; al-Mahdi 2011c). This would become a pattern in the strikes against the neoliberal offensive, as Alexander elucidated:

> Strikes lasted longer, sometimes for a week or more, and thus demanded a greater and more sustained organisational commitment than disputes that were either quickly settled or crushed by the security forces. A tactical shift by the authorities who attempted to deal with most strikes by negotiation, rather than direct repression, was also highly significant as directly elected negotiators were able to gain valuable experience in representing striking workers' interests to the employers and the state.
> ALEXANDER 2012, 112

In order to solve the new problems of organization, reproduction, and negotiation, the strike activity produced its own neoformations: fresh organic intellectuals – leaders, organizers, spokesmen, writers, singers, cartoonists, and so on; and relatively stable networks and centers to direct and organize the worker actions. As the labor representatives of the GFETU were maneuvering against the strike, a spontaneous strike committee was leading the workers' struggle.[3] The factory had to be occupied by workers in order to prevent security forces of taking over the premises and continuing production. From a sit-in or demonstration, the leading activity of the strike developed into *occupation*.

The leading activity of occupation expanded and deepened the strike project. The occupying workers needed food, shelter and protection, which stirred the formation of new committees responsible for these functions (Bassiouny and Omar 2008). Demonstrations and solidarity actions were organized outside the physical space of the workplace to obtain the practical and moral support from the whole Mahalla community. As a city of working class families, Mahalla al-Kubra citizens participated spontaneously in the proletarian activity-system of the strike, thereby drawing them into a proletarian subjectivity. The

---

2 Cf. Chapter 4.
3 Interview with Sayyid Habib, Mahalla, 12 November 2010.

contingent chain of strike actions was becoming a cohesive *system* of activity with a logic of its own.

Interiorization

The success of the activity-system that sprang from the strike actions also acted as a brake on its *immediate* development. When the workers achieved their demands after four or five days of strike, the development of their strike activity and its direct objectifications obviously came to a halt. However, during and after the strike activity, its objectifications were also being *interiorized* into the fledgling worker subject.

Firstly, victory reinforced the workers' consciousness: it had been their collective will and agency as organized striking workers that had realized their demands. Objective success was translated into subjective confidence. The Mahalla workers knew that they could deploy the same kind of activity in the future to defend their interests.

Secondly, when they faced the same problems of unpaid bonuses in 2007, they did not have to begin protesting from scratch, but they could immediately import and build upon their experiences from the previous year and take the development of the system of activity to the next level. The activity-system had continued its life-process as a developing concept in the thoughts, memories, language, and discussions of the workers. Not only the practico-inert[4] *content* of the strike (expressed, for example, in slogans, songs, poems, and pamphlets) could be rapidly reactivated, but also its *form* (the detailed technical know-how of painting banners, planning meetings, and decision-making procedures). The development of the strike illustrates how 'movement' and 'institutionalization', 'living activity' and 'practico-inert' are continuously subsuming each other in the real process of the class struggle.

Fourthly, even though the strike was initiated because of a goal *external to* the activity of striking from its own life-process emerged new goals and aims. This dynamic represents the immanent development of goals from the shared collaboration, as opposed to the original direct, economic demands that constituted the project.[5] The subjectness of the workers developed in line with the formation of a concept of themselves and their predicament. The workers' everyday critique and good sense[6] of their predicament was generalized and

---

4 Cf. Chapter 9.
5 Cf. Chapter 4.
6 Cf. Chapter 7.

concretized through their strikes. A basic economic struggle for livelihoods developed into a 'higher' conflict for national labor rights, and eventually into a confrontation with al-nizam – the régime or 'system'.

The strike stimulated a 'vertical' generalization of the Mahalla worker project, evolving from workplace-bounded demands to the trade unionist objective of a national minimum wage, and eventually bordering on political critiques and goals. This conceptual development followed the logical chain of predicaments that the workers faced. The first and direct obstacle on the road was the factory's management, which exploited and disciplined them as a workforce. Second was the GFETU, 'their' trade union, which was (re)discovered as a means for the state to sabotage the strike. Third was the state security apparatus that repressed them and which revealed the contradictory relation between the state as a political and economic actor, as a defender of the 'common good' and as a capitalist or proxy for private capitalists. The good sense of the Mahalla workers was generalized and developed from a simple criticism of the corruption of the particular factory management, over a rejection of state-subordinated trade unionism, toward a political-economic critique of the general authoritarian and capitalist nature of al-nizam. More and more workers saw the GFETU, the state, and the president no longer in terms of moral-economic guardians and patrons, but as class enemies (al-Mahdi 2011c).

During the 6 April 2008 insurrection in Mahalla, posters of Mubarak were torn apart by jubilant youth (Clément 2011, 73). This episode expressed the growing connection in thought between particular forms of economic exploitation and the general political domination of the Mubarak régime,[7] or, in other words, how the workers organic, everyday concept of the class struggle began to unite the economic and political lines of development. The politicization of the strike movement worried the régime, which explains its willingness to grant economic concessions to the workers even in the context of neoliberal counterreform. An attack on the undemocratic GFETU, which traditionally mobilized the workers in pro-government rallies and elections, was perceived as a challenge towards the authoritarian régime itself (cf. Beinin 2007).

Projection

In its development from an economic-corporate level to trade unionism, the working class not only has to overcome its 'vertical' amorphousness and incohesion

---

[7] Interview with Saud Omar, Suez, 17 October 2010.

within workplaces, but also its 'horizontal' fragmentation *between* different spatial and temporal instances of struggle. The immanent goals and objectifications of the strike were not only interiorized by the Mahalla worker subject, but they were also saliently projected 'outside' the physically-bound activity-system.

Firstly, this projection was an interpellation of other workers and non-proletarian groups to assist and participate in the strike activity-system in a solidary way. Sayyid Habib recalled that: "[...] the workers at Kafr ad-Dawwar made a symbolic strike for two hours. In Shibin al-Qom also for two hours and in Giza for three hours. Other factories made statements in solidarity with us."[8] Suez labor activist Saud Omar remembered that: "We supported the Mahalla workers by statements and by organizing protests in Cairo in front of the GFETU or parliament."[9] Spontaneous actions in other workplaces and communities in solidarity with the Mahalla workers proleptically imagined a proletarian unity that was not yet institutionalized. In this manner, the spatio-temporal individuality and isolation of the Mahalla strike was overcome through its reenactment by other worker actions.

Secondly, the Mahalla experiences projected the ability for Egyptian workers *in general* to solve their economic predicament through the means of striking. Veteran worker leader Talal Shukr explained that:

> [...] in December 2006, the workers of Ghazl al-Mahalla created a great movement. They demanded a salary raise. Other workers gained hope through the Mahalla workers' victory and struck as well. They advanced the same demands: a good salary, decrease in the cost of education, etc. A good salary is necessary: it's a means to lead a decent life. In addition, the strike was an important learning experience: it showed the workers the power of a strike as an instrument.[10]

Mahalla was not only the barometer of the Egyptian class struggle, passively indicating the low and high tides of the workers' movement, but it also actively taught other workplaces about the power of strike action. The projection of the Mahalla strikes was proleptic, in the sense that it showed other instances of the workers' movement a more advanced stage of their own activity-system in development. It was this proleptic instruction that enthused other workers, first in the textile companies, then in other industrial sectors, and ultimately in the

---

8   Interview with Sayyid Habib, Mahalla, 12 November 2010.
9   Interview with Saud Omar, Suez, 17 October 2010.
10 Interview with Talal Shukr, Cairo, 21 April 2009.

proletarian 'periphery' – for example real estate tax workers, health technicians, teachers, and pensioners – to emulate the Mahalla experience (Bassiouny and Omar 2008). Faysal Lakusha asserted that: "Ghazl al-Mahalla taught a lot of different people how to strike, e.g. teachers, doctors. When our workers got their bonus and salary, all the workers benefit from it,"[11] and: "When others saw this experience they made their own strikes. The consciousness started from Mahalla."[12] By their struggles the Mahalla workers acted as teachers toward other workers, who began to use similar methods to get the same results.

Thirdly, the development of the organization and demands of the Mahalla workers did not only imagine the strike as a leading activity, but also the neoformation of independent trade unionism, even though its concrete structures and networks did not yet exist. In practice the Mahalla worker subject was "[…] already operating as an independent trade union."[13] Moreover, during their struggle, workers implicitly realized the right to assembly, protest, and free speech that the Egyptian civildemocratic movement had explicitly, yet unsuccessfully, called for.[14] Strike objectifications such as committees, mass meetings, sit-ins, and 'tent-cities' had stimulated practices of collective debate and decision making, reinforcing already existing grassroots democratic traditions among the workers (Alexander 2010). More than just a means to an end, the strike revealed to the workers the contours of an authentic democratic society, which existed in opposition to the paternalism and the dictatorship of the factory, the community, and the state. As a faint prefiguration of workers' democracy, the strike activity-system represented also an end-in-itself: living a less alienating human life.

Mahalla's Defeat

Between 2006 and 2008 the Mahalla workers constituted the vanguard of the Egyptian workers' movement, instructing and pushing forward the vertical and

---

11 Interview with Faysal Lakusha, Mahalla, 20 May 2009.
12 Interview with Faysal Lakusha, Cairo, 20 October 2010.
13 Interview with Mustafa Bassiouny, Giza, 12 October 2010.
14 "The workers' movement is a democratic power itself […] When workers organize a demonstration in Cairo, they have to occupy the streets and arrange transport for their comrades. When they want to negotiate with the minister, they have to elect delegates from the different governorates. This is an example of workers' democracy. […] Those who talk about democracy and who advance democratic demands cannot accomplish any of these demands, but the workers accomplish these demands without using any political slogan" (Interview with Hisham Fouad, Giza, 26 October 2010). Cf. Alexander 2011a, 2011b.

horizontal economic development and generalization of the worker subject, and tentatively exploring the political domain. Even though there was no direct organizational connection between the different collective actions, the Mahalla scenario was often repeated in other workplaces, revealing the universal logic of class struggle. However, at the same time there was an unevenness in the development of class consciousness and in the radicalism of the demands. While strikers in Mahalla, Kafr al-Dawwar, and Shibin al-Kum turned against their official trade union representatives, other workers were more cautious towards the GFETU – even when their syndical officials were obstructing their actions (Beinin and Hamalawy 2007a). Faysal Lakusha remembered that it was difficult to overcome the ad hoc character of solidarity and coordination in this period: "We started to coordinate, e.g. in Kafr al-Dawwar. The coordination was not so good, however. They moved after us, not with us. We have to make additional efforts to make them move with us and to coordinate the struggle."[15]

Although the February 2008 demonstration expressed the high point of the Mahalla movement, afterwards the workers' leaders were divided over the direction of the movement. Some actors advocated a deepening of the political aspect of the strikes, while others recommended caution and moderation. In addition, the state, both at the level of factory management and state security, tried to undermine the organization of the workers by giving in to some of the protesters' demands and especially by separating and alienating the organic leadership from its rank and file.[16] Mahalla strike leaders were detained, put on early retirement, or transferred to other factories.[17] Prominent worker leaders who were given a platform in the national media were accused of opportunism and seeking 'stardom'.[18]

The Mahalla strike committees had been the seed of independent trade unionism, but the 6 April 2008 strike fiasco cut right through its developmental trajectory. Yet, even though the Mahalla workers were no longer able to play a vanguard role between 2008 and 2010,[19] the prolepsis of their strike activity roused a movement towards trade unionism in other workplaces. Although these strikes were often not as salient, vast, militant or successful as the Mahalla strikes, they set in motion a process of molecular changes in the whole working class.[20] Although

---

15   Interview with Faysal Lakusha, Mahalla, 20 May 2009.
16   Interview with Wael Tawfiq, Cairo, 16 October 2010.
17   Interview with Faysal Lakusha, Cairo, 20 October 2010.
18   Interview with Wael Tawfiq, Cairo, 16 October 2010.
19   Interview with Khaled Ali, Cairo, 25 October 2010.
20   Interview with Sabr Barakat, Cairo, 16 October 2010.

the Egyptian working class was far from being a cohesive and coherent force, centrally organized on a national level, the strike became contemporaneous in the lives of many workers. By exchanging strike experiences and organizational forms, tactics and demands, concepts and critiques, workers shared the ideal and material artifacts that mediated their strike actions, without, however, engaging in a joint collaboration as such. In other words, there were different worker projects that assisted each other directly and indirectly, but there was not yet a united proletarian activity-system, despite a development in that direction.[21] This subjective predicament of spatial and temporal fragmentation could only be overcome through the generalization of shared goals and self-concepts and the formation of a directive center and trade union *apparatus*.

The First Independent Trade Union

After 2008 the development of the workers' movement was pushed forward organizationally by the formation and consolidation of the Real Estate Tax Authority Union (RETAU) and unions of teachers, health technicians and pensioners; and discursively by the formulation of the demand of an equitable national minimum wage. Whereas the Mahalla strikes had taught workers it was possible to achieve their demands through collective struggle and organization; the successful strike of the tax workers and the establishment of the RETAU demonstrated how an effective trade union leadership and apparatus could and should be built. Kamal Abu al-Eita, leader of the RETAU, summarized their experience:

> We, the tax syndicate, were the first to organize strike committees in the whole country. When we had achieved all our demands we doubled our wages from 340 EGP. We changed our leadership of the state union and of the ministry of finance, through the strike. [...] After we achieved our own demands we came to another stage in our democratic struggle. We organized a public and independent trade union containing 30 committees in the whole country. It was by agreement of all strike committees in the whole country. A successful strike brings a successful independent trade union. By using our own trade unions in the negotiations we succeeded in doubling our wages. And in July we'll achieve another doubling of wages. We have already organized a new fund for social care in the trade union to give workers a pension. It costs 1.5 million.[22]

---

21   Interview with Inas Safti, Cairo, 27 October 2010.
22   Interview with Kamal Abu al-Eita, Giza, 20 March 2011.

Kamal Abu al-Eita's story revealed the immanent development of the worker subject through the dynamic of the strike activity. Just as the Mahalla strikers, the tax workers began by contesting a purely economic demand. The experience of the strike revealed the main immediate obstacle for the workers, i.e., the state syndicate, and its solution – the independent trade union. When the tax workers began their strike they had no idea that they would be the first since 1952 to establish a nationwide trade union independent from the state.

Among Mahalla workers the victory of the RETAU was received with mixed feelings. On the one hand, they applauded the successes of their comrades in advancing the shared cause to a level that they had not yet reached themselves, but, on the other, the creation of the RETAU glaringly confronted them with their current inability to develop their own movement. Some labor activists gossiped that the régime had 'allowed' the independent RETAU, because it was situated at the periphery of the workers' movement and did not directly threaten the GFETU as a pillar of the system. For example, Abdul Kader, a Mahalla worker, claimed that the RETAU "[...] took our example, but they already succeeded [in creating an independent trade union]. Kamal Abu al-Eita, their leader openly admits this. The government knows that if the workers of Mahalla succeed in setting up an independent union the GFETU will collapse."[23] Even veteran worker activist Talal Shukr was skeptical about the RETAU victory: "This is the first time since 1952 that there's an independent union. It sets an example for other movements. At the same time it's only a show, an illusion of liberty. The government allows this union to deceive the International Labor Organization."[24] Other activists stressed, more correctly, that the real estate tax workers succeeded where the Mahalla workers failed because of the tenacity and homogeneity of the RETAU leadership and the ambivalent attitude of the state toward a frontal and violent confrontation with the national movement.[25] CTUWS director Kamal Abbas underlined that:

23 Interview with Abdul Kader, Mahalla, 20 May 2009.
24 Interview with Talal Shukr, Cairo, 21 April 2009.
25 "After the strike of 2008 in Ghazl al-Mahalla there wasn't any labor activity anymore. The reason was that there wasn't a real worker leadership there, despite what the media was telling us. In 2008 the state union leadership started to kick out the active worker leaders in Mahalla and transferred them to Cairo and Alexandria, and it was as if they killed them slowly. If there was a real leadership, the factory would have made a strike to support those who have been kicked out. If they had been a real leadership, there would have been strikes in solidarity with them. So they were not real leaders" (interview with Siham Shewada, Cairo, 8 March 2011). Also: "After the Mahalla strike was finished, because of the bad organization there was no group able to speak for Mahalla, and this was different for the tax workers' strike" (Interview with Wael Tawfiq, Cairo, 20 October 2010).

"The ideal example for the independent union was the struggle of the real estate tax workers and of the pensioners: they had a conscious and political leadership which was able to take good decisions and prepare for strategies and tactics."[26]

Snowball Trade Unionism

The RETAU was followed by the pensioners' union in 2008, an initiative of Tagammu MP al-Badry Farghaly,[27] the health technicians' union[28] in 2009, founded by Ahmed al-Sayyid, and the teachers' union in 2010, established by Abd al-Hafiz. Whereas the instructive role of the Mahalla strike had been indirect and diffusive, the RETAU transferred its experiences directly and concentrated on other trade union formations, as Ahmed al-Sayyid recalled: "When we had a good number of members we met Kamal Abu al-Eita. We learned from him how to set up a good trade union. [...] We held a main conference in the journalists' syndicate with the help of Kamal Abu al-Eita, where we announced the creation of the trade union."[29] The RETAU's assistance was not just leading by example, but consisted of a process of dialogic education, especially transferring technical and tactical competences. Moreover, the uneven and combined development of trade unionism allowed for a 'privilege of backwardness'[30] dynamic to kick in. Instead of repeating the experience of RETAU – i.e., developing a trade unionist neoformation from the strike activity – other worker projects could skip this stage and immediately import and absorb this subjectivity into their own collaboration. In the health technicians' union, the strike was already subsumed under the trade union neoformation: "Kamal Abu al-Eita started his trade union with a strike, but we took the decision to first set up our organization, gather a lot of members, announce our demands, and only then, if we did not get our demands, would we organize a strike."[31]

Despite the assistance of the RETAU, the health technicians' union faced many problems, which also constituted obstacles for other trade union initiatives. Firstly, workers were afraid to join an independent union because of state repression.

---

26 Interview with Kamal Abbas, Cairo, 27 March 2011.
27 Interview with al-Badry Farghaly, Cairo, 21 March 2011.
28 Comprising all workers who graduated from the Health Technical Institute, such as anesthetist assistants, laboratory and machine technicians, and so on.
29 Interview with Ahmed al-Sayyid, Cairo, 23 March 2011.
30 Cf. Chapter 10.
31 Interview with Ahmed al-Sayyid, Cairo, 23 March 2011.

Moreover, trade union leaders faced being discharged as a consequence of their syndicalist activities – as happened with the health technician leaders. Secondly, workers were suspicious towards trade unionism in general, due to their negative experiences with the GFETU bureaucracy. As the membership fees for the state union were directly subtracted from the workers' wages (without their consent) the health technician union did not take any membership fees during its first year of operation. Thirdly, the ministry of manpower categorically refused to recognize the independent unions, and the only way to become a formal trade union was through legal action. This necessitated a protracted and costly struggle in court. However, this obstacle often turned into an opportunity as many solidary lawyers supported the formation of independent trade unions.[32] Finally, some local branches of the state union were active, regularly in defiance of the official leadership. These groups often did not want to sacrifice their limited but sure activity for the adventure of independent trade unionism.[33]

The teachers, for their part, had been involved in struggles since 2005. After fifteen years of employment teachers still earned a meager 600 EGP and had to obtain extra income through private lessons. This was a burden for both teachers and families, as Abd al-Nasser Ibrahim, a teacher in Giza and Tagammu activist, explained: "Families in Egypt spend 30 percent of their income on education. They look on teachers as greedy people. Our real private salary comes from the people in private classes. But once we have a higher salary, we'll stop our private classes."[34]

Mubarak had promised the teachers better working conditions and salaries, but instead a law was implemented which paved the way for the liberalization and privatization of the school system, under the guise of safeguarding the quality of education. In addition, teachers challenged their own societal position as loyal pillars of state power: "The government turns the teacher into a policeman. The books serve to keep the pupils quiet. Don't discuss, don't ask! We are the first police officers in society. We kill their ideas and deliver them to the government to take their freedom away."[35] Abd al-Hafiz, an English teacher and Tagammu activist, stressed that the school was a reflection of the authoritarian society with practices of direct control and supervision: "Every school had a spy. Every administration has someone who is the contact with the state security [...]. They make the students file reports on the teachers and the

---

32 Interview with Ahmed al-Sayyid, Cairo, 23 March 2011.
33 Interview with Ahmed al-Sayyid, Cairo, 23 March 2011; interview with Abd al-Nasser Ibrahim, Cairo, 22 May 2009.
34 Interview with Abd al-Nasser Ibrahim, Cairo, 22 May 2009.
35 Interview with Abd al-Nasser Ibrahim, Cairo, 22 May 2009.

teachers against the students and against each other [...]."[36] Because the Egyptian education system was an important space for the social and political reproduction of al-nizam, the economic protests of the teachers often included an explicit component of anti-authoritarianism, especially when they created solidary activity-systems with the students.

From 2006 onward Abd al-Hafiz began to take unpaid vacations and he established the Egyptian Center for Educational Rights, an NGO which contested the new law and defended the rights of teachers. The teachers' movements were scattered and needed a central point for coordinating their actions and demonstrations. Abd al-Hafiz had to start from scratch in organizing the teachers' protest:

> [...] there was nothing. Then some teachers from al-Arish telephoned the newspaper, and asked for my number, and they told me: "We would like to join the teachers' organization in al-Arish." I said "Ok." I have a friend in al-Arish so I called him "Ashraf, how are you, from now on you are responsible for the work in al-Arish" and so it started. It started with small groups, then bigger groups, and then came the idea of a trade union.[37]

Even though a lot of teachers agreed with the necessity to contest neoliberal reform in the domain of education, not everyone was of the opinion that an independent trade union would be the best method in achieving their goal. One group of teachers emphasized that they could and would only try to reform the existing state teachers' syndicate. Another group, chiefly consisting of Muslim Brotherhood members and sympathizers claimed that they first had to see if there was a possibility to reform and change the teachers' syndicate from inside. If not, they could still leave the syndicate and set up their own trade union. A smaller faction, led by Abd al-Hafiz, however, decided to build an independent trade union, on a class instead of corporatist basis: "we are going to build a trade union for the teachers as workers – as paid wage workers."[38] By July 2010 the teachers' union had three to four thousand members and they declared themselves officially as a trade union.[39] The 25 January Revolution

---

36   Interview with Abd al-Nasser Ibrahim, Cairo, 22 May 2009.
37   Interview with Abd al-Hafiz, Cairo, 21 March 2011.
38   Interview with Abd al-Hafiz, Cairo, 21 March 2011.
39   The development of the trade union was pushed forward by the increased exploitation by the Ministry of Education: "We planned to announce our union by the end of 2011 this year. But accidently it happened that seven teachers died, one per day during the secondary school examinations. It was because the Minister of Education decided to double the work hours and to give them no chance to get sick leaves. So those who suffered from severe diseases just started to die" (Interview with Abd al-Hafiz, Cairo, 21 March 2011).

would accelerate the maturation of the teachers' protest movements and organizations into fully-developed independent trade unions. In the fall of 2011 the general teachers' strike became one of the biggest coordinated strikes in Egyptian history (Alexander 2012, 107).

There were, of course, many other strikes before the 25 January Revolution that did not yet (fully) develop into trade unions. One example is the Voice of the Nurses Movement. Nurses in state run hospitals suffered from very low wages and appalling working conditions. Sayyida al-Sayyid Muhammad, a nurse and RS member made clear that: "[...] they work twelve hours and they only earn one pound and 25 piasters each shift in university hospitals like al-Qasr al-Aini [...]. They deduct taxes from our wages even if the shifts are like twelve hours through the night."[40] Moreover, individual hospitals economized on basic working conditions. In Tanta, for example, the management gave the nurses a lump sum instead of the hot meals, two uniforms a year, shoes, and veil stipulated by the ministry of health – but the money did not cover the costs at all. In Qasr al-Shibeen hospital management refused to pay the nurses the 125 percent bonus that was promised to them.

In addition to these economic issues nurses were treated as social pariahs. Inas Safti of the Forum for Women in Development explained that:

> [...] the nurses sector in Egypt faces enormous prejudice and they are extremely underprivileged. [...] It's very degrading to women nurses and for very awkward reasons that do not apply to female doctors or surgeons. Nurses work late at night and that's why they are perceived in a bad way socially [...] but the same applies to doctors or surgeons and they are not frowned upon.[41]

Furthermore, the nurses were represented by three different state unions. Most nurses were affiliated to the general union for nurses, but those who worked in universities were members of the Union of Education and Scientific research, and nurses related to the ministry of health were part of the Union of Health Services. Besides, nurses were spread over different hospitals – workplaces which were isolated from one another and with much variance in working conditions. Finally, there were contradictions between state institutions in dealing with the nurses, as the ministry of health promised the nurses an

---

40 Interview with Sayyida al-Sayyid Muhammad, Giza, 26 October 2010.
41 Interview with Inas Safti, Cairo, 27 October 2010.

increase in their salary, whereas the ministry of finance cancelled the decision, sowing confusion among the nurses if they would obtain a pay rise or not.[42]

Yet, nurses were quite militant and achieved some victories in the following years. What is more, from January 2010 onward, activist nurses began to contact the leaders of the various spontaneous strikes, in an attempt to coordinate the struggles. Successful strikes in Qasr al-Shibeen and Tanta created a snowball effect:

> There were five strikes in one day: in Ismailiyya, two places in Cairo, Benha, Minya. There were also strikes in Beni Suef…There were strikes in many places. And thank God they were able to achieve a part of their rights, not yet all of them, but they will demand again the rest of their rights.[43]

On 19 July 2010, the nurses' movement held its first conference in the Journalists' Syndicate, moving towards the formation of an independent trade union, and opening up possibilities to ameliorate their social status: "The nurses movement does not only represent a good example of organized labor, it is not only a role model for workers, it is also defending this sector […] and presenting a better image of nurses because they are always looked down upon."[44]

At last the economic struggle began to flirt with the political domain. Apart from the organizational development of four independent trade unions and many syndicalist movements, from 2009 onward workers also increasingly protested in front of parliament, physically introducing their local and particular strikes to the space of national politics. This chain of continuous sit-ins imagined separate instances of struggle as part of one cohesive workers' movement, and this repetition enabled workers to generalize their separate and particular experiences into shared class demands. Two main economic demands emerged from the sit-ins: a fair minimum wage and expanded rights for the temporarily employed.[45]

In conclusion, before the 25 January Revolution there was already an independent trade union movement in Egypt. The salient and successful Mahalla strikes had given workers the preferable method and the confidence to use collective struggle – the strike – as a means to overcome their economic-corporate

---

42 Interview with Sayyida al-Sayyid Muhammad, Giza, 26 October 2010.
43 Interview with Sayyida al-Sayyid Muhammad, Giza, 26 October 2010.
44 Interview with Inas Safti, Cairo, 27 October 2010.
45 Interview with Khaled Ali, Cairo, 25 October 2010.

predicament. The victory of the tax workers and the establishment of the RETAU granted workers a concrete model of institutionalizing their spontaneous project into a trade unionist form. The demand for a fair national minimum wage, which had been raised spontaneously in the Mahalla strikes, emerged as a central goal of the developing worker project, which interpellated and united different workers – at least conceptually – as members of the same working class.

The development of the worker subject remained an uneven and non-linear process, however. In the 1980s and 1990s the economic predicament of the Egyptian private sector workers went much deeper than that of the state employees, yet they were less likely to protest because they were less organized and their situation was more precarious.[46] While the neoliberal counterreforms, at first, led to passivity in most private companies, they stimulated resistance in the textile sector. The public sector workers had already developed a subjectivity of revolt in the form of collective traditions, experiences, tactics, leaderships, and concepts. Since the proletarian activity-systems in the textile sector were more developed than the fragmented worker collaborations in the private factories, it was better prepared to handle the predicament of the neoliberal offensive – as witnessed in the Mahalla strikes.

However, Jan Romein's 'law of the handicap of a head start'[47] reared its head. While the Mahalla workers put the concept and method of the strike as a tool of securing economic gains and labor rights back on the agenda of the whole Egyptian working class, at the dawn of the 25 January Revolution they were still struggling to fully develop the outcome of the strike logic: an independent trade union. Class actors in the periphery of the workers' movement had already formed their own trade union neoformations: the real estate tax workers; the teachers; the health professionals; and the pensioners. These factions came late but fresh to the scene of the strike. They were not demoralized like the Mahalla workers and because the strike movement had become a 'combined' activity-system, they could immediately import their experiences into their own struggle. Even though the workers' movement had experienced a setback, it continued its slow, gradual, and uneven development into a more coherent and cohesive subject.

---

46   Interview with Abdel Rashid Hilal, Cairo, 9 October 2010.
47   Cf. Romein 1980. It is the other side of the coin of the 'privilege of backwardness'. In economic development, pioneering a new technology grants you a head start, but when, after a while, another innovation hits the market, you are stuck with the older technology and have to make a large investment to replace the equipment.

CHAPTER 20

The Strike's Intellectuals

In the previous chapter I analyzed the developmental dynamic of the Egyptian worker subject since the mid-2000s. Although the Mahalla strikes played a key role in the resurgence of the workers' movement, proper independent trade unionism only emerged with the formation of the RETAU. In the next chapter I discuss the role of organic and especially traditional intellectuals – political activists, journalists, artists, and human rights advocates – in assisting the budding proletarian subject.

Organic Intellectuals

As neither the traditional leftist parties[1] nor the state-controlled GFETU played their part as proletarian leaderships, the task of organizing and directing the various struggles fell directly on the grassroots committees (al-Mahdi 2011b): "The trade union gives only services to the workers, but doesn't defend their demands. In reality: workers make their own leadership."[2] Proletarian organic[3] intellectuals are the product of both the present and the past of class struggle. Leaders and activists of a previous episode of the strike are interpellated and reactivated by contemporary worker actions, and new directive organic intellectuals are produced through the activity of protest itself. With regard to the Mahalla movement, strike leader Sayyid Habib explained that:

> The Mahalla workers had the advantage of a more or less continuous leadership since 1975. The strike leaders organized groups in every section of the company, incessantly discussing with the workers and calling on them to make a strike. Through the strike movement a new generation of leaders emerged, which led the strikes of 2007 and 2008.[4]

The strikes of the 1990s and 2000s called the old worker leaders of the 1970s and 1980s back into action and from the labor protests themselves emerged a layer of new, young activists. This was necessary as from 2007 onward the régime

---

1 Cf. Chapters 14, 15, and 16.
2 Interview with Muhammad Fathy, Mahalla, 20 May 2009.
3 Cf. Chapter 7.
4 Interview with Sayyid Habib, Mahalla, 12 November 2010.

started to transfer traditional strike leaders to other workplaces in order to break the strike spirit and organization.[5]

Most of the old worker leaders were not affiliated to any political organization,[6] but they were active and organized in official GFETU committees. Even though they shared an objective subjectivity of belonging to the Mahalla workforce, they were often white-collar employees: supervisors, engineers, and educated layers with a different social status in the company.[7] In fact, before the rigged trade union elections of 2006, a majority of Mahalla worker leaders were part of the labor bureaucracy and their removal from the GFETU committees was an additional and important stimulus to the organization of protests outside the formal structures of the state union.

A cynic might conclude that these worker leaders only turned to their rank and file to defend their own, narrow bureaucratic interests. Regardless of the intentions of the Mahalla proletarian intellectuals it is much more productive to conceive of the relation between organic intellectuals and their class base as a reciprocal process. The workers reappropriated 'their' intellectuals as much as these figures won the support of 'their' rank and file. It is the self-organizing activity of the workers and their constitution as a collective subject, a social force, that interpellated old intellectuals back to the proletarian project and produced new organic leaders and activists. Conversely, the lack or disintegration of such an activity-system alienated organic intellectuals from their class base, and reversed the relations of force within the worker subject, encouraging bureaucratic pathologies. This reciprocal relation is expressed in trade union circles in the good sense notions of 'pressure from the rank and file' and 'pressure from the top'. Therefore, the question is not whether this or that individual proletarian intellectual is 'essentially' a bureaucrat or a genuine defender of worker interests; the real challenge is to establish a healthy dialectical pedagogy guaranteed by a strong and critical activity from the rank and file.

In Mahalla, the old proletarian intellectuals who were ousted from the GFETU structures supported the workers in their confrontation with the official labor representatives and helped them in setting up their own independent organizations at the factory level to organize the strikes (Alexander 2012). In addition, with the help of traditional intellectuals such as political and civil activists, they established the Textile Workers' League, which played a crucial role in organizing the September 2007 strike.[8]

---

5 Interview with Sayyid Habib, Mahalla, 12 November 2010.
6 Interview with Wael Tawfiq, Cairo, 16 October 2010.
7 Conversation with Per Björklund, Cairo, 5 May 2009.
8 Interview with Sayyid Habib, Mahalla, 12 November 2010.

Workers also engaged in the aesthetic and ideological articulation of their struggle,[9] thus becoming cultural organic intellectuals. However, the art forms that workers spontaneously produced were often ad hoc creations or performances within the immediacy of the strike activity.[10] Songs, poetry, graffiti, and cartoons were reproduced within the collective memory of the working class, but without an institutionalization of the cultural dimension of the strike, it was difficult for workers to develop these art forms in a stable, coherent, and systematic way. It was still the songs of Shaykh Imam and the poetry of Ahmed Fouad Negm from the 1970s that dominated the cultural expression of the workers' protests in the new millennium. Some trade unions also engaged in cultural production, but this domain had traditionally been the domain of the Modern Prince, and required the formation of a cultural apparatus that also integrated non-proletarian cultural intellectuals.

A Return to Class

Returning to Marx's principle that the emancipation of the working class is the task of the working class itself, one could argue that the Egyptian workers were perfectly able to solve their own problems. They formed their own organic intellectuals, started to overcome their economic-corporate predicament, and even moved toward the political domain before the 25 January Revolution. On the other hand, it was clear that non-proletarian actors played an important role in developing the workers' activity-systems by raising awareness, connecting various instances of the strike, setting up organizations, expressing the struggle aesthetically and ideologically, and so on. The question of whether workers are able to develop 'autonomously' and 'in isolation' from other forces into a subject-for-itself is, in actuality, nothing but a thought experiment. In any social formation, workers confront and are confronted by other collective subjects that mediate their developmental trajectory. Conversely, non-proletarian actors are interpellated by workers to join and support their activity-system. The question is not whether workers are influenced by other actors, but how they relate to these external forces and how their formation as a subject is being shaped by this interaction.

The problem with presenting an analysis of collaboration is that the portrayal should adequately represent a matrix of actors, forms, and modes of assistance. For example, I have to choose whether to discuss assistance from

---

9 Interview with Hassanein, Cairo, 13 October 2010.
10 Interview with Wael Tawfiq, Cairo, 11 November 2010.

the perspective of either the workers or the traditional intellectuals. In the first case the mode of assistance becomes the main typology, as it is much more relevant for the proletarian activity-system *how* it is stimulated than *by whom* it is supported. The second option requires me to start with a categorization of the various types of traditional intellectuals and their organizations and then analyze their modes and forms of assistance toward the workers' movement.

In order to solve this problem of presentation I begin with an investigation from the point of view of the different traditional intellectuals and civildemocratic actors vis-à-vis the Mahalla strikes, focusing on whether the three main trends of the old left, new left, and Muslim Brotherhood were or were not called 'back to class'; and whether they did or did not assist in building the workers' movement. In the next chapter, I reinvestigate these various forms of assistance through the lens of the workers' movement, paying special attention to the different *modes* of assistance and the question to which assistance adequately pushed the development of the worker subject forward. I conclude with a discussion of the dialectical pedagogy of the strikes, which could be conceived of as the mechanism which united organic and traditional intellectuals in an authentic, shared system of activity.

Before the Mahalla protests, civil society actors were little interested in 'economic' struggles. Helmi Sha'rawi of the African Arab Research Center (AARC) admitted that:

> It is shameful that this privatization has been happening without any protest. Workers were dismissed from their factories without any protest movement. What is this? I myself am surprised. From 1975 to 1995, during 20 years the whole economy has been reorganized and transformed, the whole society was changed, dismissing people from their work, giving them pensions to leave with hundreds…If it will continue it will be a failure of the whole progressive movement in Egypt.[11]

Of course, until the Second Palestinian Intifada in 2000 there was little grassroots mobilization in general, be it around economic or political issues.[12] Although the subsequent rise of the civildemocratic movement signified a rupture with the hegemony of the Mubarak clique, it did not succeed in building its own counterhegemonic apparatus or worldview, nor in drawing workers, peasants, and broad layers of the urban middle classes and subproletariat into its activity-system. Hisham Fouad emphasized that: "If the workers did

---

11   Interview with Helmi Sha'rawi, Giza, 11 November 2010.
12   Cf. Chapter 15.

not enter in a direct way in the Movement for Change it is because of two reasons: the Change movement did not form any social demand and the workers did not add their social demands to its agenda."[13] The purely political demands of the civildemocratic subject did not offer the subaltern classes the means of overcoming their economic problems (Solidarity Center 2010, 14).

Cut off from society at large and ridden with internal disagreements, the Kefaya movement started to disintegrate – just as the Mahalla strike movement was on the rise. Baho Abdul acknowledged that:

> The urban middle-class intellectuals had failed to build relations with the workers. Before 2006 no one in the political field was interested in the workers' movement, because there did not seem to be a real movement. The strike of December 2006 changed everything. All parties went to the movement.[14]

The saliency of the Mahalla strikes led to a reappreciation of the workers' movement as a force of societal change, and called a number of traditional intellectuals 'back to class'.

The Old Left

When I confronted Tagammu chairman Rifaat al-Said about the militancy of the Mahalla strikes he remained pessimistic, pointing to the failed insurrection of 1977.[15] In al-Said's view, the political role of Tagammu had been narrowed down to an oppositional discourse in the media and during elections.[16] Leaders of Tagammu's Trend for Change explicitly went against the discourse of disengagement with the workers' movement that dominated the party leadership. In April 2009 I met with Ali al-Dhib, co-founder of Tagammu, member of the Central Committee, and secretary of the Council of Advisors, who forcefully claimed that: "[...] we should go back to the original role of a socialist party. The last five years have seen a wave of strikes, demonstrations, new NGOs, which confirm this [...]. Tagammu should join these movements and always be at the heart of the strikes."[17]

---

13   Interview with Hisham Fouad, Giza, 26 October 2010.
14   Interview with Baho Abdul, Cairo, 10 May 2009.
15   Cf. Chapter 14.
16   Interview with Rifaat Al-Said, Cairo, 12 April 2009.
17   Interview with Ali Al-Dhib, Cairo, 3 April 2009.

Al-Dhib attacked the official party line on three fronts. Firstly, Tagammu should explicitly strive for socialism, not 'national capitalism' or any other 'Third Way'. Secondly, the party should actively engage with the class struggle and street politics to raise political consciousness. Thirdly, democracy would not arise from top-down reforms; change had to come from below. These three concerns reverberated especially among the old labor activists, the youth, and the local cadres of this old left party. Tagammu labor activists such as Talal Shukr had a long tradition of assisting the workers' movement: "We support the workers' movement at any place, for example through our solidarity articles in al-Ahali. We gather workers, give them training, and raise syndicalist issues."[18] Tagammu labor leader Abd al-Rashid Hilal summarized the assistance by the party's labor committee as follows:

> First the committee sends reports to all the newspapers, not only al-Ahali. Second, the committee goes to the strike to investigate the demands of the workers and to send documents to the [state] union in name of the Tagammu labor committee. We also give legal help. If the workers need a lawyer, Tagammu will offer them for free. We will give them food, clothes, blankets, and so on.[19]

The Tagammu labor committee mostly offered practical support by acting as a middleman between strikers and the state union, giving legal aid, and distributing material goods to continue the strike. However, it would be more correct to see these labor leaders with a clear working class background as *organic* proletarian intellectuals who had been politicized in the 1970s and then became a part of the fledgling Modern Prince that Tagammu once appeared to be.[20]

Yet, from the Second Palestinian Intifada onward, there seemed to be some truth in Helmi Sha'rawi's statement that: "The political parties were sleeping but they have become better now."[21] For example, Geber Serkis of the ADNP's local Mahalla branch recalled that they not only supported the Mahalla workers through their national al-Arabi newspaper, but that they also were standing side by side with the strikers, entering the factory, issuing statements of support and offering legal aid.[22] Especially the old left's few remaining younger militants actively participated in local economic and political struggles – often

---

18   Interview with Talal Shukr, Cairo, 21 April 2009.
19   Interview with Abd al-Rashid Hilal, Cairo, 9 October 2010.
20   Interview with Saud Omar, Suez, 17 October 2010.
21   Interview with Helmi Sha'rawi, Giza, 11 November 2010.
22   Interview with Geber Serkis, Mahalla, 12 November 2010.

without support from the party leadership. Ahmed Belal, leader of the UPY, member of the Central Committee of Tagammu, and political activist in his hometown of Mahalla al-Kubra, emphasized the necessity for political activists to go to the factories and link up with the workers.[23] When I was in Mahalla in 2009 and 2010 I spoke with Belal, who attempted to turn the UPY into a vehicle of intra-party opposition, and Muhammad Fathi, who was active in the labor group of Tagammu in Mahalla. Fathi confided in me that:

> The events in Mahalla have made Tagammu members more conscious about the need to be close to the common people in the streets and the factories. But the leadership obstructs our party branch in Mahalla in working with the workers. For example, during the strike in December 2007, the leadership warned the workers not to speak with us lest the police would come and arrest them. They play a negative role.[24]

Old left activists participated in the strike collaboration by bringing food, organizing solidarity demonstrations, discussing with the workers "how we could advance their demands,"[25] forging ties between the workers and national and international media, explaining the workers their legal rights, and being "in the factories for six days, side by side with the workers."[26] Through the presence of local political activists in Mahalla with national and international connections, the spatial limits of the strikes were more easily overcome. These actors could switch between their subjectivity as an embedded individual subject within the provincial Mahalla community, and their subjectivity as Cairo-based participants in national and international civil and political society. However, the disengagement of the leadership from grassroots politics meant that these activists either stood alone, or were isolated as a branch from the whole party.[27]

The New Left

Between 2000 and 2006 the Revolutionary Socialists had focused on the democratic struggle and the recruitment of students. The rise of street politics and the civildemocratic movement in 2002 had solved the split between the RS and

---

23 Interview with Ahmed Belal, Mahalla 6 April, 2009.
24 Interview with Muhammad Fathy, Mahalla, 20 May 2009.
25 Interview with Muhammad Fathy, Mahalla, 20 May 2009.
26 Interview with Muhammad Fathy, Mahalla, 20 May 2009.
27 Interview with Saud Omar, Suez, 17 October 2010.

the Sharara[28] group in practice, and the two factions reunited. Yet the failure of Kefaya opened up new lines of discussion. One faction claimed that the RS had made a mistake with its involvement in Kefaya, and that they should have focused on building their own apparatus instead of engaging with a 'petty-bourgeois' movement, whereas the other tendency suggested that the idea of building the party through these movements had been sound and that they should analyze where Kefaya went wrong.[29]

The Mahalla strikes and the decline of Kefaya oriented the RS 'back to class'.[30] In 2006, Baho Abdul was one of the RS youth who was disappointed with the inability of Kefaya and the Youth for Change to forge close ties with the workers' movement. She saw the gap between traditional intellectuals and workers as one of the biggest problems of the struggle against the régime. While the urban, almost exclusively Cairo-based, middle-class intelligentsia busied itself with politics without movements, the protest movements that emerged spontaneously in the factories, in the slums, and in the countryside were alienated from the political field. This divide between the social and the political, and between workers and intellectuals, inspired leading members of the RS such as Fatma Ramadan to support the establishment of Tadamon (Solidarity): "a solidarity movement which tries to bridge the gap between intellectuals and workers, political and social demands."[31]

The RS developed an internal division of labor, whereby one part was engaged with the workers' struggle, while another focused on building the organization and publishing the paper. Tadamon was explicitly established to assist the workers in the development of their activity-system, by exchanging experiences, methods, and tactics, and by forging ties with other subaltern groups such as farmers and fishermen.[32] Moreover, seeing that there were different organizations such as the Tagammu Labor Committee and the Egyptian Center for Economic and Social Rights (ECESR) assisting the workers, Tadamon took the initiative of making "[...] one committee that brings all the supporters of the workers together so they can speak with one voice and give one piece of advice. Otherwise Tagammu for example advises to end the strike and Tadamon gives them the advice to continue it."[33]

---

28 Cf. Chapter 17.
29 Interview with Gihan Shabeen, Cairo, 16 March 2011.
30 Interview with Mustafa Bassiouny, Giza, 12 October 2010; Interview with Fatma Ramadan, Cairo, 11 October 2010.
31 Interview with Baho Abdul, Cairo, 15 May 2009.
32 Interview with Fatma Ramadan, Cairo, 11 October 2010.
33 Interview with Fatma Ramadan, Cairo, 11 October 2010.

Apart from Tadamon activists, the RS in general renewed its engagement with the workers' movement. Unlike the local Tagammu activists, who were often isolated and faced obstruction from their national leadership, RS militants could directly mobilize their national structures to exchange the material and conceptual means of protest from one instance of struggle to another. Mustafa Bassiouny, a leading member of the RS, recalled:

> During the Mahalla strike we used a lot of whistles and drums, and when I went to the tax workers strikes we exchanged the experience of the drums and whistles. [...] We also informed the workers on how to conduct negotiations, how to strike, and how to deal with the security.[34]

A shared theoretical perspective between the RS and the British SWP allowed for the Mahalla strikes to gain a broad international audience, and the organization of international solidarity campaigns and meetings, e.g. via the Cairo International Conference and Liberation Forum; so that "workers gain strength and hope, they are able to see the broader picture, see things in international class terms, and so on."[35] In conclusion, the explicit and committed engagement of new left organizations with the resurging workers' movement meant that they played a bigger role in the protests and exerted more influence than Tagammu and the ECP.[36]

Muslim Brothers

When in 2009 I asked Said Husayni, Muslim Brother MP for Mahalla, if the Ikhwan supported the workers in their strikes, he claimed that:

> The Muslim Brotherhood supported the first strike on 7 December, 2006, which was a historical strike. I supported it, as an MP and a businessman. The Muslim Brotherhood workers participated in the strike. I went to the workers in the company and gave their demands to the management and the parliament.[37]

---

34 Interview with Mustafa Bassiouny, Giza, 12 October 2010.
35 Interview with Baho Abdul, Cairo, 10 May 2009.
36 Interview with Saud Omar, Suez, 17 October 2010.
37 Interview with Said Husayni, Mahalla, 20 May 2009.

Talal Shukr, however, pointed out that:

> In the beginning they declared their participation. After a few days, they withdrew. They are continuously balancing. In most situations they take steps back, as they don't want to anger the government. The workers do not accept this attitude and they know that labor is not the field of the Muslim Brotherhood.[38]

Likewise, leftist blogger and RS member Hossam al-Hamalawy acknowledged that the Ikhwan had a presence during the Mahalla strikes, but that they, as an organization, failed to give the workers any real assistance. During the September 2007 strike, Said Husayni was even denounced by the workers, who refused to let him in the factory because of the lack of support from the Brotherhood.[39] Muhammad Fathi recalled that: "Said Husayni came to the strike and the Muslim Brotherhood said that he would make a statement for them. But he only came for show."[40]

When I asked Kamal Abu al-Eita if the Ikhwan played a role in the independent trade union movement, he laughed and answered:

> Nothing! No support. I only have one Muslim Brother in a union of 50,000 members. The Brotherhood owns a lot of factories that had strikes. That's it. They are adopting capitalist policies. Even if they call it an Islamic economy, it is capitalist. They are the sons of capitalism: even their trade and finance are capitalist. The government was using the Brothers to frighten the workers.[41]

The answer of al-Badry al-Farghaly, founder of the pensioners' union, when questioned if there were members of the Brotherhood in the pensioners' union, was laconic: "*Ma fish* [none]."[42] Ahmed al-Sayyid of the health technicians' union claimed: "I never met one of them during my trade union work."[43] Leftist activist Wael Tawfiq narrated how in the 2009 Helwan Cement strike Muslim Brothers were originally leading the protests, but wanted to halt the strike after the management had given in to two of the five demands raised by the strikers. Wael Tawfiq and other non-Ikhwan activists rejected the Brotherhood's maneuver and gained the support of the workers.[44]

---

38 Interview with Talal Shukr, Cairo, 21 April 2009.
39 Conversation with Hossam al-Hamalawy, Cairo, 14 May 2009.
40 Interview with Muhammad Fathy, Mahalla, 12 November 2010.
41 Interview with Kamal Abu al-Eita, Giza, 20 March 2011.
42 Interview with al-Badry Farghaly, Cairo, 21 March 2011.
43 Interview with Ahmed al-Sayyid, Cairo, 23 March 2011.
44 Interview with Wael Tawfiq, Cairo, 20 October 2010.

In general, as an organization, the Brotherhood assisted workers by helping them in their negotiations with the management and the ministry of manpower, and by providing practical support to strikers. Baho Abdul underlined: "The Muslim Brotherhood never leads, but often helps, for example, with food distribution to strikers."[45] The assistance of individual and local groups of Ikhwan, however, often went further. For example, Yosry Bayumi, a Muslim Brother MP, defended the rights of workers in parliament and the media. In Suez, the local branch of the Muslim Brothers became much more involved in strikes after the Mahalla strike, because the workers pushed them to this orientation.[46] Muslim Brother youth joined Tadamon, as the organization provided a common ground for different political factions to defend workers' rights and connect instances of protest: "When Ikhwan and other leftists joined Tadamon they joined as individuals and they had an agreement that they will never discuss the problems between the Ikhwan and the left. Tadamon is there only for the workers."[47] However, because the topic of the workers' movement traditionally belonged to the left, working class-oriented organizations such as Tadamon were generally conceived of as politically leftist, regardless of the fact that these organizations gathered "[...] a lot of members from the Ikhwan and all political organizations."[48]

Journalists

While the media did not pay much attention to working class actions before 2006, the saliency of the Mahalla strike movement drew them 'back to class', especially because the struggle immediately followed the disintegration of Kefaya. Because of the political and organizational weakness of the opposition parties, journalists often played an active role during the civildemocratic and class protests of the 2000s.[49] Khaled al-Balshy, chief editor of the leftist al-Badil newspaper, was of the opinion that: "The press in Egypt plays a big role, because the political parties are weak. Newspapers function as NGOs and parties. [...] The media enable the movement to share its experiences on a national level. People who want to strike even ask us for our advice."[50] There was an interesting

---

45   Interview with Baho Abdul, Cairo, 15 May 2009.
46   Interview with Saud Omar, Suez, 17 October 2010.
47   Interview with Fatma Ramadan, Cairo, 11 October 2010.
48   Interview with Fatma Ramadan, Cairo, 11 October 2010.
49   Interview with Muhammad Abd el-Azim, Mahalla, 12 November 2010; Interview with Saud Omar, Suez, 17 October 2010; interview with Faysal Lakusha, Cairo, 20 October 2010.
50   Interview with Khaled al-Balshy, Cairo, 8 April 2010.

reciprocal transformation process whereby, journalists covering street politics became political actors, and political activists became engaged in grassroots journalism to be closer to the workers. In Hossam al-Hamalawy's experience "the easiest way to engage with the workers is being a journalist, as any political activism is a priori suspicious. Being the media means having authority."[51] Mustafa Bassiouny, who was not only a leading member of the RS but also a journalist for al-Dostour, agreed: "For me journalism was a tool to be near to the labor movement [...]. As a journalist I could get near to the workers without worrying about security [...]."[52]

Of course, not all journalists became fellow travelers to the workers' movement. Mustafa Bassiouny remarked that the role of journalists: "[...] can be positive or negative, you have to specify if they belong to the state or not. State journalists are writing against the strikes. Other journalists can be very positive for the labor movement."[53] Medhat al-Zahed concurred that: "It depends on the journalists and the newspaper."[54] In general, journalists from newspapers such as al-Arabi, al-Ahali, al-Badil, al-Masry al-Yawm, al-Dostour, and al-Shorouk covered labor issues in a way that assisted the development of the workers' movement.

Many labor activists regarded the role of journalists as crucial in the development of the strike movement. Sabr Barakat explained that: "By their help during the past few years the voice of the workers became louder. And the workers' ability to contact each other has improved."[55] Saud Omar was of the same opinion: "There was a lot of support from the media. We gained a lot of experience: how to organize the strikes; how to define our demands; how to organize demonstrations."[56] Mahalla worker Faysal Lakusha commented that: "The role of the media was very important, and they were supporting, and covering us."[57] Abir Mehdawi, a young journalist, explained that: "[...] some journalists are also activists, more and more nowadays. They play a role in sharing experiences and bringing local issues to the regional, national or even international level. They help in spreading the culture of protest."[58]

Journalists gave different forms of assistance to the strike movement. Firstly, they diffused particular methods and forms of organization to the Egyptian

---

51   Conversation with Hossam al-Hamalawy, Cairo, 14 May 2009.
52   Interview with Mustafa Bassiouny, Giza, 12 October 2010.
53   Interview with Mustafa Bassiouny, Giza, 12 October 2010.
54   Interview with Medhat al-Zahed, Cairo, 9 November 2010.
55   Interview with Sabr Barakat, Cairo, 16 October 2010.
56   Interview with Saud Omar, Suez, 17 October 2010.
57   Interview with Faysal Lakusha, Cairo, 20 October 2010.
58   Interview with Abir Mehdawi, Cairo, 13 April 2009.

working class in general, either indirectly and vertically, by writing about specific class conflicts in the national media, or directly and horizontally by transferring experiences from one concrete struggle to another. Secondly, by bringing the story of the Mahalla strikes in the national media, they projected and imagined the workers as a social force able to challenge the system. This narrative reinforced a class subjectivity among workers in other companies and encouraged them to solve their own particular problems in the same way as the Mahalla strikers. Thirdly, by articulating the demands of the Mahalla workers in the national sphere, they encouraged the generalization and articulation of these demands as aims of the whole Egyptian working class.

Artists

While in the past the communist and left-nationalist movements had used their institutional and financial means to bring traditional intellectuals and workers together, since the 1980s the support from the old left for these initiatives dwindled. During the 1980s and 1990s, most artists became disengaged with street politics and the class movement.[59] Essam Hanafy, a young cartoonist working for the Nasserist al-Arabi newspaper, highlighted that even cartoonists in privately-owned newspapers faced censorship from their own editors, who did not want to upset the investors nor provoke state intervention: "writing a cartoon is like walking on a field with landmines."[60]

In addition to work-related pressures "[...] there is social pressure. For example there was a political cartoonist who was engaged to be married, but the family of the bride broke the engagement because it was too dangerous."[61]

---

59 Some popular and populist bands or singers only expressed the poverty of the working class and the subproletariat without offering a political alternative or presenting a concept of them as a potential collective agent capable of struggle: "Like Shaban Abd al-Rahim, he sings about the tomato prices but he does not criticize the policies let alone give an alternative. He sings that he hates Israel but in a vulgar way [...]. Abd al-Rahim is a huge star. His last song was about voting for Mubarak and if Mubarak wouldn't go to the elections he would vote for Gamal. He is one of those with interests in the régime. It is a low form of class art in order to be famous [...]" (Interview with Wael Tawfiq, Cairo, 11 November 2010). Whereas these art forms originated from the subaltern classes, they did not push forward the development of these groups into assertive social agents. They rather expressed the passivity and subalternity of these societal layers vis-à-vis al-nizam.
60 Interview with Essam Hanafy, Cairo, 25 November 2010.
61 Interview with Essam Hanafy, Cairo, 25 November 2010.

The rise of the civildemocratic and workers' movements in the last two decades also called artists back into an engagement with political and economic issues. Writer Alaa al-Aswany contemplated that: "Many writers joined these movements, especially because these movements are not political parties. They are movements for a very determinate purpose, for democracy, justice and freedom. I cannot think of any writer who could stay away from the issue of freedom [...]."[62] Despite the engagement of a new layer of traditional 'cultural' intellectuals with street politics, only a few of these artists and writers recognized the workers as a social and political force. For example, when I asked the cartoonist Salah Abd al-Azim if he dealt with the workers' movement in his art, he replied: "No, for me this was not important. Mubarak was using these elements to complicate the struggle [...] for me the struggle is foremost against Mubarak. [...] The soil is not able to grow everything. First we should change the soil, then we can plant anything we want."[63]

Those artists that did recognize the workers' movement as a social force, played a central role in the articulation and development of class demands and forms of consciousness – especially cartoonists. According to Essam Hanafy: "The cartoonist's mission is not only to make jokes, but also to make the people conscious. He expresses the situation in pictures. We were with the peasants against the landlords. Peasants were killed. Art must express the problem at hand, for example the insurrection of the Mahalla workers."[64] Art forms such as songs, graffiti, cartoons, sketches, and poems, expressed the workers' predicaments as well as possible solutions to overcome them. Hassanein explained that:

> I was trying to draw what the workers want and the things as they see them. This helps the workers to think. The cartoons help the workers know their interests and goals as a short-cut; they can understand everything from just a small picture. [...] We know the problems, but we know from them what the problem is really like: what and how they really see it.[65]

The cartoon was instrumental in the development of a 'true'[66] concept by workers of themselves as a social and political force, and of a critique of al-nizam. Firstly, cartoons are easily accessible and reproducible; they are not

---

62 Interview with Alaa al-Aswany, Cairo, 26 November 2011.
63 Interview with Salah Abd al-Azim, Cairo, 22 March 2011.
64 Interview with Essam Hanafy, Cairo, 25 November 2010.
65 Interview with Hassanein, Cairo, 13 October 2010.
66 Cf. Chapter 7.

exclusively found in art galleries, which are detached from the everyday conditions of the class, but they are "the art of the poor people,"[67] printed in newspapers and painted on walls in the streets. Secondly, a cartoon is a sign that combines a simple, primitive form or signifier with a complex content or signified (cf. Gribbon and Hawas 2012). A political cartoon has the potential to act as an index of the historical bloc, revealing implicit relations of force, hidden interests, and making connections between the local and the national, the economic and the political. Finally, the humorous nature of the cartoon *disarms* both the interpreter and the object that is being represented. Humor draws an audience that is often suspicious of politics into the message of the cartoon and it undermines the fear, awe, and prestige that hegemonic and dominating institutions, symbols, and persons evoke (cf. Colla 2012).

Human Rights Activists

During the 1990s and 2000s, similarly to journalists, human and civil rights activists often had to step in to fill the void left by the bureaucratization of the trade unions and the disengagement of political parties with grassroots politics.[68] Activists frequently established or joined NGOs to get hold of a semi-legal apparatus and a stable framework for political work. The RS created the Center for Socialist Studies in Giza and some of its members, like Hisham Fouad, were active in the Sons of Land Center for Human Rights (SLCHR); the ECP had its Afaaq Ishtirakiyya center; Saud Omar became active in the Suez Democratic Forum; and so on.

Two centers gathering activists stood out for their support for the workers' movement in general and for their role in the Mahalla strike movement in particular: the Center for Trade Union and Worker Services (CTUWS) and the Hisham Mubarak Law Center (HMLC).[69] Other noteworthy NGOs with a (partly) 'working class orientation' were the SLCHR and the New Woman Foundation.[70]

The CTUWS was one of the pioneers of grassroots-oriented NGOs in Egypt. The organization was established in 1990 in Helwan and spread to other industrial

---

67   Interview with Essam Hanafy, Cairo, 25 November 2010.
68   Interview with Inas Safti, Cairo, 27 October 2010.
69   Interview with Faysal Lakusha, Cairo, 20 March 2010; Interview with Muhammad Abd al-Azim, Mahalla, 12 November 2010; Interview with Sayyid Habib, Mahalla, 12 November 2010.
70   Interview with Nawla Darwish, Cairo, 16 February 2008.

cities such as Mahalla al-Kubra. In 1993 it was recognized and supported as a partner NGO of Oxfam Novib. The CTUWS helped workers to organize themselves, exchange experiences and problems between different workplaces, assist and advise strikers in negotiations, procure media attention, and so on.[71] In December 2006 the Mahalla branch of the CTUWS was the main focal point of the strike movement, offering practical, legal, and material support to the workers and organizing solidarity.[72]

The HMLC was established in 1999 and had its roots in legal aid associations of the 1990s. One of the key figures was Khaled Ali, a lawyer and human rights activist since 1994, who was a co-founder of HMLC and who created the Egyptian Center for Economic and Social Rights (ECESR) in 2010. Khaled Ali offered workers legal advice and defended them in court free of charge. In addition, he acted as an educator, raising awareness among workers of their rights and publishing reports about labor conditions and trade union problems. Finally, he went to court to litigate both individual cases as general issues that the Egyptian workers faced, such as the privatization of health insurance or their demand for a national minimum wage.[73]

The assistance given by human and civil rights centers was primarily oriented towards the overcoming of practical obstacles in the development of the workers' strike activity. Firstly, human rights lawyers knew the procedures, registers, codes, and performances of the legal apparatus, and by lending the workers their expertise they made sure strikers could appropriate the same concrete ideological and institutional tools that the régime and the ruling classes used against them.

Secondly, as legal specialists, these traditional intellectuals raised awareness among workers of their labor and constitutional rights, projecting and interpellating generalizing strikers as members of a national working class with its own shared system of rights. Workers had general rights, both as citizens and as wage laborers, and the consciousness of these general rights in turn generalized proletarian and civildemocratic self-concepts among the workforce.

Thirdly, human and civil rights activists such as Khaled Ali did not only fight to safeguard the existing labor conditions, but also to improve the rights and livelihoods of the workers, for example through the demand of a fair national minimum wage. From 2010 onwards the ECESR organized and supported worker protests demanding the national minimum wage, and these actions became a

---

71 Interview with Kamal Abbas, Cairo, 27 March 2011.
72 Interview with Abdul Kader, Mahalla, May 20 2009.
73 Interview with Khaled Ali, Cairo, 25 October 2010.

leading activity for the class as a whole, stimulating the unity of the workers' movement.[74]

Fourthly, because of their connection to international organizations such as the International Labor Organization (ILO) and trade union solidarity campaigns, NGOs with a working class orientation encouraged an exchange of experiences, achievements, and ideas between Egyptian and foreign syndicalists.[75] Moreover, they acted as hubs that united organic and traditional intellectuals, a diversity of traditional intellectuals, and different forms of assistance. For example, journalists often functioned as a liaison between workers and these legal organizations, bringing cases under the attention of worker-friendly lawyers. Apart from legal personnel, HMLC and ECESR also harbored political and human rights activists, who assisted workers in a more trade unionist manner, e.g. by setting up strike committees.[76]

---

[74] Interview with Muhammad Abd al-Azim, Mahalla, 12 November 2010.
[75] Interview with Saud Omar, Suez, 17 October 2010.
[76] Interview with Osama Muhammad Khalil, Cairo, 13 October 2010.

CHAPTER 21

Pedagogies of Revolt

Whereas in the preceding chapter I discussed the different groups of intellectuals that assisted in the formation of the workers' movement, in the following chapter I investigate the different *forms* – technical, cultural, and directive – and *modes* – colonization, commodification, and solidarity – of assistance provided by these intellectuals.

Forms of Assistance

When they engaged with the Mahalla strike movement, traditional intellectuals such as journalists and lawyers, human rights and political activists, writers and artists, offered the emerging worker subject different *forms* of assistance: technical, cultural, and directive.[1] Although of crucial importance for the sustenance and reproduction of the strike movements, *technical* assistance, such as organizing material and practical support and legal aid for individual strikes, did not have a *developmental* impact on the workers' activity from the perspective of subject formation. *Cultural* assistance, on the other hand, in its broadest sense, played a fundamental role in developing the worker subject. Three forms of cultural assistance can be discerned: connection, projection, and integration.

Firstly, because of their social function, mobility, and position as intellectuals in civil society at large, non-proletarian actors could more easily *generalize* the experiences, methods, and lessons from one 'horizontal' instance of struggle to another. They acted as liaisons between organic proletarian intellectuals, literally mediating the internal communication and consciousness of the decentralized worker subject. Even though workers were still 'physically' confined to the particular instances of their separate protests, their struggles became conceptually connected through shared demands and practices. This type of assistance was not only spatial, but also temporal. Traditional intellectuals sometimes acted as an auxiliary reservoir of the collective memory of the working class: when 'old' proletarian intellectuals were, for whatever reason, cut off from the embryonic 'fresh' organic layers, then traditional intellectuals

---

1 Cf. Chapter 7.

such as political activists, journalists, writers, and so on, transferred class experiences to the new generation.[2]

This form of cultural assistance can be described as *connection*. With regard to concept formation in ontogenesis, Vygotsky observed a transition from syncretism to thinking in complexes. Put simply, this developmental process contains the connection of objects on the basis of objective bonds and relations, based on association, function, sequence, and so on. Transposed to the domain of proletarian sociogenesis connective assistance brings experiences from different spatial and temporal instances of struggle together and allows workers to share their competences and methods. It mediates the horizontal, reciprocal learning process between workers, enabling them to instruct one another and push their mutual development forward. However, "[...] there is no hierarchical organization of the relations between different traits of the object [...] the structural center of the formation may be absent altogether" (Vygotsky 2012, 124). Connective assistance creates relations between worker projects, but it does not organize them as a cohesive whole.

Secondly, by a 'vertical' projection of individual worker struggles into the sphere of national civil society, e.g., in the media, traditional intellectuals made the spatially isolated strikes directly contemporaneous to the lives of many workers. Through the mediation of, especially, newspapers articles and blog posts, workers got to know that their comrades in other companies struck to overcome problems similar to their own. They realized that they shared the same goal and that the objective of their strike activity was, for all purposes, the same. Traditional intellectuals enabled workers to imagine and generalize themselves as a coherent and cohesive working class despite the fact that they were far from organized as a national workers' movement. Furthermore, this projection influenced the attitudes of other societal actors towards the workers, calling them 'back to class'.

This form of cultural assistance can be described as *projection*. With regard to concept formation in ontogenesis, Vygotsky noted that the 'bridge' between thinking in complexes and thinking in real concepts was the *pseudoconcept*: "[...] the appearance of a concept that conceals the inner structure of a complex" (Vygotsky 2012, 127). When faced with a ready-made concept, children cannot directly absorb it, but they build complexes around it: "What we see here is the complex that, in practical terms, coincides with the concept, embracing the same set of objects. Such a complex is a 'shadow' of the concept, its contour" (Vygotsky 2012, 130). Transposed to the domain of proletarian

---

[2] Interview with Hisham Fouad, Giza, 26 October 2010.

sociogenesis projective assistance helps the workers to generalize their struggle from the local, particular to the national, general level. It mediates the 'vertical' sublation of the spatial fragmentation of the working class by a heteroleptic imagining of the workers as a collective subject.

Thirdly, journalists, writers, and activists helped to develop the particular grievances of the Mahalla strikers into general demands and self-concepts of the working class. Basic conceptual generalizations, such as a fair national minimum wage and a solution for the position of temporary workers, unified workers from different sectors and lifted their struggle from the economic-particular to a national trade unionist level.[3] More advanced generalizations posited the strikes as indices of *class* activity and consciousness, and emphasized the subjectness of the proletarian subject.

This form of cultural assistance can be described as *integration*. Vygotsky observed that: "When the process of concept formation is seen in all its complexity, it appears as a movement of thought within the pyramid of concepts, constantly alternating between two directions: from the particular to the general, and from the general to the particular" (Vygotsky 2012, 152). Integration represents the intertwining of everyday and scientific lines of development: the development of a philosophy of praxis by the interpenetration of the spontaneous good sense of the strikers with a political-economic critique of capital, class, and the state.[4]

Finally, *directive* assistance represents not assistance proper, but leadership. During strikes where workers were inexperienced – especially in new, private companies – sometimes external actors such as political activists or even journalists had a leading role in the organization of the movement. When directive assistance is not connected to the formation of organic leaders, it can lead to substitutionist or colonizing (cf. infra) practices.

Modes of Assistance

Traditional intellectuals came to the budding workers' movement with various interests, attitudes, and methods, which were not all beneficial to the development of the proletarian activity-system. I return to Blunden's model of the archetypical collaborative relations between subjects or projects.[5] Unlike the

---

3　Interview with Hisham Fouad, Giza, 26 October 2010.
4　Cf. Chapter 7.
5　Cf. Chapter 4.

forms of assistance, sketched above, which elucidate the substance of the offered assistance, these *modes* of assistance deal with relations of power between subjects, opening up the ethico-political dimension of class pedagogies. Building on Blunden's typology, I recognize five fundamentally different ways in which subjects recognize each other and interact with each other: (1) non-recognition; (2) colonization; (3) commodification; (4) solidarity; (5) hegemony.

The first mode of assistance – non-recognition – is only assistance in appearance, because the object of assistance – the worker's movement – is not recognized as a subject. Even though the Mahalla strikes called many traditional intellectuals 'back to class', not all of them recognized the workers as a collective subject. Rightist leaders of the old left such as Rifaat al-Said dismissed the notion that the workers could play a role in overcoming their own economic predicament, let alone be an agent in overthrowing the régime. Some liberal political activists and artists such as Salah Abd al-Azim who believed in the power of al-sha'b to challenge al-nizam were suspicious of the workers' movement and considered strikes as a means for the régime to divert attention from the civildemocratic struggle. They discarded the notion of a proletarian subjectivity and only recognized a civildemocratic subjectivity: the right of workers to protest and mobilize as citizens against the corruption and the authoritarianism of the system.

Most Ikhwan leaders rejected the notion of a proletarian project as well. A number of them acknowledged the plight of the workforce, but advocated a new, Islamic moral economy between employers and employees as a way of softening the contradictions between labor and capital.[6] Their slogan of 'social justice' does not express a political-economic critique, but an interpellation of individual moral attitudes of the rich and wealthy who, under the influence of Islam, support those in need. Helmi Sha'rawi observed that "[...] the prestige of helping and being helpful is important for the Brothers, not their presence in the movement."[7] While this kind of charity may alleviate the direct suffering of individuals and groups, it perversely fetters the development of these subaltern categories into self-determining and autonomous social subjects by institutionalizing a relation of dependency and clientelism.

In general, however, the saliency and the militancy of the Mahalla strike movement, in combination with the disintegration of the civildemocratic movement, forced traditional intellectuals to develop an attitude towards the

---

6 Interview with Essam al-Erian, Cairo, 10 March 2008.
7 Interview with Helmi Sha'rawi, Giza, 11 November 2010.

emerging worker project. Assistance of the workers' movement took on the shape of colonization, commodification, and solidarity.

Colonization

Colonization is the subsumption of a subject under another subject. A colonizing subject presents its own forms of mediation as the best way to realize the goal of a different subject.

When encountered with the strength and confidence of the workers' movement, many Ikhwan activists could not simply ignore the workers as a social force. Some individual Muslim Brother militants came closer to the working class through their participation in a shared activity-system.[8] Others tried to subjugate the strike to the goals of the Brotherhood and incorporate its activity in their own project. Kamal Abbas, director of the CTUWS, explained that: "[…] since 2005 they were closer to the labor movement, not because of the workers, but for their own benefit."[9] Brotherhood figures such as Said Husayni projected themselves as the natural leaders of the working class. Their lack of militants in the organized labor movement was explained by a *reductio ad absurdum*: because they had a great influence in the factories, they were the primary target of the régime and security apparatus; ergo their weakness was proof of their strength.[10] Moreover, the workers' good sense of the contradictions between labor and capital was conceptually reframed within a national-culturalist paradigm. For example, Husayni translated the demand of the renationalization of privatized firms, which expressed the proletarian concept of many workers that the public companies where they labored were 'theirs' (Revolution Through Arab Eyes 2012), into a cultural-colonial or nationalist issue. He said: "The problem of privatizations in Egypt is that we have lost ownership of our industry. It is transferred to criminals or foreigners. The whole process is illegal."[11] Muhammad Abbas, a youth leader of the Brotherhood claimed that the Mubarak régime:

> […] opened the doors of Egypt widely for foreign workers and industries. It didn't take care of the national industries to be able to compete with

---

8   Interview with Saud Omar, Suez, 17 October 2010; interview with Fatma Ramadan, Cairo, 11 October 2010.
9   Interview with Kamal Abbas, Cairo, 27 March 2011.
10   Interview with Said Husayni, Mahalla, 20 May 2009.
11   Interview with Said Husayni, Mahalla, 20 May 2009.

foreign industries [...]. We will not get foreign workers to work here. [...] For sure, before we are Muslim Brothers we are Egyptians, so it is important that the Egyptian people should work and be employed. In the companies of al-Ikhwan we do not have any foreign workers.[12]

By positing Egyptian workers against foreign laborers, and Egyptian employers against foreign capitalists, the good sense of political-economic exploitation shifted away from the relation between labor and capital, toward a cultural-political contradiction between productive Egyptians and parasitic foreigners. However, as labor activists and leaders such as Kamal Abbas, Kamal Abu al-Eita, Ahmed al-Sayyid, Al-Badry al-Farghaly, Talal Shukr, and others, made clear, in general the colonizing attitude of the Brotherhood had little impact on the development of the proletarian activity-system, especially in the industrial sectors.

Colonization was also a mode of assistance found among activists of the civildemocratic movement. The episode of the 6 April 2008 'general strike' epitomized the colonization of workers' actions by civildemocratic actors. Charles Hirschkind framed the intervention from the perspective of the civildemocratic movement as follows:

> The strike, the largest anti-government mobilization to occur in Egypt in many years, had been initiated by labor activists in support of striking workers at the Mahalla textile factory who had for months been holding out for better salaries and improved work conditions. In the month leading up to the strike, however, the aim of the action enlarged beyond the scope of the specific concerns of the factory workers. Propelled by the efforts of a group of activists on Facebook, the strike shifted to become a national day of protest against the corruption of the Mubarak régime, and particularly against the régime's complete inaction in the face of steadily declining wages and rising prices.
> HIRSCHKIND 2011A

Hirschkind emphasized the importance of 6 April because "Egypt witnessed its most dramatic political mobilization in decades, an event that brought together people across the political spectrum, from Muslim Brotherhood members to Revolutionary Socialists" (Hirschkind 2011a). Yet on the ground, especially in Mahalla, most workers did not perceive the call for a general strike

---

12 Interview with Muhammad Abbas, Cairo, 28 March 2011.

by external civildemocratic forces as an extension of their struggle, but rather as a voluntarist, political hijacking of their project. Mahalla worker leaders and labor activists accused Kefaya and other civildemocratic movements, parties, and organizations of mobilizing them for their own political struggle.[13] The failure of the 6 April Mahalla strike was partly due to these civildemocratic forces, which suddenly turned an economic strike into a high-profile political action, without preparing or organizing the workers for this new type of confrontation with the state. Baho Abdul commented that: "The strike was called by some forces in Kefaya, but the timing was bad. They ignored the workers' demands and did not listen to them."[14] Khaled Ali noted that:

> It attracted many human rights activists but this didn't encourage them to work more on labor issues. Actually, it drove many political movements and political activists to jump on these movements and many politicians and political movements tried to reap the benefits of this. They were releasing conflicting statements that divided the movement itself.[15]

Instead of introducing the idea of a general strike into the workers' movement, the colonizing attitude of civildemocratic actors was one of the factors that led to the defeat of the Mahalla strike and the subsequent popular uprising. Between 6 April 2008 and the 25 January Revolution, Mahalla no longer played a leading part in the development of the Egyptian workers' movement.

A more subtle form of colonization could be found among leftists who propagated some form of 'stage theory' of the class struggle. The workers' direct social demands had to be supported by the political parties in order to win them over to the fight for democracy that took precedence. This idea was popular among most liberal, Nasserist, Tagammu and ECP intellectuals. For example, despite being a local Tagammu activist engaged in the Mahalla strike movement, Muhammad Fathy asserted that: "In Egypt you need a democracy first, then people become organized in classes and they will fight as classes."[16] ECP leader Salah Adli claimed that the class struggle in Egypt was muddled by "the problem of Israel" and "the problem of Islam," which blurred a sharp contradiction "between rightist classes and classes like farmers and workers."[17]

---

13   Interview with Abd al-Rashid Hilal, Cairo, 9 October 2010; Interview with Talal Shukr, Cairo, 21 April 2009.
14   Interview with Baho Abdul, Cairo, 15 May 2009.
15   Interview with Khaled Ali, Cairo, 25 October 2010.
16   Interview with Muhammad Fathy, Mahalla, 12 November 2010.
17   Interview with Salah Adli, Cairo, 13 November 2010.

Leftists had to first build a strong civildemocratic movement, drawing workers into this project on the basis of the right to strike, to establish trade unions, and so on.

Leftist nationalists, for their part, often emphasized that social justice was more important than democracy, but they did not conceive of the workers as a societal force with a subjectivity and subjectness distinct from al-sha'b, the people.[18] They subsumed the proletarian subject conceptually under the national-popular subject and were suspicious of any 'divisions' within 'the people'. Hamdeen Sabahi, the leader of the neo-Nasserist al-Karama party saw in the workers a force "central to any political change in the country the way they have been throughout history" (Karama Party Leader 2010), but at the same time, al-Karama hesitated to support the formation of independent trade unions – which was ironic seeing as the first independent union, the RETAU, was established by Kamal Abu el-Eita, himself a Nasserist leader.[19]

Commodification

A relation of commodification or exchange between two subjects requires a mutual process of recognition. Assistance is based on a quid pro quo basis, as each project conceives of the other as a useful instrument for its own development. The Other is only recognized as a means for the Self, and not as an end in itself. During the Mahalla strike movement, journalists, human rights activists, and leftist parties were accused of recruiting the workers' struggle for their own benefit. Many journalists covered the Mahalla strikes because they constituted, first and foremost, a newsworthy *event*. As long as the movement remained a hot topic, this attitude did not have a negative effect on the movement, as it enabled workers to use the media themselves to reach out to other layers of the working class and the political community. There was a trade between workers producing an 'event' and journalists sharing these events as news with civil society at large.

However, as soon as the saliency and novelty of the strikes diminished, they lost their status as 'event' and many journalists became disinterested and disengaged with the movement. Faysal Lakusha, a Mahalla worker who was one of the leaders of the strikes, resentfully commented:

> After the failed strike of 6 April 2008, the government started to fire worker leaders and the media did not stand by us. After the fire is out we

---

[18] Interview with Tareq Said, Cairo, 11 November 2010; Interview with Wael Tawfiq, Cairo, 11 November 2010.

[19] Interview with Wael Tawfiq, Cairo, 20 October 2010.

have victims, but the media is not talking about the victims of the fire. The chief editors don't talk about the worker victims because there were no big actions.[20]

For most journalists covering the Kefaya and Mahalla movements, 'protest' was just another exciting news product to sell. Only politicized journalists or activists dabbling in grassroots journalism continued their engagement with the workers' movement irrespective of its value as news. Yet their assistance was often based on an exchange relation that recognized the strikes primarily as a means of accumulating members and building influence amongst the working class. Hassanein criticized leftists for their instrumental relation to the workers' movement as they "[…] are jumping on the Mahalla movement and are trying to recuperate it, to gain something from it […]."[21] Sabr Barakat noted that:

> A lot of political activists are using the labor movement as a means to take off. I did this in my youth, but it is a big mistake. The working class is the strongest force at the moment and has the biggest effect, larger than any other movement. What happened in Mahalla, the rise of the workers movement, was used by political activists, but it was not good for the movement's progress. It tried to push the movement in a certain direction.[22]

Traditional intellectuals agreed with worker leaders that the role of political activists was not always beneficial in the development of a proletarian activity-system. Khaled Ali remarked that "[…] many political activists jumped on the Mahalla movement and tried to reap the benefits. They were releasing conflicting statements that divided the movement itself."[23] The different leftist trends accused each other of recruiting workers to their organization without supporting the movement itself.[24] Irrespective of the rights and wrongs committed

---

20 Interview with Faysal Lakusha, Cairo 20, October 2010.
21 Interview with Hassanein, Cairo, 13 October 2010.
22 Interview with Sabr Barakat, Cairo, 16 October 2010.
23 Interview with Khaled Ali, Cairo, 25 October 2010.
24 Tagammu activist Muhammad Fathi, for example, criticized the RS: "The Revolutionary Socialists came to join the demonstration. They came from Cairo with their Western attitudes and they did not have a big influence. The workers would not work with them. The Revolutionary Socialists said that they supported the workers, but at the same time they tried to recruit new members. It is not a problem that they came to the strike, but the workers thought that their attitude was opportunistic and that they did not really support their cause" (Interview with Muhammad Fathy, Mahalla, 12 November 2010). RS militant

by particular groups, it is clear that their intervention created problems. Ahmed Belal claimed that:

> The problem of the Mahalla movement today is the problem of the competition between leftists. When the strikes happened I said that all leftists should work together as comrades and support the workers. This did not happen. The activists of the leftist parties joined the movement as activists of their party and they tried to recruit workers' leaders for their party. We let the workers' leaders alone in Mahalla, while they tried to recruit them. The last years there were no strikes because each leftist faction has taken one worker leader each. We should support the movement, not try to lead it in the place of the workers' leaders themselves. Now the leaders are divided and they compete against each other and this destroys the movement.[25]

Wael Tawfiq concluded that: "A lot of political organizations treated the Mahalla movement as a launch pad for a new workers' movement and they didn't treat it as what it really was: a big strike."[26] Gihan Shabeen who later became a member of the Socialist Renewal Current (SRC), a split from the RS, admitted that the assistance of the Revolutionary Socialists had not always been beneficial to the development of the strike movement: "We analyzed our involvement in the strike as sectarian. Our activists were issuing very high demands and were splitting the movement. They were not issuing the demands that regrouped the movement and unified the movement, making it succeed."[27] Whereas RS leader Mustafa Bassiouny claimed that: "During the Mahalla strike we profited more than any other political power. We recruited more than any other one active in the labor movement. We believe that the resurgence of the workers class creates opportunities for all leftist and progressive forces," he also acknowledged that: "[...] the struggle for small party profits will destroy the labor movement."[28]

Political sectarianism and opportunism were distorted pedagogies that reflected problems of the left in building a counterhegemonic project. Often

---

Hossam al-Hamalawy, for his part, called the Socialist Horizons Center of the ECP a "[...] corrupting force in the left. They don't have any influence: they take a youth from a demo and call him a strike leader" (Conversation with Hossam al-Hamalawy, Cairo, 14 May 2009).

25   Interview with Ahmed Belal, Cairo, 9 October 2010.
26   Interview with Wael Tawfiq, October 16, 2010.
27   Interview with Gihan Shabeen, Cairo, 16 March 2011.
28   Interview with Mustafa Bassiouny, Cairo, 12 October 2010.

there was the difficult question of balancing between party building and supporting the development of the strike activity-system. Without an organizational apparatus and political center of some sort, which served to 'associate', 'project', and 'integrate' the workers' struggles, the left could not play a role in developing the proletarian subject. Without 'recruiting' – i.e., the organization and politicization of workers as intellectuals within the apparatus – leftist parties would remain external and alien forces vis-à-vis the workers' movement. Rejecting any organized role for the keft amounted to a political liquidationism.[29]

Yet, the criticisms of workers pointed toward the *Selbstzweck*[30] tendencies of leftist apparatuses. They explicitly accused political activists of "recuperating" and "using" the labor movement; "gaining" something from it and "reaping its benefits"; of conceiving the workers "as a means to take off" and a pool to "recruit new members." Instead of the political mediations of the workers' movement, leftist groups became ends-in-themselves, considering the workers as a means to develop their own apparatus. This resulted in "opportunism" and "competition," a "division" and "corruption" of the movement, and an "illusion of support."

Solidarity

A subject that assists another subject through solidarity conceives of the Other as an end-in-itself and considers its own agency as a scaffold for the development of the other project. The solidary subject offers its assistance under the directions and conditions of the Other. Firstly, *intra*class solidarity between different instances of struggle is a leading activity in overcoming the spatio-temporal fragmentation of the worker subject. Solidary collaboration projects the workers as a class and a force in society. It generalizes the different moments of the strike into a contemporaneous, yet still decentralized, subjectivity, clearing the path for a unified proletarian project.

Secondly, solidarity creates the possibility of an *inter*class shared activity system between, on the one hand, organic and traditional intellectuals, and, on the other, between workers and other subaltern forces such as farmers, slum dwellers, the deprived middle classes, students, and so on. The systematization and institutionalization of inter-class solidarity leads to the formation of a united front between subaltern forces.

---

29   Cf. Chapter 9.
30   Cf. Chapter 9.

A key concept in the development of a solidary system of activity is trust. Blunden explained that: "New trust between strangers comes out of participating together in a common project. So the qualification is that before I can expect that we will decide together what we do, first off, 'you decide what I can do to help you'" (Blunden 2004b). For the workers in Mahalla, trust and reciprocity were already part of their subjectivity as a unit of labor power in capitalist production:

> We spend eight hours every day together. It's more than the time we spend at home. We are all together – Christians and Muslims. At work, we are like a family. We eat together. If my Christian colleague needs some money, we make a collection. Maybe his son needs money to go to hospital. It's not important if it's for a Muslim or Christian.
> *Revolution through Arab Eyes* 2012

The Mahalla strikes expanded the relations of trust from within the factory to the local community, and to other workplaces. Mahalla was a city of working class families, who participated in the strike movement and acquired proletarian subjectivities. "It was war and the workers and the citizens were on the same side,"[31] Sayyid Habib recalled. "When a worker or his family went out to buy bread for the strikers and the vendor knew that it was to support the strike, he often refused to take money." [32]

Throughout the 1980s the embedding of worker subjects within the particular activity-systems of cities such as Mahalla al-Kubra and Helwan, and within the national context of the moral economy, had 'communalized' the class protests rather than 'proletarianized' the communities (DuBoc 2009). Sam Moore observed that: "[...] community is not a substitute for the class basis of union organisation and cannot of itself generate class politics or consciousness, although it can inform and strengthen this through a dynamic relationship which may transform both" (Moore 2011, 141). The radicalization of labor protests in the 1990s and 2000s in reaction to the neoliberal state offensive began to reverse the dynamic of 'communalization'. Instead of absorbing worker subjectivities into communal practices and concepts, the community assisted the strike movement in a solidary way. The development of the Mahalla strikes between 2006 and 2008 interpellated the citizens of the local community as solidary participants in the worker activity-system. Therefore the victory of the

---

31 Interview with Sayyid Habib, Mahalla, 12 November 2010.
32 Interview with Sayyid Habib, Mahalla, 12 November 2010.

Mahalla workers, the emulation of their strikes by other workers, and the solidarity campaigns created new bonds of trust between workers.

Traditional intellectuals played an important part in organizing forms of intraclass solidarity.[33] Before any proleptic instruction can take place, the instructor has to be recognized as a genuine participant in a shared activity-system. However, workers did not easily acknowledge political actors external to their activity-system as genuine allies. Sayyid Habib commented:

> The political trends and the intellectuals have to be more close to the workers and the people if they want to make a general strike [...] They have to grasp our way of living. The consciousness of the workers is low. Political leaders have to speak the same language of the people. They don't want to go to the workers but they want the workers to go to them. That's why the political trends and the workers are far from each other.[34]

Political activists had to prove themselves as solidary actors: "You must be present in the strike and make sure that the workers trust you."[35] Because the whole town of Mahalla was already in solidarity with the workers, political activists who were part of this community could more easily gain the trust of the strikers. Ahmed Belal clarified: "Political activity for me in Mahalla is easy, because I struggle together with the people from my community, not only with statements, but by joining their demonstration and by speaking with them every day. Our comrades in Mahalla are also our friends."[36] The part that activists such as Ahmed Belal and Muhammad Fathi were able to play in the strike movement flowed directly from their subjectivity as members of the Mahalla community.

For actors that did not share an important subjectivity with the workers, it was more difficult to present themselves as genuine participants in solidary collaboration. Establishing a relation of trust between traditional intellectuals and workers was realized by "going to the workers," standing "side by side," "struggling together," "be present," "grasping their way of living," "to support and not to influence," and "being close to the people and tell them the truth."[37] In order for assistance to be solidary, it had to be

---

33 Interview with Sayyid Habib, Cairo, 12 November 2010.
34 Interview with Sayyid Habib, Cairo, 12 November 2010.
35 Interview with Wael Tawfiq, Cairo, 16 October 2010.
36 Interview with Ahmed Belal, Cairo, 6 April 2009.
37 Interview with Abir Mehdawi, Cairo, 13 April 2009; Interview with Wael Tawfiq, Cairo, 16 October 2010; interview with Mustafa Bassiouny, Cairo, 12 October 2010.

unconditional, honest, and oriented toward the development of the assisted subject. Selfless and honest support created bonds of trust, which, in turn, facilitated a solidary mode of assistance. Within the collaboration that solidarity creates, a shared project may develop between non-proletarian and proletarian actors, provided that they establish a dialectical pedagogy: a process of reciprocal learning that pushes forward the development of the subjectness of all actors involved.

Educating the Educators

Throughout the Mahalla strike movement, traditional intellectuals pushed the development of the worker subject forward by their solidary assistance, elevating the worker subject from its economic-corporate level to a trade unionist activity-system. In turn, the autoproleptic actions of the working class acted as a heteroleptic magnet on leftist intellectuals. In the 2000s the Egyptian left, like the workers' movement, was fragmented and in the process of reconstructing itself. By establishing shared systems of activity, the workers' movement 'educated' leftists as much as they 'educated' the workers. Mustafa Bassiouny contemplated that: "The long term strikes like in Mahalla gave me a clear image of the daily struggle of the workers and how strikes change the political atmosphere [...]. I learned more from the workers than the other way around."[38] Baho Abdul stressed that: "We have much to learn from the natural leaders, especially their discourse and their ways to communicate. That's why we'll publish our newspaper in 'ammiya."[39,40]

For new left organizations such as the RS, Tadamon, and later the SRC, the active involvement in the workers' movement led to a political and social transformation. New layers of recruited workers changed the class base of these movements, which were primarily composed of students and middle-class traditional intellectuals. Politically they moved away from purely civildemocratic politics and returned to class. Old left parties such as Tagammu and the ECP continued their disengagement from class politics, but faced increased internal dissent, both from disgruntled leaders organized in factions such as the Trend for Change, and local activists who participated in the many social and political movements of the 2000s, such as Ahmed Belal.

---

38 Interview with Mustafa Bassiouny, Giza, 12 October 2010.
39 Colloquial Egyptian Arabic.
40 Interview with Baho Abdul, Cairo, 10 May 2009.

However, it would be misleading to present the emergence of a dialectical pedagogy between workers and traditional intellectuals as the defining political relation from 2006 onward. On the contrary, most political activists, journalists, artists, and so on, did not participate in a shared, solidary activity-system with workers and other subaltern classes: even those leftists who assisted subaltern subjects in solidarity did not automatically become 'democratic philosophers'.[41]

Moreover, collective subjectivities were not always successfully integrated at the level of the individual subject. For example, in Dikirnis, a small village near Mansura, the Tagammu branch had been at the forefront of the resistance of farmers, who tried to safeguard their lands against the encroachment of the local landlords. When I arrived in Dikirnis, Mahmud Foda – the secretary of Tagammu for Mansura who lived in the village – and three farmers – Hagga Zeki, Said Abd al-Mali and Ahmed Rashil – awaited me. They informed me about the self-organization of the farmers and their occupation of the lands that the landlords tried to take away from them. Together with other leftist factions and parties, Tagammu members supported and organized the farmers, while articulating their grievances in the national media and the parliament. On the local level, the activists stood up against the Muslim Brotherhood and the Wafd party, which supported the right of the landlords to reclaim their lands. Mahmud Foda denounced the Wafd as a party that defended the interests of landlords and capitalists. Yet, when we talked about national politics, his rhetoric changed. As a proponent of the 'democracy first' strategy, the Tagammu secretary emphasized the need to create a broad electoral front against the régime, including all secular and democratic forces. "Including the Wafd?" I asked. "Including the Wafd," he answered. When I asked Foda how he would convince the farmers present of voting for a coalition between Tagammu and the Wafd, he claimed that, due to the dictatorship, "Egyptian political activists have to work in a narrow framework."[42]

This anecdote illustrated the contradictions between subjectivities within the individual subject. Mahmud Foda supported the struggling farmers against their class enemies, reinforcing their activity-system with various forms of assistance. At the local level, he was a genuine participant in a grassroots collaboration of solidarity. Yet, he also defended a broad democratic front with the peasants' sworn class enemies – a subjectivity which was born from the colonizing logic of the old left that democratic change should precede structural economic reforms; i.e., a 'stage theory' of class struggle. The Mubarak dictatorship warranted the strategy of 'democracy first' in the national sphere,

---

41 Cf. Chapter 7.
42 Interview with Mahmud Foda, Hagga Zeki, Said Abd al-Mali and Ahmed Rashil, Dikirnis, 17 April 2009.

which, ironically, could only exist alongside forms of class politics in the local sphere because of the isolation of national politics from the street, and because of the separation of political and economic struggle. Foda's 'bottom-up' experience of solidary assistance to the struggle of the farmers did not reconstruct his 'top-down' political theory. Nor did his democratic stagism prevent him from supporting the peasants. There was no organic integration of economic and political, everyday and scientific lines of development, which led to a 'schizophrenic' political pedagogy.

Likewise, worker activist Faysal Lakusha remained loyal to the NDP and the Mubarak régime, despite his everyday struggle against the police and factory management. Similarly, Tagammu activist Muhammad Fathi clung to the theory that there was no 'real' class struggle in Egypt so long as there was no genuine bourgeois democracy and developed capitalism, while he actively participated in the everyday reality of the Mahalla strikes.

It is beyond the scope of this book to advance an exhaustive explanation for these hybrid and contradictory forms of political consciousness within individual subjects. A general factor why there was no automatic process of conceptual integration and 'educating the educator', was the economic-corporate level of the working class. Because of the fragmented character of the worker subject its little developed political line of development and its weak trade unionist and national neoformations, leftists were sometimes tempted to lead movements themselves instead of helping the class to create its own directive organic intellectuals.[43] This 'directive solidarity'[44] ran the risk of ending up as substitutionism,[45] by which a non-proletarian actor substituted its own agency for that of the worker subject. Understanding this danger, Mustafa Bassiouny pledged that: "We are not taking any decisions for the workers movement. If the movement takes a bad decision we will support them even if we see it's a bad decision."[46]

This insight connects the mode of assistance to the adequacy of instruction. Assistance must be *solidary* in order to be *genuine*, but it must be *instructive* in order to be *adequate*. Not all forms of assistance are productive, even if they are part of solidary collaboration. This poses the question of the zone of proximal development of the Egyptian workers' movement before the 25 January Revolution: which forms of assistance accelerated or retarded the development of the worker subject?

---

43   Interview with Wael Tawfiq, Cairo, 16 October 2010.
44   Cf. Chapter 7.
45   Cf. Chapter 9.
46   Interview with Mustafa Bassiouny, Cairo, 12 October 2010.

CHAPTER 22

Adequate Assistance

In the previous chapter I discussed in detail the different forms and modes of assistance in the Egyptian workers' movement. Having established solidarity as the authentic mode of assistance, the following chapter investigates which forms of assistance were adequate, by framing debates among worker leaders and leftist activists about the limits and possibilities of the movement within a 'zone of proximal development'-perspective.

Boundaries of Instruction

Whereas solidarity is a necessary condition for the creation of an authentic and reciprocal relation of learning between workers and non-proletarian actors (a dialectical pedagogy) in itself it does not guarantee an instructive process that advances the development of the worker subject. Vygotsky argued that instruction only leads (to) development when it fuels the maturation of the central neoformation and line of development of a subject at a certain point in its sociogenesis. There is only so much distance a subject can cross between its actual and potential development within a specific phase of its trajectory: the zone of proximal development (ZPD).[1] This does not mean that the formation of a worker subject and emancipation in general can be reduced to a linear scheme of preset stages, but that, for each concrete episode in its historical process, there is a 'zone' that delineates possibilities and constraints of further development depending on the actual circumstances (Daniels 2007, 209). The ZPD depends on the social situation of development. Obviously, the distance between actual and potential development is larger in revolutionary conditions, or when the 'privilege of backwardness'[2] allows for the direct 'import' of neoformations. A specific neoformation and concept – for example trade unionism – might advance the development of the workers' movement at one point in its trajectory, but retard it at another. Instructors, who can be either 'internal peers' (organic intellectuals) or 'external teachers' (traditional intellectuals), have to focus their efforts on elaborating those structures and

---

1 Cf. Chapters 4 and 7.
2 Cf. Chapter 10.

concepts that allow the worker subject to emancipate itself from its current predicament. Instruction that moves 'behind' or too far 'ahead of' development is either irrelevant or counterproductive. Intellectuals have to balance between assistance that is either too 'pessimistic' or 'voluntarist'.[3]

With regard to the Mahalla strike movement, the discussion about the ZPD of the Egyptian workers was not a purely theoretical analysis brought from without, for both organic worker leaders and traditional intellectuals were continuously debating the possible directions, capacities, and goals of the developing worker subject. From this perspective, political 'voluntarism' consisted of those forms of instruction that transgressed the 'upper' limit of the ZPD of the movement, projecting the working class in a potential moment of their emancipatory trajectory that was too far ahead of their actual developmental level. Conversely, forms of instruction that remained below the 'lower' limit of the ZPD of the movement acted as a brake on the development of the activity-system.

Limits of the Economic Line

In the years leading up to the 25 January uprising, almost all leftists agreed that: "The purpose for all of us is to participate in the basic union committees in the factories and on the site. But the highest and biggest union organizations are controlled by the government through the Ministry and the Security."[4] Even though the GFETU was a bureaucratic pillar of the régime, local factory committees often offered a space of activity for organic intellectuals of the working class. However, the success of the Mahalla strike committees and the formation of the RETAU in 2008 raised the question of the possibility of the institutionalization of independent trade unionism.

Some organic and traditional intellectuals recognized only the potential of a marginal development of the worker subject; as long as there was no real democracy in the national political sphere, a free, independent, and democratic trade union was unattainable. State repression, exemplified in the 6 April uprising, rendered the idea of any large scale and independent workers' movement within the framework of the Mubarak dictatorship unfeasible.[5]

---

3 Cf. Chapter 9.
4 Interview with Sabr Barakat, Cairo, 16 October 2010.
5 Muslim Brotherhood leader Said Husayni claimed that: "[...] this is not the right movement to make change against the régime, because (1) it's a hard dictatorship. The régime will use all

Leftist labor leaders and activists disagreed about the possibility of independent trade unionism in the Mubarak era. Helmi Sha'rawi claimed that:

> The great question for Marxist trade unionists is to either create new unions or fight within the existing trade union. In the movement you will find those who are pushing for independent unions. Of course we agree with this principle, but in the current atmosphere it will be very weak: how will you collect your contributions [...] and so on. How? It is not allowed under the emergency law.[6]

Abd al-Rashid Hilal, a senior worker activist in Tagammu, emphasized that workers and their strikes had to be oriented towards "a political-democratic goal" as "the independent union will not come without democracy" and while "[...] Tagammu aims to have a union that solves the social problems of the workers, until this happens, Tagammu will struggle to create new tools to fix it." [7] He rejected the possibility of a straightforward emulation of the RETAU experience in other workplaces, because the government did not formally recognize independent trade unions. Within the context of dictatorship, the mode of struggle was gradual and deliberate:

> We have to make our own local small committees in the government union so we can establish the independent union step by step. We can't work in the government unions unless the workers have a political perspective and unity. And that is what Tagammu wants to do: to organize the workers around one goal and one interest and give them political ideas and make small committees in the unions. Then we can gather all these small committees to make an independent union.[8]

Baho Abdul argued that the formation of the RETAU had been a fringe development and did not represent the main trajectory for the whole Egyptian worker subject.

---

ways to defend itself; and (2) the world régime won't support a revolution at this moment, as our government supports Israel. So a general strike will not succeed at the moment, but perhaps in the future" (Interview with Said Husayni, Mahalla, 20 May 2009).

6   Interview with Helmi Sha'rawi, Giza, 11 November 2010.
7   Interview with Abd al-Rashid Hilal, Cairo, 9 October 2010.
8   Interview with Abd al-Rashid Hilal, Cairo, 9 October 2010.

It's too soon for an independent union, because people don't yet understand what it means: they don't yet have the experience to run a union. Besides, the government will never accept it. They accept the tax collectors' union because it isn't a big threat to them. I am of course in favor of the organization of the workers, but a real union needs money and legitimacy before it can work.[9]

The orientation toward the working class and the attitude towards independent trade unions were one of the main reasons for the split of the SRC from the RS in 2010.[10] According to Gihan Shabeen:

We said that it was not enough to talk about independency because that is a merely democratic demand, but it is also necessary to build the union from below and to make it completely democratic, and that this was not the time to talk about independent unions for workers, we had to look at every place, and see how they can and want to organize themselves, even if they want to organize themselves legally. The issue is to organize themselves, or making small groups to do whatever necessary, not talking about independent unions.[11]

Fatma Ramadan explicated that:

[...] the conditions for the workers are not good to form independent trade unions on their own. The workers are on the defensive and the government is defending the state trade union, so until the workers unite and take a stand, it is not a good moment to create independent trade unions. [...] the workers need organization, however you call it: a committee, a trade union. Everyone in a factory should be organized in a committee. Step by step the workers will join, but even in Mahalla where they had the biggest strike, if the leaders would call their members to establish an independent union they would be isolated.[12]

Likewise the CTUWS, which had played an important role in the Egyptian workers' movement from the 1990s onward, was unwilling to turn the Mahalla strikes into the vanguard of independent trade unionism, and it came increasingly

---

9 Interview with Baho Abdul, Cairo, 10 May 2009.
10 Interview with Wael Tawfiq, Cairo, 20 October 2010.
11 Interview with Gihan Shabeen, Cairo, 16 March 2011.
12 Interview with Fatma Ramadan, Cairo, 11 October 2010.

into conflict with political forces such as the Revolutionary Socialists that advocated this kind of development.[13] RS leaders argued that the emergence of the RETAU had demonstrated the possibility of independent trade unionism in Egypt and that the efforts of political activists should be focused on strengthening the emerging trade union structures as they constituted the central neoformations of proletarian development at that juncture. Mustafa Bassiouny argued that:

> [...] the workers are ready when they are ready. We can't say that a movement with strikes and demonstrations and demands can't have an independent trade union – because in practice they were already operating as an independent trade union. [...] The labor movement showed it was ready. If the workers are ready we must be ready too. [...] Before the independent tax union a lot of activists were afraid of this idea. The example of the tax workers will help other workers. We believe that the workers movement is much stronger now.[14]

Khaled Ali of the ECESR agreed with the vanguard role of the RETAU, but was a little more cautious and pessimistic towards the future: "[the Egyptian workers] have to organize themselves like the real estate tax collector workers. [...] Actually the real estate trade union is confronted with many difficulties and hard measures against it and pressures to abort it. I hope, but I don't think they will be able to continue."[15] Sabr Barakat claimed that activists should:

> [...] push the workers more and more to the way of their own independent unions. Away from the government and the governmental trade union organizations [...]. The strikes are a tool to obtain the independent unions. The end solution is: independent unions because the union organization itself is a tool to get our rights and to protect them. And to further develop the labor rights.[16]

Unlike Abd al-Rashid Hilal, Talal Shukr elucidated that some members of the Tagammu labor committee had always looked favorably on the formation of new trade unions:

---

13   Beinin and al-Hamalawy 2007b; conversation with Hossam al-Hamalawy, Cairo, 14 May 2009; conversation with Sarah Carr, Cairo, 15 April 2009.
14   Interview with Mustafa Bassiouny, Giza, 12 October 2010.
15   Interview with Khaled Ali, Cairo, 25 October 2010.
16   Interview with Sabr Barakat, Cairo, 16 October 2010.

We have encouraged the workers to create their own, independent union, with their own ways, far from the régime union. Tagammu was with the independent movement and supported the demand for a new union. Already in 2001 we had a committee in the party to steer workers towards the idea of an independent movement.[17]

Mahalla workers such as Wael Abu Zaid[18] and Sayyid Habib[19] wanted to follow the example of the RETAU workers. They had collected 14,000 signatures in a petition of Mahalla workers against the state union and 1,200 resigned from the GFETU altogether. Their goal was to hand their demands over to the ministry of manpower and if the government refused their independent union they would go to court, as the RETAU had done, and seek support from the ILO. Sayyid Habib dismissed state repression as an insurmountable obstacle for the workers' movement: "If we cared for the emergency law we couldn't do anything. Our strikes were illegal under emergency law."[20]

In conclusion, the discussion in the years leading up to 25 January 2011 about independent trade unionism was not whether to support independent worker strikes or committees or not, but to what extent the institutionalization of these grassroots struggles was possible within the objective condition of dictatorship and strong, paternalist state unions and the subjective situation of a dispersed and relatively inexperienced working class. Whereas some organic and traditional intellectuals argued that independent trade unionism was the leading neoformation of the worker subject, others conjectured that this instruction transgressed the upper boundaries of the ZPD of the worker project at the time.

Limits of the Political Line

A second debate involved the margins of the politicization of the movement. Within the left there was a consensus that the separation between particular-economic and universal-political demands and movements constituted the main obstacle for the formation of a social and political force that would be able to challenge the régime.[21] Husayn Abd al-Razik claimed that:

---

17   Interview with Talal Shukr, Cairo, 21 April 2009.
18   Interview with Wael Abu Zaid, Mahalla, 20 May 2009.
19   Interview with Sayyid Habib, Mahalla, 12 November 2010.
20   Interview with Sayyid Habib, Mahalla, 12 November 2010.
21   Interview with Ahmed Belal, Cairo, 6 April 2009.

Every group fends for itself and the government attempts to buy off the different sections and layers. And when movements have a political character, they lack organisation. So there are political organisations without a social base, and social movements without a political organisation. No political party has a real connection to the common people.[22]

Al-Karama journalist Tareq Said observed that: "A lot of people in Egypt don't care about freedom or democracy, they care about their salaries, their living, how to raise their children. When people understand change will happen only connected to politics – then change will happen."[23]

Other organic and traditional intellectuals were pessimistic about the politicization of the workers' movement and did not recognize the potential in entwining the political and economic lines of development during the Mubarak era. Mahalla worker Faysal Lakusha, himself a NDP-member, claimed that: "If we will say that we are supported by political parties, the government will attack us, both the workers and the parties." [24] His colleague Abdul Kader asserted that: "[...] we see our demands as labor demands, not as political demands [...]. If we give labor demands a political form we won't succeed." [25] Talal Shukr explained that: "When the workers organize a movement, the government treats them kindly. When political parties enter to control the movement the government reacts very strongly, so the workers want to be independent from the parties."[26] Although the connection between the political and the economic was theoretically necessary, in practice: "We must wait: in the near future they will understand the relation between the economic and the politics."[27]

Other activists stressed both the necessity and possibility of politicizing the movement.[28] The Mahalla strikes, for the first time since the 1970s, and perhaps even the 1950s, "[...] had the potential of relating the social to the political domain." [29] Mahalla workers began to connect their local, particular struggle to the domination and exploitation inherent in al-nizam. Medhat al-Zahed emphasized the reciprocal relation between political and social

---

22 Interview with Husayn Abd al-Razik, Cairo, 12 April 2009.
23 Interview with Tareq Said, Cairo, 11 November 2010.
24 Interview with Faysal Lakusha, Mahalla, 20 May 2009.
25 Interview with Abdul Kader, Mahalla, 20 May 2009.
26 Interview with Talal Shukr, Cairo, 21 April 2009.
27 Interview with Talal Shukr, Cairo, 21 April 2009.
28 Interview with Muhammad Fathy, Mahalla, 20 May 2009.
29 Interview with Fatma Ramadan, Cairo, 11 October 2010.

activism as mutually reinforcing activities: political groups should incorporate trade unionist demands and social movements should develop a political perspective.[30]

Of course, there was a danger that the politicization of the worker struggle entailed its colonization, i.e., its subjugation to the civildemocratic project, as I discussed in the previous chapter. For example, Abd al-Rashid Hilal argued that Tagammu activists "[…] have the task to move these strikes toward a political-democratic goal."[31] However, the experience of the failed 6 April strike showed the devastating effect of both a colonizing politicization and a political instruction that went beyond the 'upper' limit of the workers' ZPD at that time. Fatma Ramadan explained that:

> The political movement only touched the social movement: there was not a strong connection yet. The political activists went too fast raising the idea of a strike in the whole country which was not possible at that moment. This made the government use violence against the workers, and they paid some of the workers leaders to side with the government, and the prime minister, and the minister of manpower and the minister of investments went to the workers to grant them some of their demands.[32]

Although the Mahalla workers began to develop political subjectivities, these were all but matured during the 6 April strike of 2008. The central predicament of this period was still the economic-corporate condition of the working class. Despite the offensive worker struggles, the budding movement was caught up in a war of position, primarily defending the achievements of the past against the neoliberal onslaught. The task for solidary assistance was to support the building of central neoformations that were strongly entrenched in the workers' struggle, such as independent strike committees and trade unions like the RETAU.

The entwinement of the economic and the political lines of development was essential, but could and should not be forced from outside, leading to either colonization or substitutionism of the movement. Hisham Fouad wisely commented that:

---

30 Interview with Medhat al-Zahed, Cairo, 8 April 2009.
31 Interview with Abd al-Rashid Hilal, Cairo, 9 October 2010.
32 Interview with Fatma Ramadan, Cairo, 11 October 2010.

There is often an attempt to politicize the movement without developing the demands of the movement itself. One should wait until the movement reaches a good level before turning it into a political one. When there are no labor unions or labor parties there is an absence that we cannot fill. We only have a small number of activists. We should support the workers' demands themselves. Through this process the workers' aims are developed, and they develop into an independent group and from there they start to form demands that relate to the society at large, for example the demand of the minimum wage. Through the process of creating groups like this they will develop their demands from an immediate, low state to a higher form. On the other hand, they are facing a huge enemy. This enemy has to be conquered first and only then you can pose higher demands.[33]

The dictatorship constituted a hard limit on the development of the worker subject. Mubarak's neoliberal offensive and reconfiguration of the postpopulist historical bloc propelled workers into action, but at the same time it restricted their capacity to systematize their protests (Bassiouny and Omar 2008). The régime was not a passive obstacle, waiting to be overcome by the workers' movement, but an active force that mediated its predicament. Shandro sharply remarked that: "The process of [...] elaborating the political self-definition of the working-class movement, is one in which the adversary is inevitably and actively present" (Shandro 2001, 230). Whereas the establishment of independent trade unions had shown the potential development for the whole workers' movement, the crushed Mahalla uprising on 6 April 2008 served as a warning for the industrial core of workers not to challenge state power. At the same time it was a clear message that the workers' movement had to face the political character of its predicament – capital as state power – if it wanted to continue and complete its emancipatory struggle. An alliance with the civildemocratic movement was a necessary step in this process.

Workers themselves evaluated the capacity of the left and other civildemocratic actors to offer directive, technical, and cultural assistance – and often found the existing leftist parties and organizations wanting. For example, Nagwan Soleiman of the SLCHR claimed that the lack of politicization of the workers' movement was due to the organizational weakness of the political field. The necessity of a phase of proletarian 'trade unionism' before *hizbiyya* or 'partyism' owed as much to the underdevelopment of the left as it was a

---

[33] Interview with Hisham Fouad, Giza, 26 October 2010.

consequence of the workers' economic-corporate predicament: "Before the political activists start to organize the workers they should start to organize themselves. Later on they can agree on a certain agenda on how to interact with the labor movement. But the labor movement will not be developed into a political movement without this."[34]

The cohesion, coherence, and strength of the left also constituted an important aspect of the proletarian social situation of development. The weakness of the political line of development and the lack of a concrete national-popular subject was a predicament for the working class. The only solution for both the workers' and civildemocratic movement was an integration of their economic and political, everyday and scientific developmental lines through a sustained reciprocal, solidary, and proleptic collaboration.

---

34 Interview with Nagwan Suleiman, Giza, 26 October 2010.

PART 6

Tahrir

CHAPTER 23

Story of an Uprising (I)

The previous parts discussed the neoliberal predicament that Egypt's subaltern classes faced and the gradual and non-linear development of a civildemocratic and workers' movement. These are the objective and subjective elements that constituted the prehistory of the 25 January insurrection. The next two chapters deal with the 'story' of Tahrir: a description of the events of the 25 January uprising that prepares the way for an analysis of its 'plot' in Chapters 25 and 26.

The Tension Mounts

From the perspective of the 25 January insurrection, its 'original accumulation' spanned several decades, creating different revolutionary movements that were disassembled and reassembled in response to reconfigurations of the Egyptian historical bloc. These processes of subaltern subject formation have been discussed in the previous parts. The last forward thrust of this historical ebb and flow entailed the resurgence of politics 'from below' in the decade before 25 January 2011, led by the development of two collective subjects: the civildemocratic and the workers' movement. The molecular accumulation of protests went hand in hand with the crumbling hegemony of the Mubarak state, caused by the mixture of aggressive neoliberal counterreform, an increasing reliance on violence and coercion instead of consent-generating politics, and a reduction of the social base of the régime, among both subaltern and elite classes. The narrowed delineation of the interests and forces of al-nizam meant that the substance of the abstract national-popular subject, al-sha'b, became progressively obvious to all.

The generalization of discontent was accelerated in 2010 by events such as the murder of Khaled Said and the massive fraud of the November parliamentary elections. Sinan Antoon remarked that: "If Bouazizi's self-immolation was the spark in Tunisia, the brutal beating to death of Khaled Said, a 28-year old man from Alexandria, at the hands of two undercover policemen back in June of 2010 angered many Egyptians and spurred demonstrations" (Antoon 2011). Sabry Zaky explained the significance of Khaled Said for the mobilization of the middle-class youth in the months leading up to the revolution:

> [...] Khaled Said represented every one of them. Before this incident they were thinking like "Ok, the torture in police stations is something normal, because the state uses it against criminals or baltageyya, thugs, [...] and it is happening against the lower classes, ordinary people in the streets, squatters, and so on. But when this happens to one of us, belonging to the middle class, oh my God, we are not far away from this: this can happen to us."[1]

The name of the Facebook group "We are All Khaled Said," established by Google employee Wael Ghoneim, expressed this feeling of solidarity. The murder of Said served as an exemplum of the violent degeneration of the state that was supposed to protect the 'common good'. In addition to the centralized state attacks on political and human rights activists, workers' and farmers' movements, local police officers habitually harassed, tortured, and extorted ordinary citizens (Marfleet 2011). "Police demanding bribes, harassing small microbusinesses, and beating those who refuse to submit had become standard practice in Egypt" (Amar 2011). There was a growing 'good sense' of indignation within the populace and understanding that their oppression and exploitation by petty bureaucrats and administrators were only the local and everyday expressions of the corruption of the whole nizam. The behavior of the policemen who assaulted Khaled Said was not denounced because it was an aberration, but because it had become standard practice among state representatives. The murder of Said spurred on middle-class youth to organize and protest against the police state, not only through Facebook groups such as "We are All Khaled Said" and "6 April Youth," but also in grassroots movements such as HASHD, where they were further politicized.[2]

If the murder of Khaled Said served as an example of the rottenness of the system on the local level, the parliamentary elections of November 2010 became a symbol of the complete hubris of the rulers and their estrangement from society. Amina al-Bendary commented:

> In the last parliamentary elections NDP members alienated many sectors of society, both players in the political system and the overwhelming silent majority left out of it, by monopolizing the election process from nomination to election, resorting to any and all means necessary to keep non-NDP candidates out of parliament house; gerrymandering, intimidation, detention of opponents (especially Muslim Brotherhood

---

1 Interview with Sabry Zaky, Cairo, 10 March 2011.
2 Interview with Gihan Ibrahim, Cairo, 20 March 2011.

members), old-fashioned [vote] rigging, physical violence – any and all means possible.
> AL-BENDARY 2011

Thanks to an unprecedented display of massive fraud and intimidation Mubarak's NDP secured 209 of the 211 seats in the first round of voting.[3] The Muslim Brotherhood, the biggest opposition force in parliament, almost magically lost all but one of its 88 seats. In the past, parliamentary elections had given the régime an aura of legitimacy[4]: a means to forge a base of consent with other political opposition groups, such as the Wafd, Tagammu and the Muslim Brotherhood, and a channel for distributing favors and reinforcing patron-client relations. Since the 1980s, one of the strengths of the Mubarak régime had been its ability to include and absorb political opposition forces. Now, the stubborn and disdainful rejection by the NDP's leaders of any meaningful concession for the opposition came, ironically, at a moment when the régime's overall hegemony was at a historical low point: "The government's actions seemed rash, clumsy, and a little panicked. It simply wasn't the sort of thing a confident dictatorship does" (Khalil 2012, 103). The obsession of the inner NDP circle with the creation of an obedient parliament that would secure Gamal Mubarak's succession to power, combined with a supercilious and anxious refusal of any substantive democratic reform,[5] spelled the end of the régime. The elections prompted huge protests in the Canal town of Suez, which anticipated the protests of 25 January 2011 and the vanguard role that this community would play throughout the insurrection:

> In the first day, after the result of the elections, Suez had a demonstration of five or six thousand people standing in front of the police station, the governorate, and state security buildings, which are close to each other. This day was a tryout for the revolution in Suez [...]. We had a protest in the morning demanding an end to the régime, the police, and so on. This was during the elections – three months before the revolution. By the end of the day and after the results there was a huge demonstration in the streets of Suez, 15,000 citizens, and this was a huge number in these days.[6]

---

3 BBC News, 7 December 2010.
4 Legitimacy not only based on the mere fact of holding elections, but also because it allowed the Mubarak régime to present itself as a beacon of secularism and realpolitik vis-à-vis the Islamists.
5 Sameh Naguib (2011) argued that the state was especially wary of social and political instability in the wake of the global economic crisis from 2008 onwards.
6 Interview with Saud Omar, Suez, 18 March 2011.

Tunisian Prolepsis

Whereas the murder of Khaled Said and the election fraud highlighted the arrogance and brutality of the régime and its complete disdain for the dignity and rights of its citizens, the example of the Tunisian Revolution showed a concrete way out of the predicament: "The real trigger was the Tunisian revolution. It basically showed Arabs that they are capable of overthrowing their leaders."[7]

After an authoritarian reign of 24 years, on 14 January 2011 president Zine al-Abidine Ben Ali was forced to resign and flee to Saudi Arabia. Weeks of largely peaceful, mass protests had brought the dictatorship on its knees. Like other activists, Gihan Shabeen emphasized the importance of Tunisia as a source of inspiration for the Egyptian revolution: "Since twenty years ago we couldn't convince people that things would change through the people's power itself. Tunisia changed everything. We all saw on television how Egypt could change."[8] Sabry Zaky commented that: "[...] the revolution was inspired by the Tunisian revolution. Everyone said: "oh my God, it's possible, they ousted Ben Ali; they can do that. The audacity! And we can do this too." [9] After the Tunisian uprising, Khaled al-Balshy wrote an article in al-Badil that the Egyptian régime was as weak as Ben Ali's and that what happened in Tunisia could happen in Egypt as well: "I did not really believe in the article, but I played my role in encouraging people. What happens now in the whole Middle East is copying the Tunisian experience."[10] The proleptic instruction of the Tunisian revolution offered the Egyptian masses a glimpse of their own revolutionary potentiality (cf. Khalil 2012, 123). All that was needed was a spark that allowed this potentiality to develop into actuality. The 25 January protests became the catalyst of this revolutionary process.

25 January

Because of widespread popular resentment toward the increased violence and authoritarianism of the Mubarak régime and the shining example of the Tunisian Revolution, an "unlikely alliance of youth activists, political Islamists, industrial workers and hardcore football fans" (Shenker 2011a) felt confident to call on the Egyptian people to rise in protest on National Police Day, a national

---

7   Interview with Ahmed al-Gourd, Cairo, 24 March 2011.
8   Interview with Gihan Shabeen, Cairo, 16 March 2011.
9   Interview with Sabry Zaky, Cairo, 10 March 2011.
10 Interview with Khaled al-Balshy, Cairo, 14 March 2011.

holiday on 25 January. The holiday had been established in 2010 and commemorated the Battle of Ismailiyya on 25 January 1952, when police officers sided with the anti-colonial resistance against the British occupation forces. Ironically, the liberators of 1952 who were honored on Police Day had become the loathed epitomes of the oppressive state (al-Bendary 2011a). Already in 2010, 6 April activists had organized a protest against the police (Khalil 2012, 122).

Mobilization toward the 'Day of Rage' was organized through grassroots organizations and virtual networks. In cyberspace, the two main mobilizing forces were the 6 April Youth Movement and the We are All Khaled Said Facebook networks. Whereas the We are All Khaled Said group was the more popular one, the 6 April network still had some 70,000 members and a more political profile, including both economic and democratic demands. We are All Khaled Said issued the call for a march against torture, corruption, poverty and unemployment on 25 January, and the 6 April Movement quickly joined its initiative. Facebook users changed their profile picture to indicate symbolic support for the protest. Such virtual networks were not actors in themselves, but tools and expressions of physical spaces, connections, and actors 'on the ground' (Sassen 2011, 578). Paul Amar keenly observed that: "The so-called 'Facebook revolution' is not about people mobilizing in virtual space; it is about Egyptian internet cafes and the youth and women they represent, in real social spaces and communities, utilizing the cyberspace bases they have built and developed to serve their revolt" (Amar 2011). The poet Sinaan Antoon agreed: "Yes, new technologies and social media definitely played a role and provided a new space and mode, but this discourse eliminates and erases the real agents of these revolutions: the women and men who are making history before our eyes" (Antoon 2011).

The call to protest from the new social media was strengthened by leftist e-zines such as al-Badil. Khaled a-Balshy recalled:

> I wrote on the day when Ben Ali resigned on the website: "The First One." With the start of the Tunisian revolution I put the Tunisian flag on the logo of al-Badil. When Ben Ali resigned and the protests in Egypt started, I switched to the Egyptian flag, symbolizing the shift of the revolution to Egypt. [...] On 24 January, we contacted political forces with the question: "Will you attend the revolution or not?" And I wrote an article on 24 January to invite the people to the protests of 25 January because in my opinion it was the beginning of the end. And I said: "if you don't participate in these events you will be outside of Egyptian history, which will be written tomorrow."[11]

---

11 Interview with Khaled al-Balshy, Cairo, 14 March 2011.

Apart from the call by the new and the traditional media the mobilization of thousands of protesters was realized through the organizing activities of political movements. There were four political tendencies that prepared for the Day of Rage, using the traditional means of face-to-face meetings of activists, distribution of pamphlets, and so on. The first tendency consisted of youths of the Muslim Brotherhood, who decided to join the demonstration against the wishes of the Society's leadership.[12]

The second group was the activists of the new left: young members of parties such as Tagammu and the ECP, and militants of new movements such as the RS and the SRC.[13] Gihan Ibrahim recalled:

> I went to a meeting, the Thursday before Tuesday [25 January] and there was a representative basically from each group that was taking part in the protest. We agreed on the final places, the locations, the time, on what will we do if we get to Tahrir, what will happen, and so on [laughs]. [...] We were used to holding these kind of meetings for protests against the emergency law thing, or in favor of the minimum wage, or against high prices, and so on.[14]

The supporters of Muhammad al-Baradei and the National Association for Change (NAC) constituted a third faction, grouping liberals, progressive Islamists, activists from the Democratic Front party, and middle-class professionals (Kandil 2011). In 2010 al-Baradei had become a rallying point for the civildemocratic movement, but his inability to connect with the masses and forge lasting political alliances with, for example, the Brotherhood, had marginalized the NAC by early 2011 (Khalil 2012, 115).

A fourth type of people who organized the protests 'on the ground' were human rights activists, some of whom also belonged to the new left or 6 April Movement umbrellas. For example, human right activist and 6 April member Asmaa Mahfouz distributed tens of thousands of leaflets in informal neighborhoods in Cairo the day before the protests (Amar 2011).

A last and unlikely group of apolitical organizers were the 'Ultras': a movement of hardcore football fans that was formed in 2005. Like many other independent civil society groups, the Ultras had been repressed by the security forces, which tightly controlled football matches and stadiums. Before the first

---

12   Hazem Kandil in NLR 2011.
13   Interview with Haisam Hassan, Cairo, 7 March 2011; interview with Hisham Fouad, Giza, 13 March 2011; interview with Gihan Shabeen, Cairo, 16 March 2011; interview with Mustafa Bassiouny, Giza, 17 March 2011.
14   Interview with Gihan Ibrahim, Cairo, 20 March 2011.

protests of 25 January, the Ultras reassured the demonstrators that they would protect them against the police (al-Werdani 2011).

The demands of the organizers reiterated the standard, minimal aims of the civildemocratic movement, especially ending the emergency law and limiting the president's term. No one expected the protests to become a mass insurrection with revolutionary demands.[15] "The reason why 25 January became a mass protest was that it started from below, from the popular neighborhoods,"[16] claimed leftist activist Wael Tawfiq. The tactic to start the mobilization for a big protest from the poor areas had been developed already during the anti-war demonstrations of 2003.[17] This enabled activists to gather a critical mass of protesters before they arrived at Tahrir Square, as groups of only tens of demonstrators would get arrested easily by the police (Sowers 2012, 4). Moreover, through Twitter, Facebook, and snowball text messaging, organizers changed the original hour and place of the protests at around 10 h30 in the morning, outwitting the ministry of interior (Khalil 2012, 139).

The security apparatus was overwhelmed by the massive turn-out and at first stood by and watched. Already by noon it was clear to some participants that the massive demonstrations could be "an opportunity to bring down the Mubarak régime" (Guardian News Blog 25/1, 2011). In the afternoon the CSF tried to break up the protests with water cannons, sound bombs, batons, rubber bullets, and tear gas, and the peaceful demonstrations turned violent as protesters retaliated with rocks and bricks. "We stayed in the streets for the evening and the image of the Tunisian revolution was in our mind."[18] Protesters gathered on Tahrir Square, where they planned to make a stand against the riot police. During the late evening and night they were dispersed by the CSF, however (Khalil 2012, 149). Access to mobile phone networks and internet was gradually blocked. The protests in Cairo sparked off massive demonstrations in Alexandria and in major cities in the Delta, the Canal Zone, and Upper Egypt. In Suez the protests were brutally repressed, leading to a fierce confrontation with the police.[19]

Keeping the Fire Going

The morning after 25 January downtown Cairo was empty of protesters. The interior ministry deployed thousands of riot police "[…] on bridges across the

---

15   Cf. Introduction.
16   Interview with Wael Tawfiq, Cairo, 8 March 2011.
17   Interview with Gihan Shabeen, Cairo, 16 March 2011.
18   Interview with Haissam Hassan, Cairo, 7 March 2011.
19   Interview with Saud Omar, Suez, 18 March 2011.

Nile, at major intersections and squares as well as outside key installations like the state TV building and the headquarters of Mubarak's ruling National Democratic Party in central Cairo" (Guardian News Blog 26/1, 2011). As the 25th had been a holiday, the ministry expected fewer protesters on Wednesday and was determined to forcefully crush any mobilizations of the activist vanguard. At noon, individual youth and small groups of demonstrators were rounded up in Tahrir. As the number of protesters swelled during the afternoon and the evening, the violence of the police and plainclothes state security forces increased commensurably. Throughout the evening and the night, small rallies of a few hundreds of demonstrators were repeatedly charged and broken up by police and plainclothes, only to regroup at another location and continue their protests (Khalil 2012, 149–153). The fight in the streets was complemented by a state offensive in cyberspace, as the régime "[…] did not choose merely to target a handful of the major social networking sites, but rather the internet as a whole in addition to mobile phone networks […]" (Selim 2011). Mobile phone networks, internet access, and landlines were completely cut off. The websites of al-Dostour and al-Badil were taken down.

Outside Cairo, in Asyut and Mahalla al-Kubra protests were swiftly disbanded, but in Suez "[…] an angry crowd of about 1,000 people gathered outside the city's morgue demanding to take possession and bury the body of one of three protesters who died in clashes on Tuesday" (Guardian News Blog 26/1, 2011). Violent clashes between the police and the population of the Canal Zone city ensued. Several civilians were killed and in retaliation protesters set fire to the police station and the local NDP headquarters (Guardian News Blog 27/1, 2011). With both pride and grief Saud Omar recollected that: "There are five police stations in Suez we burned three of them. We burned a lot of police trucks […]. We burned the firefighters' station, because they were using the fire brigade trucks to transport weapons and kill protesters."[20]

On the second day of the protests the Egyptian political opposition started to voice its demands. Al-Sayyid al-Badawi, chairman of the Wafd, demanded a national unity government, the dissolution of parliament and new, fair elections. He remained completely silent, however, on the spontaneously emerged aim of the movement: the removal of Mubarak and a complete end to the régime. Conversely, the NAC, led by Muhammad al-Baradei, called on the president to step down and demanded that his son Gamal should not be allowed to run for president. Other groups stressed the demand to increase the national minimum wage and/or to fire the interior minister, Habib al-Adli (al-Amrani 2011a).

20 Interview with Saud Omar, Suez, 18 March 2011.

The morning of 27 January saw a return of calm to Cairo, as most activists prepared for a massive mobilization after the Friday afternoon prayers. New spontaneous protests of hundreds of protesters took place in Suez, Ismailiyya, and Alexandria. Thursday also saw the formal entrance of the Muslim Brotherhood in the protest movement, as Muhammad Morsi declared the participation of the Society in the demonstrations planned on Friday. The official statement read:

> The movement of the Egyptian people that began January 25 and has been peaceful, mature and civilised must continue against corruption, oppression and injustice until its legitimate demands for reform are met. We are not pushing this movement, but we are moving with it. We don't wish to lead it but we want to be part of it.
> *Guardian News Blog* 27/1, 2011

In the evening Muhammad al-Baradei arrived in Cairo pledging his active participation in the protests of Friday. Yet the fact that he waited for three days after the first protests to return to Egypt gathered a lot of criticism in the streets: "Only a smattering of well-wishers made it down to greet ElBaradei, a far cry from the scenes last February when the former UN nuclear weapons chief was met by more than a thousand supporters at the beginning of his triumphant return" (Shenker 2011b).

Friday of Anger

One of the main reasons for the success of the first demonstrations on 25 January was that their mobilization had started from working class neighborhoods. This tactic was repeated on the Friday of Anger, 28 January, which became a pivotal moment for the revolution. Leftist activist Wael Tawfiq recollected the snowball effect of mobilizing in the working class areas:

> We agreed to meet in a place in Imbaba. Before we got there we ran into several, six or seven, youth who came out of a small mosque, using slogans such as "the people want to end the régime." Our number reached twenty as we started to demonstrate in a poor neighborhood. The most important thing was the attitude of the normal people, demanding their rights, and continually asking others to participate. The demonstration in the poor neighborhood attracted thousands. When we reached the Kit

Kat Square we found a huge number coming from the famous Mustafa Mahmud Mosque. I took my group and went to the square.[21]

The Egyptian régime took the call for renewed protests on Friday 28 January seriously and prepared for the worst. From Thursday night on, all major ISPs were shut down and some 88 percent of Egyptian internet connections were effectively blocked (Rashed 2011, 23). Security forces and plainclothes police were mobilized on a massive scale: "There were thousands of police on the streets, hundreds on every corner and they have been recruiting young men to help quell protesters" (Guardian News Blog 28/1, 2011). As soon as the Friday prayers were finished, security forces launched a preemptive strike against (potential) protesters, using teargas, water cannons, and sound bombs. This time, many activists were prepared for a confrontation with the police, thanks to their experience on 25 January. Some of them had gotten advice from Tunisian revolutionaries: "[…] a Tunisian friend concluded that we could make a revolution on Friday and he sent us advice on what to do if they resort to us tear gas: using cola and vinegar and onions."[22]

Thousands of demonstrators started to clash with the police, not only in Cairo, but also in Alexandria, Beni Suef, Minya, Asyut, Ismailiya, Port Said, and al-Arish. In the Delta city of Mansura some 40,000 protesters destroyed the NDP headquarters. The NDP offices in Damietta followed suit. In Suez "[…] there were 80,000 people on the streets […] in a region like Suez! There are half a million people in Suez, so there was twenty percent of the population in the streets."[23] The police station in the al-Arbain neighborhood was taken over and detained demonstrators were freed. Security forces seemed to have withdrawn from the city, as Al Jazeera reporter Jamal al-Shayyal claimed: "The police has been quite comprehensively defeated by the power of the people" (Al Jazeera Live Blog 28/1, 2011). Al Jazeera reporter Rawya Rageh observed protesters 'arresting' police officers and beating some of them with their own batons (Al Jazeera Live Blog 28/1, 2011). Peter Bouckaert of Human Rights Watch described how in Alexandria the police just gave up fighting:

> The clashes lasted for nearly two hours. Then a much larger crowd of protesters came from another direction. They were packed in four blocks deep. Police tried to hold them back with teargas and rubber bullets, but they were finally overwhelmed […]. It is a very festive atmosphere.

---

21   Interview with Wael Tawfiq, Cairo, 8 March 2011.
22   Interview with Haisam Hassan, Cairo, 7 March 2011.
23   Interview with Saud Omar, Suez, 18 March 2011.

> Women in veils, old men, children, I even saw a blind man being led. And there are no police anywhere.
> *Guardian News Blog* 28/1, 2011

Central Cairo, however, was turned into a warzone between tens of thousands of protesters, who were trying to march on Tahrir Square, and the riot police who were attempting to block roads and bridges and to disperse the demonstrators with tear gas and rubber bullets. Wael Tawfiq evoked a telling scene:

> I encountered a huge number of people who were injured and who came from the Mustafa Mahmud Mosque, the gathering place from where also a lot of Mubarak supporters started their demonstrations. I noticed a lot of political activists. We began to walk in the Corniche. The police started to shoot us and we went to the side streets. With every step we got more numbers from the streets. At 6 October Bridge we encountered a huge number of police, throwing a huge number of gas grenades. Then we went back to the Arab League street, Gama't al-Dawwal. We found huge numbers, tens of thousands gathered there. At this moment the people pushed the police away from the streets. The policemen tried to block the roads to Tahrir Square. There were a lot of clashes. The most important clash was the one on the 6 October Bridge. We tried to go back to the square through al-Gal'a Bridge. On the way to Gal'a bridge we encountered another huge number of people. At this moment in my opinion we reached 100,000. We found some 5,000 people clashing with the police on the bridge. We told the policemen: "stop and surrender." We told them: "we will not hit you." The police leaders took their forces and withdrew and even left two trucks, and the people attacked the empty trucks. From al-Gal'a Bridge to Qasr al-Nil Bridge, the Opera neighborhood had a huge number of protesters. The policemen started to watch the side streets. Some of us were thinking about attacking the policemen, but most of us shouted "peaceful, peaceful!" In the entrance of the Qasr al-Nil square there were a lot of trucks awaiting us with gas grenades. The number of protesters was huge, which made the effect of the grenades more effective, because there was no room to retreat. The police tried to push the people back. Every one or two minutes a policeman was throwing four or five bombs, and then the people threw them back. I was afraid that with all these people the bridge could collapse. There was a continuous game of going forth and back between the police and the people. This is an important image in the revolution – the most important image in this day that made me realize that the régime was going down. We did not know

what was happening at the other side, at Tahrir, but we were hearing a lot of grenades and noise and we were afraid that a lot of people were dying at the other side. And we thought that the number at the other side was less than ours. We had some 150,000 people on the bridge so there had to be less people in Tahrir. So we started to think that we had to make a lot of noise, making the police concerned about our number, and draw them to us. So they would stop shooting the other side. This mood made me realize that the régime was falling. I was afraid and the ordinary people were also afraid, but still they spontaneously took this decision. This lasted for twenty minutes and the people insisted on going to Tahrir and to save the others. We went to the NDP headquarters. At this moment the most violent clashes started at the bridge.[24]

The NDP headquarters near Tahrir were set on fire. A curfew was ordered in the whole country, but it was largely ignored by the protesters. Youth activist Ahmed al-Gourd explained how the protesters were able to defeat the security apparatus:

Usually the police tried to disperse the people in order to surround the smaller groups. That's what we did – we used their own tactics against them. We organized different focal points in different areas of the city, and most of these people marched on Tahrir. Some people did not even go to Tahrir, they had their own shit going on in their own neighborhood. All the poor neighborhoods basically had their own huge protests, for example in Matareyya. So I can remember two main routes: one from Nasr City all the way walking, all the way along the Salah Selim road to Abasseyya to Ramsis Square to Tahrir. From the other, western side: Giza, Mohandiseen, Haram, Doqqi and even Helwan, they all converged on Qasr al-Nil bridge, entering Tahrir from that area. I was in front of the Ramses Hilton and we got everybody out in that neighborhood and started to push the cops back. The police in Downtown basically got surrounded and dispersed in a lot of different areas and they got pinned. And when they got pinned they unleashed all they had got on the protesters.[25]

The police themselves began to fell unconscious because of the smog caused by tear gas in the streets and started to defect.[26] Throughout the afternoon, it

---

24 Interview with Wael Tawfiq, Cairo, 8 March 2011.
25 Interview with Ahmed al-Gourd, Cairo, 24 March 2011.
26 Interview with Haisam Hassan, Cairo, 7 March 2011.

became more and more clear that the ministry of interior was not able to stem the revolutionary tide, as Hazem Kandil noted: "Coming together from different assembly points, and gathering steam as they marched towards Tahrir Square, crowds snowballing to some 80,000-strong were now ready to take on the police. Caught off-balance by the size and persistence of the demonstrators, the police were finally overwhelmed" (Kandil 2011). Somewhere between 16 h and 17 h the police were defeated (Khalil 2012, 177; Rashed 2011, 23). Wael Tawfiq remembered that: "This was the moment the police chose to surrender and go back to... somewhere we still don't know yet. [laughs]"[27]

27   Interview with Wael Tawfiq, Cairo, 8 March 2011.

CHAPTER 24

Story of an Uprising (II)

During the Friday of Anger the mass demonstrations of 25 January turned into a popular uprising that defeated the hated police in the streets. This chapter continues the story of the insurrection after the Friday 28 January protests.

Gaining Confidence

Because of the defeat of the police and the CSF in the streets, Mubarak had to call on the army to restore order (Khalil 2012, 193). Tanks and APCs rolled into the center of Alexandria, Cairo, and Suez, where they were welcomed by demonstrators who hoped that the army would side with them against the police. This episode evoked a moment from the 1917 February Revolution in Russia, narrated by Trotsky:

> Soon the police disappeared altogether – that is, begin to act secretively. Then the soldiers appeared – bayonets lowered. Anxiously the workers ask them: "Comrades, you haven't come to help the police?" [...] The police are fierce, implacable, hated and hating foes. To win them over is out of the question. Beat them up and kill them. It is different with the soldiers: the crowd makes every effort to avoid hostile encounters with them; on the contrary, seeks ways to dispose them in its favour, convince, attract, fraternise, merge them in itself.
>
> TROTSKY 2011, 128

At this point, the Egyptian military did not intervene in clashes between protesters and police. They did, however, disperse a group of protesters who tried to storm the *Maspero* state television building, sealed off access to parliament and cabinet buildings, and took control over Tahrir Square.[1] At around midnight president Hosni Mubarak appeared on Nile TV, declaring that he would fire the cabinet and appoint a new one on Saturday. In the same breath he warned the Egyptians that he would not condone any more chaos in the streets. Even though the army called on the population to respect the curfew, thousands

---

[1] Interview with Wael Tawfiq, Cairo, 8 March 2011.

continued to protest throughout Saturday 29 January in Cairo, Alexandria, Ismailiya, Suez and Damanhur.

After the withdrawal of police forces from the streets, the revolutionary masses faced a new threat: criminal gangs, some of them escaped/released prisoners, and baltageyya, 'thugs' who terrorized neighborhoods and looted houses, shops, and supermarkets (Stacher 2011a). These attacks were widely covered by state television and framed as a consequence of the anti-régime protests (Khalil 2012, 202). Blogger Issandr al-Amrani, however, criticized this type of coverage:

> There is a discourse of army vs. police that is emerging. I don't fully buy it – the police was pulled out to create this situation of chaos, and it's very probable that agent provocateurs are operating among the looters, although of course there is also real criminal gangs and neighborhoods [sic] toughs operating too.
>
> AL-AMRANI 2011B

Civil vigilante groups were improvised during the evening and night in order to protect neighborhoods from the attackers. The people, both in popular and wealthy areas, organized themselves to maintain order "[...] while plain clothes policeman [sic] try to create the impression of anarchy" (Guardian News Blog 30/1, 2011). At around 17 h30, Mubarak appointed intelligence chief Omar Suleiman as vice-president and Ahmed Shafiq, a former air force commander and civil aviation minister, as prime minister.[2] This move did not placate the masses, who continued their protests throughout the evening and the following day. Most banks, offices, and shopping malls remained closed.

At noon on Sunday 30 January, new tanks rolled into Tahrir Square, fortifying the salient military presence in the heart of the revolution where some 20,000 protesters were still gathered, chanting slogans against the president and the régime. In a ploy to divide the revolutionary movement, Mubarak blamed the Muslim Brotherhood for the chaos and looting, and warned Egyptians that the Society was taking advantage of their economic and political grievances. Meanwhile, the Ikhwan and four other opposition movements called for a temporary 'national salvation government', headed by al-Baradei,

---

[2] Suleiman had been the régime's favored candidate for the position of vice-president for two years. He headed the General Intelligence Services, which were directly dependent on foreign funding and worked closely with the USA and Israel, and which were distrusted by the general public (Hajjar 2011). Ahmed Shafiq, for his part, had been a Chief of Staff of the Air Force, which together with the Republican Guard constituted the two elite branches of the armed forces and those sections of the military that were closest to Mubarak.

which would organize an orderly transition toward democracy. In the evening al-Baradei arrived at Tahrir Square, where he got a mixed response. "There were waves of excitement and optimism as he arrived. But a notable number chanted anti-al-Baradei slogans, asking "How can you steal our revolution now?" (Guardian News Blog 30/1, 2011) Not that it mattered much, as Ashraf Khalil observed: "He was, for all intents and purposes, irrelevant to the process" (Khalil 2012, 118). At around midnight senior judges and scholars from *al-Azhar* University visited the dwindling number of demonstrators in Tahrir Square.

On Monday 31 January most government offices, public compannies, banks, schools, the stock market, and some private businesses remained closed. A group of 200 protesters had remained in Tahrir, occupying the square, while chanting and reading poetry. By the afternoon, the hard core of occupiers at Tahrir Square was again joined by tens of thousands of protesters, including women and children. Al Jazeera estimated the number of protesters at 250,000 (Al Jazeera Live Blog 31/1, 2011).[3] In Alexandria, Mahalla al-Kubra, Tanta, Kafr al-Zayat, and Fayum the revolutionary mobilization continued as well, with thousands protesting. In Suez popular committees effectively controlled the city, organizing traffic and protecting neighborhoods (Guardian News Blog 31/1, 2011).

In the evening a surprising statement came from the army which pledged not to shoot at civilians staging protests against the president, although it warned that it would not tolerate violence and chaos. Whereas the military, in general, exercised restraint in confronting the masses, it engaged in the systematic detainment and torture of individual protesters "[...] for no more than carrying a political flyer, attending the demonstrations or even the way they look" (McGreal 2011). By the end of the second week of protests, some 10,000 people, especially, political and human rights activists, had been arrested in Cairo alone (Guardian News Blog 8/2b, 2011).

Vice president Omar Suleiman addressed the nation on state television, acknowledging the need for dialogue with the opposition, constitutional reform, fighting corruption, and unemployment and an investigation into the November 2010 parliamentary elections. The speech was meant to co-opt the most moderate wing of the movement and isolate the most radical elements of the uprising from the rest of society. Suleiman's speech had little impact on the protests: "The consensus seems to be that Suleiman's appearance was intended for USA consumption" (Guardian News Blog 31/1, 2011). Activists called for a *millioneya* or 'one million march' on Tuesday and fixed Friday as a deadline for Mubarak's departure; if not, they would march on the presidential palace in Heliopolis.

---

3   A general *caveat*: such numbers were highly speculative estimations.

Late in the evening, the first attempt of the régime to organize opposition in the streets against the mass movement produced a feeble crowd of around 300 demonstrators outside the information ministry. State television, however, paid a lot of attention to the event and claimed that the pro-Mubarak protesters numbered thousands (Guardian News Blog 31/1, 2011). During the night, the last of Egypt's main internet providers, Noor, was shut down.

In the morning of Tuesday 1 February, the army closed main roads and train services to Cairo "[…] to prevent protesters from reaching mass protests today" (Guardian News Blog 1/2, 2011). State television tried to play on "[…] fears that today's protest could lead to violence, insecurity, and looting like what happened on Friday. Again they are trying to convince people not to join protests" (Al Jazeera Live Blog 1/2, 2011). Moreover, in order to create a semblance of societal polarization: "The state owned television and the police are ordering their employees to stage pro-Mubarak protests and about a few hundred are now engaging in pro-Mubarak demonstrations outside the state owned TV building" (Guardian News Blog 1/2, 2011). Nevertheless, tens of thousands of protesters made their way to Tahrir Square until more than one million people were occupying Tahrir Square and its surrounding areas. The original plan of marching on the presidential palace, however, was abandoned. "There are a lot of people who are against that because it's too far. And there is also a fear that if they leave the square, riot police will reoccupy it" (Guardian News Blog 1/2, 2011). Some activists began preparing for a continuous occupation: "[…] erecting tent [sic], bringing in blankets, food is being distributed, either for free or at discounted prices, music is being played […] people are arranging entertainment to keep them occupied during the protest – a football tournament will be starting soon" (Al Jazeera Live Blog 1/2, 2011). Anthropologist Samuli Schielke described the moving atmosphere at Tahrir:

> This day was one of the most amazing things I have ever experienced. It was perfectly peaceful, perfectly organised by spontaneous volunteers who took care of order, security, cleanliness. The people behaved in a very peaceful and reasonable way, and there was an amazing shared sense of dignity and power…Such pride, such determination, such sense of dignity, such sense of power, and such joy prevailed today in the centre of Cairo that I cannot write about it tonight without becoming very emotional. Not a moment for detached analysis.
>
> SCHIELKE 2011

Huge protests also took place in Alexandria, Suez, Ismailiya, Mansura, Damietta, Tanta, Kafr al-Shaykh, and Mahalla al-Kubra. Most people hoped that the massive scale and continuity of the demonstrations would be enough to force Mubarak to resign.

At around 23 h the president addressed the nation in "[...] a rambling speech in which Mubarak tried to show empathy with the protesters but at the same time suggested that they have been manipulated by political forces (perhaps trying to implicate the Muslim Brotherhood, whose role has been minimal)" (Guardian News Blog 1/2, 2011). Mubarak promised not to run again for president, which did not at all satisfy the disappointed crowd in Tahrir. "'Erhal erhal', meaning 'leave leave', the crowd in Tahrir Square continue to chant after Mubarak said that he will see out his current term" (Al Jazeera Live Blog 1/2, 2011). Outside Tahrir, however, the president's speech "[...] created a real sense of sympathy for Egypt's aging leader and this provided the pro-Mubarak camp with the momentum to maintain a strong counterrevolutionary movement for approximately one week after the speech" (Taha and Combs 2012, 83).

Amr Moussa, secretary general of the Arab League and one of the leaders of the opposition, called on the political forces to study Mubarak's offer carefully, whereas a majority of parties and movements, including the Muslim Brotherhood, rejected the proposal. In Alexandria protesters clashed with pro-Mubarak supporters, a foreshadowing of the coming counterrevolutionary violence throughout the next two days.

Battle of the Camel

On Wednesday morning, some twenty pro-Mubarak supporters clashed with the 1,000 protesters who had remained at Tahrir Square. "People were becoming tired and there was a small number in the square compared to other days," [4] Wael Tawfiq remembered. A few hours later a few thousand pro-Mubarak demonstrators gathered at the Mustafa Mahmud Mosque in Mohandiseen and near the Maspero television building, chanting slogans in support of the president. Meanwhile, the army made a statement calling on the protesters to end their demonstrations as Mubarak had granted them important concessions. Internet services returned, Al Jazeera became available again, and the régime seemed bent on 'normalizing' economic life after a week of protests.

At midday, Peter Beaumont observed that: "Thousands and thousands of pro-Murabak demonstrators are now pouring into the square... It seems to have been heavily choreographed" (Guardian News Blog 2/2, 2011). The army

---

[4] Interview with Wael Tawfiq, Cairo, 8 March 2011.

stood by and allowed armed Mubarak supporters to enter the square.[5] Initially, the Tahrir occupiers were able to form a human chain, pushing back the pro-Mubarak 'demonstrators' in a peaceful way. But then, by midday, the occupiers were suddenly attacked with rocks, Molotov cocktails, and knives. In a bizarre scene, some pro-régime forces charged with riding horses and camels into the Tahrir occupiers: "At one point, a small contingent of pro-Mubarak forces on horseback and camels rushed into the anti-Mubarak crowds, swinging whips and sticks to beat people. Protesters retaliated, dragging some from their mounts, throwing them to the ground and beating their faces bloody" (Guardian News Blog 2/2, 2011). Guardian journalist Jack Shenker commented: "People continue to run away from the square. Many of them have got blood wounds. I could saw [sic] one man just brush past me carrying a child…there appeared to blood on his chest" (Guardian News Blog 2/2, 2011). With regard to the attackers, Egyptian blogger Sharif Abd al-Kouddous observed that:

> These were not the same kinds of protesters that have occupied Tahrir for the last few days. These crowds were made up mostly of men, in between 20 and 45 years old. Many wore thick leather jackets with sweaters underneath. They chanted angrily in support of Mubarak and against the pro-democracy movement. They were hostile and intimidating.
>
> ABDEL KOUDDOUS 2011

Shenker identified them as: "[…] government-employed thugs and ex-prisoners […], alongside plainclothes policemen – though it would be misleading to suggest that these are the only people making up that side of these increasingly-violent rival demonstrations" (Guardian News Blog 2/2, 2011). New York Times columnist Nicholas Kristof, who was present during the infamous 'Battle of the Camel',[6] wrote that:

> In my area of Tahrir, the thugs were armed with machetes, straight razors, clubs and stones. And they all had the same chants, the same slogans and the same hostility to journalists. They clearly had been organized and briefed. So the idea that this is some spontaneous outpouring of pro-Mubarak supporters, both in Cairo and in Alexandria, who happen to end

---

5 Paul Amar, however, claims that: "The military were trying as best they could to battle the police/thugs, but Suleiman had taken away their bullets for fear the military would side with the protesters and use the ammunition to overthrow him" (Amar 2011).

6 A nod to the Battle of Bassorah in 656 between the forces of Ali and Aisha. Aisha led her soldiers from a camel carriage.

up clashing with other side – that is preposterous. [...] to me these seem to be organized thugs sent in to crack heads, chase out journalists, intimidate the pro-democracy forces and perhaps create a pretext for an even harsher crackdown.

Guardian News Blog 2/2, 2011

Later, many of the pro-Mubarak forces were shown to be plainclothes Central Security police and rank and file NDP members (Sallam, Stacher and Toensing 2011). Nonetheless, some popular layers of the counterrevolution consisted of protesters who had switched sides after the president's speech on Tuesday night, arguing that the people's demands were met and that life should now return to normal.

Despite the assault of the baltageyya, the anti-régime forces held their ground. After 18 h the protesters gained the upper hand and the thugs withdraw from the square. By midnight the battle shifted towards the streets surrounding Tahrir and the area around the Egyptian Museum: "Mubarak's 'thugs' tried to torch the national museum so they can claim it was the protesters. The scheme failed miserably as the protesters defended the museum and reclaimed it by way of protecting it" (Haddad 2011a). A force of 2,000 anti-régime protesters succeeded in securing the area around Tahrir and the museum, putting up barricades and stamping out fires from the régime supporters' petrol bombs. Yet throughout the night the battle continued to rage, with pro-Mubarak snipers and gunmen terrorizing the protesters. Tensions ran high in Alexandria as well, with supporters of the régime challenging the anti-Mubarak protesters "[...] but nothing on the scale of civil war that seems to be erupting in central Cairo. People here are now extremely fearful and anxious; no one knows what the coming days will bring" (Guardian News Blog 2/2, 2011).

Thursday morning, PM Ahmed Shafiq apologized for the violence in Tahrir and promised an investigation into the events. A meeting between Omar Suleiman, Ahmed Shafiq, and opposition leaders was boycotted by most political forces, including the Muslim Brotherhood. Suleiman vacillated between describing the protesters as "youth with genuine demands" and "foreign infiltrators wishing to destabilize the nation" (Guardian News Blog 3/2, 2011). The state media began to spread the rumor that there were Israeli spies among the foreigners in Egypt. Journalists – especially from Al Jazeera – were harassed by pro-régime supporters and then rounded up by the military "for their own safety" (Guardian News Blog 3/2, 2011). Others were arrested by agents of the ministry of interior. The offices of HMLC and ECESR were raided and their directors, Ahmed Sayf al-Islam and Khaled Ali, were arrested by military police. "The people were being beaten and the street had been told they were Iranian and Hamas agents come to destabilise Egypt so the street was chanting against them" ('Guardian News Blog 3/2, 2011). On the other hand, some cracks appeared in the state media as figures such as Shahira Amin from Nile TV resigned in protest of the régime violence: "I quit my job because I don't want to be part of the state propaganda régime, I am with the people. I feel liberated and relieved. I have quit my job and joined the people in Tahrir Square" (Al Jazeera Live Blog 3/2, 2011).

Although the army began to clear the area around Tahrir of the 1,000 or so Mubarak supporters in the morning, around midday the pro-Mubarak forces started to throw stones at the 4,000 strong occupiers, without any intervention from the army. During the afternoon, however, it became clear that the Tahrir occupiers, whose numbers swelled to about 50,000 to 100,000, were routing the pro-Mubarak forces. "Anti-government protesters are saying that if they survive tonight, the demonstration tomorrow will be massive. They are calling it departure day, the day Mubarak will be kicked out of office. Everything hinges on the next 24 hours" (Guardian News Blog 3/2, 2011). Meanwhile, in an exclusive interview with ABC news, Mubarak indicated that, eventually, he would leave his post as president, but "if I resign today there will be chaos" (Guardian News Blog 3/2, 2011). Ironically, at the same moment, ABC journalists were carjacked and chased by pro-régime supporters.

Remaining Steadfast

On Friday 4 February protesters hoped to force an outcome in the stand-off through a mass mobilization after the midday prayers. The slow withdrawal of international support for Mubarak, combined with the president's expressed desire to stand down 'eventually', and their own victory in the Battle of the Camel, emboldened the revolutionary forces. Already in the morning people started queuing in their thousands to get into the square. By around midday, hundreds of thousands were gathered in Tahrir, with Muslims, Copts, and Catholics praying together. A sermon by Yussef al-Qaradawi, the exiled Islamist preacher, was broadcast: "O Pharaoh, the time of the Pharaohs is over...Millions of people don't want you. As long as this man is there, Egypt will not be stable" (Guardian News Blog 4/2, 2011). Opposition leaders such as Muhammad al-Baradei and Ayman Nur called on Mubarak to resign immediately. Amr Moussa was more cautious and expected the president to remain in his post until presidential elections in September. The atmosphere in the square was defiant, but festive. Journalists and foreigners, however, were blocked from entering the square and continued to be harassed by military police and NDP members. In Alexandria and Damanhur, more than 100,000 people were protesting.

Meanwhile, between a 'rightist' faction of the political opposition, dubbed 'the Council of Wise Men', and a pragmatic group within the state, a consensus was emerging on a 'transition of power', which entailed that Omar Suleiman would take over all presidential powers, while Mubarak kept the symbolic office of president for constitutional reasons until new elections. In the next two days, talks between the vice president and opposition groups resulted in some concessions from the régime, such as the promise of the freedom of press, of the release of political prisoners, and of the formation of a constitutional reform committee. However, main opposition figures such as Muhammad al-Baradei and Ayman Nur criticized the meeting, and groups such as the Muslim Brotherhood declared that the first condition for any negotiation was the resignation of Mubarak and free democratic elections. Various youth groups operating in Tahrir Square rejected both the legitimacy and the outcome of the negotiations. By Sunday 6 February, many observers agreed that the Mubarak era was almost finished, but that "[...] the spirit of his rule, the essence of his régime, and the methods of his era are far from over" (Guardian News Blog 7/2, 2011).

Even though the hopes of the masses for the swift resignation of Mubarak were dashed they continued to occupy Tahrir Square. New York Times reporter Anthony Shadid observed that: "Protesters have called this 'the Week of Steadfastness', and there is plenty here. But there is a sense of siege, too, with a lurking fear that the optimism of the people here may eventually succumb to grimmer realities" (Guardian News Blog 7/2, 2011). An Al Jazeera reporter in Alexandria noted the bewilderment of people faced with the president's stubbornness: "Some people are scratching their heads, wondering what more they need to do to make it clear to the president that they don't want him" (Al Jazeera Live Blog 5/2, 2011).

Despite the rainy and relatively cold weather, rumors of a forced evacuation of Tahrir drew in thousands of anti-régime protesters on Saturday 5 February, strengthening the continuous occupation of the square. The government promised negotiations and did its best to steer the street back to 'normality'. On Sunday morning 6 February, banks reopened for business. Protesters, however, tried to convince civil servants working near Tahrir to strike and join the occupation. Omar Suleiman held a meeting with Muhammad al-Baradei, business tycoon Naguib Sawiris, and representatives of the Muslim Brotherhood, Wafd, Tagammu, and a number of youth groups. However, the negotiations only yielded vague promises. Throughout the night thousands continued to camp out in Tahrir.

On the afternoon of Monday 7 February, the régime promised public sector employees a raise in salaries and pensions of fifteen percent. More concessions followed the next day, as Suleiman claimed to have a roadmap for the transition of power. He also promised that protesters would not be persecuted. The number of Tahrir occupiers had dwindled to a mere 1,000 and activists called for a new mass demonstration. Guardian journalist Chris McGreal commented: "What is likely to bring people out is that the government is trying to pretend that the protests in Tahrir Square are no longer relevant and that the process has moved on to political negotiations" (Guardian News Blog 8/2a, 2011).

Indeed, Tuesday 8 February saw the return of hundreds of thousands to Tahrir. Some of the protesters visited the square for the first time. In addition, the release of online activist Wael Ghoneim, one of the administrators of the Khaled Said Facebook group, on Monday 7 February, and his subsequent emotional appearance on Dream TV, galvanized new layers of youth, encouraging them to come to the square.[7] Cairo University professors and students joined the protesters. Extending the normal mid-term break Egypt's schools and universities remained closed in the following week. The cracks in the state propaganda machinery seemed to widen, with journalists from the pro-régime Rose al-Yusef striking against their editor. Even former minister of transport, Essam Sharaf, came to Tahrir Square.

Protests were not confined to Tahrir Square, but demonstrations also took place near government buildings, the People's Assembly, and the Shura Council. Moreover, in Alexandria, thousands of people protested in front of the Ibrahim Mosque. In regional cities such as Ismailiyya, Asyut, and Mahalla al-Kubra, mass actions were organized as well. In Suez, Port Said, and Ismailiyya, over 6,000 workers from the Suez Canal Company began an open-ended sit in. Thousands of employees of Telecom Egypt started to protest as well, demanding a ten percent pay rise and the resignation of the top manager (Guardian News Blog 8/2b, 2011). In the New Valley area, some 500 kilometers south of Cairo, 3,000 protesters went on the streets and clashed with security forces. In Asyut, 8,000 people, a majority of them farmers, set up barricades of flaming palm trees, blocking the main highway and railway to Cairo, contesting bread shortages. Even in remote areas, such as the desert oasis of Kharga, protesters confronted the CSF, attacking government buildings and police headquarters,

---

7   Although the impact of Wael Ghoneim should not be exaggerated, as Chris McGreal explained: "I'd also just take issue with the statement that protesters say they were inspired to turn out by release of Wael Ghonim. Undoubtedly some were, but Tuesday is one of the two days a week when mass protests are scheduled and also a lot of the people I spoke to said they were there because they wanted to show the régime that they were not going to compromise in the negotiations – that Mubarak has to go. They planned to turn out anyway, Ghonim aside" (Guardian News Blog 8/2b, 2011).

and demanding the resignation of the provincial security chief (Guardian News Blog 9/2, 2011).

In the face of renewed mass protests and emerging strikes in the whole of Egypt, the vice president warned of the possibility of a coup if the current crisis continued. An end to the régime and the immediate resignation of the president was out of the question. However, youth movements such as 6 April and opposition groups remained adamant in demanding the instant removal of Mubarak.

Day of Departure

Even though Thursday 10 February was considered by many activists to be a calm day in anticipation of the increasingly 'traditional', massive demonstrations after Friday prayers, thousands were still occupying the square. About 1,000 doctors in white coats joined the protests in Tahrir, while 3,000 lawyers gathered near Abdeen Palace, from where they marched to the square (Al Jazeera Live Blog 10/2, 2011). Faced with the stubborn continuation of protests the army made its entrance as a direct power in the public sphere under the opaque form of the 'Supreme Council of Armed Forces' (SCAF).[8] In an ominous 'Communiqué no. 1', the SCAF reassured the protesters that they were in control of the situation and that all their legitimate demands would be met. Although Mubarak had not yet formally resigned, he had been sidelined and political decision-making at the top level had, in practice, already shifted to the military.

State television radically changed its tone and coverage, showing the masses in Tahrir Square and accusing former ministers of corruption. Swiftly rumors spread that Mubarak would be announcing his resignation in the evening, or at least a transfer of power to Omar Suleiman. Triumph mixed with anxiety gripped the demonstrators in Tahrir as the prospect of Mubarak's removal from power was tainted with fear of a military coup.

At around 22 h45, Hosni Mubarak addressed the nation. He repeated his commitment not to participate in presidential elections and he promised the eventual abolishment of emergency law. Yet he did not step down as president:

---

8 The SCAF was composed of: "[…] the Defence Minister, the Chief of Staff, the heads of the five services, of the five military districts into which the country is divided, and the heads of each of the specialized departments – intelligence, legal and so on. But we can be sure it is the first twelve who call the shots" (Kandil 2011).

> Satisfied with what I have offered the nation in more than 60 years, I have announced I will stay with this post and that I will continue to shoulder my responsibilities [...]. I never sought false power or popularity. I am certain that the majority of people are aware who Hosni Mubarak is.
> *Guardian News Blog* 10/2B

In Tahrir anticipation turned into anger, as demonstrators waved their shoes at the giant screen where the president's speech was projected. After Mubarak's speech the words of Suleiman did little to appease the masses: "I call upon the young people and heroes of Egypt, go back to your houses, go back to your work" (Guardian News Blog 10/2b). Groups of protesters marched towards the state television headquarters at Maspero and towards the presidential palace. In Alexandria thousands of people rallied to the military base. The 6 April Youth Movement called for "an all-out general strike" on Friday (Guardian News Blog 11/2a, 2011).

Friday morning 11 February, the SCAF, in a second communiqué, again reassured the protesters that it would supervise a democratic transition, but it remained silent on the fate of the president. Meanwhile, Tahrir Square was filling up even before the start of prayer. Activists hoped to use this numerical advantage to mobilize people towards occupying and/or blocking other strategic locations in Cairo. At least 3,000 protesters gathered at the presidential palace, which was heavily guarded by the president's Republican Guard (Guardian News Blog 11/2a, 2011). Tens of thousands of people rallied at Maspero. In Alexandria the streets were packed with hundreds of thousands of protesters. Tens of thousands surrounded government buildings in Suez, declaring that they would not leave until Mubarak stepped down. There were also mass demonstrations in Mansura, Damanhur, Tanta, Mahalla al-Kubra, Asyut, Sohag, Beni Suef, Port Said, Damietta, Qena, and al-Arish.

In the afternoon, Egyptian streets buzzed with the news brought by state television that a new "statement from the presidency" was to be expected in the evening. At 18 h, a surprisingly brief declaration followed, given by the vice president: "In these difficult circumstances that the country is passing through, president Hosni Mubarak has decided to leave the position of the presidency. He has commissioned the armed forces council to direct the issues of the state" (Guardian News Blog 11/2a). The accumulated anger and anxiety of the Egyptian masses suddenly metamorphosed into exhilaration and joy. On its Live Blog, Al Jazeera dryly remarked: "No point any of our presenters trying to speak over the roar of Egyptians celebrating [...]. Mubarak steps down. Brought to you live on Al Jazeera" (Al Jazeera Live Blog 11/2, 2011). Guardian reporter Jack Shenker participated in the celebrations at the square:

> There was a complete eruption of humanity, I have never seen anything like it. The world's biggest street party has really kicked off here. There are huge huge crowds of people jumping up and down suddenly as one. Suddenly everyone rushed into the road. I'm being slapped in happiness and bounced around.
>
> *Guardian News Blog* 11/2B, 2011

At around 20 h30, in its third communiqué, the SCAF acknowledged the resignation of Mubarak as president and committed itself to supervising a transition of power. The political intervention of the military was positively received among many activists and protesters. Wael Ghonim, for example, declared in a tweet that: "The military statement is great. I trust our Egyptian Army" (Guardian News Blog 11/2b). This 'soft coup' was also explicitly sanctioned by the USA. president Obama praised the Egyptian army: "The military has served patriotically and responsibly as a caretaker to the state and will now have to ensure a transition that is credible in the eyes of the Egyptian people" (Guardian News Blog 11/2b).

The soft coup ended the spontaneous, insurrectionary moment of the 25 January Revolution. However, the popular war of movement continued as the Egyptian streets and Tahrir Square especially, remained a space for mass demonstrations and strike waves hit the workplaces. At the same time, the revolutionary process was increasingly subsumed under a counterrevolutionary movement, epitomized by the second moment of popular mass mobilization in June 2013, which, with support of the military, overthrew the newly elected Muslim Brother president Muhammad Morsi.

CHAPTER 25

The Activity of Tahrir

Whereas the previous two chapters offered a detailed description of the 18 Days, the next two chapters investigate the developmental dynamic of the Republic of Tahrir, paying attention to the transformation of demonstration into occupation, the instructive role of the counterrevolution, spontaneity, division of labor, forms of instruction, the formation of new goals and activities, and the projection of the square.

Extended Reproduction

The 25 January uprising marked the transition from the 'original accumulation' to the 'extended reproduction' of the revolutionary process. Although the sudden eruption of popular protests created the impression that "Before the revolution nothing happens and then during the revolution everything happens all the time,"[1] the activity of the insurrection drew heavily on the projects of revolt that came before. Civildemocratic and working class movements, organizations, networks, and individual actors were able to inject the knowledge and practice of revolt that they had acquired during the previous decade into the mass protests. Without this 'original accumulation', the uprising would not have been possible. However, this does not mean that the insurrectionary phase was but a *quantitative* – bigger and louder – continuation of earlier protests. Quite the contrary: as soon as the masses entered the political field, the activity of revolt acquired a *qualitatively* novel and autonomous dynamic. The formation of national-popular and proletarian subjects was accelerated in this war of movement mode of struggle. Revolution constituted a new social situation of development for these subjects, but also an activity and collaboration in its own right, entailing different phases of development. Previous projects of revolt were 'nested'[2] in the new revolutionary collaboration. The emerging project of revolution was, at the same time, a revolution of projects.

Conceiving of the complex and non-linear sequence of events the 25 January uprising as a single project calls forth the problem of an 'entry point'

---

1 Interview with Sabry Zaky, Cairo, 10 March 2011.
2 Cf. Chapter 4.

that allows for an understanding of the amorphous whole as a coherent and cohesive process. I suggest 'Tahrir' as a unit of analysis[3] of the insurrection (cf. De Smet 2014b). Tahrir became almost synonymous with the 25 January Revolution, although it constituted a discrete collaboration within the wider process, pushing forward the development of the entire struggle. After the defeat of the police on Friday 28 January: "[...] Tahrir [...] became the epicenter of a revolution. Protesters not only transformed it, they were themselves transformed by their presence in it. Tahrir became a revolutionary organism unto itself [...]" (Khalil 2012, 5). There were various reasons why Tahrir was able to play such a role. Firstly, from a spatial perspective, Midan Tahrir was a center of Cairo, and in turn of the whole of Egypt, as it represented: "[...] a major transport hub surrounded by vital elements of the state apparatus: the parliament, several ministerial buildings, and the imposing Mogamma' [...]" (Rashed 2011, 23). Secondly, its name, 'Liberation Square' referred to the 1919 revolutionary uprising against the British. Thus it became a favorite gathering place for national events: "Egyptians have poured into Tahrir to celebrate soccer victories, to mourn the passing of national icons, and to protest injustice" (Shokr 2012, 41). In 2003 Tahrir had become already the symbolic locale of political mobilization, when demonstrators occupied the square for ten hours in protest against the war in Iraq (Khalil 2012, 39). Thirdly, the project of Tahrir developed much faster than the revolution as a whole, constituting its collaborative vanguard, and proleptically projecting a potential line of development for the whole process: "When protesters arrived at Tahrir on January 29, they did not come with the intention of creating a radical utopia [...]. As the revolution unfolded, Tahrir was elevated from a rally site to a model for an alternative society" (Shokr 2012, 42). From a mere space of protest, Tahrir developed into a project in its own right.

Demonstration

There were two central activities that pushed forward the development of Tahrir as a project, and so, in turn, the whole revolution: demonstration and occupation. 'Demonstration' was the first form of collaboration that emerged in the square on Tuesday 25 January. As I discussed in Chapter 6 in abstract terms, the demonstration is the cell-form of the national-popular subject, initiating the political line of development. The 25 January uprising started as a demonstration, a showing of discontent: a clear message directed at those in

---

3 Cf. Chapter 4.

power and a rallying call towards potential supporters. The accumulation of anger, criticisms, and resistance since the past years, the example projected by the Tunisian revolution, and the organization of marches from popular neighborhoods allowed activists to draw in huge numbers of non-politicized citizens into showing their displeasure with the régime.

The massive turnout of the demonstrations took the riot police by surprise. Egypt's Central Security Forces (CSF) were organized for a large-scale, but short-term and focused deployment, striking swift and hard at a single point of resistance by overwhelming protesters by pure numbers – as happened in Mahalla on 6 April 2008.[4] However, as on January 25 the quantitative balance shifted in the favor of the demonstrators, the CSF was no longer able to simply 'surround' and subdue protesters (Colla 2011; Khalil 2012, 140–142). Heavy street fights broke out between demonstrators and the CSF, and in order to exercise their right to demonstrate and show their discontent, protesters attempted to hold Tahrir Square in order to make a stand against the riot police. At this point, the activity of occupation was merely instrumental to the leading collaboration of demonstration: a way to solve the immediate problem of the police preventing protestors from demonstrating.

During the late evening and the night, the emerging revolutionary project bumped into another obstacle: as Tuesday had been a national holiday, working class protesters began to leave Tahrir for their homes. The remaining hard core of activists had to keep the fire burning until the next large-scale demonstration: the Friday of Anger, 28 February. As the masses thinned out in Tahrir, its first occupation was violently dispersed, and small groups of hundreds of protesters – especially the Ultras – threw themselves into a game of cat and mouse with the security forces in nearby streets and neighborhoods (Khalil 2012, 149–153). There was a sense of urgency among the remaining protesters and an awareness of the leading role of the Tahrir occupation in the whole revolutionary process: "We must hold Tahrir through the night and tomorrow, so that every corner of Egypt can take us as an inspiration and rise up in revolt […]. It's a matter of life and death now – what happens over the next 24 hours will be vital to the history of this country" (Guardian News Blog 25/1, 2011). The constant, decentralized attacks and retreats of the 'urban guerrilla' played a crucial role in softening up the security apparatus for the Friday of Anger, as conscripts and petty officers began to suffer from physical and moral fatigue (Khalil 2012, 161). Just as occupation, the activity of urban guerrilla functioned as an auxiliary collaboration that made demonstration possible.

---

4 Cf. Chapter 18 and 19.

Friday 28 January became a key moment for the revolutionary project. The vanguard heroism of the urban guerrilla on Wednesday and Thursday had kept the demands and spirit of the revolution on the minds of the masses, who returned to the streets on their day off. Traditional religious gatherings after the Friday midday prayers organically morphed into political mass demonstrations. The protesters were again confronted with the obstacle of the CSF, which they overcame by turning their demonstration into a mass-shape of the guerrilla warfare that took place in the previous two days. At this point the Gramscian military analogy between revolution and war of movement stopped being a mere resemblance and became the substance of the struggle. Whereas the previous guerrilla collaboration had been a defensive strategy of small groups to keep the spirit of the revolution alive, now it became an offensive of the masses in order to overcome a main obstacle in their revolutionary project: the violent repression of their demonstrations: "The protesters, in the face of such violence, temporarily abandoned their signature cries of salmeya (peaceful) and responded with their own storm of rocks, concrete chunks, and, eventually, Molotov cocktails" (Khalil 2012, 1).

Occupation

The first outer defense force of the Mubarak state – the police – had been utterly defeated in the streets by the war of movement of the masses. Protesters had physically conquered social spaces that were formerly controlled by the state. This marked the transition from demonstration to occupation as the leading activity of the uprising. The CSF was replaced by military troops, which, for reasons of their own (cf. De Smet 2014a), did not confront the protesters head-on, but preferred a war of position, digging 'urban trenches' around important state sites, such as parliament, the Maspero Radio and Television building, the presidential palace, the stock exchange, and so on (cf. Khalil 2012, 208).

In addition to the ambiguous presence of the military, from Saturday 29 January onward, the release of prisoners and the semi-organized looting, violence, and vandalism, constituted a new predicament for the revolutionary masses. The intimidation of families and the vandalization of homes meant that the activity of the national-popular subject was directed from 'demonstrating in the streets' to 'securing neighborhoods'. The state tried to undermine the legitimacy of the uprising by smothering it in a wave of orchestrated chaos. However, this obstacle became a springboard for the revolutionary movement. In the absence of law and order, popular collaborations established grassroots committees to protect families, homes, and neighborhoods.[5] Ironically, often the withdrawal of the police reinforced instead of weakened the cohesion of local communities, as Ahmed al-Gourd narrated:

> [...] you live in a house and you don't know your neighbors and suddenly you know everyone from your street. Not only your own building, but the entire block. You meet people living in your own building, living in the building next to you, people living along the whole street, you start to get to know people, calling them to see if they are alright, you know. It was actually a way for people to get to know each other and it worked pretty good. And I think it was actually an awesome display of how people were self-aware of things like safety, there was no vandalism, no looting, people protected the library of Alexandria, people protected the Egyptian museum.[6]

Protesters occupied Tahrir anew and the continuous collaboration of occupation came to represent the revolution as a whole. Instead of merely being a *site* to demonstrate discontent, the collaboration of the square became an *instrument* of popular power to pressure the president to step down: we won't leave until you leave. Within the overall war of movement that the uprising represented, the occupation of Tahrir represented the protesters' own war of position as they were loath to confront the military in a violent way and still hoped that Mubarak would leave of his own accord, as Ben Ali had done in Tunisia. Often literally facing the military, protesters became occupiers, digging their own trenches for a war of attrition with the régime.

Midan Tahrir was slowly transformed into a "city of tents" (Guardian News Blog 6/2, 2011). In order to continue the occupation, housing in the form of tents was provided, blankets were distributed to overcome the chilly January nights, food and water were made available, and entertainment was arranged to keep the spirits of the occupiers high. Tahrir became a "freed zone"[7] within the belly of the dictatorship. The Square offered a miniature experience of political emancipation. The activity of occupation was transformed from an

---

5 In themselves, such committees were neither 'progressive' nor 'reactionary': their role varied from city to city and from area to area. The character of civil committees established in rich neighborhoods in Cairo such as Zamalek or Maadi was different from those in popular neighborhoods such as Imbaba, or in working class cities such as Mahalla al-Kubra and Suez (cf. Khalil 2012, 204). As a general rule, those committees that connected their viligante activity with the broader project of popular revolution constituted a further development of the emerging national-popular subject (interview with Gihan Shabeen, Cairo, 16 March 2011).
6 Interview with Ahmed al-Gourd, Cairo, 24 March 2011.
7 Declared by the occupiers themselves (Rashed 2011, 34).

instrument of liberation to a *prefiguration* (cf. van de Sande 2013) of a free society: "It is not just a protest against an oppressive régime and a demand for freedom. In itself, it is freedom. It is a real, actual, lived moment of the freedom and dignity that the pro-democracy movement demands" (Schielke 2011).

Even though the objective of the uprising, the overthrow of the Mubarak régime, remained grim, the liberating feeling among Tahrir occupiers that they could organize their own lives independent of al-nizam, allowed for a "festival of the oppressed and exploited" (cf. Lenin 1962). The occupation of Tahrir generated ways of enjoying life (cf. Rashed 2011), illustrated by "[…] the picnicking families, the raucous flag-wavers, the volunteer tea suppliers, the cheery human security cordons, the slumbering bodies curled up in the metal treads of the army's tanks, the pro-change graffiti that adorns every placard, every tent, every wall space in vision […]" (Guardian News Blog 8/2b). Many Egyptians experienced a greater authenticity of living, negating, albeit in a limited way, the realities of the oppressive nizam.

The festive activity was partly a reappearance of the modern culture of political protest that had emerged in the civildemocratic demonstrations and occupations since the 2000s, and partly a revolutionary appropriation of the traditional, popular *mulid* celebration: "[…] a popular form of carnivalesque festivities that has been celebrated in Egypt for hundreds of years and whose rituals, enacted by multitudes of demonstrators, were marshaled, politicized, and revolutionized during the massive protests and sit-ins to sustain and transform the impetus and impact of the revolt" (Keraitim and Mehrez 2012, 30). The appearance of elements of the traditional, religious feast in Tahrir illustrates how the uprising rearticulated and 'nested' a range of existing activity-systems within the Gestalt of its own project.

On Tuesday 1 February there were new mass demonstrations, coming from all over Cairo and, despite military blockades of railroads and highways, even from other places in Egypt, that filled the square. Whereas demonstrations as a form of revolutionary collaboration remained important throughout the whole 18 Days, they now played a supporting and reinforcing role within the leading activity of occupation. The revolution-as-festival reached its zenith: the police had been defeated, the military stood by, and the baltageyya had not yet made their move against the occupiers.

The Whip of Counterrevolution

The Battle of the Camel on Wednesday 2 February became another key moment in the development of the uprising. After the mass mobilizations on Tuesday 1

February, Mubarak had promised some concessions to the protesters. While the vanguard of the movement derided the president's move, some protesters were satisfied by the concessions and wanted a return to 'normalcy'. Relatively large pro-Mubarak protests were held to discredit the powerful claim of the revolutionaries that they represented 'the people', sowing additional confusion in the ranks of the less politicized protesters. This moment had the potential to split the mass movement into a moderate and a radical wing. If Mubarak had yielded to the protesters, promising a referendum on a limit to his presidential term, there was a chance that he could have diffused the uprising, remaining in power or transferring power on his own conditions.[8] If the régime had restrained itself, temporarily exchanging the stick for the carrot, it would have considerably weakened the revolutionary project. Instead, the ministry of interior initiated a clampdown on the remaining protesters who were camping in Tahrir: a vicious attack by Molotov throwing plainclothes security forces, rock throwing baltageyya, paramilitary snipers, and – in a surreal episode – charging camel drivers. Samah Selim commented: "The world is watching in awe – and anxiety – because, in these rare moments of unmediated and massive social upheaval, the naked power of the national security state is on show for all to see, in all its violence and unmitigated brutality" (Selim 2011). People who had been hesitating to continue their participation in the protests were appalled by the violence and felt "stabbed in the back" (Guardian News Blog 3/2, 2011).

The régime's attack not only called protesters back to the activity of occupation, but the square changed from a "utopian street party" into "Fortress Tahrir" (Khalil 2012, 243, 247). Wael Tawfiq explained:

> The camel battle transformed the atmosphere and attitude inside the square. […] The most important image of this day was that the square transformed into organized working groups. Everyone in the square was organized: even girls and women with a niqab. All of them were united without thinking about ideology or religion. Everyone did what he could to his ability. I had a broken arm so I started to break rocks to help others. The women with the niqab were carrying the rocks. A lot of people removed their jackets to carry rocks, even if they got cold. […].[9]

---

8 Interview with Wael Tawfiq, Cairo, 8 March 2011; interview with Sabry Zaky, Cairo, 10 March 2011.
9 Interview with Wael Tawfiq, Cairo, 8 March 2011.

As Tahrir was now a 'freed zone' its 'borders' – the 'Front' (Rashed 2011, 25) – had to be defended, which encouraged the formation of a 'military' division of labor: a first group outfitted the 'warriors' with protective layers; 'gatherers' tore rocks from the pavement as ammunition; 'foragers' supplied the 'warriors' in the frontlines with rocks, water, and food (Khalil 2012, 229). A field hospital was erected in the center of the square and a 'civil prison' was established: "In the first days when we arrested a policeman we handed them over to the army, but they released them. So now we made a prison."[10] In the prison occupiers held captured plainclothes police officers and state security personnel in custody, not least to protect them from the wrath of their co-protesters.

This episode is reminiscent of Marx's (alleged) aphorism that "[...] a revolution needs from time to time the whip of the counterrevolution" (Trotsky 2001, 774). A Vygotskian reading of this epigram emphasizes that a predicament or crisis is not merely an obstacle in the life-process of a collective subject, but may force the project to create the necessary neoformations to overcome it, which in turn drives its entire development forward (cf. Shandro 2007, 24). The dynamic of the project of Tahrir was determined by the specific solutions it developed to overcome the obstacles that were thrown on its path (cf. Bamyeh 2011). Those obstacles were objective and subjective in nature. The objective predicaments were provided by the antagonist of the uprising, the Mubarak régime, which constituted the most important motor for the development of the whole revolutionary process. Demonstration turned into a massive street battle with the police, not because protesters had such a preconceived plan, but because the CSF was an obstacle to their peaceful protests. Demonstration became occupation because this was the best way to safeguard the activity of protest. Subjective obstacles, on the other hand, were organizational and conceptual obstacles inherent to the developmental level of the mass movement itself: its lack of coherence, cohesion, structures, direction, and centralization. With every forward step in the struggle against al-nizam, the project of Tahrir was itself transformed, and its subjectivity rendered more and more concrete.

---

10   Interview with Wael Tawfiq, Cairo, 8 March 2011.

CHAPTER 26

The Organization of Tahrir

In the previous chapter I investigated the transformation of the leading activity of Tahrir from demonstration into occupation. The next chapter continues the analysis of the developmental dynamic of the square, focusing on questions of organization, instruction, and consciousness.

Spontaneous Organization

One of the features of the budding revolutionary activity-system most celebrated by activists, journalists, and political scientists alike, was its 'spontaneity'. As Rosa Luxemburg posited with regard to the Russian Revolution of 1905, the notion of spontaneity is crucial to an understanding of the revolutionary process "[…] because revolutions do not allow anyone to play the schoolmaster with them" (Luxemburg 1970, 188). It is from the masses themselves that springs, in Trotsky's words, "[…] that leaping movement of ideas and passions which seems to the police mind a mere result of the activities of 'demagogues'" (Trotsky 2001, 18). A popular revolution is not engineered by demagogues, parties or activists, but it is the activity of the people itself.

However, when spontaneity is opposed to *organization*, the concept acquires a mystical character. There was nothing unorganized about the committees that defended, cleaned,[1] entertained, and governed Tahrir. If anything, they represented "spontaneous order out of chaos" (Bamyeh 2011). The notion of spontaneity does not exclude organization or centralization; it denotes the organic, bottom-up origins of the cohesion, coherence, and systematicity of a project. Leadership and organizational centralization are not antithetical to the spontaneous self-organization of the masses, but they constitute a higher, more elaborate phase in the development of its systemic activity.

Moreover, there is no mystical emergence of 'order out of chaos': the sociogenetic logic behind 'spontaneous organization' is that of a collective learning process: performance produces competence.[2] The 'outward'-oriented activity of occupation turned 'inward', transforming structures that had been developed

---

1 "Garbage is continuously collected at the demonstration and on the main streets by volunteers in a country that until now has been full of garbage anywhere you turn" (Schielke 2011).
2 Cf. Chapter 4.

as external weapons against the state into internal means of self-governance. Revolutionary collaboration created, on the one hand, its own division of labor, organic intellectuals, rules, relations, material tools, and signs; and, on the other, it appropriated the traditions of existing systems such as the Ultras' movement and the religious *mulid* as organizational means for political protest (cf. Keraitim and Mehrez 2012).

The interiorization of the revolution also entailed a psychological struggle, which represented an attempt to correct the disturbed organic relation between everyday and scientific modes of thinking.[3] The good sense that constituted a reflection of the activity of protesting and occupation in thought, came increasingly into contradiction with the dominant ideologies, which had denied the national-popular subject any real subjectness. Salah Abd al-Azim poetically referred to this process as "tearing down the idols in ourselves."[4] Harriet Sherwood narrated that: "People are eloquent about the reasons for their uprising. [...] One of the most memorable comments in a day, a week, of memorable conversations comes from a guy who tells me he has come 'to fight the fear inside me'" (Guardian News Blog 6/2, 2011). Bamyeh (2011) explained that:

> More than one participant mentioned to me how the revolution was psychologically liberating, because all the repression that they had internalized as self-criticism and perception of inborn weakness, was in the revolutionary climate turned outwards as positive energy and a discovery of self-worth, real rather than superficial connectedness to others, and limitless power to change frozen reality.
>
> BAMYEH 2011

Technical Assistance

Tahrir became a project of life in almost all its facets and as such it required some form of governance. As the state was forcefully driven away, practices of self-governing emerged from the developed collaboration of occupation: "Daily struggles to hold the space and feed its inhabitants, without the disciplined mechanisms of an organized state, were exercises in democratic process. It was through these everyday practices that Tahrir became a truly radical space" (Shokr 2012, 44). British actor Khaled Abdallah, who was among the protesters in Tahrir, declared that: "Midan Tahrir [...] has now become like a mini state that works and will function as long as it needs to in order to get what this

---

3 Cf. Chapter 7.
4 Interview with Salah Abd al-Azim, Cairo, 22 March 2011.

country deserves" (Guardian News Blog 6/2, 2011). Thus the 'freed zone' was increasingly dubbed the 'Republic of Tahrir' by participants and observers alike (cf. Khalil 2012).

Apart from the defense of the square, as outlined earlier, the occupiers had to create a daily life routine: securing food and shelter, treating the wounded, washing clothes, providing stations for mobile charging, building restrooms, setting up nurseries for protesters' children, and so on (Keraitim and Mehrez 2012, 28).[5] This required a development of *technical* functions. Actor Muhammad Zaky Murat summarized:

> In order to hear each other within the millions we had to create a sound system, so we needed specialists with expertise in sound systems. They were using electricity from the state without permission because they stated that they owned the country and its electricity as well. So if there was an electricity engineer in the square he played his role as an electricity engineer. While the thugs attacked the people in the square we moved a lot of vehicles to the boundaries of the square and we couldn't do this without a lot of mechanic engineers who showed us how to do it. [...] The most important practical thing we all agreed about was the security and the cleaning of the square and the healing of the injured. Of course the doctors played an important role.[6]

Doctors, engineers, technicians, and all those who already possessed the relevant know-how became technical intellectuals of the revolutionary project. Ultras shared their "skills in banner writing, chanting, and the use of fireworks" (Keraitim and Mehrez 2012, 53) with other protesters. Political activists distributed leaflets with practical and tactical advice for demonstrators, for example what to do when being attacked by tear gas. In addition, the square produced its own 'organic' technical intellectuals in the form of cleaners and security.

Cultural Instruction

The continuation of the project of Tahrir did not only require basic survival skills, but also the formation of a *cultural* dimension that elaborated revolutionary thought and prefigured a more authentic living. Journalists and activists

---

[5] Survival was realized through a continuous exchange with revolutionary collaborations 'outside' Tahrir, which illustrated strong ties of solidarity, but also the impossibility of the square to exist as a society on its own.
[6] Interview with Muhammad Zaky Murat, Cairo, 30 March 2011.

who engaged with the popular activity-system in a solidary way, played an important part in rendering the mass protests more cohesive and coherent. When the internet was shut down, when the independent media were repressed, and when the battle was primarily waged in the streets, progressive journalists and 'virtual' activists were forced to go to the streets and support the masses there. By harassing and arresting independent journalists, the state turned them into activists. Journalists and political activists generalized and articulated the grievances of the masses, offering projective and integrative assistance.[7] Phrases such as: "We have started an uprising with the will of the people, the people who have suffered for thirty years under oppression, injustice and poverty [...]. Egyptians have proven today that they are capable of taking freedom by force and destroying despotism" (Guardian News Blog 25/1, 2011), projected the 'people' as a collective subject and integrated the political and economic dimensions of the struggle.

The Republic of Tahrir was also supported by established artists who joined the protests, and amateur cartoonists, actors, and singers who emerged from the activity of Tahrir itself. Classic songs of Fuad Negm and Shaykh Imam, such as 'I am the People' and 'I call on you' were sung and performed by protesters, alongside new and spontaneous creations (Antoon 2011). Catchy and humorous poems were composed in *'ammeyya*, the Egyptian colloquial register. Menal Khaled of the cinema workers' union, recalled that: "We created two stages in the square. One for the actors, the other for the professional workers, and we were supporting popular people's consciousness."[8] Zaky Murat highlighted the important function of art:

> [...] the artists in the square played the role of continuing the spirit of the revolution by songs and poems, and of entertaining the people in Tahrir Square. For example, musicians, in addition to the cartoonists. We didn't know them but we saw their works in the square. They increased awareness among the people and created a lot of new symbols and ideas by their drawings. [...] We had to give the media a message every day. So the artists inside the square made a new art, a new form, which was to write the demands and symbols in the soil, the land, the rocks, the stones. This was a message, not only to the media, but also to the people outside and inside the square in order to change the square into the real society we were dreaming of.[9]

---

7 Cf. Chapter 21.
8 Interview with Menal Khaled, Cairo, 25 March 2011.
9 Interview with Muhammad Zaky Murat, Cairo, 30 March 2011.

These cultural intellectuals not only provided entertainment, but also delivered the semiotic means for the occupiers to develop a concept of al-nizam and of themselves as al-sha'b. Art often functioned as a shortcut that elucidated, disclosed, or unpacked complex political and economic narratives: "This poetry is not an ornament to the uprising – it is its soundtrack and also composes a significant part of the action itself" (Colla 2012, 77). The art of the square was its material self-consciousness.

There was a dialectical pedagogy between, on the one hand, activists and artists becoming part of 'the people', and, on the other, of 'the people' becoming involved in politics and artistic production. Salah Abd al-Azim contemplated that: "for many Egyptians it was the first time to see artists in action, and for artists it was the first time to have a mass feedback and audience through the square."[10] Revolutionary stages were erected where every participant of the project was allowed to act, speak, or sing.[11]

Leadership

Finally, as a 'mini-state' besieged by the Mubarak régime, the square needed *directive* organs and practices of deliberation and decision. Intellectuals giving leadership and direction to the movement consisted of both those activists who had been a part of the political community before the revolution, and the leaders who materialized spontaneously within the ranks of protesters. Political activists intervened in the movement with pamphlets and slogans, convincing protesters to stay in Tahrir when Mubarak pledged to fire the cabinet,[12] putting forward concrete demands, and recommending instruments and methods to achieve the popular objectives.[13]

Political activists who supported the popular activity-system in solidarity had to prove their sincerity by standing side by side with the protesters, who were suspicious of any form of 'party politics': "We made a presence in the

---

10   Interview with Salah Abd al-Azim, Cairo, 22 March 2011.
11   Interview with Muhammad Zaky Murad, Cairo, 30 March 2011.
12   Interview with Haisam Hassan, Cairo, 7 March 2011.
13   On 4 February, for example, youth activists on Tahrir raised the joint demands of the resignation of the cabinet; the formation of a transitional government made up by senior judges, youth leaders, and military leaders; the formation of a constitutional assembly of public intellectuals and constitutional experts, which had to be ratified in a referendum; new local and national elections; an end to the emergency law; dismantling of the hated state security apparatus; a trial of key régime leaders such as president Mubarak and interior minister Habib al-Adli (Guardian News Blog 4/2, 2011).

square with Tagammu, not by our words, but by sleeping in the streets, and so on."[14] They quickly became part of the organic division of labor of the activity-system: "Hani knows a lot about media and mixing sounds, so he will do this. Haisam knows about publishing papers and leaflets and talking about demands, so he will do that."[15]

However, because of the vast numbers of protesters, the small groups of leftists were only able to give directive assistance in a fragmentary way and they were not at all able to lead the movement. Moreover, they were often the ones running behind the actual developmental level of the revolutionary project, instead of moving ahead of it.[16]

Immanence and Teleology

Are activities constituted teleologically by their goals, or do goals emerge immanently from activities? In Chapter 4 I suggested that the notion of project collaboration encompasses both movements, i.e., from motivation to activity, and from activity to final goal. A goal is the ideal form of the outcome of an activity, and the outcome is the material form of the goal. The first rallies on 25 January clearly illustrated this notion, as the activity of demonstrating was directly constituted by the call to protest of the organizing activists. Clearly the idea of the protests already existed before the materialization of the demonstrations.

However, from 25 January onward, the goals of the developing collaboration lagged behind its fast evolving activities. Even though some activists had hoped that 25 January would initiate a revolutionary uprising,[17] the majority of organizers "[...] didn't think they could do this to Mubarak. At first the protest movement went to the streets to demand the resignation of Habib al-Adli of the ministry of interior."[18] They only demanded the implementation of basic democratic reforms, not the dismissal of Mubarak, let alone a revolutionary change of the relations of power. However, the sheer numbers of protesters in the streets swiftly transformed the goals of the demonstrations 'from below'. Already at noon it was clear to some participants that the massive protests could be "an opportunity to bring down the Mubarak régime" (Guardian News

---

14 Interview with Haisam Hassan, Cairo, 7 March 2011.
15 Interview with Haisam Hassan, Cairo, 7 March 2011.
16 Interview with Hisham Fouad, Giza, 13 March 2011.
17 Interview with Khaled al-Balshy, Cairo, 14 March 2011.
18 Interview with Sabry Zaky, Cairo, 10 March 2011. Cf. Bamyeh 2011.

Blog 25/1, 2011) and the slogan of "the people want the fall of the régime" was heard among some of the demonstrators.[19]

As the actions of the protesters became more radical their aims followed suit. No one who came to the protests of 25 January would have dared to dream that in the following days they would torch NDP and state security offices throughout the whole country and by strength of numbers defeat the dreaded CSF in the streets. In successive waves, elements of the state apparatus were disorganized and defeated by the masses, and with each victory the call for a 'régime change' became louder: "by the end of the day on January 28, the immediate removal of Mubarak from office had become an unwavering principle, and indeed it seemed then that it was about to happen" (Bamyeh 2011). The Friday of Anger was the moment when most people realized that they were in the process of 'making' a revolution.[20] Whereas political activists were still cautiously chanting for the *government* to change, it was non-organized and non-politicized people who shouted for an end to the *régime*.[21] The radical demands of "the people want the fall of the régime," "leave, leave, Hosni Mubarak," and "bread, freedom, and social justice" were the explicit recognition of the masses that, during the past days, they actually had been waging a revolutionary struggle against the state. Here the goal that is rendered explicit is not an external object that constitutes the activity, but, on the contrary, it is a reflection in consciousness of the real collaborative process that is unfolding. Protesters became conscious of what they were already doing in practice: creating a revolutionary project. Again, the developmental logic that performance creates competence reared its head.

The genesis of new forms of collaboration in Tahrir, occupation, festival, and governance, stimulated the formation of new goals. Revolution appears not only as the *expression* of an already-present popular democratic will, but also as a *generative process* of self-emancipating practices and ideas. Revolution is not merely an instrument to accomplish societal change: it is the movement itself toward a transformation of society. The future social formation is not an object external to the revolutionary process, lying in wait until the masses finally 'capture' it, but it is immanent to the revolutionary activity-system itself. The forms of self-organization, democracy, and authentic living that arise during the mass mobilizations and protests are anticipations of a fully matured society based on the self-determination and self-governance of the people.

---

19   Interview with Haisam Hassan, Cairo, 7 March 2011.
20   Interview with Mustafa Bassiouni, Giza, 17 March 2011.
21   Interview with Haisam Hassan, Cairo, 7 March 2011; interview with Wael Tawfiq, Cairo, 8 March 2011.

Obviously, in the development of a project, the 'teleological' and 'immanent' movements, from goal to activity and from activity to goal, are interwoven. The trajectory of Tahrir illustrates how the imagination of a project sometimes lags behind its actual collaboration and tries to catch up theoretically with its own radical practice, or sometimes moves ahead of it, pulling the activity toward it, as it were. Demonstrators and occupiers also began to discover themselves as 'the people', or rather: their self-governing practices increasingly filled the abstract notion of al-sha'b with a concrete substance. Even during the first days of demonstrations, there were already subtle changes in the slogans of this vanguard of protesters, which pointed toward a development in the consciousness of the actors with regard to their own agency. Instead of chanting "we want change," protesters declared: "we are change" (Guardian News Blog 28/1, 2011). The slogan "we want change" implicitly addressed another actor who could achieve change for the masses. The aim expressed the formation of a popular will – the people as wanting something – but not yet the self-determining agency of al-sha'b. This slogan could still be a part of the old Arab nationalist paradigm of corporatism and a moral economy, whereby the people demanded its negotiated rights from the 'Savior-Ruler'. "We *are* change," however, forcefully rejects the paternalist mediation of an external force in the emancipation of the people. 'Change' is no longer an object external to the activity of the people that can be demanded from and granted by another power: 'change' *is* the self-directing activity of the masses. The realization that the people organized in the streets is the solution to its own problems is the realization of its political agency as a people: "we don't need politicians; this is the people's revolution!" (Schielke 2011).

Tahrir became the concept, the cell-form of the national-popular subject. The Mubarak state could no longer assert that it defended the 'common good' and the 'population in general' when its otherwise passive constituency was massively and explicitly out in the streets demanding its end. The particular class content of the universalist claims of the state was revealed by the practical-critical activity of the masses.

Projection

The collaboration of Tahrir not only entailed a *project*, in the sense of people jointly working towards a shared goal, but also a *projection*: a proleptic image that shone forth from this activity (cf. De Smet 2014b). The concept of projection denotes the capacity of a project to generalize itself and attract new participants to its cause, and, most importantly, it underscores collaboration as a process of learning and instruction. The Tunisian and Egyptian revolutions illustrated how people learnt to act democratically, not through formal education, but by the lived experience of collaborating toward shared goals of freedom, dignity, and social justice. A revolutionary insurrection is not the mop of history: an abrupt, irrational, instinctive, chaotic, blind force, in which 'the people', after decades of passivity, suddenly rise up, destroy the status-quo, and clear the path for new political actors. Grassroots democracy, self-determination, self-emancipation, and so on, are not practices and ideals extrinsic to the revolutionary project, but they are developed *within* the process of revolution. Throughout the 18 Days, Tahrir evolved from an *instrument* of political and human emancipation to a prefiguration of emancipation *itself*. The governance of Tahrir projected a concrete alternative to al-nizam: "[...] self-rule, democratic representative government, human rights, a dignified life" (Al-Bendary 2011) and "[...] community and solidarity, care for others, respect for the dignity of all, feeling of personal responsibility for everyone [...]" (Bamyeh 2011). Tahrir was not only the actual collaboration of protesters on the square (project), it was also a glimpse of a better society (projection); an imagination or potentiality that moved ahead of the current developmental level and instructed and inspired protesters to organize their activity accordingly.

Projection enabled Tahrir to play a vanguard role in the whole 25 January Revolution, making it the cell-form of the uprising. Through Al Jazeera and other international media outlets Tahrir was literally projected into the living rooms of Egyptians and the global community. This projection offered a powerful, contemporary, heteroleptic example of popular revolt, solidarity, and the building of a new society 'from below'. It interpellated protesters, either drawing them physically toward and into actual, solidary collaboration with the protesters on the square, or motivating them to appropriate and generalize the ideals and/or methods of the project for their own particular circumstances. Occupiers themselves were conscious of their instructive role in the revolution and the importance of their 'leading activity' for the rest of the movement. Even after the first day of protest, Tuesday 25 January, activist Ahmed Salah claimed that:

> We must hold Tahrir through the night and tomorrow, so that every corner of Egypt can take us as an inspiration and rise up in revolt [...]. It's a matter of life and death now – what happens over the next 24 hours will be vital to the history of this country.
> *Guardian News Blog* 25/1, 2011

With regard to the Battle of the Camel, Wael Tawfiq, observed that: "The resistance and organization of Tahrir influenced the whole of Egypt and transformed the meaning of Mubarak's speech." [22]

Tahrir captured not only the imagination of Egyptians, but also that of the global community. The slogan of "Fight like an Egyptian" (Shihade et al. 2012, 5) was heard worldwide, among the *Indignados* in Madrid, Occupy Wall Street activists in New York, workers striking in Wisconsin, students demonstrating in the UK, and Greeks protesting on Syntagma Square. Schielke contemplated that: "Egyptians have given the world an example in freedom and courage that we all should look up to as an example. This sense of admiration and respect is what has drawn so many foreigners to Tahrir Square in the past days, including myself" (Schielke 2011).

---

22   Interview with Wael Tawfiq, Cairo, 8 March 2011.

CHAPTER 27

The Mass Strike

The previous chapters focused on the organization of Tahrir as the cell-form of the uprising. In the next chapter I turn my attention to the development of the worker subject within the broader revolutionary process, discussing their war of movement mode of struggle through the paradigm of the 'mass strike'.

Workers as National-Popular Actors

It has been argued by Anne Alexander (2011b), by Sameh Naguib (2011), by Michael Schwartz (2011), and by myself (Zemni, De Smet, and Bogaert 2013), that the 'movement' of the Egyptian worker subject in the revolutionary process could be understood through Rosa Luxemburg's conception of the 'mass strike'.[1] Processing the experience of the 1905 Russian Revolution, Luxemburg approached the numerous strikes that happened throughout the revolutionary process not as a loose collection of protests, but as a Gestalt: "[…] the method of motion of the proletarian mass, the phenomenal form of the proletarian struggle in the revolution" (Luxemburg 1970, 182). The social situation of popular revolution, radically transformed the pace, scale, and content of the economic line of development: "Only in the sultry air of the period of revolution can any partial little conflict between labor and capital grow into a general explosion" (Luxemburg 1970, 186).

In Egypt, throughout the 1990s and 2000s workers were waging 'partial little conflicts' against their local and particular forms of exploitation and domination. From 2006 onward, the vanguard of the workers' movement took on a trade unionist form, but the working class at large remained stuck within an economic-corporate condition. With regard to the worker struggles leading up to the 1905 Russian Revolution, Luxemburg had comfortably posited that a general uprising "[…] cannot come in any other way than through the school of a series of preparatory partial insurrections, which therefore meantime end in partial outward 'defeats' and, considered individually, may appear to be 'premature'" (Luxemburg 1970, 181). Among leftists, there was a general consensus that the strike movements of the decade before 2011 had contributed as

---

1 Cf. Chapter 8.

much, if not more, to the 'original accumulation' of the Tahrir uprising as the civildemocratic movement.[2] With hindsight, the 6 April 2008 insurrection in Mahalla was presented as a precursor of the 25 January insurrection.[3] In addition, the uprising in Suez, three months before 25 January, "[…] was like an experiment for the revolution in my opinion."[4]

In any case, the molecular development of the strike before 25 January had spread a practical critique of Egypt's neoliberal historical bloc and a good sense of overcoming this predicament through struggle and solidarity. At the eve of the 25 January Revolution, the Egyptian workers' movement was still trying to overcome its subjective condition of fragmentation and prepared for a new wave of protests. Following the example of the RETAU, other grassroots workplace committees planned to establish independent trade unions. The development of the workers' movement had provided the 25 January Revolution with a strong undercurrent, but – unlike the 1905 and 1917 Russian Revolutions, and more in tune with the Iranian Revolution of 1978–79, for example – the uprising did not begin as an explicit class protest. Since 2000, the political and economic struggles against the neoliberal war of movement had continuously subsumed each other as moments within a broad process of accumulating popular revolt. If 2005 represented the high point of the civildemocratic 'political' moment (and its subsequent collapse), the Mahalla uprising of 2008 expressed the culmination of the economic class struggle (and its ensuing refragmentation). With the 25 January uprising, the movement's moment shifted back to the political.

From the first protests on 25 January, wage laborers participated in the 25 January uprising, but it took a while before these individual subjects intervened in the revolutionary process with a proletarian subjectivity: "workers were taking part as 'demonstrators' and not necessarily as 'workers'– meaning, they were not moving independently" (al-Hamalawy 2011). Workers joined the popular demonstrations and occupations and as such became participants of the developing national-popular subject. The closure of companies, banks, and shops by the government during the first week and a half of the uprising locked workers outside of their workplaces. In the streets, specific working class subjectivities were absorbed by the massive street protests. This reflected the general subsumption of the economic developmental line under the political one.

---

2 Interview with Sabry Zaky, Cairo, 10 March 2011; interview with Fatma Ramadan, Cairo, 15 March 2011; interview with Mustafa Bassiouny, Giza, 17 March 2011; interview with Gihan Ibrahim, Cairo, 20 March 2011.
3 Cf. Part 5.
4 Interview with Saud Omar, Suez, 18 March 2011.

Workers as Class Actors

As soon as the government reopened businesses from 7 February onward, workers brought the insurrection back into their workplaces and started to strike or demonstrate as class actors. "Within the last three days before Mubarak left, there were mass strikes in the whole of Egypt."[5] On Thursday 10 February the bus drivers went on strike, paralyzing transport, and adding to the general disorganization of the state.[6] Whereas the battle between the state and Tahrir had become a static war of attrition, the strikes reignited the uprising as a popular war of movement. Hossam al-Hamalawy claimed that:

> The whole time we were in Tahrir we could exert control over Tahrir, but we didn't control the rest of the country [...]. But the workers, if they strike, it's 'game over.' [...] It's finished, because the machine won't work. There's no money coming in. No trains are moving. No buses are moving. No factories are working. No ships are moving. No ports are operating. It's 'game over' – finished.
>
> HADDAD 2011B

The 25 January Revolution "[...] for the first time awoke class feeling and class consciousness in millions upon millions as if by an electric shock" (Luxemburg 1970, 171), forcefully interpellating all layers and sections of the Egyptian workforce as proletarians. From 8 February on, Egyptian workers began to protest on a massive scale. Their demands were primarily economically oriented, both

---

5   Interview with Mustafa Bassiouny, Giza, 17 March 2011. On Tuesday 8 February, over 6,000 workers of the Suez Canal company in Suez, Port Said, and Ismailia began an open-ended sit-in. Also in Suez some 13,000 steel workers went on strike. Cairo public transport and telecom workers also began to protest. Wednesday 9 February saw a further strengthening of the strike wave: workers from all sections, layers, and regions engaged in work-stoppages, sit-ins, demonstrations, road-blockages, and other protests: thousands of factory workers in Mahalla, and Helwan; 5,000 workers of textile, medicine bottle, and ship repair companies in Suez; court workers in Cairo and Helwan; thousands of workers in the Luxor tourism industry; more than 2,000 workers in Qena; some 5,000 unemployed youth in Aswan; three public transportation garages in Cairo; thousands of workers in front of the Cairo Petroleum Ministry; sanitation workers in Dokki (Cairo); 3,000 Egyptian National Railways workers; railway technicians in Beni Suef; state electricity staff; service technicians at the Suez Canal company; workers of at least one hospital; employees of a factory of beverages; more than a hundred journalists of al-Ahram; the armed forces' music corps; and so on (all numbers from Al Jazeera 2011 Live Blogs and Guardian 2011 News Blogs).
6   Interview with Hisham Fouad, Giza, 13 March 2011.

particular to the workplace, and general for the whole class: "[...] the minimum wage, employment of temporary workers, return privatized companies back to the state and to reinstate workers who were fired because of their strikes, and equal pay for workers [...]."[7]

Before the 25 January uprising, worker leaders and leftist activists were discussing the zone of proximal development of the workers' movement, disagreeing whether independent trade unionism exceeded its upper limit or not. The insurrection forcefully solved the question. Workers could 'nest' their own strike projects within the larger collaborative framework of the uprising: "The Egyptian revolution was for us a safe place, a safe haven against the repression of the Mubarak régime and the state syndicate."[8] Irrespective of the motivations of the strikers – genuine solidarity with the popular insurrection or its opportunist 'colonization' or 'commodification'[9] – their interactions with the national-popular subject politicized their own struggles. The uprising became a "living political school" (Luxemburg 1970, 172) that instructed the workers and developed new and already existing proletarian activity-systems. Trade unionism was no longer a future moment in the trajectory of the worker subject, it became the actual line of development.

Although workers often did not list the fall of the régime among their formal demands, they chanted the same radical slogans as the occupiers on Tahrir (al-Hamalawy 2011). Other strikers began to formulate general political demands, such as democracy and the right to establish independent trade unions. There was also a growing good sense that integrated everyday economic with political criticisms of the Mubarak régime: "Workers were motivated to strike when they heard about how many billions the Mubarak family was worth [...]. They said: 'How much longer should we be silent?'" (Guardian News Blog 9/2, 2011).

The Economic and the Political

The awakening of the proletarian subject within the broad process of insurrection frightened the state and the ruling classes. Labor activist Fatma Ramadan,[10] SRC leader Gihan Shabeen,[11] independent activist Wael Tawfiq,[12] RS militant

---

7   Interview with Fatma Ramadan, Cairo, 15 March 2011.
8   Interview with Kamal Abu al-Eita, Giza, 20 March 2011.
9   Cf. Chapters 4 and 7.
10 Interview with Fatma Ramadan, Cairo, 15 March 2011.
11 Interview with Gihan Shabeen, Cairo, 16 March 2011.
12 Interview with Wael Tawfiq, Cairo, 16 March 2011.

Gihan Ibrahim,[13] many other leftists, even liberal activists[14] and some Muslim Brothers,[15] agreed that the worker strikes definitely tipped the balance of power in the favor of the protesters. The decision of the government to reopen businesses was primarily aimed at insulating Egyptian society at large from the pockets of resistance. Yet, the régime's 'capital strike' was replaced with workers' strikes that imported the uprising to workplaces in the whole country.

Reuters observed that: "If the strikes spread across the country, and paralyse key sectors, it could push Egypt's army to take sides, after trying to maintain an appearance of neutrality" (Guardian News Blog 10/2a, 2011). Shenker noted that important Egyptian companies were: "[...] explicitly distancing themselves from the Mubarak régime [...] if key business figures now see fit to disassociate themselves from a governing clique that served them so well for so long, that can't be a good sign for Omar Suleiman and those around him" (Guardian News Blog 9/2, 2011). Not only did the strikes directly damage the short-term interests of private capitalists, public companies, and military entrepreneurs, unlike the civildemocratic movement the workers' movement posed a threat to the economic structure of the historical bloc. Nevertheless, Alexander pointed out that the independent trade unionist neoformations that had developed over the past years "[...] were too small in relation to the scale of the movement for their presence as an organised force to shape the overall outcome of the uprising, or even influence its direction much" (Alexander 2012, 113). Independent trade unions, autonomous strike committees, and individual worker leaders and leftist activists played a role in organizing some political strikes in solidarity with the insurrection, but they could not direct the spontaneous development of the strike as a 'mass strike'. At this point in the trajectory of the mass strike there was no coordinated and concentrated collaboration, but only a contemporaneity of the worker protests, which inspired solidarity between individual strike activity-systems and a horizontal connection of demands and methods. The trade unionist vanguard was but a drop in the ocean of thousands of spontaneously striking workers.

However, the revolution also presented an opportunity for the vanguard of the workers' movement to consolidate and expand the leading trade unionist neoformation. In Tahrir Square representatives of the four independent unions decided to constitute the Egyptian Federation of Independent Trade Unions

---

13   Interview with Gihan Ibrahim, Cairo, 20 March 2011.
14   Interview with Ahmed al-Gourd, Cairo, 24 March 2011.
15   Interview with Muhammad Abbas, Cairo, 28 March 2011.

(EFITU) as a potential center for the workers' movement.[16] They formulated a class program that was based on demands that had emerged spontaneously from the strike since 2006, including: a national minimum and maximum wage; the right to establish independent trade unions and the abolition of the GFETU; the right to strike and protest; the renationalization of privatized companies; the cleansing of the public sector of corrupt managers; improved healthcare; and the abolition of temporary contracts.[17] The disciplined and politicized presence of EFITU militants in the square – one of the discrete activity-systems within the broad collaborative project of Tahrir – directly instructed workers and their leaders from other sectors and governorates to form their own independent unions when they returned to their homes and workplaces (Alexander 2012).

Nuancing the role of the workers' movement, Saud Omar drew attention to the *convergence* of two processes that led to Mubarak's fall: on the one hand, the powerful entrance of the workers as class actors in the revolution; and on the other, the tendency of the revolutionary masses in Tahrir to move from a mere occupation and war of attrition strategy to a 'frontal assault' of state institutions: "The people marching on Europa palace in Cairo and calling labor strikes in Suez had an equal impact on the outcome of the revolution. These two were revolutionary actions that put pressure on the president to resign."[18] It is exactly the specter of the increasing interpenetration of the political and economic moments of the revolution that scared the SCAF and led the generals to dispose of Mubarak as the leader of the neoliberal bloc.

Despite a few specific collaborations where the political and economic lines were entwined and integrated, the fall of Mubarak on 11 February cut through this general process. Whereas the political mobilization of the masses ran out of breath, the strike movement expanded and intensified until early March. Unlike the bulk of protesters, the strikers did not put their fate in the military 'transitional' government. In the words of Luxemburg: "[...] after the possible content of political action in the given situation and at the given stage of the revolution was exhausted, it broke, or rather changed, into economic action" (Luxemburg 1970, 172). Workers returning to their workplaces transposed their revolutionary experience to their predicament as wage laborers. Feeling empowered by the mass strike and the popular uprising, they began to set up their own trade unionist neoformations vis-à-vis the factory management and

---

16 Interview with Fatma Ramadan, Cairo, 15 March 2011; Interview with Kamal Abu al-Eita, Giza, 20 March 2011.
17 Interview with Saud Omar, Suez, 18 March 2011.
18 Interview with Saud Omar, Suez, 18 March 2011.

the structures of the GFETU: "A lot of people are now coming to us to ask for advice to make their own independent unions and to join our independent union. We haven't enough time to answer all applications for new unions [...]."[19]

Instead of the pinnacle of the uprising, the mass strikes initiated a new, protracted phase of the 25 January Revolution. In the months and years following the uprising, almost every section of the Egyptian working class rose in protest against bad working conditions, low wages, and the petty dictatorships of the 'little Mubaraks' presiding over the public and private companies (cf. Alexander 2012).

---

19 Interview with Kamal Abu al-Eita, Giza, 20 March 2011.

CHAPTER 28

Revolutionary Pathologies

Despite its size and militancy, the popular uprising of 25 January uprising did not lead to a transformation of the neoliberal-capitalist historical bloc. The next chapter investigates the main reasons why the insurrection could not accomplish its central demand of the 'fall of the régime'.

Lack of a Center

Friday 5 February was dubbed the Friday of Departure as an ultimatum to Mubarak. This episode expressed both the strength and the weakness of the revolutionary project at that moment. Whereas the movement had been able to set its own concrete timetable and demands, it had not yet developed the means to enforce them. Tunisia's projection of successful revolution, which had been instructive in drawing in participants to the project of Tahrir, now became a brake, as protesters hoped that Mubarak would, like Ben Ali, just leave in the face of their mass demonstrations and occupations alone. State institutions were paralyzed and disorganized due to the demonstrations and sit-ins, but they were not captured and transformed. As long as the main institutions, such as the Maspero television and radio building, parliament, the presidential palace, and army barracks, were protected by the military, the state dug in, enduring the protests in the hope that the demonstrators' physical and mental constitution would wear down quickly. The occupation form of collaboration, which had been the motor of the revolution in the previous week, now became a bottleneck for its development.

Already on the first Friday of Anger, 28 January, there were activists who tried to rally and direct people towards occupying not only the largely symbolic location of Tahrir, but also 'real' spaces of state power. During the Friday of Departure there was a renewed attempt to orient the masses toward a march on the presidential Palace, but this call did not materialize. Conversely, the régime, after its disastrous attempts to repress the revolutionary uprising by force, was content to wage a war of attrition with the occupiers. Whereas the majority of protesters remained stuck in the occupation-strategy, from Tuesday 8 February onward some participants tried to develop a 'second front' of occupation near the parliament and the presidential palace. Alexandria protesters sent a message to Tahrir that they should occupy the Maspero building

(Schielke 2011). Moreover, workers opened up a new form of collaboration in the revolutionary struggle by organizing strikes, while peasants mobilized in the countryside, dealing blows to the economic pillars of the régime.

These novel collaborations expressed the potential, on the one hand, to deepen the political line of development of the uprising, and, on the other, to integrate the political and economic protests. The ideal projection of the Republic of Tahrir was insufficient to act as motor for development: the revolutionary collaboration had to expand its activity in material form as well by occupying and conquering all the strongholds of power throughout Egypt. However, in order to transform the projection of its collaboration to the nation into a nationwide collaboration, Tahrir had to negate itself. Its revolutionary 'governance' had to be shared with neighborhoods and workplaces all over Egypt. Instead of being just a particular within the revolution, the Republic of Tahrir had to become a universal connecting its vanguard, projective role in the revolution to the particular struggles waged by the popular masses outside its borders. In other words: Tahrir had to become the active, self-conscious center of the revolution.

From the beginning of the uprising, there had been a continuous exchange between Tahrir and participants from local projects of resistances in other Cairo neighborhoods or even towns and cities. In the square these 'delegations' enjoyed the freedom to debate the strategy of the movement and the future of Egypt. When they returned to their own, particular collaborations, they transposed their participation in the self-governance of the square to the local sites of protests, sharing and diffusing the experience of the Republic of Tahrir. However, these connections were anything but systemic and coherent. With regard to the 1917 Russian Revolution, Trotsky remarked that: "Without a guiding organization the energy of the masses would dissipate like steam not enclosed in a piston-box" (Trotsky 2001, 19). The expansion of Tahrir required a specific neoformation, a grassroots political center and apparatus of some kind, that represented both the plurality and the concentrated will of the masses: a Modern Prince.

In the final days of the Mubarak era there was a shy push for such a development. There was a growing sense of urgency that the Tuesday and Friday momentum of mass mobilization should not be allowed to evaporate, but channeled in a march on the state's institutions. When in his speech on Thursday 10 February the president still refused to step down, out of the anger and confusion among the masses rose "[...] a feeling that people want to get on the move now. I can hear this chant: We'll go to the palace and tear him out" (Guardian News Blog 10/2b, 2011). This illustrates the growing consciousness of the occupiers that staying in Tahrir would not lead to a breakthrough in the stand-off between al-sha'b and al-nizam.

The fact that the movement lacked a 'center' had been, in its early stage, rather a springboard than an obstacle. Without a center it was much more difficult for the state to defeat the masses by absorbing or liquidating their leadership.[1] However, when the masses needed to strike a decisive blow against the 'system' the lack of a directive center that "[showed] them the shortest and most direct route to complete, absolute and decisive victory" (Lenin 1962, 113) locked the movement in its war of attrition. The absence of a political center that could direct the masses was temporarily compensated by the presence of cultural expressions, which imagined and projected the next step in the development of the revolution: "Many signs functioned as organizational tools. They enabled protesters to communicate with one another, and made the aims of the revolution an ever-present, explicit call to action" (Gribbon and Hawas 2012, 104). Salah Abd al-Azim recalled:

> […] I made a cartoon of Mubarak sitting in his chair and a lot of spiders climbing on it. As a symbol to say: 'stay in your palace, don't move, and we will come to you'. I made a lot of copies, small and big ones. […] After the speech of Mubarak when he said I will remain in the chair, a lot of people carried small copies of the cartoon in a demonstration to Mubarak's palace. The biggest one is four to three meters, they carried it on a car and people wrote on it: "don't leave, we're coming to you […]"[2]

However, the success of this semiotic stopgap illustrated the weakness of the national-popular subject as a self-directing force. The predicament of its own decentralized and unstructured subjectivity was further deepened by the 'soft coup' of the armed forces.

Caesarism Again?

The movement of the masses toward key sites of state power – in particular the presidential palace and the parliament (Khalil 2012, 259–260) – and the parallel explosion of nation-wide strikes, prompted the military to intervene in the process, cutting short the developmental process. Through its 'communiqués', the SCAF began to operate openly and explicitly as a power independent from the presidency (Kandil 2011). The best option for the survival of the Egyptian ruling classes was that the armed forces placed themselves at the

---

1 Interview with Sabry Zaky, Cairo, 10 March 2011. Cf. Bamyeh 2011, Schielke 2011.
2 Interview with Salah Abd al-Azim, Cairo, 22 March 2011.

head of the revolution and 'lead' it, in order to defeat it. Before the laconic statement of Omar Suleiman that spelled the end of Mubarak's presidency, soldiers and officers were joining protesters at Tahrir, while people in the square chanted that the army and the people were one. The confusion about the role of the armed forces in Egyptian society among many of the protesters, and the absence of a grassroots political center, allowed the military leaders to step in and represent themselves as revolutionary arbiters or even leaders (De Smet 2014a). On Sunday afternoon 13 February, in its fourth communiqué, the SCAF declared that parliament was dissolved and the constitution suspended and that it would run the country until presidential and parliamentary elections were held. It also called upon the population "[...] to head back to work, and stop the strikes that have disrupted Egypt's economy" (Al Jazeera Live Blog 14/2, 2011).

Although the 25 January protesters had constructed their goal as the straightforward overthrow of the unequivocal evil that Mubarak's reign represented, in reality they faced a multitentacled monster. The Egyptian nizam – the neoliberal historical bloc – was vertically and horizontally layered. As the ruling classes, especially in a complex capitalist society, cannot rule directly they create forms of mediation to dominate and oppress the subaltern classes.[3] These mediations often acquire a logic and agency of their own, and sometimes attain a far-reaching autonomy vis-à-vis their original, constituting classes – as happened, for example, with the military during Nasser's rule. Every so often state elites such as high-positioned bureaucratic and military layers are even able to establish themselves as a ruling class in their own right. Since the 1970s and 1980s Egyptian state elites close to Sadat and Mubarak had been able to transform themselves into a private capitalist class, at the expense of the political and economic power of the generals.

When the 25 January protests turned into a general insurrection, subordinated factions within the armed forces were not inclined to save their civil political and economic 'competitors' within the ruling stratum: i.e., the interior

---

3   At the eve of the 25 January Revolution, the main structures of class rule were the military, the NDP, and the ministry of interior with its diverse civil repressive apparatus. I consider parliament, the cabinet, ministries, universities, the office of the Grand Mufti, the GFETU, and so on, as secondary sources of class rule, because they were more or less directly supervised, infiltrated, and subjugated by the institutions above. A third category is the most contended 'civil' space of class rule represented by the professional syndicates, the GFETU factory committees, the media, the legal parties, the Church, the Sufi Orders, and so on. These more localized and particularist institutions often acted as sites of state coercion and consent as well as spaces of political and economic resistance.

ministry, the NDP, and the crony capitalists around Gamal Mubarak.[4] For the military elites the uprising was as much a *threat* as an *opportunity* to reconfigure the relations of power within the ruling stratum to their advantage. Therefore, they stood passively by when protesters burned down the NDP headquarters in Cairo (Amar 2012). To be clear: the generals were not against the neoliberal offensive in principle, but, apart from the danger of political destabilization it caused, they contested the fact that they did not sufficiently participate in the cannibalization of the public sector (Armbrust 2012).

The disorganization of al-nizam through incessant mass demonstrations, occupations, and strikes put pressure on the armed forces to find a way out of the régime's crisis. When it became obvious that the masses would not even accept an 'honorary' exit for the president, Mubarak had to be sacrificed on the altar of the counterrevolution. CNN quoted an anonymous senior Egyptian official claiming that "It's not a coup, it's a consensus" (Guardian News Blog 10/2a, 2011). The emerging consensus among Egypt's ruling classes and foreign allies, such as the USA, was that Mubarak's days were numbered and that the military was the only state structure able to contain the revolutionary flood. The balance of power, which began to shift from the ministry of interior and the NDP to the armed forces after the first Friday of Anger, had now swung decisively in the favor of the military. Omar Suleiman's laconic statement that Mubarak had resigned, not only signified the end of his presidency, it also established the SCAF as the sole *supra*-constitutional ruling power.

The SCAF had to balance carefully between defending their own particular interests, and representing their intervention as a continuation of the revolution and a protection of the common good. As a historical state institution, the Egyptian military has been an essentially counterrevolutionary force, in the sense that it actively blocked the self-organization and self-determination of al-sha'b. Between 1952 and 1967 it had been a transformative or revolutionizing power, but its execution of increasingly radical changes to the Egyptian social formations was meant to *prevent* the development of an autonomous national-popular

---

4 Among the military elites, there were also differences of interest. Whereas the air force, military intelligence, and presidential guard generals were generally favored by the Mubarak clique, others, such as the general chief of the armed forces, Muhammad Tantawi, were less privileged (Amar 2012). In addition to the swings in the revolutionary atmosphere, the contradictory actions of soldiers and officers vis-à-vis the protesters – sometimes protecting them against the police and baltageyya, sometimes siding with the interior ministry against the demonstrators and occupiers – were determined by their discrete loyalties to particular departments and interest groups within the armed forces.

subject, instead of encouraging it.[5] In 1952 the Free Officers had *substituted*[6] their own 'revolutionary' agency for that of the masses. Ironically, in 2011 the generals were able to repeat this Caesarist intervention and play the role of Savior-Ruler, because of their forced retreat from political society, which inoculated the military from the popular criticisms of the escalated domination, oppression, and exploitation during the last two decades.[7] Simply put, the armed forces were, in the eyes of the majority of protesters, no longer a salient pillar of al-nizam. On the contrary, in contradistinction to the civil institutions of the Mubarak régime, the Egyptian military had retained an aura of being a national and popular social force – of a genuine participant in the national-popular subject.

Already on Saturday 29 January, the people called on the army to pick a side in the conflict by the slogan "the people and the army: one hand." A joint statement of youth activists in Tahrir declared that:

> We the people and the youth of Egypt demand that our brothers in the national armed forces clearly define their stance by either lining up with the real legitimacy provided by millions of Egyptians on strike on the streets, or standing in the camp of the régime that has killed our people, terrorized them and stole from them.
>
> *Guardian News Blog* 31/1, 2011

The recognition of "our brothers in the national armed forces" as a potential revolutionary ally was an interpellation of the army as being a part of al-sha'b against al-nizam. The protesters were anxious when the armed forces entered the physical spaces of the uprising, since they recognized the decisive role of the military in the struggle against the Mubarak régime. In their slogans, but also in their actions of embracing and kissing soldiers, giving them flowers, food and drink, discussing with them, and so on, the protesters spontaneously tried to draw the armed forces in their revolutionary activity-system, encouraging them to assist the national-popular subject in a solidary way. The spontaneous instruction of the military by protesters was always directed 'horizontally': at the soldiers and conscripts and "[...] many were unaware of how stark the differences were between the interests of the soldiers and the generals" (Armbrust 2012, 119).

The SCAF profited from this confusion about the nature of the armed forces, seen as both a potentially liberating force through its soldiers developing toward solidarity and as one of the central pillars of al-nizam. Taking the lead in the

---

5   Cf. Chapter 13.
6   Cf. Chapter 9.
7   For a detailed comparison: Alexander 2011c; De Smet 2014a.

revolutionary process seemed to agree with the dominant sentiment among protesters that the armed forces were on their side. Conversely, the generals were pressured to act because the interpellation of "the people and the army: one hand" started to affect the rank and file soldiers.[8] The generals could not command their troops to open fire on the protesters because that would have broken the spell that conjured the image of the armed forces as the defenders of the national popular interest. In order to block the spontaneously emerging solidary mode of assistance between soldiers and protesters, the SCAF had to initiate a colonizing mode of assistance towards the mass movement, which, at face value, satisfied the expectations of both popular masses and soldiers (cf. Stacher 2011b).

The End of the People

The Caesarist pathology of the uprising was a consequence of the low development of national-popular subjectness: its structural and self-conscious capacity to act as a political force in its own right. The strength of the SCAF consisted mainly of the weakness of the national-popular counterhegemony. The masses accepted the leadership of the SCAF because they had no directive center and hegemonic apparatus of their own.

Moreover, the political interventions of the left were insufficient to enrich the everyday, practical critiques of the system with a scientific, theoretical understanding of al-nizam as a historical bloc. The concrete figure of Mubarak had been a physical icon of everything that was structurally wrong with the Egyptian social formation, just as the iconicity of the mass protests represented the tangible substance of the national-popular subject. Once the president had been removed, the system was no longer immediately represented in a concentrated form and its attributes – corruption, violence, authoritarianism, poverty, and so on – became disembodied and abstracted. The concretization of al-nizam in thought required a thorough critique of the economic structure and the relations of domination and hegemony – a critique that would unmask the interests of the military, the Brotherhood, and other forces that claimed leadership in the ensuing struggle for hegemony.

In the absence of a national-popular Modern Prince that could offer both a directive center and a philosophy of praxis, integrating an everyday with a scientific critique, the masses confused the military's substitutionism for revolutionary leadership, and the great majority returned back to their homes (cf. Khalil 2012,

---

8 Interview with Khaled al-Balshy, Cairo, 14 March 2011.

266). The failure to expand the Republic of Tahrir to the whole of Egypt reduced the square to a symbolic site for ritualistic protest. Although Tahrir continued to play a role as a key locale for demonstrations and occupations, it no longer determined the development of the revolutionary process. For most of the protesters who accepted the SCAF as the leader of the 'democratic transition process' this was but a temporary and conditional guardianship. For example, Alaa Abd al-Fattah, a youth activist, argued that: "The military are the custodians of this particular stage in the process, and we're fine with that, but it has to be temporary" (Shenker 2011c). People often expressed their confidence in their own collective agency to keep the SCAF in check and claimed that they knew now that they could and would return to the streets when something did not work out as they wanted it to be. Such statements highlighted a general rise in political consciousness and subjectness that the uprising had stimulated. Although the SCAF governed, it was the people that had given the military a provisional mandate.

At the same time, without real structures that organized and concentrated popular power, this revolutionary awareness became difficult to mobilize. Moreover, the separation of political consciousness from everyday practices of mass protest increasingly emptied the national-popular subject of its content. The moment of general insurrection, which had united different activity-systems into a single collaboration, was dissolved back into its constituent parts – although it had thoroughly transformed many of the participating projects. The past and present of the revolution were rewritten: some revolutionary actors were excluded as genuine participants in the activity-system of al-sha'b, such as striking workers, while other, counterrevolutionary, forces were included (Sallam 2011b), hiding, sometimes literally, behind the Egyptian flag. Mobinil and Vodaphone set up giant billboards in the national colors with the slogan 'We are all Egyptians'. Shops like Adidas painted their windows as Egyptian flags in order to prevent people from smashing them. The form of the national-popular subject survived its real collaborative activity as a nationalist metanarrative, that could be easily appropriated and colonized by each of the political forces involved in the post-Mubarak hegemonic struggle: "The revolution was a group work. But now everyone is talking about the revolution as if he owns it."[9]

Soviets?

Just as there was no revolutionary neoformation that offered a directive center and an integration of the everyday and scientific developmental lines of critique,

---

9 Interview with Saud Omar, Suez, 18 March 2011.

the uprising lacked a structure that integrated political and economic lines, and the national-popular and proletarian subjects. The investigation in Chapters 25 and 26 revealed Tahrir not as the unit of analysis of *revolution*, but as the mass form of the *demonstration* and thus the cell-form of the revolutionary *uprising*. Tahrir was unable to embody the plurality of collaborations that had led up to 25 January. Although there were elements of the particular struggles of farmers, workers, women, students, and so on, within the square, these were largely subsumed under the banner of the fight for democracy and civil rights. It is hard to say if the 'Republic of Tahrir' would have been able to articulate and unite the class, gender, and socio-geographical[10] subjectivities of the popular revolution, if its development had not been interrupted by the soft coup.

Saud Omar stressed that: "The most important benefit of the revolution is this image: the alliance between the régime and capital."[11] If the substance of the 25 January Revolution was a war of movement against the neoliberal offensive, then it could only be completed by changing the domestic and transnational class alliances and the political economy of accumulation by dispossession (Maher 2011). The democratic revolution could not succeed except by a reconfiguration of the economic structure, and the economic structure could not be transformed unless political power was captured and appropriated by the subaltern classes.

Unlike the Russian Revolution of 1905 and 1917, where workers and peasants (as soldiers) constituted joint political organs – soviets – that connected the class struggle with the fight for democracy, the 25 January uprising lacked such directive neoformations that organically connected the political and economic lines of development. In Egypt, workers were either subsumed under the national-popular subject, or fought their own struggles through the embryonic structures of trade unionism. Perhaps, if the Republic of Tahrir had been able to develop its own directive organs that concentrated the revolutionary process in the whole country, trade union structures such as the EFITU would have injected proletarian subjectivities directly into the national-popular subject. The Caesarist intervention and the concomitant demobilization of the square made such an outcome impossible. Instead of growing toward each other, the political and economic lines seemed to separate.

On 14 February, the SCAF demanded that worker leaders stop their strikes. Rightwing nationalist, Islamist, liberal, and even some leftist[12] forces concurred

---

10   The opposition between urban and rural areas; between the metropolises of Cairo and Alexandria and provincial towns; between Upper and Lower Egypt; and so on.
11   Interview with Saud Omar, Suez, 18 March 2011.
12   Interview with Hisham Fouad, Giza, 13 March 2011.

and rejected workers' protests for being 'parochialist', counterrevolutionary, and against the national interest (cf. Clément 2011, Sallam 2011b, Naguib 2011). Even independent media outlets such as al-Masry al-Youm showed the continuation of the strike movement in a negative light.[13] This narrative also began to affect the ranks of non-proletarian revolutionary youth organizations and networks, which argued that "[...] those who are taking part in [the strikes] were classes with limited interests that primarily concerned them and weren't of concern to the rest of the classes in society, from their point of view. There was a situation of hostility between the workers and middle class youth" (Haddad 2011b). Workers were no longer taken for granted as legitimate, solidary participants in the national-popular project.

Workers, for their part, were reluctant to engage in 'politics'. Although politicized worker leaders and leftist activists noticed the presence of a good sense that moved toward political consciousness,[14] most trade unions and strike committees refrained from elaborating an explicit political program. Labor leaders often had a pragmatic and gradual view on the development of the workers' movement: "[a workers' party] will be positive in the future, but right now we should focus on developing the trade unions and the federation and we use up a lot of energy in organizing this."[15] Even though trade unionism was the negation of the workers' economic-corporate condition, it already showed signs of becoming a future obstacle for the development of the worker subject. The more or less stable trade union neoformations had to be brought into a continuous organic relation with the workers themselves, lest organizational 'bureaucratism' and ideological 'economism' distorted the dialectical pedagogy of the proletarian project.

---

13 Interview with Fatma Ramadan, Cairo, 15 March 2011; Interview with Gihan Ibrahim, Cairo, 20 March 2011; Interview with Mustafa Bassiouny, Giza, 17 March 2011; Interview with Saud Omar, Suez, 18 March 2011.
14 Interview with Gihan Ibrahim, Cairo, 20 March 2011.
15 Interview with Kamal Abbas, Cairo, 27 March 2011.

CHAPTER 29

Revolution Beyond Tahrir

Whereas the previous chapter elucidated the direct, pathological outcome of the 25 January uprising, the following chapter discusses the further development of the revolutionary process. It investigates the changing role of Tahrir, the counterrevolution, and the difficulties in developing a Modern Prince that could integrate the different lines of development.

From Cell-Form to Symbol

Thousands of euphoric protesters remained overnight in the square to celebrate Mubarak's departure. On Saturday morning, however, the question arose as to whether the occupation of Tahrir should continue until there was more clarity about the promised transition to democracy.[1] The main democratic demands that had emerged from the movement were the end of emergency law, the release of political prisoners, the formation of a presidential committee dominated by civilians, and of a constitutional committee, in addition to full freedoms for the press, syndicates, trade unions, and political parties. Hossam al-Hamalawy warned that: "The war hasn't ended. The first battle of the revolution ended with Mubarak's stepping down from power, but the revolution hasn't been completed" (Haddad 2011b). The hard core of occupiers argued that they should remain in Tahrir in order to pressure the SCAF for real reforms. In the past two weeks, the occupation of the square had proved to be an effective strategy to enforce concessions from the régime. Moreover, life at Tahrir projected the capability of popular self-governance and a vision of a new, solidary society. Tahrir was the soul of the revolution, and to abandon this liberated space would jeopardize the entire revolutionary process. The role of political activists was "[...] pushing people to collect themselves again in the square on Fridays and stop this normalization of revolutionary activity."[2]

The Tahrir mobilizations still had an effect after the fall of Mubarak. For example, protesters succeeded in putting enough pressure on the SCAF to fire prime minister Ahmed Shafiq on 3 March and replace him with Essam Sharaf who had a better standing with the masses, because he had participated in the

---

1 Interview with Wael Tawfiq, Cairo, 16 March 2011.
2 Interview with Muhammad Zaky Murat, 30 March 2011.

25 January protests – even though he had served as minister of transportation in 2004 and 2005. Under pressure of the Tahrir occupiers, Sharaf reshuffled his cabinet, removing many figures that were perceived as too close to the old régime. After March, Tahrir still welcomed tens of thousands of protesters and occupiers, for example during the Friday of Cleaning on 8 April 2011, the Second Friday of Anger on 27 May 2011, throughout July, the Friday of Correcting the Path on 9 September 2011, and at the eve of the 2011 parliamentary and 2012 presidential elections. Those protesting were increasingly disappointed with the lack of real change and the counterrevolutionary role of the SCAF.

However, it became more and more clear that the Caesarist intervention had succeeded in demobilizing and pacifying the majority of protesters. Already in March 2011, Menal Khaled of the cinema workers' union confided in me that: "[...] I don't love Tahrir anymore. I went to Tahrir and I found people as if they were going to the zoo with their children, taking photos of the tents, and so on."[3] Apart from a space for ritualistic protest, Midan Tahrir had become a tourist site of commemoration of the revolutionary uprising where t-shirts and souvenirs were sold – already celebrating the past of the revolt instead of its presence or future (Gribbon and Hawas 2012, 135). Whereas the Republic of Tahrir had appropriated the organizational traditions of the carnivalesque *mulid* during the 18 Days, now the revolutionary activity of the square had been subjugated to the festival's atmosphere.[4]

Sabry Zaky moved that: "Now, staying in Tahrir is an old game. I think it has brought us many successes and gains, but we have to be creative, because a revolution by definition is a creative thing [...] we have to think about other venues and other ways to spread this revolution."[5] Menal Khaled agreed: "Being in the square now is only a symbolic movement. You should be in the neighborhoods. Conscious actors and artists should go to the neighborhoods, especially the poor neighborhoods, to raise consciousness, and through their work and movies they should raise awareness."[6]

The moment of the uprising, the explicitly revolutionary phase that began with the 25 January protests and ended with the fall of Mubarak (and which is often identified with 'revolution' in a narrow sense) drew in, at its high point,

---

3   Interview with Gihan Shabeen, Cairo, 16 March 2011.
4   Keraitim and Mehrez (2012) were too optimistic when they described the transformation of Tahrir into a spectacle as an empowering tendency. For a while, Tahrir remained a projection, but only as a lingering echo of its past dynamic, for it no longer represented a real, developing activity-system.
5   Interview with Sabry Zaky, Cairo, 10 March 2011.
6   Interview with Menal Khaled, Cairo, 25 March 2011.

millions of ordinary Egyptians. However, even the street politics of the revolutionary uprising could not immediately instruct the whole population. Although thousands continued to protest and occupy Tahrir, the real masses, the millions who had poured into the streets during the uprising, returned to their homes after the Caesarist intervention, implicitly granting the SCAF a mandate for its emancipation and explicitly voting for the most conservative political forces in the following referenda and parliamentary and presidential elections.

In the eyes of many leftists, the offspring of the revolution seemed monstrous. SCAF-organized referenda and elections represented a counterrevolutionary consolidation of the ruling stratum's power in a civildemocratic form. Nevertheless, already in March 2011 Gihan Ibrahim rejected "[...] these huge assumptions that [...] because now the people are in favor of revolution they will never vote for someone who is part of the old régime, or the NDP, which is nonsense in my view [...]".[7] With regard to the similar anticlimactic outcome of the 1917 February Revolution in Russia, Trotsky observed: "But in voting for them they created a partition-wall between themselves and their own aims. They could not now move forward at all without bumping into this wall erected by themselves, and knocking it over" (Trotsky 2001, 192).

For the revolutionary project, not the 'inherent' conservatism of the 'silent majority' was the main obstacle – this had been overcome in the praxis of struggle and it could be overcome again – but the practical divide between 'the masses' and 'the vanguard'. The soft coup had cut off the vanguard from its mass base. The first task for leftists wanting to assist in the development of the disintegrating national-popular subject was to reconnect the vanguard to its mass basis and reconstitute the revolutionary activity-system. While opinions within the left differed strongly on the validity and usefulness of participating in SCAF-organized elections, most activists of the new left realized that, if the vanguard could not mobilize the masses into the streets, it would have to go to the masses and bring the 'spirit of Tahrir' to the popular neighborhoods and workplaces. "We have to take Tahrir to the factories now," exclaimed Hossam al-Hamalawy (2011a). Likewise, Gihan Ibrahim asserted that: "[...] our battles are not in parliament, but in the factories, in the unions, in setting up the workers' party, in using these strikes and workers' power into a political weapon."[8]

Although the situation remained far from stable and the masses far from passive, the salient insurrectionary phase had ended, and the difficult, molecular work of building a counterhegemonic alternative had just begun.

---

[7] Interview with Gihan Ibrahim, Cairo, 20 March 2011.
[8] Interview with Gihan Ibrahim, Cairo, 20 March 2011.

A Civil Counterrevolution

Once the bulk of the masses had been demobilized, Egypt's ruling classes regained the political initiative. The military elites were able to improve their position within the ruling stratum at the expense of the capitalist groups close to Gamal Mubarak and the NDP elites. The Brotherhood bourgeoisie, for its part, tried to take advantage of the situation to advance its own political and economic standing within the ensemble of dominating classes. To a certain extent the trajectory of the Muslim Brotherhood reflected that of the military during the 25 January uprising. The Society's leadership was anxious of the régime's repression should it join the 25 January protests, and suspicious of the development of the national-popular subject as a self-determining and self-organizing force. Nevertheless it participated in the revolutionary activity-system because it was pushed by its enthusiastic youth membership (Alexander 2011c, 544),[9] and because it realized that the insurrection constituted an opportunity to swing the balance of power in its favor. Even with its formidable apparatus of relatively loyal, organized activists, the Brotherhood would not, and could not, *lead* the protests of millions (Bayat 2011; Sallam, Stacher and Toensing 2011). For most secular activists and observers this was a reassuring fact, as its presence in the revolution had conjured images of the Iranian Revolution of 1979. During the uprising Muslim Brothers generally stood side by side with the other protesters and were often the most militant and resilient demonstrators and occupiers.[10]

After the fall of Mubarak, the attitude of the leadership changed, however, as it cautiously supported the soft coup and called upon protesters to leave the square and start negotiations with the SCAF – much to the anger of radical liberals, socialists, and nationalists (cf. Alexander 2011c). The collapse of the NDP left a political vacuum that neither the SCAF nor the existing opposition parties could fill. The Brotherhood leadership was conscious of its potential as a power broker between the generals and the popular masses (Alexander 2011c, 536). It desired a small reconfiguration of the neoliberal historical bloc: the addition of its own capitalist leaders such as Khayrat al-Shater to the dominant stratum within the ruling classes (cf. Teti and Gervasio 2012).

The military had little interest in ruling Egypt directly, firstly because it was unfit to deal with domestic crowd control; and secondly because it rather

---

9   Interview with Muhammad Ali, Cairo, 27 March 2011; interview with Muhammad Abbas, Cairo, 28 March 2011.
10 Interview with Gihan Shabeen, Cairo, 16 March 2011; interview with Muhammad Abbas, Cairo, 28 March 2011.

wished to elevate itself above civil and political society, playing the part of arbiter between different political and economic factions of the ruling classes (Kandil 2011). While the NDP was formally dissolved on 16 April 2011 by court order, the SCAF left the apparatus of the interior ministry largely intact (Khalil 2012, 302), because it was still a useful and necessary instrument of coercion.

The continuation of workplace strikes and street demonstrations 'from below' stood in stark contrast to the normalization and consolidation of political society 'from above', spearheaded by the SCAF and supported by the Muslim Brotherhood and the Salafists. The direct military Caesarism of the SCAF gave quickly way to a civil counterrevolution that took on the form of military-supervised representative politics (De Smet 2014a). Instead of representing a genuine process of revolutionary democratic change, elections and referenda were deployed by the 'transition government' as weapons of restoration. Firstly, they narrowed the meaning and space of 'revolutionary politics' from spontaneous street and workplace protests to the limited and top-down controlled domain of the state. Political activists were diverted from the more pressing task of reconnecting the vanguard with the masses and reforging ties between the various collaborations of the disintegrating revolutionary project. The focus on formal democratic practice also served to sever the link between the struggle for democracy of the political opposition and urban middle classes and the economic demands of workers, peasants, and the urban poor. Secondly, elections atomized the active national-popular subject into individual 'voters', which were politically drowned in the wider population: the 'qualitative' majority in the streets was reduced to a 'quantitative' minority in the polling booths. Thirdly, by controlling the pace of elections and the agenda of referenda, new cleavages were created – especially the sectarian divide between 'secularists' and 'Islamists' – and certain political factions, such as the Brotherhood and the Salafists, were favored at the expense of more revolutionary but less organized groups.

The Brotherhood's landslide in the parliamentary elections of fall 2011 and a growing discontent among the population with the SCAF's failing and heavy-handed 'transitional' policies,[11] encouraged the Ikhwan to raise the stakes. The Muslim Brotherhood and the Salafists realized their parliamentary victory was a pyrrhic one, as parliament was still governed by the old constitution that did not even grant them the right to form a cabinet of their own choice. A race

---

11   The intimidation, harassment, and torture of political activists, especially women, the failure to democratise authoritarian institutions such as the ministry of interior and the army itself, the inability to secure economic prosperity and pursue 'social justice', and so on.

began between parliament, which established a committee to write a new constitution that would expand its powers, and the executive – i.e., the SCAF – which began legal proceedings to contest the constitutionality of parliament. On 14 June 2012 the High Constitutional Court dissolved parliament, and the SCAF took over legislative powers: preparing the outcome of the final round of the presidential elections that were held on Saturday 16 and Sunday 17 June 2012.

In the first round of the 2012 presidential elections, the more 'revolutionary' candidates Hamdeen Sabahi and Abdel Moneim Abul Futuh were beaten by a slim margin into third and fourth place respectively by Muslim Brotherhood contender Muhammad Morsi and régime runner Ahmed Shafiq. In the second round, Egyptians were forced to choose between the lesser of these two evils and Morsi won.[12] This episode represented an increasing polarization between Islamist and secular subjectivities, which cut right through the national-popular subject. Even though the Brotherhood and the Salafists profited from the sectarianization of the political debate in the short term, in the long run it made it much more difficult for these forces to present themselves as the defenders of the national 'common good' (cf. Sallam 2011a). The stronger the Islamist factions became, the more the military leadership would be able to play up fears among secular liberal, nationalist, and 'old' leftist opposition forces about the danger of an imminent Islamization of society. Without the will or ability to mobilize an independent social base against the Islamists, secular parties could not but look for protection among the armed forces against the bigger 'threat' of Islamism.

Popular Uprising and Military Coup

By June 2012, after a year in power, the SCAF had shown itself a select and self-centered clique that was unable to consolidate its domination over the whole armed forces, let alone the other ruling class factions, or society at large. The victory of Muhammad Morsi was an opportunity for the military to share the burden of ruling with a civil ally. In exchange for a protection of the political and economic interests and privileges of the generals, the armed forces would leave the reorganization of the state to the Ikhwan. Instead of a

---

12   Although there were allegations that, in fact, Ahmed Shafiq had won the elections but the military chose to reverse the results in order not to provoke the streets (Beilin 2013). True or not, it was clear that in the Spring of 2012 the generals were not too upset with a Muslim Brother as president.

demilitarization and democratization of the state, Morsi's constitutional declaration of 12 August 2012, which retired old heavy-weight SCAF generals such as Hussein Tantawi and Sami Anan, signaled a pragmatic compromise between the Brotherhood and the armed forces. Morsi catapulted Brotherhood sympathizer Abdul Fattah al-Sisi into the position of defense minister and chief of staff of the armed forces. The constitution of 26 December 2012, which shielded the defense budget from parliamentary oversight and asserted that the minister of defense was chosen from the ranks of the military, affirmed this alliance (De Smet 2014a).

After initial enthusiasm about Egypt's first 'democratically elected', civil president, in the fall of 2012 there was a growing discontent among broad layers of the population with the Brotherhood's inability or unwillingness to forge a national consensus, to dismantle and democratize state structures such as the interior ministry, to solve the economic crisis, and so on. Morsi's constitutional declaration on 22 November 2012, which temporarily granted him absolute executive and legislative powers, seemed to confirm the worst fears among secular opposition forces about a 'Brotherhoodization' of political and civil society (De Smet and Matthies-Boon 2013). The next few months saw an escalation of violent mass protests between pro-Morsi and anti-Brotherhood demonstrators. While both camps claimed to represent the revolutionary path, they contained a mix of revolutionary and counterrevolutionary forces subsumed by two factions of the counterrevolution. The National Salvation Front (NSF) united rightists such as Amr Moussa, liberal-democrats such as Muhammed al-Baradei, leftist Nasserists such as Hamdeen Sabahi, and *feloul* (Mubakarist elements) under one broad umbrella against the Brotherhood.

The struggle in political and civil society remobilized the masses in the streets. At the end of April 2013 the petition campaign *Tamarod* (Rebel) was established, which collected signatures calling on president Morsi to step down. Although infiltrated by anti-Morsi elements of the security apparatus (al-Sharif and Saleh 2013), it became a huge mass movement, which gathered numbers in the streets that were only comparable to those of the January 25 uprising. A wide range of leftist and rightist opposition forces participated in the door-to-door campaign, reconnecting national politics to the popular spaces of the streets and workplaces. Popular layers that had remained passive throughout the 2011 insurrection were galvanized into action. Seeing that the Ikhwan were incapable of securing political and economic stability, let alone hegemonic leadership, the military leaders opened up negotiations with Tamarod and the NSF. After collecting millions of signatures from ordinary Egyptians, Tamarod launched the 30 June Front to organize protests against the president on the day that commemorated his first year in power. Already on 28 and 29 June preparatory demonstrations turned violent when they clashed with pro-Morsi supporters. Massive demonstrations and strikes mobilizing millions of Egyptians in the streets erupted on 30 June, demanding nothing less than the resignation of the president. In an echo of 28 January 2011, Tahrir Square reached its maximum capacity of demonstrators. However, Morsi, stressing his legitimacy as democratically elected president, refused to give in.

When the mass protests entered their second day on 1 July, Abdel Fattah al-Sisi, head of the armed forces, issued an ultimatum to both camps to solve the crisis within 48 hours or else the military would intervene. After two more days of deadly clashes between pro and anti-Morsi protesters, the 30 June Front met with the military leaders, and shortly thereafter al-Sisi declared that the president had been removed from his position and that chief Justice Adli Mansour would head a transitional government as interim president. Morsi was arrested and the army occupied key political and economic sites in the country, cheered by the anti-Morsi masses. Mirroring February 2011, a popular uprising was 'crowned' with a military coup.

The Tamarod insurrection was a new high point in the revolutionary process, remobilizing and repoliticizing broad layers of the population, and creating grassroots committees that organized the collection of signatures and the organization of demonstrations and strikes. Although the character of the movement was marred by the presence of feloul, opportunist political forces, and members of the security apparatus, such elements could not possibly control a movement of millions. As in 2011, the armed forces had to intervene before the uprising produced its own organic political center opposed to the 30 June Front. Again, the only means of controlling and dispersing the insurrection was to substitute its own agency for that of the masses, forcing the president to resign and imposing its own 'roadmap'. Neither a completed revolution, nor a simple top-down military coup, the events of June and July 2013 constituted a genuine uprising that was successfully 'deflected'[13] by the agency of the generals.

Many Princes

Since 11 February 2011, the revolutionary project faced two intertwined challenges. The first was its disembodiment from street politics and its refragmentation in

---

13   Cf. Chapters 10 and 13.

a diversity of disconnected collaborations and collective subjects. The second was its colonization by new and old political forces, especially the military and the Brotherhood, but also 'secular' and 'democratic' projects. The victory of Islamist forces in the referenda and elections in 2011 and 2012 conjured anew the specter of an Islamist takeover. Old left parties such as Tagammu, but also the newly formed Egyptian Social Democratic Party (ESDP) allied with rightwing formations such as the Free Egyptians Party of Naguib Sawiris around a shared program of a more or less secular state.

Whereas the 'secular bloc' was constructed against the threat of Islamism, a 'civildemocratic' bloc was built around the idea that the main challenge for Egypt was to establish a democratic society and a civil state, i.e., a political and civil community not controlled by the military. The feloul and the generals constituted the biggest threat to the revolutionary process. Moderate Islamist formations such as al-Wasat or individuals such as Abd al-Moneim Abu al-Fotouh were not excluded from the bloc and joined the ranks of progressive liberals, parties such as al-Ghad and al-Gabha, al-Baradei supporters, urban middle-class youth movements such as 6 April, human rights activists, and so on. The battle for hegemony was not understood as a struggle between subaltern and ruling classes, but in terms of a conflict between the military-dominated 'state' and 'civil society'. Activists were to encourage the creation of parties, civil organizations, grassroots committees, NGOs, trade unions, syndicates, of whatever class composition or political orientation, for the development and multiplication of these organs would create a dynamic civil society that would act as a counterweight against the state – i.e., the military, the interior ministry, and so on.[14] Such an artificial separation between 'state' and 'civil society' was a liberal conception. It also represented a variation on the stagist concept of "democracy first, social reforms later."

Among leftist formations that did not join the secular or civildemocratic collaborations, a debate emerged which kind of political party they should build or support: an explicitly leftist party; a popular party; or a workers' party. The relative freedom to create parties meant that the left, for the first time since 1952, could openly establish itself as a socialist, social-democratic, or communist party. Inevitably, the revolution spawned a host of leftist groups, and some activists voiced the need for unity between the left in Tagammu, the RS, the ECP, the SRC, the Democratic Left, the ESDP, and so on. They perceived the fragmentation of the left as the main obstacle for leftists to assist the revolutionary project in its development: "Most groups […] are waiting for a big

---

14 Interview with Sabry Zaky, Cairo, 10 March 2011.

leftist party to join it and support it demands. We need a huge leftist organization to attract these groups and individuals."[15]

The Socialist Popular Alliance Party (SPAP) aimed to take over Tagammu's traditional role of the 'house of the Left'. Nevertheless, its leaders realized that they shouldn't waste too much time on courting the various tendencies: "[...] there are still a lot of leftist forces outside it, like Tagammu [...] like the Egyptian Communist Party, which treats Tagammu as its own party, and the Revolutionary Socialists, which established the Democratic Labor Party. We do our thing and we'll see."[16] The RS was skeptical towards the project of uniting the different strands of the left and claimed that:

> [...] collecting all the small leftist groups will not have the same impact of that of a good strong party. It is better to orient yourself directly toward the people than toward other parties. It is only when the left is active in the streets that the new, leftist leadership will become clear.[17]

For most leftist activists, the real challenge was the construction of a revolutionary subaltern project that could transform the neoliberal-capitalist historical bloc, which remained firmly in place after the fall of Mubarak: "The most important thing is to organize the people themselves, not only the leftists. We should create groups from the popular committees to protect the people's demands. Furthermore, we should organize the workers in independent unions. [...] This is the most important step in this phase of the revolution."[18]

All over Egypt, the 25 January uprising had spawned spontaneous structures of self-organization: the popular or civil committees and strike committees.

---

15 Interview with Fatma Ramadan, Cairo, 15 March 2011. Ironically, the project of an explicitly leftist platform encouraged both centripetal and centrifugal forces. Muhammad Zaky Murat remarked that: "In my opinion, there is now a perfect atmosphere to create a truly leftist party in Egypt, but it is the left itself that does not want it" (interview with Muhammad Zaky Murat, Cairo, 30 March 2011). Leftists could only constitute a counterbalance against liberal, nationalist, Islamist, and military rightist forces by uniting themselves in a single fist. This perspective led to tactical discussions about the shape of Left unity. Should it be an alliance between different, existing leftist groups? Should it be a new, pluralist party with room for different platforms, factions and voices? Or should the Left simply join the formation with the most resources and authority? Posing these tactical questions already ripped the Left apart. No sizeable, organized group was willing to absorb their often slowly and painfully built apparatus into another party.

16 Interview with Fatma Ramadan, Cairo, 15 March 2011.
17 Interview with Mustafa Bassiouny, Giza, 17 March 2011.
18 Interview with Wael Tawfiq, Cairo, 16 March 2011.

When Tahrir disintegrated as the centralized cell-form of the insurrection, these neoformations represented the seeds of the national-popular and proletarian subject, respectively. However, a lot of energetic activists were still thinking in terms of a war of movement struggle and the *mobilization* instead of the *institutionalization* of popular power. A distrust and disdain for 'party politics', especially among new layers of activists, were instrumental in the formation of various youth movements. Most of these had their roots in prerevolutionary political activities, such as the 6 April Youth Movement, but others were born in the Republic of Tahrir and other subsystems of revolutionary activity, such as the Coalition of (the) Youth (of the) Revolution (CYR). These youth movements were horizontally organized and constituted a loose collection of discrete groups and networks. Although they played an important role in the continued mobilization of protesters after the fall of Mubarak, they were unable and/or unwilling to construct themselves as a more cohesive and centralized political force.

Leftists who had been engaged in the struggles of subaltern actors since the 1990s had often developed an integral concept of the revolution as a process of both political and economic struggle. Just as al-nizam did not only represent political dictatorship, but also economic exploitation, al-sha'b had a clear social dimension. In the suffering and resistance of workers, farmers, impoverished urban professionals and students, slum dwellers, and so on, the abstract national-popular subject found its class substance.

Popular or Proletarian?

Within the small group of leftist actors that recognized the necessary entwinement of political and economic struggles a debate ensued on the hegemonic relations *within* the revolutionary subaltern project. The RS positioned themselves firmly on the standpoint of the proletariat and stressed the historical necessity of the workers' politicization and independence: "We want the workers, the true workers, represented and be part of the political process that they have completely been out of for decades."[19] Hisham Fouad underlined that: "[…] we have to help the workers to build their party."[20] Because of their economic position within Egyptian society and the experiences and structures of self-governance that emerged from the development of strike and trade unionist movements, the proletariat was the most able class to direct the subaltern

---

19 Interview with Gihan Ibrahim, Cairo, 20 March 2011.
20 Interview with Hisham Fouad, Giza, 13 March 2011.

bloc. However, in order to lead an alliance of subaltern groups, the workers needed their own, independent political structures. Mustafa Bassiouny emphasized that the goal of the RS was to assist the workers in creating their own party: "We will help the workers in developing their own demands, which are not necessarily the demands of the RS."[21] With the support of some of the leaders of the independent trade unions, the RS established the Workers National Democratic Party (WNDP). The class character of the workers' party was more important than the purity of its revolutionary credentials or socialist program.[22] Saud Omar explained that:

> There should be a new labor party because the political parties should be rooted in social reality. A lot of leftists say that we need a new Egyptian Communist Party. I am not against this, of course. But I think that building a party on a class basis is more effective and powerful in society. Having a new labor party without any ideology, like communism or something, will grant it a larger influence than a communist labor party. It will allow the 'bearded men', women, Christians, poor men, and so on, to join and become involved in this party.[23]

The subsumption of the worker subject under the national-popular project would obfuscate the fundamental conflict between labor and capital, and the task of overcoming capitalism as a concrete mode of production. Moreover, a purely proletarian political formation would draw in important layers that were suspicious of socialism or communism, and through a joint struggle with leftist workers their everyday good sense could be integrated with a scientific understanding of their antagonist: the neoliberal-capitalist historical bloc.

Other leftists, however, criticized the initiative of the WNDP as it came too soon with regard to the actual developmental level of the workers' movement.

---

21 Interview with Mustafa Bassiouny, Giza, 17 March 2011.
22 This line of thought was reminiscent of Trotsky's argument in favor of a proletarian organization: "[...] of course, 95 percent of the population, if not 98 percent, is exploited by finance capital. But this exploitation is organized hierarchically: there are exploiters, there are subexploiters, sub-subexploiters, etc. Only thanks to this hierarchy do the superexploiters keep in subjection the majority of the nation. In order that the nation should indeed be able to reconstruct itself around a new class core, it must be reconstructed ideologically and this can be achieved only if the proletariat does not dissolve itself into the 'people', into the 'nation', but on the contrary develops a program of its proletarian revolution and compels the petty bourgeoisie to choose between two régimes" (Trotsky 1931).
23 Interview with Saud Omar, Suez, 18 March 2011.

Wael Tawfiq moved that: "I think we should start from the base, from the unions. We should establish strong unions before a workers' party. Establishing a new workers' party now only brings about a new leadership."[24] Gihan Shabeen explained that: "It is not enough for workers to have a party calling itself the workers' party in order to join it. [...] The most important thing is to let the worker feel that the party is a real alternative for change."[25] Ahmed al-Sayyid, the leader of the health technicians' union, was of the same opinion: "First we have to make solid trade unions, then we can have a party, but it takes a long time to create it. The ex-régime made fake parties, so people will not trust the parties."[26]

The difference of opinion between the RS and the SRC on the necessity of either a workers' party or a national-popular party concerned the 'upper limit' of the proletarian ZPD. Whereas the SRC asserted that first the trade unionist movement had to be developed before there could be any real, mass, organic workers' party, the RS believed in the proleptic role of a 'high profile' proletarian party in the politicization of the workers' movement at large. These perspectives also reflected their diverging views on the dominant mode of struggle of the subaltern bloc in the post-insurrectionary period. The 'transitory' national-popular strategy of the SRC was based on the perspective of a gradual and protracted development of the revolutionary process, in which the workers had to wage an offensive war of position to consolidate their trade unionist neoformations vis-à-vis the dominant military and Islamist forces of the counterrevolution. Conversely, the strategy of the RS was much more oriented towards a war of movement of the working class, and a high tide of the mass strike. In this volatile and crisis-ridden social situation of development, the workers' movement could become quickly politicized, if provided with an effective proleptic instruction that projected the proletariat as a hegemonic force.

In general, new left activists tried to consolidate those grassroots popular committees with subaltern roots and to transform and politicize them into committees for the defense of the revolution. However, their influence was small and they could not prevent popular power sliding back into passivity. The demobilization of the democratic protesters in the streets was in inverse proportion to the mobilizations of workers in the factories and companies. While the civil committees were facing disintegration, the strike committees flourished. New left activists tried to "[...] transform these committees into independent

---

24   Interview with Wael Tawfiq, Cairo, 16 March 2011.
25   Interview with Gihan Shabeen, Cairo, 16 March 2011.
26   Interview with Ahmed al-Sayyid, Cairo, 21 March 2011.

unions in the factory [...]. If the leftists and the people succeed in creating these committees, it will be a precious instrument in winning the revolution."[27] The assistance at the level of the workplace was complemented with support for the formation of trade union federations, which consisted of connecting and coordinating isolated instances of class struggle.[28] Strike and civil committees sometimes entwined and fused into committees for the defense of the revolution, as Wael Tawfiq remembered: "In the iron factory in Helwan we organized a committee to protect the revolution. We were the first ones to do so."[29]

The September 2011 strike wave represented a growing generalization of workers' coordination and consciousness. In contradistinction to the unplanned and ad hoc worker protests from February until March 2011, these strikes were organized by the independent unions. Conversely, the September strikes instructed other workers to coordinate their protests and form trade unionist organizations themselves (Alexander 2012). Trade unionism also reached out to layers of the working class that hitherto had remained relatively passive: "[...] Hospital doctors, mosque imams, fishermen, Tuk-Tuk drivers, skilled craftsmen, intellectual property rights consultants, daily-paid labourers and the operators of the "scarab boats" that take tourists on Nile river trips [...]" (Alexander 2012, 114–115). Whereas the workplace 'strike committee' had been the leading neoformation of the workers' movement between 2006–2010, from 2011 onward, trade unionist forms increasingly overcame the local and sectoral fragmentation of the proletarian subject. However, at the level of national leadership, independent trade unionism became divided between the radical and vanguardist EFITU of Kamal Abu Eita and the more moderate and cautious Egyptian Democratic Labor Congress (EDLC) of Kamal Abbas (Beinin 2013b). The appointment of Kamal Abu Eita as minister of manpower in July 2013 illustrated the challenge of state 'transformism' that lied ahead of the trade unionist movement.

The 'bottom-up' formation of a Modern Prince from the fragments of popular and proletarian structures of self-governance remained obstructed by the colonizing 'secular' and 'civildemocratic' political projects that emerged after the fall of Mubarak and limited by organizational weakness, political confusion, and divisions among leftist actors, who, despite valiant efforts, did not succeed in building a strong workers' party nor a mass popular party. Thus, the sudden upsurge in mass demonstrations and strikes in May and June 2013 could not be concentrated or led by a proletarian or popular hegemonic apparatus, and could be easily appropriated by the armed forces.

27 Interview with Hisham Fouad, Giza, 13 March 2011.
28 Interview with Gihan Ibrahim, Cairo, 20 March 2011.
29 Interview with Wael Tawfiq, Cairo, 16 March 2011.

Conclusions

Permanent Deflections of Revolution

As a work of synthesis, this book has tried to weave different philosophical, historical, and political threads together in order to reveal the contours of a theory of the emancipatory subject centered around the notion of learning by struggling. In this regard, such a theory is necessarily a 'pedagogy of revolt', in the sense of a system of thought and practice that not only understands the sociogenesis of emancipatory subjects, but also proposes a methodology and deontology of active intervention and instruction that advances their development – what Gramsci called a 'philosophy of praxis'. I summarize the insights developed in the book with regard to, firstly, the Egyptian case and, secondly, the theoretical encounter between Vygotsky and Gramsci that resulted in a 'pedagogy of revolt'. To end with, I reflect briefly on my own position as a 'fellow traveler' within the project of the Egyptian revolution.

Class Formation and Anti-Imperialism

The logical unfolding of the 'strike' and 'demonstration' in Part 2 was used as a framework to investigate the Egyptian national-popular and proletarian lines of development within the historical process. The starting predicament was reconstructed as a colonial historical bloc. From the end of the nineteenth century onward, the dominance of imperialist forces and precapitalist landed and commercial groups created a combined capitalist-feudal form with only a small group of proletarianized laborers. The strikes of this period were rooted in both 'traditional' and 'modern' subjectivities and their hybrid and corporatist character was expressed in the first trade union organizations such as the MTWU. The colonial state was the most advanced capitalist actor in the bloc. Its infrastructure and service sector created the most modern layer of wage workers. Through their struggles they produced neoformations such as the CTWU, which were much more representative of an emerging class subjectivity.

The hybridity of the workers' movement was further complicated by the nature of its antagonist. Although foreign capital acted in coalition with Egyptian class forces, capitalist exploitation was mainly understood in terms of alien political domination. The concept that the the budding worker subject developed of its predicament was a critique of colonialism and imperialism, and its negation was political sovereignty and independent economic development.

This allowed the workers' movement to be subsumed under the broad national-popular movement of 1919 that was led by a half-hearted coalition of Egyptian landlords, commercial capitalists, peasants, effendiyya, and an impotent industrial bourgeoisie. The revolution was incomplete as both imperialism and domestic landed groups (especially the king) were able to keep their positions of power within the bloc.

Throughout its developmental trajectory, the Egyptian workers' movement would enjoy, as well as suffer, the intervention and assistance of non-proletarian actors in its activity-system. Because of its salient class activities, the workers' movement attracted the attention of other forces, and of the intellectuals that were organically produced within these classes. The nationalist movement understood the potential of the workers as a social force – well before the workers themselves. Actors such as the National Party assisted workers to set up their first economic structures, such as the MTWU. However, they supported the workers in a colonizing way: instead of stimulating the organic and independent development of trade unions, they controlled and dominated these mediations. Conversely, the worker subject recognized itself as a trade union subject via the paternalist mediations of the nationalist movement. The economic-corporate level of the Egyptian workers was artificially transcended by external mediations such as the GFLU or Prince Halim's NFTUE.

Independent Trade Unionism
Nevertheless, in the 1920s and 1930s the worker subject began to realize that the riddle of its exploitation was not simply solved by nationalism. Foreign domination continued, but it was complemented and complicated by the feeble attempts of domestic capitalists to carve out a niche for themselves in Egypt's industries. For the workers' movement this period represented an important developmental phase. Firstly, the absolute and relative number of wage laborers increased by the domestic industrialization efforts, and the military production of the Second World War. This expanded the proletarian subject as a population that is the object of the capitalist production process; i.e., as a class-in-itself. The saliency of modern wage labor differentiated the 'wage laborer' conceptually from the artisan and other precapitalist types of laborers.

Secondly, the strikes in this period pushed the workers' development as a class-for-itself. The trade unionist line of development – which had its roots in the colonial period, but only now became the central neoformation – gradually negated the economic-corporate predicament of the workers. Strikes challenged both foreign domination and capitalist exploitation. The colonization of trade union neoformations by non-proletarian actors was slowly overcome by independent trade unions led by workers themselves. Prince Halim's patronage constituted a transition phase for the workers' movement, as organic proletarian intellectuals began to replace the Wafdist non-proletarian leaders.

Politically, however, the worker subject continued to identify itself with the nationalist project. Nonetheless, there was a reconfiguration of the relations of power within the counterhegemonic alliance. The shared activity between the workers' movement and the Wafd took on the dominant form of commodification: in exchange for economic concessions, the workers recognized the Wafd as the directive counterhegemonic force. By the early 1950s the workers' movement had become one of the primary subjects within the counterhegemonic collaboration, supporting the shared national-popular project on its own conditions. This opened up the possibility for a permanent revolution, in which the proletariat substituted its agency for that of the non-existing 'progressive' bourgeoisie. In this manner, the 'nationalist' deformation of the Egyptian worker subject would become its organic solution: the subsumption of workers' emancipation under the national-popular project of nationalist emancipation would be reversed, and turned into the realization of the national-democratic revolution through proletarian hegemony.

Nasserist Deflection

The inability to forge an alliance with the mass of peasants, the often inadequate assistance by communist intellectuals, the precedence of anti-imperialism over class politics, and the strength of precapitalist structures expressed by the Muslim Brotherhood made it difficult for the worker subject to develop a political expression of its own and become a hegemonic force. In 1952 the Nasserist Caesarist intervention deflected the revolutionary process and solved the colonial question by substituting its own agency for that of the national-popular project. From the perspective of the sociogenesis of proletarian subject, this episode constituted a more profound developmental pathology than the 'nationalist' colonization of the previous decades. Firstly, its independent trade unionist neoformations were subsumed under the state, losing their organic nature as historical mediations of the strike, and becoming 'practico-inert' objectifications of the working class. This did not mean that workers could no longer negotiate wages and working conditions through these structures: it signaled the end of these institutions as forces in the development of a proletarian project. Secondly, the 'octroyal socialism' and corporatism of the state transformed a political-economic critique of property relations into a moral-economic consciousness of paternalist rights and duties between workers and the Savior-Ruler. The dominant form of the strike – a brief work-in instead of a protracted work stoppage – generally prevented the organic development of new trade unionist neoformations. Thirdly, the confusion among leftists about the nature of Nasserism and their own liquidation as an organized tendency spelled the end of their support for the workers' movement.

Neoliberal War of Movement

The global shift toward a neoliberal strategy for accumulation from the 1970s onward, initiated a new predicament for the global workers' movement. In Egypt, Sadat's Infitah launched a new war of movement in the streets, remobilizing the national-popular and worker subjects and starting new lines of development. However, the mode of assistance of the left remained largely entangled in the previous hybrid mode of assistance, flowing from an incorrect concept of the historical bloc and the tasks of the revolution and calling on the workers to unite with a phantom progressive bourgeoisie. Repression by state and Islamist forces, inadequate assistance from communist actors, a failure to connect the political and the economic, and the contingent emergence of a rentier economy halted the developmental trajectory and enabled the ruling classes to reconfigure the Nasserist bloc in a 'postpopulist' way. Thanks to the distribution of rent income and the successful 'transformism' of oppositional forces, Mubarak decelerated neoliberal reform and succeeded in blocking the development of strikes and demonstrations in the 1980s. In general, the left proved incapable of offering the workers' movement any coherent and centralized directive, cultural, or technical assistance, and it collapsed. In adverse subjective and objective conditions grassroots leftist intellectuals continued to support the workers struggles in genuine and solidary ways, but were unwilling or unable to instruct the workers' movement adequately as a potential social force.

The debt crisis and a fall in rentier income forced the ruling stratum to go on the offensive and implement far-reaching neoliberal reforms, backed up by increased state domination and coercion. The rising rate of exploitation changed the social situation of development of the worker subject, while the traditional paternalist means of mediating their predicament, the GFETU, loyally executed the state's bidding. In order to overcome its objective predicament the population of workers had to overcome its fragmentation and organize itself as a project. Although elements of historical subjectivity were appropriated by the strikes of the 1990s and 2000s – in the form of elderly activists, traditions, texts, songs, slogans, and memories – for the most part, the workers' movement had to reinvent and reinstruct itself as a collective subject. The Mahalla strikes constituted both the conceptual and historical 'jump-start' of novel trade unionist neoformations and a new line of economic development.

The protracted and militant work stoppages of the Mahalla workers inspired the tax collectors strikes, which led to the first independent trade union, and, in turn, stimulated the teachers, pensioners, and health technicians to form such structures of their own.

In the meantime, the increase of political and social state violence against the population and the contraction of the ruling stratum's class base had alienated the people from 'its' political expression. A new left reengaged with street, community, and workplace politics. The emergence of the demonstration in the first decade of the 21st century at first was outwardly oriented as a solidarity movement with Palestine and Iraq. Subsequently it 'turned inward' and reconstructed a project of the people as an active force. The demise of Kefaya and the salient and militant strike movement led many non-proletarian actors to 'return to class'. Their assistance toward the developing worker subject took on different forms and modes, and not all of them were genuine and adequate. For leftists it was tempting to treat the workers' movement in a colonizing or commodifying way: as a springboard for political emancipation or as a shortcut to a mass leftist party. The defeat of the 6 April uprising in 2008 serves as a warning of the damage that inauthentic and inadequate assistance could cause.

Nevertheless, thanks to the internal development of the worker subject – e.g. the formation of the RETAU – and the proleptic and solidary assistance of some non-proletarian actors, the workers' movement gradually matured independent trade union neoformations. The national-popular subject, however, remained primarily a civildemocratic movement and was unable to integrate its political line of development with the economic struggle of the worker subject and of other more feeble subaltern forces.

Uprising and Deflection

The 25 January insurrection massified the demonstration and accelerated the political line of development. The national-popular subject gained a social body by the massive turnout of demonstrators in the streets, the shared demands of "freedom, bread, and social justice," and the occupation of Tahrir. The 'Republic of Tahrir' became the cell-form of popular power and projected a free society by its prefiguration of emancipatory practices.

The uprising first subsumed the workers' movement under the grand movement of al-sha'b, but then the class differentiated itself from other actors by its strike activities: the best manner in which workers could assist the further development of the revolutionary project was by constructing themselves as an organized and militant subject in its own right. The insurrection and the concomitant disorganization of state power created a favorable social situation of development for the formation of trade unionist structures and self-concepts.

The 'mass strike' as "the method of motion of the proletariat" within revolutionary conditions continued well beyond the actual moment of the uprising.

The lack of a directive center in Tahrir, its failure to physically conquer state institutions and expand its activity-system to the whole of Egypt, and its inability to formulate a profound critique of al-nizam allowed the military to step in and deflect the revolutionary process. The process of formation of a national-popular subject was partly subsumed under the Caesarist intervention, and partly refragmented in the local activity-systems of popular committees and various party and coalition projects in the national political sphere. After a brief Muslim Brotherhood intermezzo a new mass uprising in 2013 reaffirmed the military as the leading societal force.

Although the Republic of Tahrir was unable to extend itself to the whole Egyptian social formation, the seeds of trade unionism continued to grow on fertile soil, resulting in the highest number of strikes since the 1950s. Whereas the development of the national-popular subject became locked in a war of position with counterrevolutionary forces, the proletarian subject still engaged in a war of movement against state and capital, although it became increasingly alienated from the political line of development. This is problematic, because the success of the revolution depends on the integration of the political and economic developmental lines. The future of trade unionism and worker emancipation is interwoven with the development of a revolutionary national-popular counterhegemony. When workers and other subaltern actors join the national-popular project, the development of trade unionism is reinforced by political emancipation, and political emancipation by the agency of a strong trade union movement. Within the instructive process of political emancipation and the maturation of its own trade union neoformations, the worker subject may recognize the means of a universal, human emancipation in the development of its own, particular emancipation from capital. Conversely, the challenge for civildemocratic actors is to see the means of their own emancipation in the building of the proletarian subject.

Although precapitalist social forms have since long been absorbed by the capitalist mode of production, the continued uneven and combined development of global capitalism, imperialism, and the incompleteness of the national-democratic revolutions in the Global South reinforce the concept of 'permanent revolution' as the strategic expression of the necessity to integrate the 'political' and 'economic' lines of emancipatory development. In Egypt, freedom, civil rights, and democracy cannot be achieved unless by a radical transformation of the historical bloc: the overthrow of the alliance between foreign capital, the USA, the domestic military establishment and their capitalist clients. The only actor able to accomplish this momentous task is an alliance of subaltern actors that constructs itself as 'the people', a broad national-popular collaboration, led by the most cohesive and coherent participating project: the working class. The permanent deflection of revolution can only be prevented by the formation of a Modern Prince: a hegemonic apparatus that integrates not only political and economic struggles, but also everyday good sense and scientific critique into a philosophy of praxis. This general, logical formula has to be grounded in actual grassroots popular and proletarian struggles. For organic and traditional intellectuals wishing to support the development of the popular-proletarian project there is no linear, external model to implement, only a pedagogy of solidary, reciprocal, and adequate assistance.

A Pedagogy of Revolt

In classical texts such as "The History of the Russian Revolution" (Trotsky 2001) and "The Making of the English Working Class" (Thompson 1963) there is a strong, yet implicit and undeveloped recognition that subject formation entails a process of collective learning and instruction. Likewise, pamphlets such as Lenin's "April Theses" and Trotsky's "Transitional Program" contain an implied political pedagogy of adequate and necessary forms of instruction. However, there has not been a systematic and critical reflection of the nature and dynamic of political pedagogy in the construction of emancipatory subjects. Political intervention has been largely guided by common sense notions instead of a scientific understanding of the developmental limits, opportunities, dangers, and necessesities of instruction. This work aimed to be a modest contribution to the active construction of a theory of the emancipatory subject, in which processes of learning, instruction, and assistance take a central place.

Interiorization

If we understand genuine emancipation as self-emancipation, then the means of emancipation must be found within the actor itself. Probably Marx's greatest humanist achievement was that he saw the ragtag industrial proletariat of his age not merely as a collection of dejected and tormented beings that had to be 'saved' from the ills of capitalism, but as powerful saviors in their own right. Where the humanitarians saw only the suffering of the wretched of the earth, he saw their agency as the 'gravediggers of capitalism'. However, Marx never elaborated the process of proletarian class formation, let alone sociogenesis in general. By combining insights from Marxist authors, especially Gramsci, and cultural-historical activity theory, such as Blunden and Vygotsky, collective subject formation becomes understandable as a collaborative process of learning.

Vygotsky's revolutionary understanding of the social situation of development as a predicament that the child has to overcome by creating the necessary psychological functions, immediately appeared to me as a key insight. The simple observation that performance creates competence lies also at the core of the process of self-emancipation. Historically, national-popular and class subjects are the products of struggle, not its producers. Outward-oriented, problem solving activity turns inward and constructs the behavioral functions that find a solution to the predicament. Obviously, Vygotsky's ontogenetic insights could not simply be transposed to the domain of sociogenesis, let alone class formation. Blunden's critical appropriation of Hegel and Vygotsky and his concept of collaborative project offered one part of the answer: Gramsci's notions of intellectuals, dialectical pedagogy, and the Modern Prince another.

Put simply, I understood collective subjectivity as a process of interiorization of shared, outward-directed performances. The traditional concept of the working class as a subject-in-itself was grasped as the specific activity-system of wage labor, produced by historical processes of proletarianization and capital accumulation. Workers cannot find the means to emancipate themselves in the activity of wage labor – which is externally enforced upon them – but instead they do so through the 'strike'. Workers' collaborative material and ideal objectifications that emerge throughout the strike activity not only constitute forms of mediation with factory management, capitalist owners, and/or the state, but they also turn inward, developing the internal cohesion and coherence of the fledgling proletarian subject. Proletarian subjectivity is the interior form of the external struggle against capital and the state. Analogous to Vygotsky's concept of neoformations the trade union, the political party, and the Modern Prince appear as central or leading structures that organize the whole process of development.

Vygotsky stressed that instruction must *lead* child development instead of slavishly following its 'natural' course: it must be 'proleptic'. Gramsci's notion of organic and traditional intellectuals pointed the way to an understanding of instruction in the context of the internal division of labor of an activity-system and external relations of assistance to a project. The distinction between organic and traditional intellectuals elucidates, on the one hand, that the worker subject is fully capable of producing its 'own' intellectuals and, on the other, that non-proletarian actors can and should play a role in proletarian sociogenesis. In line with Meschcheryakov I comprehended the proleptic instructive role of organic intellectuals as 'autoprolepsis', whereas traditional intellectuals engage in 'heterolepsis'.

Forms and Modes of Assistance

Gramsci observed that the division of labor within a collective subject meant that intellectuals engaged in different types of activities, which I abstracted into the archetypical functions of technical, cultural, and directive assistance. Technical assistance enables sociogenetic development by making available material resources and expertise, but in itself it does not fuel development. The accountant that helps in setting up a strike fund or the lawyer who offers workers' legal advice when they create a trade union creates a technical framework for development, but their assistance in itself does not enhance the learning processes that take place within the subject.

Cultural assistance, on the other hand, directly influences the formation of organizational structures and concepts ('consciousness'). Taking a cue from Vygotsky's different lines of concept development in ontogenesis, I distinguished between connective, projective, and integrative forms of cultural assistance. Firstly, connective assistance generalizes different spatial and temporal instances of fragmented strikes and demonstrations and their goals and critiques by a decentralized, 'horizontal' association. For example, journalists and political and human rights activists offered connective assistance by exchanging the experiences of different moments of struggle. Secondly, projective assistance generalizes the proletarian and national-popular subject by a 'vertical' concentration of its atomized activities and concepts, representing the potentiality of their future unification. For example, by writing about *the* workers' movement, journalists, scholars, and leftists imagined the dispersed collaborations as a united actor. Thirdly, integrative assistance is the real entwinement and interpenetration of different lines of development: 'everyday' and 'scientific', 'political' and 'economic'. 'Good sense' is integrated with 'political-economic critique' into a 'philosophy of praxis' and the struggle against capital is melded with the revolt against the state. Take, for example, the popular committees for the defense of the revolution that also became trade unionist committees and vice versa.

Finally, directive assistance is leadership: the art to tactically and strategically assess the strengths and weakness of the subject and its social situation of development, and to make informed decisions that express the organic, collective will of the subject. When organic leadership becomes disconnected from a continuous and reciprocal learning process with the rank and file a bureaucratic pathology may develop. Likewise, when an undeveloped subject is assisted in a directive way by external actors, there is a danger of domination or substitutionism of the project. In other words, there is a clear ethico-political dimension to assistance.

In order to understand this dimension I distinguished between three different archetypical modes of assistance – colonization, commodification, and solidarity –

based on Blunden's appropriation of Hegel's 'theory of recognition'. Giving assistance entails the formation of a new collaboration between subjects.

Firstly, colonization represents an asymmetrical relation of domination and subjugation within the collaboration. For example, the civildemocratic 'hijacking' of the 6 April 2008 Mahalla strikes or the military's Caesarist intervention in the uprisings of 2011 and 2013.

Secondly, commodification is a relation of exchange whereby each subject sees the other as a mere means to its own end; e.g. strikes that recognized the 25 January uprising primarily as an opportunity to formulate their own demands.

Lastly, solidarity is a relation of genuine support. I distinguished between directive and directed solidarity. Directive solidarity arises when a project supports an activity-system that is (currently) weaker in terms of subjectness, but under the direction of the weaker subject. The RETAU assisting the health technicians' union is a good example of this. Directed solidarity is the freely given support of the (currently) weaker subject for the stronger project, recognizing its leadership, which could also be understood as an authentic relation of hegemony. The support of the Mahalla community to the strikers is exemplary of this relation. Furthermore, the collaboration that arises through the solidarity relation may lead to the integration of both subjects into a new project. This Modern Prince is the ideal and necessary trajectory of the national-popular and proletarian subjects that allow it to transform the exploitation and domination inherent to the capitalist and imperialist historical bloc. In this manner, ethical relations of political assistance (solidarity) are entwined with the long-term strategic rationale of emancipatory struggle. Apart from the ethico-political and strategic dimension, such a dialectical pedagogy has to take into account also the short-term actual limits and opportunities of development: the zone of proximal development.

Zone of Proximal Development

In order to stimulate development, instruction must move proleptically ahead of the actual developmental level of the subject – but not too much. Therefore actors who want to offer adequate instruction to the proletarian and national-popular subjects must investigate and understand the subjects' current social situation of development, both in its objective aspect – the external 'conditions' – and its subjective character – its actual developmental level. Developmental situations of gradual change – war of position – are alternated by moments of crisis – war of movement.

These modes of struggle inform a general and abstract assessment of proleptic instruction. Phases of 'permanent revolution' punctuate the molecular process of reciprocal education and subject formation. For example, the possibilities for independent trade unionism during and after the 25 January 2011 uprising increased exponentially compared to the previous period. 'Transitional demands' are the most comprehensive expressions of adequate instruction with regard to the general tasks that the national and international subaltern forces face in a particular historical era. In itself, theory, however, cannot offer concrete and detailed advice with regard to specific instances of struggle. Here adequate instruction has to be deduced by a correct assessment of the social situation of development, which requires a capable leadership that is organically connected to the rank and file and the situation 'on the ground'.

When transgressing the upper limits of the zone of proximal development instruction becomes voluntarist and either loses its own organic connection with the masses or alienates and separates a vanguard from the less advanced layers within the subject. For example, from 12 February 2011 onward, the occupation of Tahrir became an increasingly voluntarist instruction with regard to the actual level of the political will and consciousness of the masses. When instruction remains at or below the actual developmental level it is pessimist and does not encourage development at all. Such was the case with the old left's support for the workers' and civildemocratic movement, continuously fettering its drive toward more advanced and radical forms of self-organization.

A Self-Reflecting Note

Any comprehensive, critical theory should be able to explain its emergence and formation in terms of its own paradigm. In the Introduction I argued that the resurgence of mass revolts such as the Arab Spring revealed the inadequacy of poststructuralist criticism to understand and guide processes of collective agency. The intellectual rediscovery of 'the subject' addresses the salient expressions of mass struggles. Moreover, from a 'collaborative project'-understanding of subjectivity, theoretical reflection and the theoretician herself are not separated from the process of subject formation. The objects of social science and the humanities are subjects in their own right. Theory is one of the tools that mediate the construction of the emancipatory subject, possibly rendering its concepts more coherent, imagining potential lines of development, and informing adequate forms of instruction. The research activity of social scientists or other 'theoreticians' creates a relation with their subject, which means that there is a clear ethico-political dimension to the development of theory – especially with regard to emancipatory projects.

Of course, one could simply ignore the object of study as a subject in its own right. In this case subaltern actors become mere statistics or passive populations subjected to political and economic processes that happen to them. The theoretician is not interpellated by the subject, and he does not interpellate any form of subjectivity in his object. Personally, I remember that when I read the Communist Manifesto for the first time as an adolescent, I was not at all interpellated by the concept of a working class – particularly because in Dutch the word for workers, *arbeiders*, has the connotation of blue-collar laborers. Why not take 'the people' as the ultimate emancipatory force, I wondered? At that point in my life, neither everyday experience nor scientific understanding had allowed me to recognize workers as a powerful collective actor. Eventually I gained this insight, both by a more profound comprehension of theory and the direct observation of and modest participation in workers' strikes and demonstrations. Now I take this agency almost for granted and I have to remind myself that this recognition has been a gradual learning process. This personal experience has supported my understanding of Egyptian civildemocratic actors' slow and often reluctant recognition of the workers' struggles as a proletarian project. Without a participation in the development of the strike – ranging from distant observation by mediation of newspapers, television, texts, and stories over direct perception to actual collaboration – recognition is impossible.

Colonization is the forceful subsumption of a subject under another subject. With regard to a colonizing science, it's easy to discern the historical examples of the 'white man's burden', modernization theory, orientalism, and so on. However, less aggressive forms of colonization are much more pervasive and, perhaps, unavoidable. For example, my historical narrative of the Egyptian social formation was largely written from the perspective of the development of the workers' movement and it drowned out the voices of other subaltern actors such as peasants, women, ethnic and religious minorities, LGBT groups, and so on. The personal friendships – a splendid form of collaboration – I developed during my time in Egypt are also suppressed in the text and only formally recognized as elements in the story of the Egyptian revolution.

The activity of academic research also renders commodification of the subject matter inevitable – up to a point. Even with the best of intentions our objects of study are not only ends-in-themselves, but they are also appropriated as pragmatic means to an end: primarily (continued) employment and scholarly prestige. The activity of emancipatory subjects is mediated and articulated into articles, books, and conferences, which are exchanged for wages, scholarships, and personal status. This is reminiscent of Marx's observation that: "The criminal produces not only crimes but also criminal law, and with this also the professor who gives lectures on criminal law and in addition to this the inevitable compendium in which this same professor throws his lectures onto the general market as 'commodities'" (Marx 1988, 306).

A purely commodifying attitude toward the object of research entails the mere extraction of valuable and relevant knowledge and the appreciation of these subjects only on the basis of their being a resource for research. My mode of research unavoidably contained an objective commodifying component, personified, for example, in this very work. Nevertheless, I aimed to integrate this necessary commodification into a shared activity of solidarity. Research that aims to be emancipatory has to engage in a solidary mode of assistance with the activity-system it studies. An engaged researcher finds herself drawn to the activity of the subject, and has to make a choice between 'keeping her distance' – i.e., minimize her participation in the shared project – becoming a 'fellow traveler' – i.e., become a genuine participant in an explicit shared system of solidarity – or fully merging with the collaborative project – i.e., becoming a 'democratic philosopher'.

Due to my own political engagement and sympathies I moved toward a clear and open position of solidarity that tried to assist and reinforce the developing proletarian and national-popular in the modest and limited ways available to me. My assistance consisted, firstly, in numerous informal discussion with some of my close respondents, which became an important reciprocal learning process. Secondly, throughout the past years I regularly offered an analysis of the unfolding events in Belgian newspapers, radio, and television, which cast the movement in terms of a genuine popular revolution struggling against a dictatorship, instead of societal chaos or an Islamist takeover. In addition, I wrote a few pieces directed at an Egyptian rather than a Belgian or international audience, engaging with the debate on the political tasks of leftists at the time. Thirdly, in my home town I supported the creation of a committee in solidarity with Tunisian and Egyptian revolution, and when I returned to Egypt in March 2011 I brought the leaders of the independent trade unions a declaration of solidarity from the Belgian socialist public sector trade union. I also helped some leftists in establishing contacts with international solidarity organizations and movements. Obviously, such individual forms of technical and cultural assistance were but drops in the ocean of the Egyptian revolution. The most relevant and powerful form of assistance I can offer is probably in theoretical efforts such as the work at hand, for a bird is known by its note and a man by his talk.

Clearly a 'pedagogy of revolt' does not stand 'above' or 'outside' the subject it engages with. Theory is an integral element of the sociogenesis of an emancipatory subject and has to develop itself intellectually from the standpoint of this project. This does not mean that an emancipatory science should be the uncritical expression of collective subjectivity. On the contrary, as 'trust', 'honesty', and 'reciprocity' are pillars of the solidary mode of assistance any 'pedagogy of revolt', however partisan, should remain critical and scientific toward the subject it supports. The most important conclusion is that political instruction matters and that any intellectual, organic or traditional, has the responsibility to critically and systematically investigate the adequacy and authenticity of the forms and modes of instruction they have to offer.

References

Interviews

All interviews were conducted formally and tape recorded with the consent of the interviewee.

Abd al-Hafiz, Cairo, 21 March 2011.
Abd al-Nasser Ibrahim, Cairo, 22 May 2009.
Abd al-Rahman Yusuf, Cairo, 21 March 2011.
Abd al-Rashid Hilal, Cairo, 9 October 2010.
Abdul Kader, Mahalla, 20 May 2009.
Abir Mehdawi, Cairo, 13 April 2009.
Ahmed al-Gourd, Cairo, 24 March 2011.
Ahmed al-Sayyid, Cairo, 23 March 2011.
Ahmed Belal, Cairo, 6 April 2009.
Ahmed Belal, Mahalla, 20 May 2009.
Ahmed Belal, Cairo, 9 October 2010.
Alaa al-Aswany, Cairo, 26 November 2010.
Al-Badry Farghaly, Cairo, 21 March 2011.
Ali al-Dhib, Cairo, 3 April 2009.
Baho Abdul, Cairo, 10 May 2009.
Fatma Ramadan, Cairo, 11 October 2010.
Faysal Lakusha, Mahalla, 20 May 2009.
Faysal Lakusha, Cairo, 20 October 2010.
Haisam Hassan, Cairo, 7 March 2011.
Hassanein, Cairo, 14 April 2009.
Gihan Ibrahim, Cairo, 20 March 2011.
Gihan Shabeen, Cairo, 16 March 2011.
Helmi Sha'rawi, Giza, 11 November 2010.
Husayn Abd al-Razek, Cairo 12 April 2009.
Inas Safti, Cairo, 27 October 2010.
Kamal Abu al-Eita, Giza, 20 March 2011.
Khaled al-Balshy, Cairo, 14 March 2011.
Khaled Ali, Cairo, 25 October 2010.
Mahmud Foda, Hagga Zeki, Said Abd al-Mali, Ahmed Rashil, Dikirnis, 17 April 2009.
Medhat al-Zahed, Cairo, 8 April 2009.
Muhammad Abbas, Cairo, 28 March 2011.
Muhammad Abd al-Azim, Mahalla, 12 November 2010.
Muhammad Ali, Cairo, 27 March 2011.

Muhammad Fathy, Mahalla, 20 May 2009.
Muhammad Zaky Murat, Cairo, 30 March 2011.
Mustafa Bassiouny, Giza, 12 October 2010.
Osama Muhammad Khalil, Cairo, 13 October 2010.
Per Björklund, Cairo, 5 May 2009.
Sabry Zaki, Cairo, 10 March 2011.
Said Husayni, Mahalla, 20 May 2009.
Salah Abd al-Azim, Cairo, 22 March 2011.
Salah Adli, Cairo, 13 November 2010.
Sayyida al-Sayyid Muhammad, Giza, 26 October 2010.
Sayyid Habib, Mahalla, 12 November 2010.
Saud Omar, Suez, 17 October 2010.
Saud Omar, Suez, 18 March 2011.
Sabr Barakat, Cairo, 16 October 2010.
Talal Shukr, Cairo, 21 April 2009.
Tareq Said, Cairo, 11 November 2010.
Wael Abu Zaid, Mahalla, 20 May 2009.
Wael Tawfiq, Cairo, 7 October 2010.
Wael Tawfiq Cairo, 16 October 2010.
Wael Tawfiq, Cairo, 20 October 2010.
Wael Tawfiq, Cairo, 8 March 2011.

Literature

Abbink, Jon, and Klaas van Walraven. 2003. "Rethinking Resistance in African History: An Introduction." In: *Rethinking Resistance: Revolt and Violence in African History*, edited by Jon Abbink, Mirjam de Bruijn, and Klaas van Walraven, 1–40. Leiden: Brill.

Abdalla, Ahmed. 1993. "Egypt's Islamists and the State." *Middle East Research and Information Project* 183: 28–31.

Abdel Kouddous, Sharif. 2011. "Live from Egypt: The True Face of the Mubarak Regime." *Democracy Now*. Available at: <http://www.democracynow.org/blog/2011/2/2/live_from_egypt_the_true_face_of_the_mubarak_regime>.

Abdelrahman, Maha. 2004. *Civil Society Exposed. The Politics of NGOs in Egypt*. Cairo: The American University in Cairo Press.

———. 2009. "With the Islamists? – Sometimes. With the State? – Never! Cooperation between the Left and Islamists in Egypt." *British Journal of Middle Eastern Studies* 36(1): 37–54.

Achcar, Gilbert. 2013. *The People Want. A Radical Exploration of the Arab Uprising*. London: Saqi Books.

REFERENCES

Afary, Janet, and Kevin Anderson. 2005. *Foucault and the Iranian Revolution. Gender and the Seductions of Islamism*. Chicago: University of Chicago Press.

Akhavi, Shahrough. 1975. "Egypt's Socialism and Marxist Thought: Some Preliminary Observations on Social Theory and Metaphysics." *Comparative Studies in Society and History* 17(2): 190–211.

Al-Amrani, Issandr. 2011a. "The Opposition Makes Its First Move." *The Arabist*. January 26. Available at: <http://www.arabist.net/blog/2011/1/26/the-opposition-makes-its-first-move.html>.

———. 2011b. "Manipulation." *The Arabist*. February 3. Available at: <http://www.arabist.net/blog/2011/1/30/manipulation.html>.

Al-Aswany, Alaa. 2006. *The Yacoubian Building*. Cairo: The American University in Cairo Press.

Al-Bendary, Amina. 2008. "Recalling 1968" [interview with Hossam Issa]. *Al-Ahram Weekly* 898. May. Available at: <http://weekly.ahram.org.eg/2008/898/fe2.htm>.

———. 2011. "Making History in Tahrir." *Jadaliyya*, February 7. Available at: <http://www.jadaliyya.com/pages/index/578/making-history-in-tahrir>.

Alexander, Anne. 2010. "Leadership and Collective Action in the Egyptian Trade Unions." *Work, Employment and Society* 24(2): 241–259.

———. 2011a. "The Gravedigger of Dictatorship." *Socialist Review*. March. Available at: <http://www.socialistreview.org.uk/article.php?articlenumber=11580>.

———. 2011b. "The Growing Social Soul of Egypt's Democratic Revolution." *International Socialism* 131. Available at: <http://www.isj.org.uk/index.php4?id=741andissue=131>.

———. 2011c. "Brothers-in-Arms? The Egyptian Military, the Ikhwan and the Revolutions of 1952 and 2011." *The Journal of North African Studies* 16(4): 533–4.

———. 2012. "The Egyptian Workers' Movement and the 25 January Revolution." *International Socialism* 133. January 9. Available at: <http://www.isj.org.uk/index.php4?id=778andissue=133>.

Al-Ghobashy, Mona. 2005. "The Metamorphosis of the Egyptian Muslim Brothers." *International Journal of Middle East Studies* 37 (3): 373–95.

———. 2012. "The Praxis of the Egyptian Revolution." In: *The Journey to Tahrir. Revolution, Protest, and Social Change in Egypt*, edited by Jeannie Sowers and Chris Toensing, 21–40. London, New York: Verso.

Al-Hamalawy, Hossam. 2007. "Comrades and Brothers." *Middle East Research and Information Project* 242. Available at: <http://www.merip.org/mer/mer242/comrades-brothers>.

———. 2008. "Revolt in Mahalla. As Food Prices Rise in Egypt, Class Struggle is Heating Up." *International Socialist Review* 59. May–June. Available at: <http://www.isreview.org/issues/59/rep-mahalla.shtml>.

———. 2011. "#Jan25 The Workers, Middle Class, Military Junta and the Permanent Revolution." *Arabawy*. February 12. Available at: <http://www.arabawy.org/2011/02/12/permanent-revolution>.

———. 2012. "Egypt's Working Class and the Question of Organization." *Jadaliyya*. Available at: <http://www.jadaliyya.com/pages/index/5645/egypts-working-class-and-the-question-of-organizat>.
Al Jazeera. 2011. "Live Blog 28/1 – Egypt Protests." Available at: <http://blogs.aljazeera.net/middle-east/2011/01/28/live-blog-281-egypt-protests>.
———. 2011. "Live Blog 31/1 – Egypt Protests." Available at: <http://blogs.aljazeera.net/middle-east/2011/01/30/live-blog-311-egypt-protests>.
———. 2011. "Live Blog Feb 1 – Egypt Protests." Available at: <http://blogs.aljazeera.net/middle-east/2011/01/31/live-blog-feb-1-egypt-protests>.
———. 2011. "Live Blog Feb 3 – Egypt Protests." Available at: <http://blogs.aljazeera.net/middle-east/2011/02/02/live-blog-feb-3-egypt-protests>.
———. 2011. "Live Blog Feb 5 – Egypt Protests." Available at: <http://blogs.aljazeera.net/middle-east/2011/02/04/live-blog-feb-5-egypt-protests>.
———. 2011. "Live Blog Feb 10 – Egypt Protests." Available at: <http://blogs.aljazeera.net/middle-east/2011/02/10/live-blog-feb-10-egypt-protests>.
———. 2011. "Live Blog Feb 11 – Egypt Protests." Available at: <http://blogs.aljazeera.net/middle-east/2011/02/10/live-blog-feb-11-egypt-protests>.
———. 2011. "Live Blog Feb 14 – Egypt." Available at: <http://blogs.aljazeera.net/middle-east/2011/02/13/live-blog-feb-14-Egypt>.
Al-Khafaji, Isam. 2004. *Tormented Births: Passages to Modernity in Europe and the Middle East*. New York: I.B. Tauris.
Al-Khashab, Karim. 2007. "Concerted campaigns [interview with Joel Beinin]." *Al-Ahram Weekly* 841. April. Available at: <http://weekly.ahram.org.eg/2007/841/eg7.htm>.
Allinson, Jamie C., and Alexander Anievas. 2009. "The Uses and Misuses of Uneven and Combined Development: an Anatomy of a Concept." *Cambridge Review of International Affairs* 22(1): 47–67.
Al-Mahdi, Rabab. 2011a. "Orientalising the Egyptian Uprising." *Jadaliyya*. April 11. Available at: <http://www.jadaliyya.com/pages/index/1214/orientalising-the-egyptian-uprising>.
———. 2011b. "Labour Protests in Egypt: Causes and Meanings." *Review of African Political Economy* 38(129): 387–402.
———. 2011c [2009]. "Labour as a Pro-democracy Actor in Egypt and Brazil." Paper presented at the American Political Science Association 2009 Toronto Meeting, Toronto. Revised version: September 23, 2011. Available at: <http://www.psa.ac.uk/journals/pdf/5/2010/1092_1356.pdf>.
Al-Shakry, Omnia. 2012. "Egypt's Three Revolutions: The Force of History behind This Popular Uprising." In: *The Dawn of the Arab Uprisings. End of an Old Order?* edited by Bassam Haddad, Rosie Bsheer, and Ziad Abu-Rish, 97–103. London: Pluto Books.
Al-Sharif, Asma, and Yasmine Saleh. 2013. "Special Report: The Real Force behind Egypt's 'Revolution of the State'." *Reuters*, October 10. Available at: <http://www.reuters.com/article/2013/10/10/us-egypt-interior-specialreport-idUSBRE99908D20131010>.

REFERENCES

Alteras, Isaac. 1993. *Eisenhower and Israel: United States-Israeli relations, 1953–1960.* Gainesville: University Press of Florida.

Althusser, Louis. 1969. *For Marx.* London: Allen Lane, The Penguin Press.

———. 1976. *Essays in Self-criticism.* London: New Left Books.

Althusser, Louis, and Etienne Balibar. 1970. *Reading Capital.* London: New Left Books.

Al-Werdani, Mahmoud. 2011. "The Ultras and the Egyptian Revolution." *Jadaliyya.* December 25. Available at: <http://www.jadaliyya.com/pages/index/3759/the-ultras-and-the-egyptian-revolution>.

Amar, Paul. 2011. "Why Egypt's Progressives Win." *Jadaliyya.* February 8. Available at: <http://www.jadaliyya.com/pages/index/586/why-egypts-progressives-win>.

———. 2012. "Why Mubarak Is Out." In: *The Dawn of the Arab Uprisings. End of an Old Order?* edited by Bassam Haddad, Rosie Bsheer, and Ziad Abu-Rish, 83–90. London: Pluto Books.

Amin, Samir. 1976. *Unequal Development: An Essay on the Social Formation of Peripheral Capitalism.* New York: Monthly Review Press.

———. 2011. *Global History: A View from the South.* Cape Town: Pambazuka Press.

Anderson, Perry, 1976. "Antinomies of Antonio Gramsci." *New Left Review* 100: 5–78.

Anderson, Betty S. 2011. "The Student Movement in 1968." *Jadaliyya.* March 9. Available at: <http://www.jadaliyya.com/pages/index/838/the-student-movement-in-1968>.

Ansari, Hamied. 1986. *Egypt, the Stalled Society.* Albany: State University of New York Press.

Antoon, Sinan, 2011. "Singing for the Revolution." *Jadaliyya.* January 31. Available at: <http://www.jadaliyya.com/pages/index/508/singing-for-the-revolution>.

———. 2012. "Impromptu: A Word." In: *The Dawn of the Arab Uprisings. End of an Old Order?* edited by Bassam Haddad, Rosie Bsheer, and Ziad Abu-Rish, 7–8. London: Pluto Books.

Aoude, Ibrahim G. 1994. "From National Bourgeois Development to Infitah: Egypt 1952: 1992." *Arab Studies Quarterly* 16(1): 1–23.

Armbrust, Walter. 2012. "The Revolution against Neoliberalism." In: *The Dawn of the Arab Uprisings. End of an Old Order?* edited by Bassam Haddad, Rosie Bsheer, and Ziad Abu-Rish, 113–123. London: Pluto Books.

Assaad, Ragui. 2009. "Labor Supply, Employment, and Unemployment in the Egyptian Economy, 1988–2006." In: *The Egyptian Labor Market Revisited,* edited by Ragui Assaad, 1–52. Cairo: The American University in Cairo Press.

Ates, Davut. 2005. "Economic Liberalization and Changes in Fundamentalism: The Case of Egypt." *Middle East Policy* 12(4): 133–144.

Attewell, Paul A. 1984. *Radical Political Economy since the Sixties: A Sociology of Knowledge Analysis.* New Brunswick: Rutgers University Press.

Ayubi, Nazih N. 1991. *The State and Public Policies in Egypt since Sadat.* London: Ithaca Press.

Au, Wayne. 2007. "Vygotsky and Lenin on Learning: The Parallel Structures of Individual and Social Development." *Science & Society* 71(3): 273–298.

Bakhtin, Mikhail. 1984. *Rabelais and His World*. Bloomington and Indianapolis: Indiana University Press.

——. 1985. "A Critique of Marxist Pologias." *Soviet Psychology* 23(3): 213–220.

Bakhurst, Daniel. 2007. "Vygotsky's Demons." In: *The Cambridge Companion to Vygotsky*, edited by Harry Daniels, Michael Cole, and James Wertsch, 50–76. Cambridge: Cambridge University Press.

Bamyeh, Muhammad. 2011. "The Egyptian Revolution: First Impressions from the Field [Updated]." *Jadaliyya*. February 11. Available at: <http://www.jadaliyya.com/pages/index/561/the-egyptian-revolution_first-impressions-from-the>.

Baran, Paul. 1957. *The Political Economy of Growth*. New York: Monthly Review Press.

Bardawil, Fadi. 2011. "Sunken Mythologies." *Jadaliyya*. February 18. Available at: <http://www.jadaliyya.com/pages/index/669/sunken-mythologies>.

Barker, Colin, Laurence Cox, John Krinsky, and Alf Gunvald Nilsen. 2013. *Marxism and Social Movements*. Leiden, Boston: Brill.

Barker, Colin, Alan Johnson, and Michael Lavalette. 2001. *Leadership and Social Movements*. Manchester, New York: Manchester University Press.

Bassiouny, Mustafa, and Omar Said. 2008. "A New Workers' Movement: The Strike Wave of 2007." *International Socialism* 118. March 31. Available at: <http://www.isj.org.uk/index.php4?id=429&issue=118>.

Bayat, Asef. 1993. "Populism, Liberalization and Popular Participation: Industrial Democracy in Egypt." *Economic and Industrial Democracy* 14: 65–87.

——. 1996. "Historiography, Class, and Iranian Workers." In: *Workers and Working Classes in the Middle East. Struggles, Histories, Historiographies*, edited by Zachary Lockman, 165–203. Albany: New York State University Press.

——. 2011. "Egypt, and the Post-Islamist Middle East." *Jadaliyya*. February 10. Available at: <http://www.jadaliyya.com/pages/index/603/egypt-and-the-post-islamist-middle-east->.

——. 2012. "The 'Arab Street'." In: *The Journey to Tahrir. Revolution, Protest, and Social Change in Egypt*, edited by Jeannie Sowers and Chris Toensing, 73–84. London, New York: Verso.

Bayat, Asef, and Eric Denis. 2000. "Who Is Afraid of Ashwaiyyat? Urban Change and Politics in Egypt." *Environment and Urbanization* 12(2): 185–199.

Beattie, Kirk J. 2000. *Egypt during the Sadat Years*. New York: Palgrave.

Beilin, Yossi. 2013. "Morsi Didn't Win the Elections." *Israel Hayom*. August 18. Available at: <http://www.israelhayom.com/site/newsletter_opinion.php?id=5395>.

Beinin, Joel. 1981. "Formation of the Egyptian Working Class." *Middle East Research and Information Project Reports* 94: 14–23.

——. 1989. "Labor, Capital, and the State in Nasserist Egypt, 1952–1961." *International Journal of Middle East Studies* 21(1): 71–90.

———. 1996. "Will the Real Egyptian Working Class Please Stand Up?" In: *Workers and Working Class in the Middle East. Struggles, Histories and Historiographies*, edited by Zachary Lockman, 247–270. Albany: New York State University Press.

———. 1999. "The Working Class and Peasantry in the Middle East: From Economic Nationalism to Neoliberalism." *Middle East Report* 210: 18–22.

———. 2001. *Workers and Peasants in the Modern Middle East*. Cambridge: Cambridge University Press.

———. 2005a. "Political Islam and the New Global Economy." *The New Centennial Review* 5(1): 111–139.

———. 2005b. "Popular Social Movements and the Future of Egyptian Politics." *Middle East Research and Information Project Online*. March 10. Available at: <http://www.merip.org/mero/mero031005>.

———. 2007. "The Militancy of Mahalla al-Kubra." *Middle East Research and Information Project Online*. September 29. Available at: <http://www.merip.org/mero/mero0092907>.

———. 2009. "Neo-liberal Structural Adjustment, Political Demobilization, and Neo-authoritarianism in Egypt." In: *The Arab State and Neo-Liberal Globalization. The Restructuring of State Power in the Middle East*, edited by Laura Guazzone and Daniela Pioppi, 19–46. Reading: Ithaca Press.

———. 2011. "A Workers' Social Movement on the Margin of the Global Neoliberal Order, Egypt 2004–2009." In: *Social Movements, Mobilization, and Contestation in the Middle East and North Africa*, edited by Joel Beinin and Frédéric Vairel, 181–201. Stanford: Stanford University Press.

———. 2013a. "Was There a January 25 Revolution?" *Jadaliyya*. January 25. Available at: <http://www.jadaliyya.com/pages/index/9766/was-there-a-january-25-revolution>

———. 2013b. "Workers, Trade Unions and Egypt's Political Future." *Middle East Research and Information Project*. January 18, 2013. Available at: <http://www.merip.org/mero/mero011813>.

Beinin, Joel, and Hossam al-Hamalawy. 2007a. "Egyptian Textile Workers Confront the New Economic Order." *Middle East Research and Information Project Online*. March 25. Available at: <http://www.merip.org/mero/mero032507>.

———. 2007b. "Strikes in Egypt Spread from Center of Gravity." *Middle East Research and Information Project Online*. May 9. Available at: <http://www.merip.org/mero/mero050907>.

Beinin, Joel, and Zachary Lockman. 1987. *Workers on the Nile: Nationalism, Communism, Islam, and the Egyptian Working Class, 1882–1954*. Princeton: Princeton University Press.

Beinin, Joel, and Frédéric Vairel. 2011. "Introduction: The Middle East and North Africa. Beyond Classical Social Movement Theory." In: *Social Movements, Mobilization, and*

Contestation in the Middle East and North Africa, edited by Joel Beinin and Frédéric Vairel, 1–23. Stanford: Stanford University Press.

Bernstein, Basil. 1999. "Vertical and Horizontal Discourse." *British Journal of Sociology of Education* 20(2): 157–173.

Blunden, Andy. 2003. *For Ethical Politics*. Heidelberg: Heidelberg Press. Available at: <http://home.mira.net/~andy/blackwood/fep/>.

———. 2004a. "Recognition, Trust and Emancipation." *Talk for the Atheists Society, Melbourne*. August 10. Available at: <http://home.mira.net/~andy/works/atheists.htm>.

———. 2004b. "Solidarity, Recognition, Subjectivity and Mediation." *Presentation at the Hegel Summer School 2004, University of Melbourne, Melbourne*. February 20. Available at: <http:/home.mira.net/~andy/seminars/solidarity.htm>.

———. 2005/6. "Johann Fichte: The Subject as Activity." In: *The Subject. Philosophical Foundations* [draft in progress]. Available at: <http://home.mira.net/~andy/works/fichte.htm>.

———. 2007. "Mediation and Intersubjectivist Interpretations of Hegel." Available at: <https://www.academia.edu/2026177/Intersubjectivist_Interpretations_of_Hegel_and_Mediation>.

———. 2010. *An Interdisciplinary Theory of Activity*. Leiden: Brill.

———. 2012a. *Concepts. A Critical Approach*. Leiden: Brill.

———.2012b. "Jamison: The Life and Death of Social Movements." Available at: <http://home.mira.net/~andy/works/jamison.htm>.

——— ed. 2014. *Collaborative Projects. An Interdisciplinary Study*. Leiden: Brill.

Booth, Marilyn. 2009. "Exploding into the Seventies: Ahmed Fu'ad Nigm, Sheikh Imam, and the Aesthetics of a New Youth Politics." *Cairo Papers in Social Science. Political and Social Protest in Egypt* 29(2–3): 19–44.

Bradley, John R. 2008. *Inside Egypt: The Land of the Pharaohs on the Brink of a Revolution*. New York: Palgrave MacMillan.

Burgat, François. 1995. *L'Islamisme en Face*. Paris: La Découverte.

Burke, Edmund III. 1996. "The History of the Working Class in the Middle East: Some Methodological Considerations." In: *Workers and Working Classes in the Middle East. Struggles, Histories, Historiographies*, edited by Zachary Lockman, 303–319. Albany: New York State University Press,.

Bush, Ray. 2000. "An Agricultural Strategy without Farmers: Egypt's Countryside in the New Millennium." *Review of African Political Economy* 27(84): 235–249.

———. 2007. "Politics, Power and Poverty: Twenty Years of Agricultural Reform and Market Liberalisation in Egypt." *Third World Quarterly* 26(8): 1599–1615.

———. 2009. "When "Enough" Is Not Enough: Resistance during Accumulation by Dispossessio." *Cairo Papers in Social Science. Political and Social Protest in Egypt* 29(2–3): 85–99.

Butler, Judith. 1993. "Gender Is Burning: Questions of Appropriation and Subversion." In: *Bodies That Matter: On the Discursive Limits of Sex*, compiled by Eddie Yeghiayan, 121–140. Routledge: New York.

Callinicos, Alex. 1989. *Postmodernism: A Marxist Critique*. Cambridge: Polity Press.

———. 2001. "Toni Negri in Perspective." *International Socialism* 92. Available at: <http://pubs.socialistreviewindex.org.uk/isj92/callinicos.htm>.

———. 2004. "Marxism and the Multitude." *Multitudes: revue politique, artistique, philosophique*. December 4. Available at: <http://multitudes.samizdat.net/Marxism-and-the-Multitude>.

———. 2011. "The Return of the Arab Revolution." *International Socialism* 130. April 1. Available at: <http://www.isj.org.uk/index.php4?id=717andissue=130>.

Chaichian, Muhammad A. 1988. "The Effects of World Capitalist Economy on Urbanization in Egypt, 1800–1970." *International Journal of Middle East Studies* 20(1): 23–43.

Chalcraft, John T. 2001. "The Coal Heavers of Port Sa'id: State-Making and Worker Protest, 1869–1914." *International Labor and Working-Class History* 60: 110–124.

Chilcote, Ronald H. 1981. "Issues of Theory in Dependency and Marxism." *Latin American Perspectives* 8(3–4): 3–16.

Clawson, Patrick. 1978. "Egyptian Industrialization: A Critique of Dependency Theory." *Middle East Research and Information Project Reports* 72: 17–23.

Clément, Françoise. 2009. "Worker Protests under Economic Liberalization in Egypt." *Cairo Papers in Social Science. Political and Social Protest in Egypt* 29(2/3): 100–116.

———. 2011. "Le rôle des mobilisations des travailleurs et du mouvement syndical dans la chute de Moubarak." *Mouvements* 66(2): 69–78.

Cliff, Tony. 2000. *Marxism at the Millennium*. London: Bookmarks.

Cohen, Robin. 1980. "Resistance and Hidden Forms of Consciousness amongst African Workers." *Review of African Political Economy* 19(9): 9–22.

Colla, Elliott. 2011. "State Culture, State Anarchy." *Jadaliyya*. February 5. Available at: <http://www.jadaliyya.com/pages/index/558/state-culture-state-anarchy>.

———. 2012. "The Poetry of Revolt." In: *The Journey to Tahrir. Revolution, Protest, and Social Change in Egypt*, edited by Jeannie Sowers and Chris Toensing, 47–52. London, New York: Verso.

Colucci, Francesco P. 1999. "The Relevance to Psychology of Antonio Gramsci's Ideas on Activity and Common Sense." In: *Perspectives on Activity Theory*, edited by Y. Engeström, R. Miettinen, and R.L. Punamki, 147–162. Cambridge: Cambridge University Press.

Cooper, Linda H. 2005. "Towards a Theory of Pedagogy, Learning and Knowledge in an 'Everyday' Context: A Case Study of a South African Trade Union." PhD diss.,

University of Cape Town. Accessed September 9, 2011. Available at: <http://www.haesdu.uct.ac.za/usr/haesdu/staff/downloads/Cooper_PhD.pdf>.

Cooper, Mark. 1979. "Egyptian State Capitalism in Crisis: Economic Policies and Political Interests, 1967–1971." *International Journal of Middle East Studies* 10(4): 481–516.

Cox, Laurence. 2010. "Book Review: Mastaneh Shah-Shuja Zones of Proletarian Development." *Review of Zones of Proletarian Development* by Mastaneh Shah-Shuja, *Capital and Class* 34(2): 292–293.

Cox, Robert W. 1987. *Production, Power, and World Order. Social Forces in the Making of History*. Chichester: Columbia University Press.

Cuno, Kenneth M. 2005 [1980]. "The Origins of Private Ownership of Land in Egypt: A Reappraisal." In: *The Modern Middle East: A Reader*, edited by Albert H. Hourani, Philip S. Khoury, and Mary C. Wilson, 195–228. New York: I.B. Tauris.

Daniels, Harry. 2007. "Pedagogy." In: *The Cambridge Companion to Vygotsky*, edited by Harry Daniels, Michael Cole, and James Wertsch, 307–331. Cambridge: Cambridge University Press.

Davis, Donagh. 2010. "Shah-Shuja, Mastaneh (2008). Zones of Proletarian Development." *Review of Zones of Proletarian Development* by Mastaneh Shah-Shuja. *Interface: A Journal for and About Social Movements* 2(1): 394–398.

Deeb, Marius. 1976. "Bank Misr and the Emergence of the Local Bourgeoisie in Egypt." *Middle Eastern Studies* 12(3): 69–86.

Del Rio, Pablo, and Amelia Alvarez. 2007. "Inside and Outside the Zone of Proximal Development. An Ecofunctional Reading of Vygotsky." In: *The Cambridge Companion to Vygotsky*, edited by Harry Daniels, Michael Cole, and James Wertsch, 267–303. Cambridge: Cambridge University Press.

De Smet, Brecht. 2012. "Egyptian Workers and 'Their' Intellectuals: The Dialectical Pedagogy of the Mahalla Strike Movement." *Mind, Culture, and Activity* 19(2): 139–155.

———. 2014a. "Revolution and Counter-Revolution in Egypt." *Science & Society* 78(1): 11–40.

———. 2014b. "Tahrir: A Project(ion) of Revolutionary Change." In: *Collaborative Projects. An Interdisciplinary Study*, edited by Andy Blunden, 282–307. Leiden: Brill.

De Smet, Brecht, and Vivienne Matthies-Boon. 2013. "From Rebel to Revolution?" *openDemocracy*. July 8. Available at: <http://www.opendemocracy.net/brecht-de-smet-vivienne-matthies-boon/egypt-from-rebel-to-revolution>.

Down to Earth. 2000. "Down to Earth with Few Grassroots." *Al Ahram Weekly* 500. September. Available at: <http://weekly.ahram.org.eg/2000/500/elec1.htm>.

Draper, Hal. 1971. "The Principle of Self-Emancipation in Marx and Engels." *Socialist Register* 8:81–109.

———. 1990. "The Myth of Lenin's 'Concept of the Party' or What They Did to What Is to Be Done?" Available at: <http://www.marxists.org/archive/draper/1990/myth/myth.htm>.

DuBoc, Marie. 2009. "Strikes without Organisation? Workers' Local Networks and Belonging in the Textile Sector." Paper presented at the workshop on The Egyptian Labour movement: Possibilities and Constraints, SOAS, London, July 7, 2009.

Dyer, Graham. 1997. *Class, State and Agricultural Productivity in Egypt: Study of the Inverse Relationship between Farm Size and Land Productivity*. London: Routledge.

Egypt Protests. 2011. "Egypt Protests: Three Killed in 'Day of Revolt.'" *BBC News*. Available at: <http://www.bbc.co.uk/news/world-africa-12272836>.

Engeström, Yrjö. 1987. *Learning by Expanding: An Activity-Theoretical Approach*. Helsinki: Orienta-Konsultit.

———. 1990. *Learning, Working, and Imaging. Twelve Studies in Activity Theory*. Helsinki: Orienta-Konsultit.

Eyerman, Ron, and Jamison, Andrew. 1991. *Social Movements: A Cognitive Approach*. University Park: Pennsylvania State University Press.

Fanon, Frantz. 1963. *Wretched of the Earth*. New York: Grove Press.

Farag, Fatemah. 1999. "Cleansing the Party." *Al-Ahram Weekly* 440. July–August. Available at: <http://weekly.ahram.org.eg/1999/440/eg10.htm>.

———. 2007. "Chronicles of an Uprising." *Al-Ahram Weekly* 828. January. Available at: <http://weekly.ahram.org.eg/2007/828/special.htm>.

Farah, Nadia R. 1986. *Religious Strife in Egypt: Crisis and Ideological Conflict in the Seventies*. New York: Gordon and Breach Science Publishers.

———. 2009. *Egypt's Political Economy, Power Relations in Development*. Cairo: The American University in Cairo Press.

Fichte, Johann Gottlieb. 1994. *Introductions to the Wissensschaftslehre and Other Writings, 1797–1800*. Indianapolis: Hackett Publishing.

Flores, Alexander. 1993. "Secularism, Integralism, and Political Islam: The Egyptian Debate." *Middle East Research and Information Project* 183 (July–August): 32–38.

Foucault, Michel. 1980. *Power/Knowledge. Selected Interviews & Other Writings, 1972–1977*. Brighton: Harvester.

Frank, Andre G. 1969. *Latin America: Underdevelopment or Revolution*. New York: Monthly Review Press.

Fraser, Nancy. 2013. *Fortunes of Feminism: From State-Managed Capitalism to Neoliberal Crisis*. New York: Verso Books.

Gaddis, John L. 1997. *We Now Know: Rethinking Cold War History*. New York: Oxford University Press.

Goldstone, Jack A. 2001. "Toward a Fourth Generation of Revolutionary Theory." *Annual Review of Political Science* 4: 139–187.

Gramsci, Antonio. 1971. *Selections from the Prison Notebooks*. New York: International Publishers.

———. 1996a [1921]. "Real Dialectics." In: *From Marx to Gramsci. A Reader in Revolutionary Marxist Politics*, edited by Paul Le Blanc, 284–285. New York: Humanity Books.

———. 1996b [1923]. "What Is to Be Done." In: *From Marx to Gramsci. A Reader in Revolutionary Marxist Politics*, edited by Paul Le Blanc, 285–288. New York: Humanity Books.

———. 2005 [1926]. *The Southern Question*. Toronto: University of Toronto Press.

Gribbon, Laura, and Sarah Hawas. 2012. "Signs and Signifiers: Visual Translations of Revolt." In: *Translating Egypt's Revolution: The Language of Tahrir*, edited by Samia Mehrez, 103–142. Cairo: The American University in Cairo Press.

Guardian. 2011. "News Blog 25/1: Protests in Egypt and Unrest in Middle East – As it Happened." Available at: <http://www.guardian.co.uk/global/blog/2011/jan/25/middleeast-tunisia>.

———. 2011. "News Blog 26/1: Protests in Egypt – As it Happened." Available at: <http://www.guardian.co.uk/world/blog/2011/jan/26/egypt-protests>.

———. 2011. "News Blog 27/1: Protests in Egypt – Live Updates." Available at: <http://www.guardian.co.uk/world/series/egypt- protests?page=2>.

———. 2011. "News Blog 28/1: Protests in Egypt – As They Happened." Available at: <http://www.guardian.co.uk/news/blog/2011/jan/28/egypt-protests-live-updates>.

———. 2011. "News Blog 30/1: Egypt Protests – As They Happened." Available at: <http://www.guardian.co.uk/news/blog/2011/jan/30/egypt-protests-live-updates>.

———. 2011. "News Blog 31/1: Egypt Protests – Monday 31 January." Available at: <http://www.guardian.co.uk/news/blog/2011/jan/31/egypt-protests-live-updates>.

———. 2011. "News Blog 1/2: Egypt Protests – Tuesday 1 February." Available at: <http://www.guardian.co.uk/news/blog/2011/feb/01/egypt-protests-live-updates>.

———. 2011. "News Blog 2/2: Egypt Protests – Wednesday 2 February." Available at: <http://www.guardian.co.uk/news/blog/2011/feb/02/egypt-protests-live-updates>.

———. 2011. "News Blog 3/2: Egypt Protests – Thursday 3 February." Available at: <http://www.guardian.co.uk/news/blog/2011/feb/03/egypt-protests-live-updates>.

———. 2011. "News Blog 4/2: Egypt Protests – Friday 4 February." Available at: <http://www.guardian.co.uk/world/blog/2011/feb/04/egypt-protests-day-departure-live>.

———. 2011. "News Blog 6/2: Egypt Protests – Sunday 6 February." Available at: <http://www.guardian.co.uk/news/blog/2011/feb/06/egypt-hosni-mubarak>.

———. 2011. "News Blog 7/2: Egypt Protests – Monday 7 February." Available at: <http://www.guardian.co.uk/news/blog/2011/feb/07/egypt-protests-live-updates>.

———. 2011. "News Blog 8/2a: Egypt Protests – Tuesday 8 February." Available at: <http://www.guardian.co.uk/news/blog/2011/feb/08/egypt-protests-live-updates>.

———. 2011. "News Blog 8/2b: Egypt Protests – Tuesday 8 February (Part 2)." Available at: <http://www.guardian.co.uk/news/blog/2011/feb/08/egypt-protests-live-updates1>.

———. 2011. "News Blog 9/2: Egypt Protests – Wednesday 9 February." Available at: <http://www.guardian.co.uk/news/blog/2011/feb/09/egypt-protests-live-updates-9-february>.

———. 2011. "News Blog 10/2a: Egypt Protests – Thursday 10 February." Available at: <http://www.guardian.co.uk/world/blog/2011/feb/10/egypt-middleeast>.

———. 2011. "News Blog 10/2b: Mubarak Refuses to Resign – Thursday 10 February [sic]." Available at: <http://www.guardian.co.uk/world/blog/2011/feb/10/egypt-hosni-mubarak-resignation-rumours>.

———. 2011. "News Blog 11/2a: Egypt Protests – Friday 11 February." Available at: <http://www.guardian.co.uk/world/blog/2011/feb/11/egypt-protests-mubarak>.

———. 2011. "News Blog 11/2b: Mubarak Resigns – Friday 11 February." Available at: <http://www.guardian.co.uk/world/blog/2011/feb/11/egypt-hosni-mubarak-left-cairo>.

———. 2011. "News Blog 14/2: Unrest in the Middle East – Monday 14 February." Available at: <http://www.guardian.co.uk/world/blog/2011/feb/14/middleeast-unrest>.

Haddad, Bassam. 2011a. "Brief Report of Cautious Triumph." *Jadaliyya*. February 3. Available at: <http://www.jadaliyya.com/pages/index/524/9-am-in-cairo-after-a-hellish-night_a-brief-report>.

———. 2011b. "English Translation of Interview with Hossam El-Hamalawy on the Role of Labor/Unions in the Egyptian Revolution." *Jadaliyya*. April 30. Available at: <http://www.jadaliyya.com/pages/index/1387/english-translation-of-interview-with-hossam-el-ha>.

Hajjar, Lisa. 2011. "Omar Suleiman, the CIA's Man in Cairo and Egypt's Torturer-in-Chief." *Jadaliyya*, January 30. Available at: <http://www.jadaliyya.com/pages/index/503/omar-suleiman-the-cias-man-in-cairo-and-egypts-tor>.

Haldon, John F. 1993. *The State and the Tributary Mode of Production.* Oxford: Oxford University Press.

Halpern, Manfred. 1963. *The Politics of Social Change in the Middle East and North Africa.* Princeton: Princeton University Press.

Hanieh, Adam. 2013. *Lineages of Revolt. Issues of Contemporary Capitalism in the Middle East.* Chicago: Haymarket Books.

Hardt, Michael, and Negri, Antonio. 2006. *Multitude: War and Democracy in the Age of Empire.* New York: Penguin Books.

Harman, Chris. 1994. "The Prophet and the Proletariat." *International Socialism* 64. Available at: <http://www.marxists.de/religion/harman>.

———. 2002. "The Workers of the World." *International Socialism* 96. Available at: <http://www.marxists.org/archive/harman/2002/xx/workers.htm>.

Harvey, David. 1990. *The Condition of Postmodernity.* Cambridge: Blackwell.

———. 2003. *The New Imperialism.* Oxford: Oxford University Press.

Hegel, Georg W.F. 1969 [1812]. *Science of Logic.* London: George Allen & Unwin

———. 2001 [1830]. *Encylopaedia of the Philosophical Sciences. Part One.* Blackmask Online (eBook). Available at: <http://www.hegel.net/en/pdf/Hegel-Enc-1.pdf>.

Hirschkind, Charles. 2011a. "From the Blogosphere to the Street: The Role of Social Media in the Egyptian Uprising." *Jadaliyya*. February 9. Available at: <http://www.jadaliyya.com/pages/index/599/from-the-blogosphere-to-the-street_the-role-of-soc>.

——. 2011b. "The Road to Tahrir." *Economic and Political Weekly* 46(7): 13–15.

Howeidy, Amira. 2005. "A Chronology of Dissent." *Al-Ahram Weekly* 748. June. Available at: <http://weekly.ahram.org.eg/2005/748/eg10.htm>.

——. 2006. "What's Left of the Left?" *Al-Ahram Weekly* 778. January. Available at: <http://weekly.ahram.org.eg/2006/778/eg8.htm>.

Huntington, Samuel P. 1991. *The Third Wave: Democratization in the Late Twentieth Century*. Oklahoma: University of Oklahoma Press.

——. 2006. *Political Order in Changing Societies*. Yale: Yale University Press.

Hurewitz, Jacob C. 1969. *Middle Eastern Politics: the Military Dimension*. New York: Praeger.

Ilyenkov, Evald V. 2008a. *Dialectical Logic. Essays on Its History and Theory*. Delhi: Aakar Books.

——. 2008b. *The Dialectics of the Abstract and the Concrete in Marx's Capital*. Delhi: Aakar Books.

Ismail, Salwa. 2011. "Civilities, Subjectivities and Collective Action: Preliminary Reflections in Light of the Egyptian Revolution." *Third World Quarterly* 32(5): 989–995.

Ismael, Tareq Y., and Rifa'at al-Sa'id. 1990. *The Communist Movement in Egypt 1920–1988*. Syracuse: Syracuse University Press.

Issawi, Charles. 2005 [1970]. "Middle East Economic Development, 1815–1914: The General and the Specific". In: *The Modern Middle East: A Reader*, edited by Albert H. Hourani, Philip S. Khoury, and Mary C. Wilson, 177–194. New York: I.B. Tauris.

Johnson, Alan. 2001. "Self-emancipation and Leadership: The Case of Martin Luther King." In: *Leadership and Social Movements*, edited by Colin Barker, Alan Johnson, and Michael Lavalette, 96–115. Manchester, New York: Manchester University Press.

Johnson, Peter. 1973. "Retreat of the Revolution in Egypt." *Middle East Research and Information Project Reports* 17(May): 3–6.

Johnston, Hank. 2009. "Protest Cultures: Performance, Artifacts, and Ideations." In: *Culture, Social Movements, and Protest*, edited by Hank Johnston, 3–29. Burlington: Ashgate.

Joya, Angela. 2011. "The Egyptian Revolution: Crisis of Neoliberalism and the Potential for Democratic Politics." *Review of African Political Economy* 38(129): 367–386.

Kandil, Hazem. 2011. "Hazem Kandil. Revolt in Egypt. Interview." *New Left Review* 68. March–April. Available at: <http://www.newleftreview.org/?view=2884>.

——. 2012. *Soldiers, Spies, and Statesmen. Egypt's Road to Revolt*. London/New York: Verso.

Kant, Immanuel. 2008 [1797]. *On the Metaphysics of Morals and Ethics*. Radford: Wilder Publications.

Karama Party Leader. 2010. "Karama Party Leader Calls for Revival of Nasser's Policies", *Daily News Egypt*. September 30. Available at: <http://thedailynewsegypt.com/people/karama-party-leader-calls-for-revival-of-nassers- policies-dp1.html>.

Kepel, Gilles. 1985. *The Prophet and Pharaoh. Muslim Extremism in Egypt.* London: Al-Saqi Books.

Keraitim Sahar and Samia Mehrez. 2012. "Mulid al-Tahrir. Semiotics of a Revolution." In: *Translating Egypt's Revolution: The Language of Tahrir*, edited by Samia Mehrez, 25–68. Cairo: The American University in Cairo Press.

Khalil, Ashraf. 2012. *Liberation Square. Inside the Egyptian Revolution and the Rebirth of a Nation.* Cairo: American University in Cairo Press.

Kiely, Ray. 2009. *The Clash of Globalizations. Neo-liberalism, the Third Way and Anti-globalization.* Chicago: Haymarket Books.

Kilgore, Deborah. 1999. "Understanding Learning in Social Movements: A Theory of Collective Learning." *International Journal of Lifelong Education* 18(3): 191–202.

Kinsman, Jeremy. 2011. "Democracy Rising: Tunisia and Egypt, When Idealists Got it Right." *Policy Options* (April): 37–43.

Koptiuch, Kristin. 1996. "Other Workers: A Critical Reading of Representations of Egyptian Petty Commodity Production at the Turn of the Twentieth Century." In: *Workers and the Working Classes in the Middle East. Struggles, Histories, Historiographies*, edited by Zachary Lockman, 41–70. Albany: State University of New York Press.

Kurzman, Charles, and Owens, Lynn. 2002. "The Sociology of Intellectuals." *Annual Review of Sociology* 28: 63–90.

Lachine, Nadim. 1977. "Class Roots of the Sadat Regime: Reflections of an Egyptian Leftist." *Middle East Research and Information Project* 56(April): 3–7.

Lavalette, Michael. 2001. "Defending the 'Sefton Two'." In: *Leadership and Social Movements*, edited by Colin Barker, Alan Johnson, and Michael Lavalette, 116–136. Manchester, New York: Manchester University Press.

Le Blanc, Paul, ed. 1996. *From Marx to Gramsci. A Reader in Revolutionary Marxist Politics.* New York: Humanity Books.

Lektorsky, Vladimir. 1999. "Activity Theory in a New Era." In: *Perspectives on Activity Theory*, edited by Yrjö Engeström, Reijo Miettinen, and Raija-Leena Punamäki, 65–69. Cambridge: Cambridge University Press.

Lenin, Vladimir I.U. 1962 [1905]. "Two Tactics of Social Democracy in the Democratic Revolution." In: *Collected Works* Volume 9, 15–140. Moscow: Progress Publishers.

———. 1964a [1920]. "Left-Wing Communism: An Infantile Disorder." In: *Collected Works* Volume 31, 17–118. Moscow: Progress Publishers.

———. 1964b [1917]. "The State and Revolution." In: *Collected Works* Volume 25, 381–492. Moscow: Progress Publishers.

———. 1973 [1901]. *What Is to Be Done?* Moscow: Foreign Languages Press.

———. 1974 [1915–1916]. "Opportunism and the Collapse of the Second International." In: *Collected Works* Volume 21, 205–259. Moscow: Progress Publishers.

———. 1977 [1917]. "Lessons of the Revolution." In: *Collected Works* Volume 25, 227–243. Moscow: Progress Publishers.

Leontyev, Aleksei N. 1978. *Activity, Consciousness, and Personality*. Englewood Cliffs: Prentice-Hall.

Levant, Alex. 2012. "Rethinking Spontaneity beyond Classical Marxism: Re-reading Luxemburg through Benjamin, Gramsci and Thompson." *Critique* 40(3): 367–387.

Lia, Brynjar. 1998. *The Society of the Muslim Brothers in Egypt: The Rise of an Islamic Mass Movement 1928–1942*. Reading: Garnet.

Lockman, Zachary (ed.). 1994a. *Workers and Working Classes in the Middle East. Struggles, Histories, Historiographies*. Albany: State University of New York Press.

——. 1994b. " 'Worker' and 'Working Class' in pre-1914 Egypt: A Rereading." In: Workers and Working Class in the Middle East. Struggles, Histories and Historiographies, edited by Zachary Lockman, 71–110. Albany: New York State University Press.

Lukács, Georg. 2000. *A Defence of History and Class Consciousness. Tailism and the Dialectic*. London: Verso.

Luxemburg, Rosa. 1970. *Rosa Luxemburg Speaks*. New York: Pathfinder Press.

Lyotard, Jean-François. 1984. *The Postmodern Condition: A Report on Knowledge*. Minneapolis: University of Minnesota Press.

Mackell, Austin. 2012. "Weaving Revolution: Harassment by the Egyptian Regime." *Interface: Journal for and about Social Movements* 4(1): 17–19.

Maeckelbergh, Marianne. 2013. Learning from Conflict: Innovative Approaches to Democratic Decision Making in the Alterglobalization Movement." *Transforming Anthropology* 21(1): 27–40.

Maher, Stephen. 2011. "The Political Economy of the Egyptian Uprising." *Monthly Review* 63(6). Available at: <http://monthlyreview.org/2011/11/01/the-political-economy-of-the-egyptian-uprising>.

Mahfouz, Naguib. 2001. *Sugar Street*. Cairo: The American University in Cairo Press.

Makar, Farida. 2011. "'Let Them Have Some Fun': Political and Artistic Forms of Expression in the Egyptian Revolution." *Mediterranean Politics* 16(2): 307–312.

Mandel, Ernest 1976. *Late Capitalism*. New York: Monthly Review Press.

Marfleet, Philip. 2011. "Act One of the Egyptian Revolution." *International Socialism* 130. April 4. Available at: <http://www.isj.org.uk/index.php4?id=721>.

Marx, Karl. 1976a [1845–1847]. "Theses on Feuerbach." In: *Marx/Engels Collected Works* Volume 5, 6–9. Moscow: Progress Publishers.

——. 1976b [1847]. "The Poverty of Philosophy." In: *Marx/Engels Collected Works* Volume 6. Moscow: Progress Publishers.

——. 1979 [1851–1852]. "The Eighteenth Brumaire of Louis Bonaparte." In: *Marx/Engels Collected Works* Volume 11, 99–197. Moscow: Progress Publishers.

——. 1982 [1868]. "Letter to Kugelmann 6/3/1868." In: *Marx/Engels Collected Works* Volume 42, 543–544. Moscow: Progress Publishers.

——. 1986 [1857–1861]. "Economic Manuscripts of 1857–8." In: *Marx/Engels Collected Works* Volume 28, 1–430.

——. 1988 [1863]. "Theories of Surplus Value." In: *Marx/Engels Collected Works* Volume 30, 348–454. Moscow: Progress Publishers.
——. 1990 [1867]. *Capital.* Volume 1. London: Penguin Group.
——. 1992 [1843–1844]. *Early Writings.* London: Penguin Group.
——. 2008 [1875]. *Critique of the Gotha Program.* s.l.: Wildside Press
Marx, Karl, and Friedrich Engels. 1975 [1844]. "The Holy Family, or Critique of Critical Criticism." In: *Marx/Engels Collected Works* Volume 4, 78–143. Moscow: Progress Publishers.
——. 1976 [1845–1846]. "The German Ideology." In: *Marx/Engels Collected Works* Volume 5, 19–538. New York: International Publishers Co.
——. 1998 [1848]. *The Communist Manifesto: A Modern Edition.* London: Verso.
Masoud, Tarek. 2011. "The Road to (and from) Liberation Square." *Journal of Democracy* 22(3): 20–34.
McGreal, Chris. 2011. "Egypt's Army 'Involved in Detentions and Torture'." *The Guardian.* February 15. Available at: <http://www.guardian.co.uk/world/2011/feb/09/egypt-army-detentions-torture-accused>.
Meijer, Roel, ed. 2009a. *Global Salafism, Islam's New Religious Movement.* New York: Columbia University Press.
——. 2009b. "Commanding Right and Forbidding Wrong as a Principle of Social Action. The Case of the Egyptian al-Jama'a al-Islamiyya." In: *Global Salafism: Islam's New Religious Movement,* edited by Roel Meijer, 189–220. New York: Columbia University Press.
Meshcheryakov, Boris G. 2007. "Terminology in L.S. Vygotsky's Writings." In: *The Cambridge Companion to Vygotsky,* edited by Harry Daniels, Michael Cole, and James Wertsch, 155–177. Cambridge: Cambridge University Press.
Michels, Robert. 1968 [1911]. *Political Parties: A Sociological Study of the Oligarchical Tendencies of Modern Democracy.* New York: Free Press.
Mitchell, Richard P. 1993. *The Society of the Muslim Brothers.* New York: Oxford University Press.
Mitchell, Timothy. 1999. "No Factories, No Problems: The Logic of Neo-liberalism in Egypt." *Review of African Political Economy* 26(82): 455–68.
——. 2002. *Rule of Experts. Egypt, Techno-politics, Modernity.* Berkeley: University of California Press.
Moore, Sam. 2011. *New Trade Union Activism. Class Consciousness or Social Identity.* New York: Palgrave MacMillan.
Morris, Aldon. 2000. "Reflections on Social Movement Theory: Criticisms and Proposals." *Contemporary Sociology* 29(3): 445–454.
Morton, Adam D. 2007. *Unravelling Gramsci. Hegemony and Passive Revolution in the Global Economy.* London: Pluto Press.
Mouffe, Chantal. 1993. *The Return of the Political.* London: Verso.
Naguib, Sameh. 2009. "The Muslim Brotherhood. Contradictions and Transformations." *Cairo Papers in Social Science. Political and Social Protest in Egypt* 29(2–3): 155–174.

——. 2011. "Egypt's Unfinished Revolution." *International Socialist Review* 79. September–October. Available at: <http://isreview.org/issues/79/feature-egyptian-revolution.shtml>.

Nigam, Aditya. 2012. "The Arab Upsurge and the "Viral" Revolutions of Our Times." *Interface: A Journal for and about Social Movements* 4(1): 165–77.

Oliver, Pamela E., and Johnston, Hank. 2000. "What a Good Idea! Ideologies and Frames in Social Movement Research." *Mobilization* 5(1): 37–54.

Opposition Is Not About Loud Voices. 2000. "Opposition Is Not about Loud Voices." *Al Ahram Weekly*, 500. September. Available at: <http://weekly.ahram.org.eg/2000/500/elec2.htm>.

Owen, Roger. 2005 [1972]. "Egypt and Europe: From French Expedition to British Occupation." In: *The Modern Middle East: A Reader*, edited by Albert H. Hourani, Philip S. Khoury, and Mary C. Wilson, 111–124. New York: I.B. Tauris.

Parties and Movements. 2011. "Parties and Movements." *Jadaliyya*, December 8. Available at: <http://www.jadaliyya.com/pages/index/3161/egyptian-bloc>.

Perelman, Michael. 2000. *The Invention of Capitalism. Classical Political Economy and the Secret History of Primitive Accumulation*. Durham: Duke University Press.

Perlmutter, Amos. 1974. *Egypt, the Praetorian State*. New Brunswick: Transaction Books.

Picard, Elizabeth. 1990. "Arab Military in Politics: From Revolutionary Plot to Authoritarian State." In: *The Arab State*, edited by Giacomo Luciani, 189–219. London: Routledge.

Posusney, Marsha P. 1996. "Collective Action and Workers' Consciousness in Contemporary Egypt." In: *Workers and Working Classes in the Middle East. Struggles, Histories, Historiographies*, edited by Zachary Lockman, 211–246. Albany: New York State University Press.

Rashed, Muhammad A. 2011. "The Egyptian Revolution. A Participant's Account from Tahrir Square, January and February 2011." *Anthropology Today* 27(2): 22–27.

Ratner, Carl. 1991. *Vygotsky's Sociohistorical Psychology and Its Contemporary Applications*. New York and London: Plenum Press.

Revolutionary Socialists' Statement. 2012. "Revolutionary Socialists' Statement on Egypt's Presidential Elections." *Socialist Worker* 2305. May 28. Available at: <http://www.socialistworker.co.uk/art.php?id=28595>.

Revolution through Arab Eyes: The Factory. 2012. "Revolution through Arab Eyes: The Factory." Documentary directed by Bocchialini, Cristina, and Ayman al-Gawzy. *Al Jazeera*. February 22. Available at: <http://www.aljazeera.com/programmes/revolutionthrougharabeyes/2012/01/201213013135991429.html>.

Richards, Alan, and John Waterbury. 2008. *A Political Economy of the Middle East*. Boulder: Westview Press.

Romein, Jan. 1980 [1935]. "De Dialektiek van de Vooruitgang." *Forum* 4(752–771): 828–855.

Rosenberg, Justin. 2009. "Problems in the Theory of Uneven and Combined Development. Part I: Introduction." *Cambridge Review of International Affairs* 22(1): 107–110.

———. 2010. "Basic Problems in the Theory of Uneven and Combined Development. Part II: Unevenness and Political Multiplicity." *Cambridge Review of International Affairs* 23(1): 165–189.

Rostow, Walt W. 1960. *The Stages of Economic Growth: A Non-communist Manifesto*. Cambridge: Cambridge University Press.

Sallam, Hesham. 2011a. "Reflections on Egypt after March 19." *Jadaliyya*, May 31, 2011. Accessed February 17, 2012. Available at: <http://www.jadaliyya.com/pages/index/1728/reflections-on-egypt-after-march-19>.

———. 2011b. "Striking Back at Egyptian Workers." *Middle East Research and Information Project* 259. Available at: <http://www.merip.org/mer/mer259/striking-back-egyptian-workers>.

Sallam, Hesham, Joshua Stacher, and Chris Toensing. 2011. "Into Egypt's Uncharted Territory." *Jadaliyya*. February 3. Available at: <http://www.jadaliyya.com/pages/index/523/into-egypts-uncharted-territory>.

Salvatore, Armando. 2013. "New Media, the 'Arab Spring', and the Metamorphosis of the Public Sphere: Beyond Western Assumptions on Collective Agency and Democratic Politics." *Constellations* 20(2): 217–228.

Sami, Azizi. 2005. "Rifaat Al-Said: Which Way Will He Bend Next." *Al-Ahram Weekly* 750. July. Available at: <http://weekly.ahram.org.eg/2005/750/profile.htm>.

Sartre, Jean-Paul. 2004 [1960]. *Critique of Dialectical Reason*. London: Verso.

Sassen, Saskia. 2011. "The Global Street: Making the Political." *Globalizations* 8(5): 573–579.

Schielke, Samuli. 2011. "'You'll Be Late for the Revolution!' An Anthropologist's Diary of the Egyptian Revolution." *Jadaliyya*. February 8. Available at: <http://www.jadaliyya.com/pages/index/580/youll-be-late-for-the-revolution-an-anthropologist>.

Schlesinger, Arthur M. 1999. *The Cycles of American History*. New York: Mariner Books.

Scott, James C. 1985. *Weapons of the Weak: Everyday Forms of Peasant Resistance*. Yale University Press.

Schwartz, Michael. 2011. "The Egyptian Uprising. The Mass Strike in the Time of Neoliberal Globalization." *New Labor Forum* 20(3): 33–43.

Schwedler, Jillian, and Janine A. Clark. 2006. "Islamist-Leftist Cooperation in the Arab World." *ISIM Review* 18: 10–11.

Seeking a New Style. 1995. "Seeking a New Style." *Al Ahram Weekly* 245. November. Available at: <http://weekly.ahram.org.eg/archives/parties/tagammu/nstyle.htm>.

Seikaly, Sherene, and Pascale Ghazaleh. 2011. "Abduh al-Fallah: Elite Myths and Popular Uprisings." *Jadaliyya*. Mach 15. Available at: <http://www.jadaliyya.com/pages/index/910/abduh-al-fallah_elite-myths-and-popular-uprisings->.

Selim, Samah. 2011. "Egypt and the Future of the Corporate Grid." *Jadaliyya*. February 1. Available at: <http://www.jadaliyya.com/pages/index/510/egypt-and-the-future-of-the-corporate-grid>.

Shah-Shuja, Mastaneh. 2008. *Zones of Proletarian Development*. London: Openmute.

Shandro, Alan. 2001. "Lenin and Hegemony." In: *Leadership and Social Movements*, edited by Colin Barker, Alan Johnson, and Michael Lavalette, 213–231. Manchester and New York: Manchester University Press.

———. 2007. "Lenin and Marxism. Class Struggle, the Theory of Politics and the Politics of Theory." In: *Twentieth-Century Marxism. A Global Introduction*, edited by Daryl Glaser and David M. Walker, 15–29. New York, Oxon: Routledge.

Shenker, Jack. 2011a. "Egypt Braced for 'Day of Revolution' Protests. Youth Activists, Islamists, Workers and Football Fans to Hold Rallies and Marches against Mubarak Government." *The Guardian*. January 24. Available at: <http://www.guardian.co.uk/world/2011/jan/24/egypt-day-revolution-protests>.

———. 2011b. "Muhammad ElBaradei Lands in Cairo: 'There's No Going Back'." *The Guardian*. January 27. Available at: <http://www.guardian.co.uk/world/2011/jan/27/elbaradei-return-cairo-egypt>.

———. 2011c. "Egyptian Army Hijacking Revolution, Activists Fear." *The Guardian*. February 15. Available at: <http://www.guardian.co.uk/world/2011/feb/15/egyptian-army-hijacking-revolution-fear>.

Shihade, Magid, Cristina F. Flesher, and Laurence Cox. 2012. "The Season of Revolution: The Arab Spring and European Mobilizations." *Interface: Journal for and about Social Movements* 4(1): 1–16.

Shokr, Ahmed. 2012. "The Eighteen Days of Tahrir." In: *The Journey to Tahrir. Revolution, Protest, and Social Change in Egypt*, edited by Jeannie Sowers and Chris C. Toensing, 41–46. New York: Verso.

Sid-Ahmed, Muhammad. 2005. "Mohieddin for president." *Al-Ahram Weekly* 741. May. Available at: <http://weekly.ahram.org.eg/2005/741/op5.htm>.

Skocpol, Theda. 1979. *States and Social Revolutions*. Cambridge: Cambridge University Press.

Solidarity Center. 2010. *Justice for All. The Struggle for Worker Rights in Egypt. A Report by the Solidarity Center*. Washington: Solidarity Center.

Sowers, Jeannie. 2012. "Egypt in Transformation." In: *The Journey to Tahrir. Revolution, Protest, and Social Change in Egypt*, edited by Jeannie Sowers and Chris C. Toensing, 1–20. London, New York: Verso.

Springborg, Robert. 2009. "Protest against a Hybrid State. Words without Meaning?" *Cairo Papers in Social Science. Political and Social Protest in Egypt* 29(2–3): 6–18.

Stacher, Joshua. 2011a. "Egypt's Democratic Mirage." *Foreign Affairs*. February 7. Available at: <http://www.foreignaffairs.com/articles/67351/joshua-stacher/egypts-democratic-mirage?page=2>.

———. 2011b. "Egypt without Mubarak." *Middle East Report Online*. April 7. Available at: <http://www.merip.org/mero/mero040711?utm_source=twitterfeedandutm_medium=twitter>.

Tagammu Gets Tougher. 2003. "Tagammu Gets Tougher." *Al Ahram Weekly*, 655. September. Available at: <http://weekly.ahram.org.eg/2003/655/eg3.htm>.

Taha, Amira, and Christopher Combs. 2012. "Of Drama and Performance: Transformative Discourses of the Revolution." In: *Translating Egypt's Revolution: The Language of Tahrir*, edited by Samia Mehrez, 69–102. Cairo: The American University in Cairo Press.

Teti, Andrea, and Gervasio, Gennaro. 2012. "After Mubarak, before Transition: The Challenges for Egypt's Democratic Opposition (Interview and Event Analysis)." *Interface: Journal for and about Social Movements* 4(1): 102–112.

Thatcher, Ian D. 2007. "Left-communism: Rosa Luxemburg and Leon Trotsky Compared." In: *Twentieth-Century Marxism. A Global Introduction*, edited by Daryl Glaser and David M. Walker, 30–45. New York, Oxon: Routledge.

Thomas, Peter D. 2009. *The Gramscian Moment. Philosophy, Hegemony and Marxism*. Leiden: Brill.

Thompson, E.P. 1963. *The Making of the English Working Class*. London: Victor Gollancz.

———. 1978. "Eighteenth Century English Society: Class Struggle without Class?" *Social History* 3(2): 133–165.

Tihanov, Galin. 1998. "Voloshinov, Ideology, and Language: The Birth of Marxist Sociology from the Spirit of Lebensphilosophie." *South Atlantic Quarterly* 97(3/4): 599–621.

Townshend, Jules. 1996. *The Politics of Marxism. The Critical Debates*. London: Leicester University Press.

———. 2007. "Right-wing Marxism," In: *Twentieth-Century Marxism. A Global Introduction*, edited by Daryl Glaser and David M. Walker, 46–58. New York, Oxon: Routledge.

Tronti, Mario. 2005 [1966]. *Workers and Capital*. Available at: <http://libcom.org/library/workers-and-capital-mario-tronti>.

Trotsky, Lev D. 1904. *Our Political Tasks. Part II: Tactical Tasks. The Content of Our Activity in the Proletariat*, translated by New Park Publications. Available at: <http://www.marxists.org/archive/trotsky/1904/tasks/>.

———. 1931. "Thälmann and the 'People's Revolution'." *The Militant*. April 14. Available at: <http://www.marxists.org/archive/trotsky/germany/1931/310414.htm>.

———. 1962 [1931]. *The Permanent Revolution Results and Prospects*. London: New Park Publications Ltd. Available at: <http://www.marxists.org/archive/trotsky/1931/tpr/pr-index.htm>.

———. 1969 [1944]. *Fascism: What It Is and How to Fight It*. New York: Pathfinder Press.

———. 1991 [1936]. *The Revolution Betrayed. What Is the Soviet Union and Where Is It Going?* Sheffield: Mehring Books.

———. 1996 [1938]. "The Transitional Program (excerpts)." In: *From Marx to Gramsci. A Reader in Revolutionary Marxist Politics*, edited by Paul Le Blanc, 272–280. New York: Humanity Books.

———. 2001 [1930]. *History of the Russian Revolution*. New York: Pathfinder Press.

Tucker, Judith. 1978. "While Sadat Shuffles: Economic Decay, Political Ferment in Egypt." *Middle East Research and Information Project Reports* 65(March): 3–9, 26.

———. 2005 [1979]. "Decline of the Family Economy in Mid-nineteenth-century Egypt." In: *The Modern Middle East: A Reader*, edited by Albert H. Hourani, Philip S. Khoury, and Mary C. Wilson, 229–254. New York: I.B. Tauris.

Vairel, Frédéric. 2011. "Protesting in Authoritarian Situations. Egypt and Morocco in Comparative Perspective." In: *Social Movements, Mobilization, and Contestation in the Middle East and North Africa*, edited by Joel Beinin and Frédéric Vairel, 27–42. Stanford: Stanford University Press.

Van der Linden, Marcel. 2007. "The 'Law' of Uneven and Combined Development: Some Underdeveloped Thoughts." *Historical Materialism* 15: 145–165.

van de Sande, M. 2013. "The Prefigurative Politics of Tahrir Square-An Alternative Perspective on the 2011 Revolutions." *Res Publica* 19(3): 223–39.

Vatikiotis, Panayiotis J. 1972. *Revolutions in the Middle East and Other Case Studies*. London: Allen and Unwin.

Versieren, Jelle, and Brecht De Smet. 2014. "Urban Culture as Passive Revolution: A Gramscian Sketch of the Uneven and Combined Transitional Development of Rural and Urban Modern Culture in Europe and Egypt." In: *Marxism and Urban Culture*, edited by Ben Fraser, 191–212. Plymouth: Lexington Books.

Voloshinov, Valentin. 1973 [1929]. *Marxism and the Philosophy of Language*. New York: Seminar.

Vygotsky, Lev S. 1978. *Mind in Society. The Development of Higher Psychological Processes*. Cambridge: Harvard University Press.

———. 1987a. "Problem and Method of Investigation." In: *Collected Works* Volume 1, 42–52. New York: Plenum Press.

———. 1987b. "The Development of Scientific Concepts in Childhood." In: *Collected Works* Volume 1, 167–242. New York: Plenum Press.

———. 1987c. "Memory and Its Development in Childhood." In: *Collected Works* Volume 1, 301–319. New York: Plenum Press.

———. 1998. "Imagination and Creativity in the Adolescent." In: *Collected Works* Volume 5, 151–166. New York: Plenum Press.

———. 2004. *The Essential Vygotsky*, edited by Robert W. Rieber, David K. Robinson. New York: Kluwer Academic/Plenum Publishers.

———. 2012 [1934]. *Thought and Language. Revised and Expanded Edition*. Cambridge, London: MIT Press.

Warren 1973. "Imperialism and Capitalist Industrialization." *New Left Review* 1(81): 3–45.

Wallerstein, Immanuel. 1974. *The Modern World System I: Capitalist Agriculture and the Origins of the European World-Economy in the Sixteenth Century*. New York: Academic Press.

Wertsch, James V. 1985. *Vygotsky and the Social Formation of Mind*. Cambridge, Massachusetts and London: Harvard University Press.

REFERENCES

———. 2007. "Mediation." In: *The Cambridge Companion to Vygotsky*, edited by Harry Daniels, Michael Cole, and James Wertsch, 178–192. Cambridge: Cambridge University Press.

Winegar, Jessica. 2011. "Egypt: A Multi-generational Revolt." *Jadaliyya*. February 12. Available at: <http://www.jadaliyya.com/pages/index/703/-egypt_a-multi-generational-revolt->.

Wood, Ellen M. 2002. *The Origin of Capitalism: A Longer View*. New York: Verso.

———. 2012. *The Ellen Meiksins Wood Reader*. Leiden: Brill.

Yasnitsky, Anton. 2012. "Lev Vygotsky: Philologist and Defectologist, A Sociointellectual Biography." In: *Portraits of Pioneers in Developmental Psychology*, edited by Wade E. Pickren, Donald A. Dewsbury, and Michael Wertheimer, 109–134. New York: Psychology Press.

Yates, Douglas A. 1996. *The Rentier State in Africa: Oil Rent Dependency and Neocolonialism in the Republic of Gabon*. Trenton: Africa World Press.

Zemni, Sami, Brecht De Smet, and Koen Bogaert. 2013. "Luxemburg on Tahrir Square: Reading the Arab Revolutions with Rosa Luxemburg's the Mass Strike." *Antipode* 45(4): 888–907.

Index

6 April
    2008 uprising   237–239, 243, 246, 277–279, 289, 295–296, 329, 346, 380, 385
    Movement   218, 302, 305–306, 324–325, 370–372
18 Days *see* 25 January protests
25 January protests   xiii, 1, 3–4, 11, 17, 21–25, 33, 39–41, 57–8, 60, 103–104, 123–126, 227–228, 233, 239, 251–254, 257, 278, 287–289, 293, 301–328, 340–343, 346–348, 351–352, 355, 360–362, 365, 371, 380, 385–386
    Of 1952   158–159
    Revolution *see* revolution
    Uprising *see* 25 January protests
1919 Revolution *see* revolution
1952 Free Officers' Coup *see* Free Officers
1977 uprising *see* bread riots
2011 uprising *see* 25 January protests
2013 Coup *see* 2013 Uprising
2013 Uprising   326, 368–369, 375, 381, 385

Abbas, Kamal   217, 248, 276–277, 375
Abu al-Fotouh, Abd al-Moneim   186, 223, 223n, 370
Abu Eita, Kamal   247–249, 264, 277, 279, 375
Accumulation
    By dispossession   208–209, 360
    Capital   x, 9, 59–60, 67, 69, 74–75, 127, 130, 132, 157, 163, 176–177, 179, 188, 194, 206, 209, 214, 279, 383
    Original and primitive   17, 60, 67, 75, 124–126, 301, 327, 346
Activity   21–60, 240–253, 327–333
    Activity-system   16, 53–55, 59–60, 68–69, 86–87, 90, 107, 110, 113, 125, 183, 241–247, 254, 258, 335, 364
    Cultural-Historical Activity Theory *see* Cultural-Historical Activity Theory
    Theory   ix, xi, 12, 14, 53, 55
Adli, Habib al-   308, 339–340
Adli, Mansour al-   369
Afaaq Ishitirakiyya   168–169

Agency   5–8, 10, 27, 30, 32–33, 36, 42, 55–57, 63, 112, 282, 342, 355, 387
    Class   78, 118, 134, 287, 368, 381–382
    Collective   2, 4–5, 8, 26, 57, 71, 242, 342, 359, 386
    Subaltern   101, 143, 357, 369, 378
Ahali, al- (newspaper)   123, 200–201, 260, 266
Ahrar, al- (party)   178–179
Amal, al- (party)   197, 225
Alexandria   2, 23n, 126, 144, 147, 181, 185n, 189, 198, 212, 222n, 237, 248n, 301, 307, 309–310, 314–323, 325, 331, 352, 360n
Ali, Khaled   270, 278, 280, 292
Alienation   23, 43, 45–46, 63, 68, 111, 151
Alterglobalization   9, 111
Althusser, Louis   6, 7
Amn al-Dawla   178, 212n
Amn al-Markazi, al- *see* Central Security Forces
Arab Spring   2, 3, 386
Arabi, al- (newspaper)   260, 266, 267
Armed forces   158, 160, 178–179, 212–213, 315n, 354–358, 367–369, 375
    Supreme Council of (SCAF)   104, 324–326, 350, 354–360, 362–368
Army *see* armed forces
Art   95, 257, 267–269
    Artists   99–100, 212, 255, 267–269, 272, 275, 286, 338–339, 363
Assistance
    Adequate   116–117, 288–297, 385–386
    By traditional intellectuals   99, 190, 257–271, 337, 377, 383
    Commodifying   276, 279–282, 384–385, 387–388
    Colonial   144, 203–204 258, 276–279, 287, 358, 385
    Connective   273, 384
    Cultural   272–273, 337–339, 384
    Directive   101, 274, 339–340, 384
    Forms of   11, 257–258, 272–274, 336–340, 384
    Instructive   90–91, 116–117
    Integrative   274

INDEX

Modes of 100, 144, 257–258, 274–285, 384–385
  Projective 273
  Solidary 56, 88, 101, 282–285, 358, 385
  Technical 272, 336, 384
Aswany, Alaa al- 123, 141, 168–169, 195, 268
Authority 11, 75, 99, 105, 110, 146, 178, 221, 266, 371n
Autonomism 8, 72–73

Badil, al- (newspaper) 123, 199, 227, 265–266, 304–305, 308
Baradei, Muhammed al- 227, 306, 308–309, 315–316, 321–322, 368
Battle of the Camel 25, 318–321, 332–333, 344
Baltageyya 302, 315, 320, 332–333, 356n
Behaviorism 14, 48
Beinin, Joel 72, 103–104, 156–157, 183, 186, 202
Bekhterev, Vladimir 13
Bildung 37–40, 47, 54
Blunden, Andy ix–xii, 14, 16, 37, 42–43, 48–49, 53–59, 72, 100–101, 111–112, 274–275, 283, 382–383, 385
Bolshevik 15
Bordiga, Amadeo 15
Bourgeoisie see class
Bread riots (1977) 189, 191
Brotherhood see Muslim Brotherhood
Butler, Judith 6
Bureaucracy 79, 136, 165–166, 175–176, 194, 202, 250, 256
  Bureaucratism 17, 87, 113, 361

Caesarism 119–120, 134, 158, 169–171, 175, 179, 354–358, 360, 363–364, 366, 378, 381, 385
Cairo 1–2, 126, 144, 159, 164, 181, 189, 197, 208, 211, 213, 218–219, 224, 244, 253, 261–262, 306–311, 315–317, 319, 323–325, 328, 331n, 332, 347, 350, 353
Capital (Marx) ix–xi, 47–48, 59–60
  Accumulation see accumulation
Capitalism x, xii, 4, 7–9, 43, 64, 67–68, 70, 72–73, 81, 93, 108, 114, 116, 118, 126–32, 135–136, 145, 148, 151, 154, 157, 182, 186, 260, 287, 373, 381–382
  Class see class
  Mode of production see mode of production

Rentier see rentier economy
Society x, 27, 64, 75, 81–83, 89, 94, 98, 102, 355
State 163, 176, 194
Cartoon 267–269
Center for Trade Union and Workers' Services (CTUWS) 217, 269, 276, 291
Central Security Forces (CSF) 1, 58, 178, 212n, 213, 219, 307, 323, 329, 330
Charity 56, 151, 185n, 186, 196, 275
Christians 23, 39, 283, 321, 373
Civildemocratic
  Project 17, 214–230
  Movement 222–223, 226, 228–229, 234, 245, 258, 261, 268, 270, 275, 277–279, 296–297, 301, 307, 328, 346, 349, 380–381, 386
Class
  Bourgeois and capitalist 65–67, 115, 127, 135, 147, 176, 150, 194, 209, 212, 355
  Consciousness 70, 72, 144, 234, 246, 274, 347
  Formation 68, 70, 73–74, 76, 78–79, 81, 84, 90, 97, 99, 101–103, 107, 170, 376, 382–383
  Middle 15, 22, 117, 139, 143, 176, 186, 188–189, 196–197, 228, 258, 262, 282, 285, 301–302, 306, 361, 366, 370
  Petty-bourgeois 168
  Ruling 66, 92, 96, 98, 114–115, 119, 124, 128, 131, 137, 139, 145–146, 167, 176–178, 187, 201, 206, 209–210, 213, 270, 348, 354–356, 365–367, 370, 379
  Society 10, 64, 96
  Struggle ix, 47, 73, 77, 87, 97, 100, 103, 130, 133, 147, 156, 188, 203–204, 242–244, 246, 255, 260, 278, 286–287, 346, 360, 375
  Subaltern 115, 124, 126–128, 132, 145–146, 156, 169, 171, 191, 206, 210, 217, 259, 286, 301, 355, 360
  Working x, 10–11, 15–17, 63, 68, 72, 74, 81, 87, 91, 98–100, 109, 115–119, 127, 132–134, 140–142, 146–148, 150–151, 153, 156, 166–167, 170, 168, 182, 188, 190, 199, 202–204, 209, 226, 228, 233, 240–241, 243, 246–247, 254, 257, 260, 265, 267, 269–274, 276, 279–281, 283, 285, 287, 289, 291, 293, 295–297, 309, 327, 329, 345–346, 351, 374–375, 378, 382–383, 387

Coercion   76, 75, 83, 108, 127, 136, 140, 158, 160, 170, 210, 301, 355, 366, 379
  Coercive consent   87, 100, 165–166
Cognition   29–31, 33, 41
Cole, Michael   12, 14
Collaboration   ix, 13, 16, 33–34, 36, 52–53, 55–58, 60, 72, 76, 78, 90, 100–101, 103–104, 106, 111, 126, 204, 219, 221, 223–227, 229, 242, 247, 249, 254, 257, 261, 282, 284–287, 297, 327–332, 336, 340, 342, 343, 349–350, 353, 359–360, 366, 370, 378, 382, 384–385, 387
  Collaborative project   48, 54–55, 57–58, 63, 191, 350, 383, 386, 388
  Form of   56, 60, 77, 80, 224, 328, 341, 352–353, 387
  Mode of   100–101
Colonialism   2, 126, 128, 132, 139n, 141, 143, 150, 155, 160n, 164, 376
  Colonial bloc   139, 144, 155, 158, 169
  Colonial mode of assistance see assistance
Commodity   ix–x, 47, 59, 67, 145
  Commodity production   127, 138, 141–142
  Commodification   55–56, 68, 101, 106, 272, 275, 384–385, 387–388
  Mode of assistance see assistance
Common sense   93, 95–97, 382
Communism   6, 70, 90, 373
  First Wave   147
  Second Wave   152–153
  Third Wave   181, 189
Concept   xi, 40–43
  Everyday   94–97, 99, 117, 202, 242–243, 336, 358
  Scientific   54, 95–96–97, 186, 336, 358, 373, 382, 387
  True   96, 268
  Pseudoconcept   273
Copts see Christians
Corporatism   130, 142, 150–151, 165, 342, 378
  Economic-corporate   80, 115, 141, 148, 150, 166, 178, 190, 203, 226, 243, 253, 257, 285, 287, 295, 297, 345, 361, 377
Counterrevolution   104, 189, 318, 320, 326, 332–334, 356, 359, 361, 363–369, 374, 381

Crisis   8, 51, 102, 119, 124, 143, 145–146, 152, 174, 189, 199, 214, 334, 356, 368, 374, 385
  Conjunctural   131
  Debt   138, 206, 369
  Developmental   118
  Oil   131
  Organic   131, 153–158, 177
Croce, Benedetto   15
Cultural-Historical Activity Theory (CHAT)   11–14, 16, 37, 382

Day of Rage see 25 January protests
Delta, Nile   2, 126, 233, 307, 310
Democracy   8–9, 85, 91, 104, 125, 128, 147, 159, 167–168, 177, 181–182, 195, 214, 217, 222–223, 226–227, 260, 268, 278–279, 289–290, 316, 341, 348, 360, 362, 366, 381
  Bourgeois   4, 132n, 133, 143, 178, 287
  From above   195
  Grassroots   343
  Workers'   78, 132n, 245
Demonstration   33, 84–85, 102–103, 105, 126, 181, 223–224, 227, 241, 245, 328–329, 330–332, 334, 340, 346, 360, 380
Descartes, René   28–29, 32
Determinism   6, 70
Development
  Lines of   51, 83, 86, 93–94, 96–97, 102–103, 105–106, 116, 126, 152, 182, 243, 274, 287, 294–295, 360, 362, 376, 384, 386
  Social situation of   16, 50–52, 69, 75–76, 78–79, 81, 90, 101–102, 105, 107–109, 115–116, 124, 170, 182, 191, 202, 288, 297, 345, 374, 397, 381, 383–384
  Uneven and combined   17, 108, 126–131, 135, 138, 381
Dialectic   xii, 46, 56, 106, 111
  Logic see logic
  Pedagogy see pedagogy
Dialogical   113, 204
Dictatorship   4, 22, 132–133, 160, 169, 171, 178, 188, 195, 223, 225, 245, 286, 289–290, 296, 303–304, 331, 351, 372, 388
Discourse   2, 6–7, 23, 33, 92, 95n, 141, 150–151, 192, 200, 210–211, 223, 229, 259, 285, 305

INDEX

Division of labor   9, 63–64, 68, 91, 97, 110, 129, 133, 136, 262, 334, 336, 340, 383–384
  Social   10–11, 113
  Technical   11, 91, 113
Dostour al- (newspaper)   227, 266, 308

Education   3, 9, 11, 13–14, 65, 67, 89, 165, 169–170, 181, 195–196, 235, 249–251, 343, 386
Effendiyya   139–140, 143–144, 149n, 150, 153, 155, 170, 377
Emancipation   xiii, xv, 2, 6, 8–11, 36, 43, 45, 57, 63–68, 75, 85, 88, 91, 93, 101, 119, 156, 191, 257, 288, 331, 342–343, 364, 378, 380–383
Emergency law   1, 159, 195, 290, 293, 306–307, 324, 339n, 362
Engeström, Yrjö   12, 14, 53–54
Egyptian Center for Economic and Social Rights (ECESR)   262, 270–271, 292, 320
Egyptian Federation of Independent Trade Unions (EFITU)   350, 360, 375
Entryism   221
Epistemology   26
Epoch   177–178
Eschatologism   6
Ethics   55, 95
  Ethico-political   9, 72, 158, 170, 177–178, 185, 275, 384–386

Facebook   39, 125, 302, 305, 307, 323
Fanon, Frantz   8
Farmers   15, 66, 68, 82, 97, 125, 131–133, 135–136, 138, 140–141, 143, 151, 154, 156, 162–163, 166–167, 170, 180, 182, 200, 207–208, 210, 215, 228, 258, 262, 278, 282, 286–287, 302, 360, 366, 377–378, 387
  Struggle   125, 137, 143, 268, 286–287, 323, 353, 360, 372
Fascism   6, 15, 107, 149, 187–188, 201
  Islamic   185, 189, 200, 203, 223
Fellow traveler   139, 266, 376
Feloul   368–370
Feudalism   64–65, 108, 128, 135, 137–138, 140, 143, 159, 161–162, 169, 194n
Feuerbach and Theses of   43–45, 100
Fichte, Johann Gottlieb   31–32
First World War   15–17, 87, 143, 147
Foucault, Michel   6–7, 71n

Frame theory   5
Free Officers   158, 161–164, 166, 169, 357
  Coup   143, 157–159, 169, 175, 234
Friday of Anger   309–314, 329, 331, 352, 356, 363
Friday of Departure   316, 324–326, 352
Front   152, 183, 190, 196, 201, 126, 219, 222, 225–227, 260, 282, 286, 334, 352
  Popular   167, 227
  United   15, 156, 165, 219, 224–226

al-Gama'a(t) al-Islamiyya(t) *see* Islamic Group
German Ideology, The   10, 91, 97
General Federation of Egyptian Trade Unions (GFETU)   165, 236, 243–244, 246, 350–351, 379,
Generalization   47, 81, 93, 97, 99, 102–103, 106, 243, 246–247, 267, 375
Gestalt   37–40, 47–49, 131, 332–345
Global South   131, 133, 179, 381
Goethe, Johann   9, 14, 16, 37–41, 46–49, 53, 77
Good sense   87, 93, 97, 202, 204, 242–243, 256, 274, 276, 3023, 336, 361, 382, 384
Google   22, 302
Gramsci, Antonio   ix–xii, 12–13, 15–16, 34, 64–66, 73, 80, 85–86, 88, 91, 93–100, 107, 114–115, 119, 127–128, 130–131, 133, 156n, 138n, 169–170, 188, 376, 382–384
Gulf   160n, 180, 185n, 191, 194, 201, 206, 222
  Gulf War (1991)   222

Hamas   222, 320
Handicap of a head start   254
Harvey, David   8
Health technicians   245
  Union of   247, 249, 254, 264, 374, 380, 385
Hegel, Georg   ix–xii, 40–47, 55, 59, 63, 111,
  Hegelianism   6, 12n, 15, 35, 48, 56, 59
Hegemony   x, xii, 13, 65–67, 86–88, 92, 100, 115, 120, 131, 145, 148, 150, 157, 165, 167, 169, 178, 182, 194, 210, 226, 258, 275, 301, 303, 358, 370, 378, 381, 385
Hisham Mubarak Law Center (HMLC)   217–218, 220, 269–271, 320

Historical bloc   17, 130–131, 133, 135, 138–139, 142–143, 150, 154, 157–159, 161, 175, 177–180, 193–194, 203, 212, 228, 240, 269, 296, 301, 346, 349, 352, 355, 358, 365, 373, 376, 379, 381, 385
Hizbiyya   296
Human rights   64, 83, 149, 210, 222–223, 227, 255, 343
    Activists   1, 21, 210, 216, 269–272, 278–279, 302, 306, 316, 370, 384
Humanist   6, 28, 382
Hypokeimenon   28

Identity   5n, 6–8, 30, 43, 73, 128, 131, 141, 147, 171
Ikhwan *see* Muslim Brotherhood
Ilyenkov, Evald   7, 14, 31, 35, 40, 42, 44, 59, 112n
Imbaba   211, 309, 331n
IMF *see* International Monetary Fund
Immanence   55, 57, 70, 340–342
Imperialism   129, 132, 139n, 143, 159, 161, 191, 200, 219, 226, 377, 381
    Anti-imperialism   128, 165n, 167, 184, 217, 222, 226, 376–378
Import-substituting industrialization (ISI)   136, 163, 193
Indignados   2, 344
Infitah   175–193, 194, 234, 379
Institutionalization   9, 88, 112–113, 257, 282, 293, 372
Instruction   11, 12n, 17, 52, 59, 72, 89–97, 116–118, 134, 254, 284, 287–289, 293, 295, 304, 327, 335, 337–339, 343, 374, 376, 382, 385–386
    Leads development   52, 383, 386, 398
Intellectual   3–4, 8, 10, 13, 72–73, 87–88, 91–92, 97–102, 106, 134, 147, 152–153, 168, 170, 183, 191, 201, 203, 210–212, 221, 228, 233, 237, 257, 262, 268, 272, 278, 282, 285, 289, 337, 339, 375, 377–79, 383–384, 386, 388–389
    Organic   xii, 12n, 16–17, 89, 114, 117, 124, 139, 144, 156, 165–166, 170, 183, 241, 255–257, 260, 271–272, 282, 287, 289, 294, 336–337, 378, 382–383
    Proletarian   255–256, 260, 272, 378
    Subaltern   115, 170
    Traditional   12n, 16–17, 89, 117, 124, 156, 256, 258–259, 262, 267–268, 270–275, 280, 282, 284–286, 288–289, 293–294, 382–383
Interiorization   52, 242–243, 336, 382–383
International Labor Organization (ILO)   271, 293
International Monetary Fund (IMF)   179, 201, 207
Intifada, Second Palestinian   125, 218–219, 222, 258, 260
Iranian Revolution (1979)   71n, 187, 192, 200, 346, 365
ISI *see* import-substituting industrialization
Islam   178, 186, 188, 278
    Islamism   23, 151, 160n, 181, 186–188, 192, 196, 198, 200–201, 211–212, 222, 224–226, 367, 370
    Islamic Alliance   196
    Islamic fascism *see* Fascism
    Islamic Group   185–186, 192, 196n, 210, 211n
Israel   161, 176, 179, 181, 192, 195, 200, 219, 267, 278, 290, 315n

Jazeera, Al   310, 316–318, 320–322, 324–325, 343
Jihad   160, 192
    al-Jihad (organization)   192, 210n
Journalists   99–100, 139, 196, 210, 265–267, 273–274, 279–280, 319–321, 335, 337–338, 384

Karama (party) al-   217, 220, 279, 294
Kant, Immanuel   29–32, 37, 42
Kautsky, Karl   10, 92–93
Kefaya   125, 220, 222, 227–229, 259, 262, 265, 278, 280, 380

Labor
    Activism *see* workers' movement
    As activity   44, 58, 63
    Division of *see* division of labor
    Laborers *see* class
    Mental and material *see* division of labor
    Movement *see* workers' movement
    Power *see* wage labor
    Process *see* wage labor
    Subsumption under capital, formal and real   68, 127, 136, 164
    Wage   64, 67–69, 74, 76–79, 81–82, 84, 100, 127, 148, 283

INDEX

Labriola, Antonio   15
Leadership   11, 66, 86–87, 99–101, 106, 114–115, 119, 213, 246, 248n, 250, 255, 274, 335, 339–340, 358, 368, 384
  also see hegemony
Learning *see* instruction
Left, the   147, 157, 166, 180, 183, 185, 187–188, 190, 195, 197–205, 211, 224, 229, 281–282, 285
  Legal   210, 214–218, 221, 226
  Nasserist   178, 183
  New Left   8, 216n
  New left (Egypt)   215–218, 220–221, 223, 225–227, 237, 258, 261–263
  Old left   215–218, 223–227, 259–261, 267, 275
  Secular *see* secularism   224–225
Lenin, Vladimir   xi, 10, 12n, 15, 21, 48, 66, 95n, 99n, 124, 132, 382
Leontyev, Alexei   12–14, 49, 53, 55, 57, 63
LGBT   387
Liberalization   7, 125, 168, 175–177, 179, 180, 186, 189, 191, 193, 197, 201, 207–208, 210–211, 214, 218, 221, 223–224, 227, 229, 234, 250, 278, 306, 349, 360, 365, 367–368, 370
  Neoliberalism *see* neoliberalism
Liberation Square *see* Tahrir Square
Liquidationism   204, 282
Lines of development   51, 72, 83, 84, 99, 102–103, 105, 116, 379, 384
  Economic and political   84, 86, 97, 99, 105–106, 126, 152, 170, 182, 243, 287, 294–295, 297, 350, 360, 376, 381, 384
  Everyday and scientific   93, 94, 96, 97, 99, 114n, 118, 274, 287, 297, 359, 384
L'Ordine Nuovo   15, 87
Lukács, György   68, 78, 90n, 93–94, 119n
Luria, Alexander   13–14, 37
Luxemburg, Rosa   10, 335, 345
Lyotard, Jean-François   8

Mahalla, city and strikes   145, 198, 226, 233–248, 253–296, 308, 316–317, 323, 325, 329, 346, 379–380
Mansura   199, 286, 310, 317, 325
Maoism   8
Maspero   314, 318, 325, 330, 352

419

Marx, Karl   ix–xi, 9–10, 44–47, 50, 54n, 57, 59–60, 63–71, 77, 89, 91–92, 97, 99, 111, 119, 128, 194n, 257, 334, 382, 387
Marxism   4, 6, 15, 35, 111, 183
Mediation   14, 40, 44, 51, 56, 59, 68, 72, 78, 100, 111, 120, 144, 148, 157, 182, 203, 276, 282, 342, 355, 377–378, 383
Meshcheryakov, Alexander   14, 52
Method and methodology   2, 14, 46–47, 48–50, 69–74, 117–118, 127, 131, 374
  Methodological individualism and collectivism   28–36
Midan Tahrir *see* Tahrir Square
Michels, Robert   110–111
Military *see* armed forces
Minority   83, 143, 192, 211, 219, 366
Mode of production   x, 8n, 194n, 373
  Capitalist *see* capitalism, also see *accumulation*
  Colonial *see* colonialism
  Feudal *see* feudalism
  Precapitalist   64, 128, 131–132, 137n, 137, 139, 141–142, 146, 151, 154, 156n, 163, 378, 381
  Tributary   132, 135
Modern Prince, the   75–87, 90, 97, 107, 133–134, 171, 204, 257, 260, 353, 358, 369, 375, 382–383, 385
Modernism   6–7, 151
  Modernity   6, 8–10, 32, 151
Monologism   6
Morsi, Mohammed   212, 225, 309, 326, 367–369
Moussa, Amr   318, 321, 368
Mubarak
  Gamal   213, 219, 228, 303, 356, 365
  Hosni   187, 193–194, 199, 209, 211, 212n, 213, 215, 228, 234–235, 240, 243, 250, 308, 314–315, 318, 321–322, 333, 339, 356, 358
  Resignation of   308, 316, 318, 321–322, 324–326, 331, 341, 350, 352, 354–356, 362
Muslim Brotherhood   149–152, 155–156, 159, 160n, 180, 185n, 187, 195–196, 200–201, 210, 216, 220–227, 251, 263–265, 276–277, 286, 303, 306, 309, 315, 318, 320, 322, 349, 365–367, 378

Nasser, Gamal Abd al-
National Association for Change
    (NAC)   227n, 306, 308
National Democratic Party (NDP)   2, 24,
    26, 58, 178, 195, 197, 212, 222, 287, 294, 303,
    308, 310, 312, 320–321, 341, 355n, 356,
    364–366
Nationalism   147, 149, 181, 377
National-popular   21, 84–85, 106–107, 115,
    126, 131, 143, 149–150, 155–156, 158–161, 164,
    166, 169, 176–178, 182, 185, 188, 190, 223, 227,
    229, 279, 301, 327–328, 330, 336, 342,
    345–346, 348, 354, 356–361, 364–367,
    372–374, 376–385
National Salvation Front (NSF)   368
Negation   7–9, 112n, 361, 376
Neoformation   50–53
    Central   51, 69, 79–80, 97, 288, 292,
        295, 377
    Party see Modern Prince
    Trade union see trade unionism
Neoliberalism and neoliberal reform   7–8,
    17, 74, 166, 175–229, 179, 185, 189, 191, 194,
    197n, 201–202, 206–213, 215, 240–241, 243,
    251, 254, 283, 295–296, 301, 346, 350,
    355–356, 360, 365, 371, 373, 379
New Social Movements   4, 8
New Tenancy Law (1991)   207
Nurses' strikes   252–253

Objectivism   6, 13, 26, 45, 49
    Objectification   40, 44, 45–46, 52,
        55–57, 89, 100, 111–113, 242, 378, 383
Occupy Wall Street   2, 344
October War (1973)   181–182, 190, 192, 234
Oligarchy   110–114, 209
Ontogenesis   14, 52, 59, 69, 76, 80, 90, 96,
    273, 384
Ontology   8, 32, 57
Opportunism   246, 281–282
Oriental Despotism   4

Palestine and Palestinians   125, 218–220,
    222, 227, 258, 260, 380
Paternalism   150, 245
Pathology   71, 110, 112n
    Bureaucratic see bureaucracy
    Caesarist see Caesarism
    Inadequate instruction see instruction

Liquidationist see liquidationism
Passive revolution see revolution
Substitutionist see substitutionism
Pavlov, Ivan   13–14, 48
Peasants see farmers
Pedagogy
    Dialectical   87, 89–101, 113, 156, 190,
        203, 256, 285–286, 288, 339, 361, 383, 385
    Paternalist   4, 215
    Political   11, 117–118, 287, 382
    Schizophrenic   287
Pensioners   245
    Union of   247, 249, 254, 264, 380
Philosophy of praxis   91–97, 191, 204, 274,
    358, 376, 382, 384
Piaget, Jean   xi, xii, 13, 50, 52
Postcolonialism   8, 129, 202, 226
Postmodernism   7, 8
Poststructuralism   6, 7, 8–9, 386
Practical-critical   111–112, 112n, 183,
    222, 242
Practico-inert   111–112, 183, 222, 242, 378
Privatization   177, 186, 189, 191, 193, 201,
    208, 214, 226, 229, 234, 250, 270
Privilege of backwardness   129, 145, 249,
    254n, 288
Project   54–60
    Projection   57, 60, 243–245, 273–274,
        342–344, 353, 363n
    Prolepsis   52–53, 60, 91, 100, 103, 117–118,
        183, 244, 246, 284, 297, 304, 328, 343, 374,
        380, 383, 385
        Autoprolepsis   52–53, 91, 99,
            285, 383
        Heterolepsis   52–53, 91, 285, 383
Proletariat see working class
    Proletarianization   9, 127, 140, 383
Psychology   ix–xi, 13–14, 28, 48
    Cultural   ix, 13–14, 59
    Social   95n, 110

Qaradawi, Yussef al-   227, 321

Real Estate Tax Authority Union
    (RETAU)   239, 247–249, 254–255, 279,
    289–290, 292–293, 295, 346, 380, 385
Recognition see assistance
Reformism (left)   71, 107, 115, 130
    Reformism (Islamic)   160n, 211n

INDEX 421

Religion   2, 93, 95, 142, 216, 333
Rentier economy   193–195, 206–208
Reproduction, extended   59–60, 124–125, 208, 327–328
Revolution   102–109
  25 January *see* 25 January protests
  Counter- see counterrevolution
  Deflected   169, 369, 378
  Egyptian (1919)   4, 143–144, 220, 328, 377
  Iranian *see* Iranian Revolution
  Passive   114–116
  Permanent   131–134, 217, 226, 378, 381, 385
  Russian (1905)   21, 106, 109, 335, 345–346, 360
  Russian (1917)   48, 109, 125, 147, 314, 346, 353, 360, 364
Revolutionary Socialists (RS)   216–227, 236, 262–263, 285, 373–374
Rights
  Civil   64, 125, 128, 168, 195, 222, 226, 360, 381
  Human *see* human rights
  Labor   217, 243, 254, 292
Romein, Jan   254

Sabahi, Hamdeen   217, 279, 367–368
Sadat, Anwar   17, 160n, 168, 175–192, 193–194, 197, 199, 234, 355, 379
Said, Khaled   301–302, 304–305, 323
Said, Rifaat al-   198–199, 214–215, 259, 275
Salafism and salafists   160n, 366–367
Sartre, Jean-Paul   8, 111–112
Sawiris, Naguib   322, 370
Selbstzweck   110–114, 282
Second World War   16, 145–147, 150, 152–153, 155, 164, 169, 185, 377
Sectarianism   23, 281, 367
Secularism   211, 234, 303n, 367
  Secular bloc and front   211–212, 214–216, 225–226, 368, 370, 375
  Secular left   186, 201, 211
Self-emancipation *see* emancipation
Shafiq, Ahmed   225, 315, 315n, 320, 362, 367
Sharara   216, 262
Sisi, Abdul Fattah al-   368–369

Six Day War (1967)   131, 160, 176–178, 181, 234
Social democracy *see* reformism
Social formation
  Capitalist *see* capitalism
  Precapitalist *see* mode of production
Social Movement Theory (SMT)   5
Socialism   10, 81, 87, 90, 92, 118, 133, 147, 149, 167, 191, 214, 224, 260, 373
  Actually existing   8, 133, 164
  Arab   163–166, 168, 177–178
  Democratic cooperative *see* Arab socialism
  Octroyal   120, 170, 175, 378
Socialist Renewal Current (SRC)   281, 285, 291, 306, 348, 370, 374
Socialist Workers Party (SWP)   217, 263
Society of Muslim Brothers *see* Muslim Brotherhood
Sociogenesis   59, 69, 78, 84, 90–93, 102, 107, 116, 119, 298, 382–383, 388
Solidarity *see* assistance
Soviet (council)   106–107, 359–361
  USSR   7, 14, 161, 163n, 164, 166–167, 181, 204, 214
Spontaneity   220, 335–336
  Spontaneous philosophy   93–97
Stalin, Joseph   14, 48
  Stalinism   8, 88, 156, 206, 216–217
State   47, 63–65, 82–85, 108, 119
  Integral   82, 115, 146
  Universal Capitalist, as   209
Strike
  As cell-form   75–79
  Mahalla *see* Mahalla
  Mass Strike, the   105–109, 345–351, 374, 381
Subject   37–46
  Collective   28–36, 42, 47, 55, 60, 63, 68–69, 73, 76, 78, 105, 256, 274, 334, 379, 383
  Development and formation of   27, 57, 60, 69–70, 104–105, 116, 119, 170, 256, 272, 379, 383
  Individual   28–36, 45, 48–49, 52, 59, 65, 261, 286
  Worker *see* working class
Substitutionism   118–120, 134, 384

Suez
  Canal zone   137, 143, 147, 149, 194
  Crisis   161, 163n, 165n
  City protests   303, 307–310, 316, 323, 325, 346, 347n
Suleiman, Omar   315–316, 320, 322–325, 349, 355–356
Surplus extraction   26, 64, 68, 75, 83, 108, 132, 206, 209
Syncretism   80, 273
Systematization   240–242, 282

Tadamon   216, 218, 262–263, 265, 285
Tagammu   178, 183–184, 197–201, 204–205, 210–211, 214–218, 221, 224–227, 249–250, 259–263, 278, 285–287, 290, 292, 295, 303, 306, 322, 340, 370, 371
Tahrir al-'Umal   216
Tahrir Square   xiii, 1–2, 26, 39, 104, 189, 219, 299–375, 380–381, 386
  Republic of   18, 327, 337–338, 353, 359–360, 363, 372, 380–381
Tamarod   368–369
Tantawi, Hussein   368
Teachers   xi, 91, 100, 139, 150, 228, 245, 250–251, 288
  Strikes   245, 250–252
  Union of   247, 249, 251, 254, 380
Teleology   57, 70, 340–342
Thompson, Edward P.   76–77, 382
Trade unionism   73, 78–81, 86, 146–150, 243–245, 249–254, 289–293, 296, 348, 360–361, 375, 377–378, 381
Transformism   115, 170, 194, 211, 213, 375, 379
Transitional demands and program   118, 382
Trend for Change   259, 285
Trotsky, Leon   xi, 105–106, 118, 125, 127, 132–133, 217, 314, 335, 353, 364, 373n, 382
True concepts *see* concepts
Trust   283–285, 368
Tunisia   2–3, 21, 304, 331
  Tunisian uprising   21, 104, 123, 304, 307, 310, 329, 343, 352, 388

Ultras   1, 306–307, 329, 336–337
Upper Egypt   2, 140, 197, 307
Urphänomen   37–39, 41, 46, 49, 77
USA   74, 129, 161, 167, 177, 179, 181, 199, 200, 206, 212, 219, 326, 356, 381

Volksgeist   37
Voloshinov, Valentin   34, 94–95
Vygotsky, Lev   ix–xv, 12–14, 18, 35, 37, 48–53, 59, 69, 72, 76, 79–80, 83–84, 90, 94–96, 102, 116–117, 273–274, 288, 376, 382–384

Wafd   143, 147–153, 196, 220, 226, 286, 303, 308, 322, 378
Washington Consensus   206
War
  First World War *see* First World War
  October War *see* October War
  Of movement   107–109, 124, 133, 144, 157, 182, 185, 189, 206, 326–327, 330–331, 346–347, 360, 372, 374, 379, 381, 385
  Of position   107–109, 115, 124, 152, 155, 185, 191, 295, 330–331, 374, 381, 385
  Second World War *see* Second World War
  Six Day War *see* Six Day War
  Yemen   176
Women   123–124
  Protesters   22–23, 39, 333, 360, 366n
  Workers   73–74, 235, 252–253
Workers National Democratic Party (WNDP)   373
Worker
  Workerism   8, 73
  Workers' movement *see* class, working
  Working class *see* class, working
  Worker subject *see* class, working
World Bank   163n, 206

Zionism   184, 191, 200, 219
Zone of proximal development (ZPD)   52, 90, 91n, 116–118, 191, 288–289, 293–295, 374